Empire Without End

A NEW HISTORY OF
BRITAIN
AND THE
CARIBBEAN

Imaobong Umoren

SCRIBNER
New York   Amsterdam/Antwerp   London
Toronto   Sydney/Melbourne   New Delhi

Scribner
An Imprint of Simon & Schuster, LLC
1230 Avenue of the Americas
New York, NY 10020

For more than 100 years, Simon & Schuster has championed authors and the stories they create. By respecting the copyright of an author's intellectual property, you enable Simon & Schuster and the author to continue publishing exceptional books for years to come. We thank you for supporting the author's copyright by purchasing an authorized edition of this book.

No amount of this book may be reproduced or stored in any format, nor may it be uploaded to any website, database, language-learning model, or other repository, retrieval, or artificial intelligence system without express permission. All rights reserved. Inquiries may be directed to Simon & Schuster, 1230 Avenue of the Americas, New York, NY 10020 or permissions@simonandschuster.com.

Copyright © 2025 by Imaobong Umoren

Originally published in Great Britain in 2025 by Fern Press,
an imprint of Vintage, part of Penguin Random House UK

All rights reserved, including the right to reproduce this book or portions thereof in any form whatsoever. For information, address Scribner Subsidiary Rights Department, 1230 Avenue of the Americas, New York, NY 10020.

First Scribner hardcover edition October 2025

SCRIBNER and design are trademarks of Simon & Schuster, LLC

Simon & Schuster strongly believes in freedom of expression and stands against censorship in all its forms. For more information, visit BooksBelong.com.

For information about special discounts for bulk purchases, please contact Simon & Schuster Special Sales at 1-866-506-1949 or business@simonandschuster.com.

The Simon & Schuster Speakers Bureau can bring authors to your live event. For more information or to book an event, contact the Simon & Schuster Speakers Bureau at 1-866-248-3049 or visit our website at www.simonspeakers.com.

Manufactured in the United States of America

1 3 5 7 9 10 8 6 4 2

Library of Congress Cataloging-in-Publication Data has been applied for.

ISBN 978-1-9821-7501-6
ISBN 978-1-9821-7500-9 (ebook)

Contents

Introduction   xi

1 "One of the richest spots of ground in the world": Indigenous Communities, Early Colonialism, and Hereditary Racial Slavery   1

2 "A dreadful state": The Making of the Racial-Caste Hierarchy   39

3 "The sooner all this mass of impolicy, crime and suffering, is got rid of, the better": Anti-Black Racism in Britain, Abolition, and Emancipation   77

4 "Our freedom can be taken away from us": Struggles for Economic Justice After Emancipation   129

5 "Fighting to prove that we are no longer merely subjects, but citizens": War, Anti-Colonialism, and Rebellion   165

6 "One united family": The Second World War   207

7 "Still colonial at heart": Constitutional Decolonization and the Global Cold War   227

8 "Colonization in Reverse": Caribbean Migration, State Racism, and Black Radicalism   267

9 "Flag independence": Caribbean Black Power and the Rise of Neocolonialism, Neoliberalism, and US Imperialism   315

10 "Menace to society": (Post)-Colonial Melancholia   355

Acknowledgments   397
Illustration Credits   399
Notes   401
Index   455

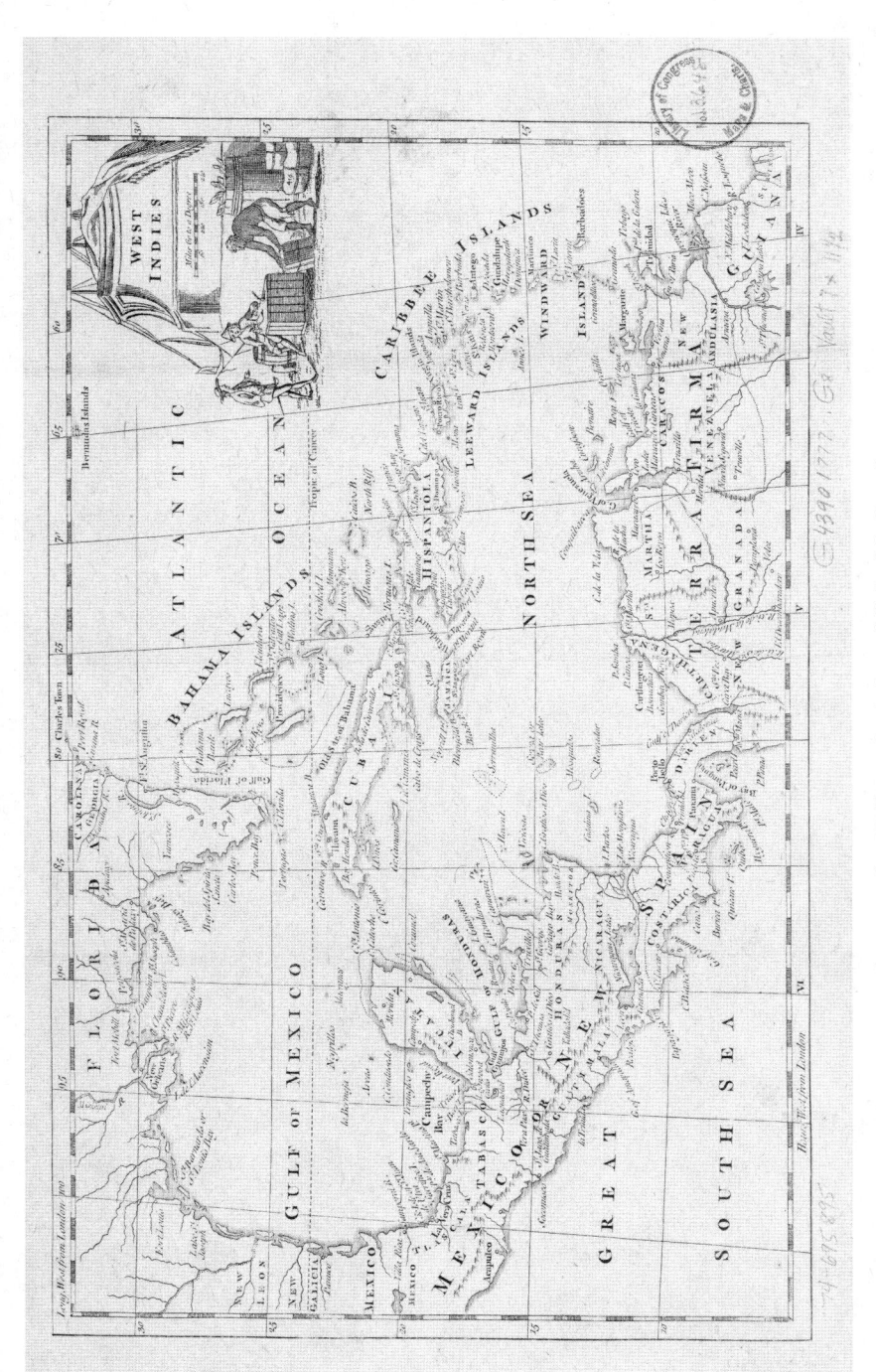

West Indies map by William Guthrie, published in London c. 1777.

The past does not exist independently from the present.

                              Michel-Rolph Trouillot

The English have become such a pitiful lot these days, with hardly any idea what to do with themselves now that they no longer have one quarter of the earth's human population bowing and scraping before them. They don't seem to know that this empire business was all wrong and they should, at least, be wearing sackcloth and ashes in token penance of the wrongs committed, the irrevocableness of their bad deeds, for no natural disaster imaginable could equal the harm they did. Actual death might have been better. And so all this fuss over empire—what went wrong here, what went wrong there—always makes me quite crazy, for I can say to them what went wrong: they should never have left their home, their precious England, a place they loved so much, a place they had to leave but could never forget.

                              Jamaica Kincaid

As such, in this post-colonial moment, the sensibilities of colonialism are still potent. We—all of us—are still its inheritors, still living in its terrifying aftermath.

                              Stuart Hall

Introduction

In June 1730, sixty-eight-year-old Sally Bassett was burned alive.[1] Her burning body hung in Hamilton, the capital of Bermuda. Bassett, an elderly enslaved woman, whose father was a white European and mother a black African, was sentenced to death for her attempt to kill by poison Sarah and Thomas Foster, the white slave owners of her granddaughter Beck, and Nancy, an enslaved woman she considered more foe than friend. Although Bassett professed her innocence during her trial, the court concluded that she had been "moved and seduced by [the] instigation of the Devil."[2] Bassett was found guilty by the all-white male jury. Bassett's attempt at murder was not the first time she had committed a crime: in 1712, she had been charged with trying to poison the cattle and damage the property of two white Bermudians.[3] She is best remembered, however, for her gruesome death.

Bassett's identity as a mixed-race enslaved woman was crucial to her life and death. The status of being enslaved passed down through women, meaning that the children of enslaved women were considered enslaved from birth. The society in which Bassett lived was built on distinctions between humans based on skin color. White elite European men, already accustomed to placing humans in a hierarchy, created a structure that assigned those with more melanin as inferior to those with less. The latter group was fit for freedom; the former branded unfree. As a mixed-race enslaved woman, Bassett's gender shaped what types of labor she would perform, who could have unrestricted access to her body, and what forms of resistance she could enact. This society was maintained by extreme levels of racial- and gender-based violence; that Bassett turned to violence herself, therefore, should come as little surprise. The specific form of violence—poison—considered a woman's crime in England and commonly used by enslaved women who drew on West African forms of knowledge—reveals that although Bassett may have never set foot either in Britain or on the African continent from which some of her ancestors came, its ideas ricocheted across the Atlantic Ocean. For Bassett and other enslaved women, poison became what social scientist James C. Scott called their "weapons of the weak," a subtle, silent, yet deadly form of resistance that existed alongside louder revolts and uprisings.[4] That Bassett died by burning—a harsh punishment for a severe crime—reflects white elite fraught fears of death by poison.

Sally Bassett's life and crime became the center of controversy once again 279 years after her death. In 2009, a bronze sculpture of Bassett was erected in Bermuda, Britain's oldest colony.[5] Occupied by the English since 1609, the island, covering fifty-four square kilometers and located in the North Atlantic, still belongs to Britain. As a non-sovereign state, it is one of six territories located in and around the Caribbean that are no longer called colonies but rather British Overseas Territories.

The idea of Bassett's statue began with the island's ruling local party, the Progressive Labour Party (PLP). Founded in the 1960s, the PLP represented the voice of the island's majority: Bermudians of African descent. But only in 1998 did the party finally win its first electoral victory against the United Bermuda Party (UBP), which tended to represent the island's white residents. Bassett's statue was created as part of celebrations commemorating the island's upcoming four hundredth anniversary and is the first monument of an enslaved person on the island. Its sculptor, Bermudian artist Carlos Dowling, titled the work *Spirit of Freedom*.

INTRODUCTION

Initially, the PLP wanted the statue placed in a central position in Hamilton's City Hall, but Sutherland Madeiros, the mayor of Hamilton, said there was no space for it. Madeiros's position as mayor is part of the Corporation of Hamilton, which administers the capital and has long represented the island's white elites.[6]

Sally Bassett statue, Bermuda, sculpted by Carlos Dowling.

His response sparked a "race row" with the PLP, which argued that the mayor did not want a "prominent reminder of slavery greeting visitors to City Hall."[7] Eventually, the statue ended up in its current location in the grounds of the Bermudian government's cabinet office.

INTRODUCTION

Yet the controversy that became divided along racial lines concerned not just the statue's location but its very existence. For some white Bermudians, the image of Sally Bassett at the stake, staring to the sky, was an unwanted reminder of a dark and depressing historical moment that tainted a (supposedly) racially harmonious society. Others argued that the statue would discourage tourism, a critical part of the island's economy.[8] Those who disliked the statue focused their rage on Dowling's portrayal of Bassett rising above the flames with her hands chained behind her back and a protruding stomach to signify that she was "pregnant with the spirit of freedom."[9] Black Bermudians were more inclined to celebrate the statue, arguing that Bassett belonged to a long litany of women who resisted their enslavement. Others praised the statue for helping refute the myth that enslavement in Bermuda was more benign than in other parts of the Caribbean.

At the statue's unveiling in 2009, Richard Gozney, the British governor of Bermuda, compared Bassett's statue to monuments commemorating none other than English statesman and soldier Oliver Cromwell; US Confederate general Robert E. Lee, whom he lauded for his "strengths of character"; and the 1838 Boer Blood River battle waged against the Zulus.[10] Black Bermudians denounced Gozney, especially his egregious references to white supremacist Lee and to African colonizers, and some called on him to apologize.[11] But he offered no regrets.

This history of Britain and the Anglophone Caribbean is, in a sense, about Sally Bassett—how she and millions of others like her came to live in a society dominated by a powerful racial hierarchy, and what occurred in the centuries afterward. The heated debates about racism, memory, history, and the British Empire that are provoked by statues—Bassett's being, of course, just one of them—resonate as much in Britain as they do in the Caribbean because, although the hereditary racial slavery that dominated Bassett's life no longer exists, the "racial-caste hierarchy" that

INTRODUCTION

was tied to it still does. And that hierarchy is historically rooted in and still shapes the Caribbean, as well as Britain.

Historians have been writing about the racial-caste hierarchy in the Caribbean for a long time, albeit without always labeling it as such. Stuart Hall called it the "colonial class pyramid."[12] Others have called it a pigmentocracy or a "white/brown/black pyramidal socioeconomic structure."[13] Whatever its name, it refers to a hierarchy based on race, skin color (that shaped colorism), class, status, and gender. At the core of this hierarchy is the construction of race: the creation of distinctions between men and women based on skin color and the linked process of racialization whereby an individual's racial identity becomes critical to their place within society. Ideas about whiteness and blackness existed long before the early modern European project of colonialism, but it was in this process, alongside the rise of hereditary racial slavery and capitalism, that modern ideas of race were codified.[14]

The construction of race had little to do with biology and everything to do with power, because it underpinned hereditary racial slavery—a racially based capitalist system that produced generational wealth for European nations and a small group of elites. White supremacy—defined by legal scholar Frances Lee Ansley as "a political, economic and cultural system in which whites overwhelmingly control power and material resources, conscious and unconscious ideas of white superiority and entitlement are widespread, and relations of white dominance and non-white subordination are daily re-enacted across a broad array of institutions and social settings"—was critical to the construction of race.[15]

Under hereditary racial slavery, social stratification ordered society. The racial-caste hierarchy became this structure and helped solidify "race" as a group identity. Unlike other forms of

INTRODUCTION

human hierarchy, the Caribbean-derived racial-caste hierarchy was never static: at times it could be fluid, with different groups moving up or down. And although it was an overarching structure across the Anglophone region, there were nuances in individual colonies.

What made the racial-caste hierarchy so distinct was that it always interacted with other forms of category—such as class, gender, legal status, and religion—which exacerbated inequality further. Moreover, as the centuries wore on, new groups would fit into this hierarchy, including those from Asia and the Middle East. Ultimately, however, white men and women and especially elites maintained their power at the top of the racial-caste hierarchy. This hierarchy was the basis for the colonialism that explicitly structured society from the seventeenth to the mid-twentieth century. In the late twentieth century, this racial-caste system changed but did not disappear.

In Britain the racial-caste hierarchy operated differently. It was central and inherent to the economy and wealth accumulation that Britain experienced due to colonialism. It underpinned the powerful form of anti-black racism that became institutionalized through the country's "color bar"—a system that saw black and other people of color denied the same opportunities and rights as white Britons. It seeped into exclusionary laws designed to curtail the black presence in Britain and shaped policies that pitted white working-class communities against black Britons. Aspects of these instances of anti-black racism in Britain persist to this day, above all in the gaping racialized and class disparities in the criminal justice system, healthcare, education, media, politics . . . (the list goes on).[16] The overwhelming evidence of specifically anti-black, institutionalized, blatant, and subtle forms of racism occurs alongside historic and ongoing attempts to deny its existence.[17] In the Caribbean from the 1660s, the racial-caste hierarchy was explicit and codified by specific laws.

INTRODUCTION

As the centuries progressed, however, in both the Caribbean and Britain, the racial-caste hierarchy became more implicit, though no less insidious or violent.

The racial-caste hierarchy is not an all-encompassing concept. It does not consider all forms of anti-black racism. But it helps us center and understand the structural nature of racist hierarchies—how they shift and adapt over time and space; how they are made, remade, and resisted; and how they impact everyone, in different ways. The places where skin color, class, capitalism, sexuality, gender, legal status, politics, the economy, and geography intersect are never seamless or frictionless. In different ways and at different times, some of these categories overrode, undercut, or conflicted with others, but together they all helped determine how power remained in the hands of a few.

Paying close attention to the racial-caste hierarchy is also a reminder of how the British Empire (and empires in general) functioned—by adopting an overarching framework of "politics of difference" that included a variety of different people within society but that sustained distinctions and hierarchies among them.[18] This was especially the case when new groups from Asia moved to the Caribbean and had to be slotted into the hierarchy, creating tensions and collaborations with people of African descent. Moreover, the racial-caste hierarchy helps highlight one of the reasons racism is so enduring: because it keeps reinventing itself, adapting to different situations and contexts but still functioning in ways that discriminate.

Within this book run two (braided) arguments. The first is that the roots of contemporary racial and linked class divisions in Britain and the Anglophone Caribbean today lie in the racial-caste hierarchy created in the Caribbean in the early days of the British Empire. (Caste is understood specifically as a form of social stratification—a division of society dependent on different forms of identity. This usage of the term avoids comparisons

INTRODUCTION

to other caste systems that operate globally but differently and are not always tied to colonialism.)[19] And this first argument flows into the second: that the racial-caste hierarchy's endurance is based on the British Empire's *continued* survival. Indeed, the British Empire is inseparable from the racial-caste hierarchy. Both grew in tandem.

The British Empire was a system of global white supremacy and class domination buttressed by violence, exploitation, extraction, and capital accumulation.[20] It was never a legitimate form of political power. Throughout its long existence, the empire has always been contested, especially by those who suffered its worst effects.[21] Mid-twentieth-century constitutional decolonization—the granting of political independence and sovereignty to former colonies—reinscribed British power more than it ended it, as British-led neocolonialism (that is, the persistence of colonialism), alongside US imperialism and neoliberalism, influenced the region. The British Empire lives on in the region's overseas territories, which show little interest in becoming sovereign partly because of their economic dependency on both Britain and the US.

The realities of neocolonialism reflect how decolonization did not confer a radical break with empire. The process was never designed to do so. Colonial-derived political, social, economic, and cultural ties endured deliberately, not just in former colonies but in Britain too, and not just in policies but also in ideas, ideologies, and institutions. Decolonization was and remains incomplete. And that is why the work to undo the legacies of colonialism—to, in effect, *decolonize decolonization*—reflected in the variety of decolonizing initiatives and projects (in part, including this book) remains vital. Indeed, this book is not only about the physical presence of the British Empire but also the ideological vestiges and legacies of colonial practice and thought that persisted beyond the diminution of that empire and that are ever-present today.[22] In the Caribbean, decolonization processes have begun, but the work is far from over. As of 2024, eight sovereign Caribbean states retain Britain's monarch as their head of state (although some are trying to change this), which is just one example of the continuing presence of empire.[23] Documented here are the struggles between those who sought to maintain the racial-caste hierarchy and those who tried to end it; between those who tried to maintain empire and those who tried to challenge it.

Consisting of over seven hundred islands and mainland countries in South and Central America, the Caribbean is a small part of the world, and home to around 45 million people today.[24] Despite its relatively small size, the events that have taken place in the Caribbean have been crucial to the creation of the modern world. The Caribbean is the only region to have experienced colonization for a period of over five hundred years, and with this came a series of phenomena—including mass migration, forced relocation and displacement of populations, a brutal economic capitalist system (plantation-based hereditary racial slavery), revolutions, and the creation of entirely new cultures—all of which have tied the region to other parts of the world: the Americas, Europe, Africa, Asia, and the Middle East. Indeed, the history of the Caribbean has led to the region being described as the engine of globalization; a place that was "modern before modernity."[25] From the 1500s to the 1900s, the English (from 1707, "British"), Spanish, French, Dutch, Swedish, Danish, and the Americans carved out different parts of the Caribbean, which became critical to their global empires.[26] But ultimately, the British came to dominate the region, amassing more colonies there than any other Western power.

Caribbean geography shaped British dominance. The islands were accessible by sea routes, which led to their "discovery" and directed thousands of newcomers to the region. The Caribbean's beauty attracted, and continues to entice, travelers and tourists, but its geography can be severe. The stereotype of the Caribbean as a tropical paradise runs parallel to its reputation for death and destruction following in the wake of hurricanes, earthquakes, and volcanic eruptions. Yet the region is not monolithic. From the relatively flat islands, like Barbados, to the volcanic St. Vincent or the mountainous Dominica; from large islands like Jamaica to the small cays of the Bahamas, one of the distinguishing features of the region is its diversity. Although widely used, the term *Caribbean* is not entirely accurate.[27] It usually refers to all the islands and mainland countries bordering the Caribbean Sea. But the Bahamian archipelago that lies in the southern North Atlantic is also considered part of the Caribbean.

This book takes an expansive view of the Anglophone Caribbean: it explores all the British-controlled areas—from islands located in and around the Caribbean and North Atlantic seas like Bermuda to countries that lie in Central and South America, such as Belize and Guyana. This approach puts into sharp perspective the complexities and variations of the region. And racial diversity matches geographic diversity: throughout the Anglophone Caribbean, one will find African, Chinese, Indian, Lebanese, Syrian, European, and indigenous communities. Together, these cultures lived alongside and interacted with each other, leading to a process of what is known as *creolization*. As a metaphor, used by various Caribbean writers and intellectuals (like Barbadian Edward Kamau Brathwaite, Martinican Édouard Glissant, and scholars like Richard Price) creolization describes the "process by which enslaved and self-liberated Africans, against all odds, created new institutions (languages, religions, legal systems, and more)—for the ways that these people coming from a diversity of Old World societies, drew on their knowledge of homeland institutions to create new ones."[28] From the ashes of violent colonialism new creolized Caribbean cultures and societies were formed that are both hybrid and heterogenous. And of course, within these societies, hierarchies, all rooted in colonialism, continue to exist.

In the early days of England's fledgling empire in the seventeenth century, the Caribbean provided the wealth that fueled Britain's growth as a superpower. When hereditary racial slavery ended, the region's economic significance waned. Former prime minister David Lloyd George derided the Caribbean as the "slums of the Empire."[29] Nevertheless, the intimate entanglement between the Caribbean and Britain endured even as empire withered away because the colonial connection was so deeply embedded. Britain was never far away from the Caribbean—and the Caribbean was never far away from Britain.

Indeed, and foremost, *Empire Without End* compresses the space between the British and Caribbean archipelagos, arguing that the two regions became deeply entangled with one another. It is also a history of the legacies of the British Empire in Britain and the Caribbean, which centers the Caribbean in key parts of British history. Previous scholarship may have overlooked the "Caribbeanization" of Britain or considered it only in relation to the period of racial slavery, or when larger numbers from the Caribbean moved into post-1945 Britain. This book considers these entangled histories over a much longer period, adopting a *longue durée* approach up to the present.[30] In doing so, racism is placed at the heart of both regions.[31] Telling a history of empire means reckoning with many things—identity, society, the state, capitalism and neoliberalism, policing, education, housing—and these topics were indelibly shaped by racism and therefore feature throughout.

The British Empire was vast and varied, but in its focus on the Anglophone Caribbean, this book hopes to challenge generalizations about it, which are often dominated by a combination of nostalgia or amnesia, or emotions of shame, guilt, and pride.

INTRODUCTION

All are evident in polls that reveal, for instance, that Britons in 2020 were more likely than people in Germany, Japan, France, and any other former colonial powers to say that they would like their country to still have an empire.[32] And that many Britons have not only pride in the British Empire but also deep dismay, and even regret, over its demise.

Part of this nostalgia comes from an inability to connect the British Empire to contemporary racial and globally unequal divisions.[33] It is also influenced by the sweeping Victorian-era image of the British Empire, which, in the aftermath of the genocide of indigenous communities and the terror of hereditary racial slavery, reinvented itself as a supposed liberal, benevolent empire, determined to spread "civilization" and "modernization" (euphemistic terms for white supremacist ideology) to the purportedly backward peoples of Asia and Africa.

By returning to the origins of the British Empire in the seventeenth-century Caribbean, *Empire Without End* tries to dispel this image, notwithstanding the hostility toward histories of Britain that foreground white supremacy, which often provoke a loud defense and violent backlash. Remaining invested in myths of the British Empire (often shaped by a cheap patriotism) is dangerous because it fuels persistent inequalities that stem from colonialism, and which perpetuate violence today, just as they have done in the past.[34]

While seeking to contribute to British as well as black British history, this book also intervenes in Caribbean history. Centering attention on the creation and long life of the racial-caste hierarchy allows for the complexity of Caribbean society and the various groups in the region to be seen more sharply. To focus on it serves as a reminder of the centrality of racial slavery to the political, economic, cultural, and social issues that have dogged the Caribbean's past and that bear heavily on its present. This history also shines a light on some of the smaller islands in the Caribbean, often overlooked in studies of the region due to their size or relative obscurity, to highlight the diversity of the Anglophone area.

A global system built on the fiction of white supremacy, and one maintained through physical and psychological torture across centuries, whose ongoing presence shapes contemporary racial, political, economic, and spiraling environmental inequalities, is something to oppose. Admonitions to tell "both sides of the story"—especially to emphasize the supposed good of this global system, as popularised by historian Niall Ferguson or the theologian Nigel Biggar—are troubling,[35] as they contribute to curtailing ongoing anti-racist movements, deny the reality of institutionalized racism in Britain, undermine the growing reparations movement, and energize violent white nationalism. Moreover, they fail to consider that no amount of balanced or "both sides" history will obliterate the racist roots of the British Empire.

The racial-caste hierarchy that emerged amid racial slavery was never a betrayal of Britain's purported image of being a freedom-loving land. It was central to its foundation. If there is pride to be had in the British Empire, it lies in the fact that there were always those, like Sally Bassett, who tried to resist it. And in attempts to resist, new forms of Caribbean and British identity and culture were created—in language, religion, music, dress, and literature. Indeed, cultural resistance to the racial-caste hierarchy was endemic throughout this period.

Included here too are the stories of those who went to great lengths to ensure that the empire endured. In telling these stories it is important to remember that not everyone who was invested in upholding empire was the stereotypical rabid racist or die-hard imperialist. Many more were complicit, knowingly and unknowingly, through indifference or willful ignorance of supporting systems of domination. While others, especially African-Caribbean men and women, were heavily invested in empire, seeing it as an important political community that they were just as much a part of as white Britons. Indeed, Caribbean people played a critical role in expanding British identity, as they saw themselves not as outsiders but rather as insiders, and in turn helped inspire new forms of British-Caribbean identity. However, over the course of centuries, Caribbean people's service to empire was often responded to with violent denial and exclusion.

Empire Without End focuses on key moments to tell the history of the racial-caste hierarchy and the persistence of the British Empire, concentrating on the black-white-mixed-race (people of African and European heritage) racial dichotomy. Occasionally it stretches beyond Britain and the Caribbean—in particular to consider how British colonialism in the region shaped the intensification of control in North American colonies and Asia and expansion in Africa. The British Empire did not operate in isolation from its European counterparts or the US's growing empire. Its interactions with other empires provoked change, competition, and innovation that influenced its mission in the Caribbean and the racial-caste hierarchy. Moreover, the racial-caste hierarchy, while specific to the Caribbean and Britain, spread its tentacles across the globe, overlapping with other racist structures in different colonial locations, or with Jim Crow segregation in the US. Just as the racial-caste hierarchy interacted with broader racialized global empires, there were always those who tried to challenge it. Detailed here are the coalitions across the "Black Atlantic" that African-Caribbean people forged with other people of color in the US, Africa, and Asia. Black politics and culture were never confined to one nation-state or ethnic group; it was intrinsically transnational, drawing on how the legacies of hereditary racial slavery created transoceanic networks and ties between Africa, Europe, the Caribbean, the US, and Asia.[36]

Empire Without End builds on (and is indebted to) current and emerging scholarship and draws on numerous sources. It follows

INTRODUCTION

a broad chronological structure, starting in the 1400s and ending today, and features the voices and stories of Caribbean men and women. This is not an even or linear history: some chapters dwell more on the Caribbean or British side of the story. Simultaneous global connections and the ways that events in one part of the world impact the other are highlighted throughout. Ultimately, it seeks to contribute to "reparatory history" through its attempt to consider how a violent past—one example being the life and death of Sally Bassett—that still shapes the present can pave the way for a radically different future. As historian Catherine Hall has aptly described: "Reparatory history must be about more than identifying wrongdoers and seeking redress: it begins with the descendants, trauma and loss, but the hope is that the work of mourning can be linked—to hopes for reconciliation, the repair of relations damaged by historical injustice."[37]

This book is not just written to enlighten. It is written with the optimism that it may contribute to a willingness to dismantle unsustainable five-hundred-year-old hierarchies.

1

"One of the richest spots of ground in the world"

Indigenous Communities, Early Colonialism, and Hereditary Racial Slavery

In 1542 Dominican friar Bartolomé de Las Casas wrote to Prince Philip of Spain about his encounter with the "poorest people on the face of the earth," who were "unassuming, long-suffering, unassertive, and submissive." Las Casas continued: they "are among the least robust of human beings: their delicate constitutions make them unable to withstand hard work or suffering and render them liable to succumb to almost any illness, no matter how mild." Reassuring the prince that Spanish colonization and Catholic conversion spearheaded by the monarchy would thrive, Las Casas explained that the indigenous peoples in the Caribbean were "innocent and pure in mind and have a lively intelligence, all of which makes them particularly receptive to learning and understanding the truths of our Catholic faith."[1]

Las Casas's tone changed when he wrote about relations between indigenous peoples and the newcomers. According to Las Casas, the Spanish settlers "tear the natives to shreds, murder them and inflict upon them untold misery, suffering and distress, tormenting, harrying and persecuting them mercilessly."

These "despotic and diabolical" behaviors were leading to a demographic disaster. Las Casas's estimate, which is contested by scholars today, was that "over the last forty years . . . more than twelve million souls, women and children among them," had lost their lives due to "unjust, cruel, bloody and tyrannical war" and murder.[2] In trying to explain this searing level of violence, Las Casas succinctly stated: "the reason the Christians have murdered on such a vast scale and killed anyone and everyone in their way is purely and simply greed."[3] Here Las Casas was correct. But subsequent discourses about colonialism would come to overlook its economically opportunistic origins and inherent violence.

Interacting with people who looked or shared different beliefs and practices was not uncommon to Las Casas. Born in 1484 in the bustling city of Seville, the heart of the Spanish Empire, into a merchant family, he grew up interacting with Christians and Muslims of high, low, and enslaved status from across Europe, the Mediterranean, and North and sub-Saharan Africa. But his observations of the indigenous peoples in the Caribbean, documented in *A Short Account of the Destruction of the Indies*, were particularly important given the consequences of his assumptions about them.

For Las Casas, it is clear that indigenous peoples were not only physically, intellectually, and morally different; they were also *inferior* to Europeans. Their inferiority justified Spanish colonization, which would supposedly civilize them. Although Las Casas saw the indigenous peoples as beneath Europeans in the "great chain of being"—a concept describing a hierarchical structure with God at the top, followed by angels, humans, animals, and plants—he did not see them as subhuman. Owing to his staunch defense of the indigenous peoples in the Caribbean and other parts of the Americas, he would acquire the sobriquet "Protector of the Indians."

"ONE OF THE RICHEST SPOTS OF GROUND IN THE WORLD"

FRAY BARTOLOMÉ DE LAS CASAS

Varon apostolico, y el mas zeloso de la felicidad de los indios.

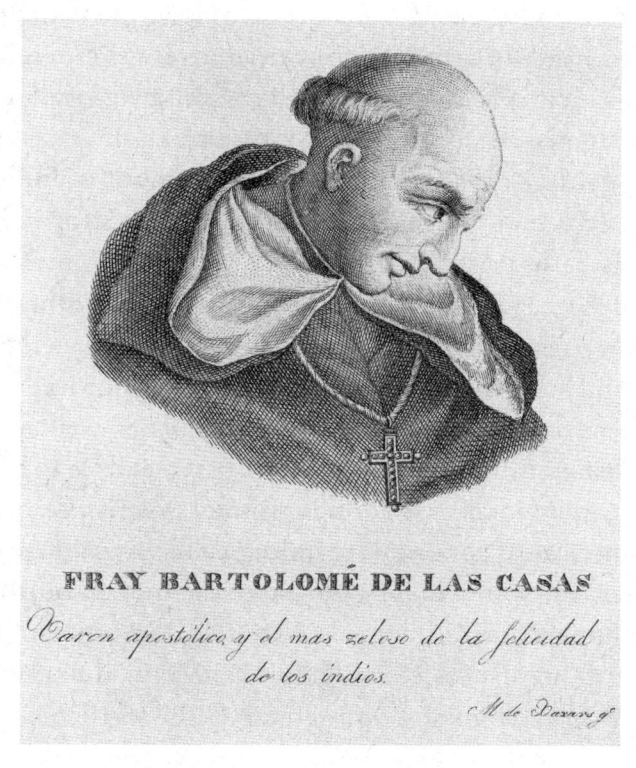

Fray Bartolomé de las Casas.

Las Casas first arrived in Santo Domingo, the capital of Spanish Hispaniola, the first Spanish colony in the Caribbean (what is today Haiti and the Dominican Republic) in April 1502. He landed as part of the largest fleet to leave Spain for the New World and quickly became immersed in settler society. Like other ordained men, Las Casas profited from the labor of indigenous peoples, which he possessed under the *encomienda* arrangement. This system originated with King Ferdinand and Queen Isabella of Spain, who decreed that the indigenous peoples had to develop the land on behalf of the colonists. In exchange, they would receive protection from the Crown, Christian conversion, and a small wage. Las Casas came to despise his status as an *encomendero*.

3

Two events in 1511 would transform his views: he witnessed the violent massacres of indigenous peoples on the neighboring island of Cuba, and then he heard a searing sermon delivered by Spanish missionary Antonio Montesinos, who chastised the Spanish settlers for their inhumane treatment of indigenous peoples. Together, these events inspired Las Casas to pen his *Short Account*. In 1515, he returned to Spain with Montesinos and informed King Ferdinand of the violence he had witnessed. But even laws passed to end settler excesses and the vicious treatment of the indigenous peoples had only a minor impact.

A Short Account of the Destruction of the Indies, written in 1542 and published in 1552, was one of the first treatises to highlight the abuse and violence that underpinned Spanish colonization in the Americas. It continues to influence Las Casas's controversial legacy. For some, in his defense of the indigenous peoples, he was the voice of Christian conscience. For others, he was a dangerous and dishonest antagonist determined to undermine the rewards of Spanish colonialism. Ultimately, his writings remain a seminal source not only for his descriptions of indigenous peoples, subjective though they are, but also because they foreground economic capital extraction and violence as central to colonization. Las Casas was one of many important critics of colonial violence. But his position was complicated because he was also complicit in it due to his involvement in the project of conversion and colonization.

Las Casas's defense of indigenous peoples did not initially extend to Africans, another group increasingly construed as inferior "others." Las Casas argued that as indigenous peoples were ripe for conversion to Christianity, their enslavement was a sin. Rather than enslaving indigenous peoples, Las Casas and many others turned to Africans, especially those captured in war or already enslaved, as a more acceptable option.[4] Yet by 1561, when he completed his three-volume *History of the Indies*

"ONE OF THE RICHEST SPOTS OF GROUND IN THE WORLD"

(*Historia de las Indias*), Las Casas had changed his mind, declaring "that the enslavement of blacks was every bit as unjust as that of the Indians."[5] But by this time the use of enslaved Africans had gathered momentum.

The decades of exploration in the Caribbean and Spanish encounters with indigenous peoples, and the use of enslaved labor in mining, would lead to the cultivation of critical crops—namely, sugar—that would soon come to be developed using enslaved African labor. Spanish control of the Caribbean paved the way for English, and later British, domination in the region, following the 1707 Acts of Union with Scotland. This early modern period would set the foundations of the rise of the transatlantic slave trade and a new form of slavery—hereditary racial slavery—that would be central to the creation of the racial-caste hierarchy and to the rise of Britain's wealthy and brutal Caribbean slave empire. It would come to usher in a key moment within the history of modernity. And it would come to completely upend, forever, the Caribbean.

FIRST ENCOUNTERS

Around seven thousand years ago, indigenous peoples embarked on a northern migratory path from South America to Trinidad, then still a part of mainland South America. Over the course of thousands of years, more continued this journey, moving beyond the Eastern Caribbean and reaching what is today Puerto Rico. In around 4000 BCE others from Central America moved from the Yucatán peninsula to Cuba, Hispaniola, and Puerto Rico. Most of these migrants were fisher-hunter-gatherers and belonged to numerous ethnic groups who left vital evidence of their presence in stones, burial sites, and artifacts.

Another wave of migration occurred around 2500 BCE. Coming from the Orinoco Basin in South America, groups of agriculturalists settled in villages in the western and eastern parts of the Caribbean, speaking languages derived from the language family known as Arawakan. Over time, more developed societies began to appear in Hispaniola and Puerto Rico.[6] Some of these peoples are collectively known as Taíno, which does not necessarily describe a specific group but rather is an adjective, loosely defined as noble or good.[7] The Taíno enacted a broad set of sophisticated cultural practices shared by several cultures that occupied the Caribbean.

It is difficult to know all aspects of Taíno daily life due to a lack of sources, but Spanish chroniclers (such as Las Casas) recorded a considerable amount of information about them. Using new archeological and ethnohistorical research, recent scholars have built on these works. They suggest that over hundreds of years Taíno society developed from being organized along tribal lines to chiefdoms.[8] Chiefs or *caciques* held godlike powers and could order laborers to cultivate land or serve in military encounters. Their society was hierarchical, with those below the *caciques* known as the *nitaínos* (elites), *behiques* (perhaps shamans), and the *naborías* (usually servants and commoners).[9] Taíno societies were matrilineal in their descent, meaning that women could be chiefs and that power was transferred from the chief's mother's relatives.[10] Labor was gendered: men took to hunting, while women focused on agricultural work, cooking, cloth-making, child-rearing and harvesting. Taínos cultivated different crops ranging from fruits to sweet potatoes, yams, and peanuts.[11]

The Taíno were not the only indigenous peoples residing in the Caribbean at this time. Another group, known as the Caribs, moved from South America and lived in the Lesser Antilles, the eastern part of the Caribbean. "Caribs" is a Taíno term meaning islanders, but the Caribs referred to themselves as Kalinagos, or sometimes Kalipuna.[12] The surrounding sea, the Caribbean, is named after this group. While Europeans regarded the Taíno as peaceful, they called the Kalinago "careless and lazy creatures," and "so vindictive there are no people more ready to take vengeance on anyone who has offended them."[13] Unlike Taínos, Kalinago activity tended to focus on trade and war. When they encountered Europeans, they would often put up a daring defense. In response, Europeans spread the myth of their cannibalism, which would be used to justify their enslavement. But there is no evidence that Kalinago peoples were cannibals.

Alongside Taínos and Kalinagos, the Caribbean was home to other groups: the Guanahatabeys, who occupied parts of Cuba, and the Lucayans, who lived in the Bahamas.[14] While many details about indigenous peoples' lives remain mostly unknown, what is certain is that by the fifteenth century they inhabited most of the islands in the Caribbean, with suggestions that their population was, adopting a conservative assessment, around 2 million by 1492.[15] In this year, indigenous peoples first met European explorers, ushering in a new phase of globalization that would connect the Caribbean to the rest of the world.

On August 3, 1492, the Genoese captain Christopher Columbus set sail on the *Santa María* from Palos, in the Bay of Cádiz on the coast of Spain, with around forty crewmen, alongside two smaller caravels, the *Niña* and the *Pinta*. They ventured first toward the Canary Islands before setting off across the Atlantic. Six thousand kilometers later, they arrived on the Caribbean island known by the Taíno as Guanahaní, which today is part of the Bahamas. Columbus took control of the land in the name of Ferdinand and Isabella of Spain and gave it a new name—San Salvador, meaning Holy Savior. Next, he and his crew moved along the north coast toward what was known as Quisqueya/Haiti, which he renamed Española or Hispaniola.[16] Here, his ship ran aground. He sent some of his crew to find the Taíno *cacique* Guacanagarí, who sent for canoes to aid the Spaniards. Later Columbus made an agreement with Guacanagarí whereby he agreed to fight the chief's enemies—in this case the Kalinago—for information on the location of gold mines.[17] Columbus continued to search for gold before sailing to the neighboring island, now known as Cuba. He eventually arrived back in Palos in March 1493, bringing with him some indigenous peoples.

Columbus's historic journey to the Caribbean occurred amid significant changes in the fourteenth and fifteenth centuries, including the exploration of the Canary Islands and Cape Verde, the weakening of Islam, and the rise of Christianity in the form of Catholicism. Born in 1451 or 1452, Columbus grew up in Genoa, a commercial and financial center. His career began on Portuguese ships, where he learned how to navigate the Atlantic on voyages to the African coast. Columbus was involved in transporting sugar, a profitable and popular new crop, from Madeira to Genoa. Around 1478 or 1479, he married a Portuguese woman from an aristocratic family and went on to climb the ranks as a mercantile agent before sealing his reputation as an intrepid geographer. Passionate about the discovery of new lands, he set his sights on the gold and riches rumored to exist in Asia. Indeed, when Columbus arrived in the Bahamas, he thought he had reached Asia.

Columbus's voyage occurred during a pivotal moment of change within European politics and political economy. In this age of discovery, new maritime technologies including the caravel, information tools like the printing press, and changes in the process of loaning money all helped contribute to an upswell of European traders looking for new markets to conquer by force. Often romanticized and glorified as a triumphant moment in Western histories, Columbus's travels wreaked havoc in the Caribbean, which became one of the key areas for European expansion and subsequently violent accumulation.

Etching of Christopher Columbus landing on the Caribbean island of Hispaniola in 1492 by Theodore de Bry, 1592.

A sense of surprise, wonder, and intrigue likely shaped the moment the Taíno and Spanish first set eyes on each other. The Spanish were small in number, and so they possibly did not spark immediate fear. In his diary, Columbus noted that the Taíno:

> all go naked as their mothers bore them, including the women . . . They were very well built with fine bodies and handsome faces. Their hair is coarse, almost like that of a horse's tail and short; they wear it down over their eyebrows except for a few strands at the back, which they wear long and never cut. They are the colour of the Canary Islanders (neither black

nor white) . . . They do not carry arms or know them. For when I showed them swords, they took them by the edge and cut themselves out of ignorance.[18]

Columbus identified the Taíno as inferior to Europeans, noting: "They should be good servants and very intelligent, for I have observed that they soon repeat anything that is said to them, and I believe that they would easily be made Christians, for they appeared to me to have no religion."[19] His initial categorization of Taínos was to have profound consequences for the success of Spanish colonization.

Encouraged by his first voyage, where he found small amounts of gold, Columbus embarked on a second in 1493. This time he went with the clear goal of establishing a trade colony with a royal monopoly in Hispaniola for his patrons Ferdinand and Isabella. The marriage in 1469 of the cousins Ferdinand II of Aragon and Isabella I of Castille united the Spanish Crown and would see Spain become a major European power. Known as the Catholic Monarchs, around 1478 they founded the Spanish Inquisition, which sought the homogenization of Spanish society, by means of brutal force, if necessary. Together they would resume the Reconquest: the campaigns by Christian states to recapture Muslim territories from parts of the Iberian Peninsula. In 1492 they gained control of Granada from the Islamic Moors, and they ordered all Spanish Jews and later Spanish Muslims to convert to Christianity or face expulsion from Spain. Ferdinand and Isabella's encouragement of colonial expansion was part of their attempt to increase the power and wealth of Spain.

As part of Columbus's mission, the monarchs urged him to convert indigenous peoples to Christianity, search for more gold, and develop trading relations. For this endeavor they introduced new rules: settlers received wages, and Columbus was made admiral, with the right to receive one-tenth of all profits

"ONE OF THE RICHEST SPOTS OF GROUND IN THE WORLD"

as commission. His expedition was equipped with seventeen ships and 1,500 male settlers, including priests.[20] The settlers also brought crops and livestock with them.

Charting a southerly route, Columbus ventured across the Atlantic from the Canary Islands to the Dominica Passage between the islands of Guadeloupe and Dominica.[21] Navigating the Lesser Antilles, he began to observe and remark on the supposed savage and hostile Kalinago occupants.

When Columbus finally reached his destination, La Navidad, in 1493—the first Spanish settlement in the Americas forged from the wreckage of the *Santa María* during his first voyage less than a year earlier—he was shocked by what he saw. The town had burned to the ground, and most of the Spanish settlers were dead, either of disease or in violent disputes about gold with indigenous peoples.[22] The indigenous peoples informed Columbus that they had tried to defend the Europeans against attacks from a rival cacique known as Caonabó, the incident foreshadowing tensions between Spaniards and indigenous peoples that would arise in the coming years. After leaving La Navidad, Columbus sailed along the north coast of Hispaniola and discovered a new settlement, La Isabela. In April 1494 he resumed exploration of Cuba, inhabiting the southern coast before heading to Jamaica, known by the indigenous peoples as Xaymaca, meaning "land of wood and water." As Columbus traveled to different islands and interacted with more indigenous peoples, he abandoned the initial plan of establishing trading relations with them. He had a new idea: to force the Taíno to work to develop Spanish colonization.[23] In 1497 he assigned groups of indigenous people to some Spaniards in a system called *repartimiento*. This saw groups of indigenous people allocated to Spaniards to perform different tasks.[24]

Many indigenous people began to flee their villages to escape from the Spanish. Others chose to rebel. When Columbus instructed settlers to build forts in large towns, Taínos attacked the settlers in large numbers. In 1495 Columbus retaliated by assailing Taíno villages and capturing chiefs. When Caonabó was arrested and sent to La Isabela, a group of chiefs raided Spanish settlements: joining with the indigenous peoples of Guacanagarí and other Taíno allies, Columbus and the Spanish fended off this attack.[25] That year, Columbus ramped up his assault on dissenting Taínos and sent out armed groups, instructing them to take captives if they encountered any hostility. As a result, around 1,600 Taínos across Hispaniola became captives—of these, 550 were sent to Spain and 650 given to settlers. The majority of the released Taínos fled from La Isabela.[26] Famine increased in 1495 and 1496 due to some Taíno attacks on Spanish crops, and this further diminished their population, along with increased labor demands and the spread of unfamiliar European-borne diseases against which the Taíno had no immunity, such as smallpox, influenza, malaria, measles, yellow fever, and the bubonic plague. Alongside famine and disease, the fall in the Taíno population was linked to waning fertility rates, partly due to attacks on Taíno villages.[27]

In 1500, the Catholic Monarchs removed Columbus from power in Hispaniola, due partly to disagreements around the treatment of indigenous peoples. In his place, they sent leading Spanish judge Francisco de Bobadilla to govern the colony as viceroy from 1500 to 1502. The monarchs introduced a range of other changes. They granted licences to other explorers and freed all indigenous peoples who had been enslaved and brought to Spain. However, Bobadilla's rule was to be short-lived: he died two years after being appointed when his ship was hit by a hurricane. His replacement was a military officer, Nicolás de Ovando, who served as governor of the Indies from 1502 to 1509. Ovando arrived in Hispaniola with 2,500 settlers, including Las Casas, and his rule marked a new phase in Spanish–indigenous peoples' relations.[28]

Ovando was granted enhanced powers in dealing with indigenous peoples, which he took as license to further suppress them. He dismantled a considerable amount of Taíno leadership and introduced the *encomienda* system to organize forced labor of indigenous peoples to work in mines and agriculture. The *encomienda* system dealt the Taíno another blow, and as a form of resistance, some died by suicide.[29] More military clashes occurred in 1503 and 1504, and these saw numerous chiefs captured, assigned to Spanish settlers, and compelled to labor in the construction of towns. They were also made to convert to Catholicism.

Alongside increasing assaults on indigenous peoples, the next few years saw mass Spanish expeditions and the establishment of new colonies. In 1508 the Spanish acquired Puerto Rico, the following year Jamaica, and Cuba in 1511. While these islands did have gold deposits, they were not as abundant as had been believed. By around 1508 gold mining had reached its peak, and in later years gold would be in short supply—colonists then turned their attention to sustainable crops that they could sell.[30] This meant drastic alterations in the ecology of the land by clearing the dense rainforest and burning trees for the planting of sugar.

In the early modern era, sugar was a valuable luxurious commodity, replacing honey as a sweetener. The process of developing sugar was long, arduous, and would remain labor-intensive, associated with enslaved labor on large plantations.

The Portuguese were the first to develop sugarcane in Brazil, on Madeira and on the West African coast in São Tomé, using the labor of enslaved Africans from various places. Following them, the Spanish began cultivating sugar in the Canary Islands, which they had begun colonizing in the fifteenth century. The Spanish subjugated and enslaved the indigenous population of the Canaries—the Guanches—exporting some of them to Madeira or Europe, while others were forced to labor on Canarian sugar plantations. The sugar development on Madeira and the Canary Islands would become a model for the growth of sugar in the Caribbean.

In search of more laborers, in 1509 the Spanish Crown granted permission for the forced movement and enslavement of the Lucayans in the Bahamas to Hispaniola, and this was followed by raids in Jamaica, Barbados, and Trinidad.[31] Indigenous peoples resisted these practices. Some began attacking Spanish settlements, and others fled to the mountains. Those who escaped became known as Maroons—runaways involved in the wars with the Spanish in 1519 and 1533. Their guerrilla tactics were effective, and in 1533 the Spanish signed a treaty with their chief leader, Enriquillo, that ended hostilities in exchange for land and freedom.

Coercion and violence were not the only features of indigenous peoples' interaction with the Spanish, however. Marriages between Taíno women and Spanish men were common, and in 1514 these unions were sanctioned by the Church and state. The offspring of these partnerships shaped the mixed—or *mestizo*—population. They also helped in the development of creole—meaning "born on the island"—society. But intermarriage could not protect the indigenous peoples, and through wars, disease, and famine their numbers continued to wane. In 1508 there were an estimated sixty thousand Taínos in Hispaniola; by 1514 their numbers had plummeted to around thirty thousand; and by 1518, eleven thousand.[32]

Ascertaining accurate figures for the decrease in indigenous communities in the Caribbean is challenging. While Spanish chroniclers numbered the population around the time of European contact to have been 1 million, anthropologists have disputed this, arguing instead for the population to have been 6–12 million.[33] If these more recent figures are taken as more accurate, they reveal the utter devastation of the indigenous population caused by European contact. Their dwindling population contributed to a labor shortage, which led the Spanish to turn their attention to another group.

By the time the Spanish took an interest in the trade of enslaved Africans, enslavement was already a long-established global institution that operated in various ways. In Africa, men and women could be captured in warfare and enslaved, or taken as part payment for a debt or as punishment for a criminal offense.[34] The Portuguese were an early European power to enslave Africans, doing so with approval in 1452 and 1455 from Pope Nicholas V, who issued papal bulls arguing that slavery provided a Christianizing influence to supposed pagans. In this era, several justifications were offered for enslaving Africans. Europeans, including Las Casas initially, claimed superiority as Christians, as most of the Africans Europeans encountered were either Muslim or animist. The idea that God used Africans' black skin color as a mark of their lack of morality and inferiority was another factor (shaped by the biblical curse of Ham and his descendants, who were assumed to be of African descent), as were hierarchical notions of difference that positioned Africans in the lower levels of the "great chain of being."

Modern notions of "race" did not yet exist, but physical differences and complexion played a role in how Europeans perceived Africans, which would prove precursors to later ideas about whiteness and blackness. For the Spanish, in one sense, the justification for the enslavement of Africans was complex and varied. Some arguments for it relied on religion: the pope had denied Spain land in Africa (based on attempts to limit competition with them and their Portuguese rivals), and many considered enslavement a good way to convert those considered pagans or who shared different faiths to Christianity. But in another sense, justification for the enslavement of Africans was stark and simple:

it served as a way to eke out cheap labor for surplus value from newly claimed territory.

Enslaved Africans were initially only a small part of Spanish colonization in the Caribbean. The Spanish did not have any forts on the African coast, so they depended on other states, like Portugal, to supply them with enslaved people. The first enslaved Africans began to arrive in the 1500s and were ordered by King Ferdinand to work alongside indigenous peoples to build forts in gold mines. In 1502 Ovando brought over more enslaved Africans, but many escaped and found refuge with indigenous peoples who had fled to the mountains. From 1518, a new series of contracts—the *asiento de negros*—began, which allowed private figures to transport enslaved Africans on the condition of paying a fee to the royal treasury.[35] It was believed that Africans could withstand the tropical climate of the Caribbean and were more resistant to disease than the Taíno, and this helped spread the stereotype that enslaved Africans were physically stronger workers. In the mid-sixteenth century, the enslaved African population of Hispaniola was around thirty thousand; by the end of the century their number in the Spanish Caribbean had grown to about one hundred thousand.[36]

The use of enslaved labor was critical to the success of Spanish colonialism in the Caribbean, but the islands were just the first stage of a period of conquest during which the Spanish Empire expanded to include Florida, Mexico, Panama, Cartagena, and Peru. Crucially, however, the Spanish did not extend their reach into the Eastern Caribbean, for reasons still debated today. One argument is that these areas did not have the resources the Spanish sought to accumulate, while another casts the Kalinago as more difficult to subdue than the Taíno. Nevertheless, the Eastern Caribbean became a place of refuge for both indigenous peoples and enslaved Africans who had escaped from Spanish territories. It would soon also become a space for the arrival of new colonial powers who, having heard stories of successful Spanish exploits in the region, were eager to see if they too could prosper in the New World.

EUROPEAN RULE AND RIVALRY

Attempts to shatter the Spanish monopoly in the Caribbean accelerated in the 1540s. The French started to plunder Spanish ships on their voyages to Spain, and the English quickly joined in—their attacks shaped, in part, by the Protestant Reformation of the sixteenth century, which spawned anti-Catholic and anti-Spanish sentiment. In 1572, Queen Elizabeth I sent English troops to help the Dutch win back independence from Spain and continued encouraging privateers—effectively pirates with a royal licence to plunder—to attack Spanish ships. As the Spanish hold over the Caribbean Sea weakened in the 1560s, English voyages to the region increased.

Naval commander, administrator, and buccaneer John Hawkins led an early English expedition to the Caribbean around 1562, taking three ships via what is today Sierra Leone. On their way, he and his crew attacked a Portuguese ship, captured the enslaved people on board, and traded them in the Caribbean, making a profit for the London merchants who had invested in the expedition. With the approval of Elizabeth I, and with his second cousin and protégé Francis Drake in tow, Hawkins continued privateering, traveling to the West African coast, where he purchased more enslaved Africans to trade in the Spanish Americas. In response, the Spanish attacked his ships.

Drake, who would become England's most famous privateer, pressed on regardless, and in 1585 he sacked Santo Domingo, the capital of Hispaniola. Men like Hawkins, Drake, and other privateers were joined by other, unlicensed, pirates who raided and plundered. Often diverse, pirate crews consisted of men and women of varied racial and ethnic backgrounds, including runaway enslaved people.[37] Yet privateering and pirate activity did not break the Spanish hold. That happened with the Anglo-Spanish Wars of 1585–1604, which prevented Spain from attacking other nascent European settlements in the region. From the 1590s, the Dutch joined the French and English in their quest for control of the Caribbean.

European powers made new discoveries as they ventured farther into the Caribbean. Hawkins was one of the first to bring tobacco to England in the 1560s. Consumed by indigenous peoples, tobacco was considered by some Europeans to be vulgar and pagan. King James VI of Scotland and I of England would notoriously describe it as "a custom loathsome to the eye, hateful to the nose, harmful to the brain, dangerous to the lungs, and in the black stinking fume thereof, nearest resembling the horrible Stygian smoke of the pit that is bottomless."[38] Despite such disdain, many quickly became enamored and addicted. As the English did not want to pay a high price for Spanish-controlled tobacco, this spurred the development of the tobacco colony of Virginia, established in 1607, followed in 1612 with Bermuda when the island became an official colony. It was the potential of tobacco that encouraged European interest in the Lesser Antilles in the early 1600s. Unlike Spain, merchants looking to invest in emerging markets, rather than the Crown, spearheaded English colonization.

St. Christopher, later St. Kitts, became in 1623 the first non-Spanish colony in the Lesser Antilles captured by the English. In 1624 the French and English jointly controlled the island and defended it against the Spanish. Both European powers also attacked the majority of the indigenous Kalinago people and planted tobacco and established plantation societies. Planting was not a new practice for the English; they had done the same in the conquest of Ireland from 1529 to 1603. The English settlers who began planting in St. Kitts were led by London merchant Thomas Warner, who was commissioned as lieutenant governor by King Charles I in 1625. But a year later, profit-seeking settlers faced another Kalinago uprising, which the English and French quickly fended off, and in 1629 the Spanish also attacked and briefly captured the island, only to be eventually driven out. Although indigenous communities' numbers dwindled, they continued to exist, and still do, in various parts of the Caribbean such as Dominica, St. Vincent, Trinidad, and Guyana.

Anglo-French control of St. Kitts was precarious, but another island would transform English colonialism. On the far eastern side of the Lesser Antilles lay the relatively flat 439-kilometer-square island of Barbados. In 1625 English captain John Powell arrived there, joined two years later by his brother Henry, who came with a group of settlers and enslaved people captured from Portuguese ships. The two began working with the London-based merchant Sir William Courteen to develop tobacco with labor from indigenous peoples, and they quickly succeeded. In 1629, Courteen's settlement was taken over by James Hay, the Earl of Carlisle.

To develop tobacco plantations, settlers relied on indentured servants and laborers from England. Indentured servitude was a long-established practice throughout Europe. Some people, lured by rags-to-riches stories, voluntarily indentured themselves for four to seven years, working for planters in return for "freedom dues"—usually a roughly ten-acre plot of land. Others, such as Irish Catholics, considered prisoners of war, came to Barbados involuntarily, as did those who were kidnapped and convicts.

While most planters treated indentured laborers well, providing them with lodgings and ensuring they had time off work, some did not, and stories of their mistreatment circulated widely. Richard Ligon provided one of the most memorable observations about the lives of these laborers. An English writer, Ligon traveled to Barbados in 1647 with a group of royalist exiles to help the barrister and planter Thomas Modyford. While in Barbados, Ligon spent time as a planter before returning to England in 1650 due to ill health and later serving time in prison for debt. Over the course of his three-year sentence, he compiled the *True and Exact History of the Island of Barbados*—a survey of the natural, social, and economic phenomena (published in 1657). The popular book was one of the first English accounts of life in Barbados. In it, Ligon described servants as leading "wearisome and miserable lives" who did "very hard labour" and were provided with poor lodgings.[39] He believed that they, rather than the enslaved, had "the worser lives" because, he surmised, Africans were more suited to work in the tropics.[40]

As Barbados was developing tobacco plantations, other islands came under English control. The English settled in Nevis in 1628, and Antigua and Montserrat in 1632. Colonists in Montserrat were largely English and Irish Catholics who had moved from the Protestant-dominated St. Kitts (although its official church was the Church of England).[41] Land on Montserrat was more widely available than on other islands, allowing the extension of property ownership to those, like the Irish, who managed to climb up the social ladder.[42]

Tobacco boomed between the 1630s and 1650s, but trouble was looming. The Caribbean produced poor-quality tobacco, and planters faced stiff competition from the superior Virginian tobacco. When the market became saturated, prices dropped, which forced planters to turn to the production of other goods, such as indigo, timber, coffee, and cotton. However, alongside changing environmental conditions and the effects of drought, these crops struggled, and their prices dropped as well, which again forced planters to follow in Spain's footsteps. The switch to sugar was spearheaded in Barbados by planter James Drax. Drax arrived on the island in the 1620s and a decade later held a portion of land with his brother William. In 1640, James Drax

"ONE OF THE RICHEST SPOTS OF GROUND IN THE WORLD"

ventured to Brazil, where he heard the Dutch were growing sugarcane. He returned to Barbados to start experimenting.

Meanwhile, back in England, political change would soon influence the Caribbean. During the English Civil Wars of 1642–51, the Dutch began to threaten English naval power. Following the success of Parliamentarians and the execution of Charles I in 1649, the Rump Parliament passed the Navigation Act in 1651, which was designed to damage the Dutch. Part of the act mandated that goods from English colonies or foreign countries must be transported in English ships, which meant that neither the Dutch nor other foreign powers could bring their products to English ports, including those in the Americas. The act led to the first Anglo-Dutch War of 1652–54.

As soon as this war had ended, the English quickly entered another. Disputes with Spain over trade routes led to the Anglo-Spanish War of 1654–60. During this time, Oliver Cromwell, who organized and led the New Model Army against Charles I during the Civil Wars, served as Lord Protector of the Commonwealth of England, Scotland, and Ireland and was keen to expand his Puritan revolution into the Americas as part of his "Western Design," which marked a new phase in English colonial activity. This phrase referred to English expeditions against the Spanish Caribbean amid the 1654–60 Anglo-Spanish War that sought to thwart Spanish control in the Americas. This was the first time a colonizing mission had come under the direct control of the government rather than a private company. Cromwell sanctioned an expedition force led by Admiral William Penn and General Robert Venables that departed from England in 1654, first arriving in Barbados and then going to Hispaniola in April 1655. On May 10, 1655, they landed and fought off the Spanish to add Jamaica as another English colony.

In 1660, King Charles II passed a second Navigation Act. In trying to overpower the Dutch, the act stipulated that all goods had to be carried to and from the colonies in English ships with a predominantly English crew. This sparked another war in 1665 that ended two years later with the Peace of Breda. In this treaty, the Dutch gained the colony of Suriname on the northeastern coast of South America in exchange for New Netherland, its outpost on the east coast of North America, which provided England with more territory and power.

Back in Barbados, Drax's experimentation in sugar was gaining ground, and a sugar revolution was imminent.

THE SUGAR REVOLUTION

Drax found that Barbados had the ideal topography for cultivating sugar. But the enterprise required a vast amount of land and capital, meaning that wealthier planters tended to spearhead sugar production. Many received money from the Dutch, who were simultaneously their competitors and collaborators. The Dutch anticipated sizable profits from sugar production and provided credit, enslaved people, and equipment to planters in Barbados. English merchants also had a hand in providing credit, investing in land, and supplying planters with enslaved labor.[43] It was strictly illegal for planters in Barbados to have links with the Dutch, who were at war with England during this period, but contact occurred nevertheless due to the distraction caused by the English Civil Wars. With Parliament preoccupied by machinations against the monarchy, Barbados became something of an independent state: the planter class gained control of legislation and at times circumvented English law, though this would end in 1651 when the British Parliament sent a fleet to the island to restore metropolitan colonial control.

Planters like Drax planned to have a small number of enslaved men and women working side by side with indentured laborers, in a sort of mixed-labor economy. Early on, Drax reaped the benefits of this combined black-and-white labor system. In 1642 he began purchasing enslaved Africans from other European powers. By the early 1650s, his wealth had significantly grown, so much so that he built on Barbados the vast and imposing Drax Hall estate, which housed around two hundred enslaved Africans. By the late 1650s, he had become an absentee planter, enjoying his riches in London.

Yet the increased wealth of planters like Drax exacted a cost from indentured laborers. The demanding process of sugar production worked and punished indentured laborers harder than before and, in turn, more servants ran away or rebelled. And as the construction of plantations devoured more land, less was available for servants. "Freedom due" land grants (given to indentured laborers after they had served their period of indentureship) were replaced by a fixed sum of money of less value. As news began to spread back to England about the strenuous work on sugar plantations, indentured laborers started to look elsewhere.

By the mid-seventeenth century, English people who saw indentureship or migration as an opportunity to improve their lives sought new opportunities in more desirable parts of the British Empire, such as the North American colonies of Virginia, the provinces of Maryland (established in 1632), and South Carolina (established in 1663). In response, planters in the Caribbean tried to make indentureship appear more attractive. Some reduced the length of servitude, but this led to prohibitive increases in the cost of servant labor. In 1652 the indentured population in Barbados was thirteen thousand (a figure that included waged laborers); by 1683 it was down to 2,301.[44] As the cost of indentured servants rose and their numbers dwindled, the number of enslaved people began to rise. The choice of enslaved Africans had less to do with complexion than profit. As Oxford-educated historian and later first prime minister of Trinidad and Tobago, Eric Williams, succinctly describes it: "Slavery was not born of racism: rather, racism was the consequence of slavery."[45] In the first decades of colonization, race was used as a legitimizing pretext for capitalist expansion and economic wealth. The turn to invest more in enslaved African labor drove the sugar revolution in the Caribbean.

Various arguments have arisen in attempts to understand the "sugar revolution"—the transformation of Caribbean society from one built on white labor to one dominated by enslaved Africans and sugar plantations. The climatic theory—that white servants failed to work on sugar plantations due to physiological factors while enslaved Africans were successful because of their race—has been widely refuted. The consensus today is one of complexity, with many situating the change within a much longer historical and larger Atlantic and global context.

While planters like Drax were initially independently involved in the purchase of enslaved Africans, the first companies to play a part in the slave trade to English Caribbean colonies were established in the 1660s. One, the "Company of Royal Adventurers of England Trading into Africa," created after the restoration of the monarchy in 1663, built forts on the West African coast and by 1664 had sent three thousand enslaved people to Barbados.[46] The then Duke of York, later King James II, was a principal leader in this company, and enslaved men, women, and children sent to the island were branded with the letters DY. Its successor, the Royal African Company, was unable to keep up with the colonial demand for enslaved people and had difficulty maintaining forts on the African coast. In 1698 Parliament rearranged the trade and gave private traders the right to be involved legally on payment of a duty to the Royal African Company.[47] Consequently, the trade flourished. This duty ended in the 1700s, and so private traders from major port cities in England, including Bristol, Liverpool, London, Lancaster, and Manchester, grew as the Royal African Company declined.[48] In its place a group of merchants joined

"ONE OF THE RICHEST SPOTS OF GROUND IN THE WORLD"

forces to create the Company of Merchants Trading to Africa and maintained forts on the African coast that were financed by Parliament.

Some European slave traders cultivated friendly relations with African leaders as they ventured up and down the West African coast to procure enslaved people. The enslaved were often prisoners of war, criminals, victims of abductions, or dependents with no kinship ties.[49] Gift-giving became an established practice to form positive bonds. African collaborators also helped European traders. Often of mixed heritage, the offspring of European slave traders and local African women, African-European men worked alongside European traders to capture Africans.

In exchange for enslaved people, English traders also provided commodities that Africans wanted. Many gave tobacco, rum, or valuable military weapons, leading to European entanglement in West African wars. While there were traders who interacted with African elites to access and capture Africans, there were plenty who did not. Some traders simply abducted Africans as they traversed the West African coast. Others raided villages in the early hours of the morning, capturing whomever they could. Olaudah Equiano, later an important abolitionist, was one of those captured in this manner. He was from the Igbo group of what is today Nigeria. In his famous autobiography, *The Interesting Narrative of the Life of Olaudah Equiano, or Gustavus Vassa*, published in 1789, he wrote that at the age of eleven, while he was at home with his sister, "two men and a woman got over our walls, and in a moment seized us both."[50] After being separated from his sister, Equiano "cried and grieved continually; and for several days did not eat any thing but what they forced into my mouth."[51]

Trading in enslaved people was a dangerous activity. European traders in West Africa contracted various diseases such as jaundice, dysentery, and fevers. Between 1684 and 1732, Royal African Company records show that the average annual death toll for men in their service on the Gold Coast was 27 percent.[52] Likewise, the enslaved fell victim to diseases brought by Europeans.

Though slavery had been considered a form of trade in West Africa, it was the transatlantic slave trade that inaugurated hereditary racial slavery—a form of enslavement premised on the creation of racial differences, passed on through the reproduction of enslaved African women, and sustained by violence and codified into law. Hereditary racial slavery was also based on the chattel principle by placing an enslaved person in the position of being sold like movable property and able to be placed and priced anywhere in the Americas. In this way, hereditary racial slavery was inescapably wrapped up with capitalism—treating individuals as trading labor entities tied to property.

Olaudah Equiano. Frontispiece from *The Interesting Narrative of the Life of Olaudah Equiano, Or Gustavus Vassa, the African*, London, 1790.

"ONE OF THE RICHEST SPOTS OF GROUND IN THE WORLD"

Capitalism and racism were inextricable. Chattel slavery made money for the English Empire; racial hierarchies were a useful justification for a profitable and powerful new system.

In the seventeenth century, race was still an emerging category and was often used to refer to lineage or family rather than skin color, but it would take on its modern meaning through hereditary racial slavery, which shared links with preexisting forms of human hierarchy. For instance, before the seventeenth century Europeans had divided themselves into hierarchical groups, with Jews, Irish Catholics, Roma, and Slavs considered "other" and subject to forms of slavery and colonialism for the purpose of capitalist development.[53]

In the era of hereditary racial slavery, a wide-ranging set of ideas about the character of sub-Saharan black Africans supported white supremacist ideology about the alleged inferiority of black Africans. For example, Dalby Thomas, an agent for the Royal African Company, noted in 1709 that

> the natives here have neither religion nor law binding them to humanity, good behaviour or honesty ... They frequently for their grandeur sacrifice an innocent man, that is a person they have no crime to charge with, and to train their children up to cruelty, they give them knives to cut and slash the person that is to be killed, neither have they any knowledge of liberty and property.[54]

"Besides," he continued, "the Blacks are naturally such rogues and bred up with such roguish principles that what they can get by force or deceit and can defend themselves from those they robb [sic] they reckon it as honestly their own, as if they paid for it."[55] Surgeon Dr. James Houston went further, commenting from Africa in 1725:

> [The African's] natural Temper is barbarously cruel, selfish, and deceitful, and their Government equally barbarous and uncivil;

and consequently the Men of greatest Eminency amongst them, are those that are most capable of being the greatest Rogues; Vice, being left without any Check on it, becomes a virtue. As for their customs, they exactly resemble their Fellow Creatures and Natives, the Monkeys.[56]

The assumptions made by Thomas and Houston deemed people of African descent not only naturally inferior to white people but also akin to animals—arguments used to justify what became one of the deadliest systems of slavery in the Americas and one that uniquely stripped the enslaved of human status and rights.

Because accounts were mostly written by Europeans and told from a European perspective, it is hard to capture from contemporaneous sources what Africans felt in the early process of their enslavement on the coasts of the continent. But what is clear is that both violence and resistance to enslavement occurred first in West Africa. Before boarding ships, captives were inspected, and if they did not pass the visual test, some—perhaps because of their age or physique—faced execution. Surgeon Alexander Falconbridge saw this occur at New Calabar (in today's Nigeria) in the 1780s: "the traders, when any of their negroes have been objected to, have dropped their canoes under the stern of the vessel and instantly beheaded them, in the sight of the captain."[57] Once captured, many tried to escape, but Europeans often overpowered them. Various methods, including heavy metal chains around the neck, hands, and feet, were used to prevent Africans from escaping.

Once on board, conditions were no better. The ships contained what Equiano described as "a multitude of black people of every description chained together, every one of their countenances expressing dejection and sorrow."[58] High mortality rates were frequent, and diseases such as smallpox, malaria, measles, and dysentery spread quickly on cramped ships where food and water were in short supply. These vessels were also spaces of frequent physical and sexual violence as well as enslaved resistance.

In 1721, seventeen enslaved people led a mutiny on the sloop *Cape Coast* at Anomabo fort (in what is today Ghana). While on board, some went on hunger strike while others died by suicide. Sold into slavery at the age of thirteen on the Gold Coast, Quobna Ottobah Cugoano said of his time aboard a ship: "Death was more preferable than life, and a plan was concerted amongst us, that we might burn and blow up the ship, and to perish all together in the flames."[59] When they reached the Caribbean, captives were usually emaciated, dehydrated, ill, and traumatized, and here plantation owners began their selection. Ligon wrote that in Barbados: "The planters . . . chose them as they do Horses in a Market; the strongest, youthfullest, and most beautiful, yield the greatest prices."[60] How the enslaved looked and their sex were important factors too. Defined as the property of their masters, and branded as such, around 3.4 million Africans were transported across the Atlantic on British ships between 1640 and 1807.[61] In all, during the period of transatlantic slavery, from 1526 to 1867, estimates show that 12.5 million enslaved adults and children were transported on ships in Africa, with 10.7 million arriving in various areas in the Americas.[62]

The union of sugar and racial slavery transformed the demography of the Caribbean. Previously, enslaved people often formed a minority of the population, and in places like Southern Europe and the Middle East the enslaved population had diverse origins. In the Caribbean, however, racial slavery would come to be associated with one group—sub-Saharan Africans.

Barbados became the most prosperous Caribbean colony in the late 1600s, while Anglo-French conflicts on the Leeward Islands of Montserrat, Nevis, Antigua, and St. Kitts delayed development of these English colonies. In addition, planters on some of these islands had limited funds to buy enslaved people and develop large plantations, with many opting to continue producing tobacco.[63] This would change as the eighteenth century progressed. Sugar planters in Jamaica, an island thirty times the size of Barbados, brought over large numbers of enslaved people. By 1713, the colony's black-to-white ratio was eight to one.[64]

As the Caribbean became a capitalized sugar monoculture, sugar thrived in Britain. The six largest sugar-producing colonies—Barbados, Montserrat, Jamaica, St. Kitts, Nevis, and Antigua—produced 90 percent of the molasses, sugar, and rum imported into England up to 1763.[65] Other crops produced in the Caribbean also made their way to Britain. Barbados cultivated ginger and cotton, and Jamaica developed cocoa. But sugar was the most popular, and it enriched planters in previously unimagined ways. When the price of sugar increased, the fortunes of those selling it became great, which in turn allowed them to establish monopolies on land. This concentration of land in the hands of elite planters would become an enduring feature of the racial-caste order: by 1680, planters had control of around 95 percent of the island.[66]

The most successful planters, like Modyford and Drax, owned many plantations, often located near each other, or on different islands, and to ensure profit and efficiency, planters introduced a complex management system. Each plantation had a resident manager, known as an overseer, who tended to be a free white man who aspired to be an owner. Modyford's and Drax's stories, however, show only one side of the experience of the English in the Caribbean.[67] For every wealthy sugar planter, thousands of English settlers struggled to get rich quick on dangerous islands, contending with tropical diseases and epidemics. Planters in the Caribbean did not operate as isolated individuals. Rather, slavery in the Caribbean was developed by those who were involved in power hierarchies, Stuart court politics, and policies about hereditary status and legal structures that encompassed England too.[68] Indeed, the notion of property rights as being foundational to all individual rights was a key part of liberalism that informed English legal policies and that underpinned legal justifications for the mass enslavement of Africans.

Enslaved Africans, indentured laborers, wealthy planters, plantation officials, and ordinary settlers all came to create new societies in the Caribbean that drew attention from visitors. In 1655, English traveler Henry Whistler offered a vivid description of Barbados, nicknamed "Little England." He described the island as

> one of the richest spots of ground in the world and fully inhabited ... with English, French, Dutch, Scots, Irish, Spaniards they being Jews, with Indians and miserable Negroes born to perpetual slavery, they and their seed ... This island is the dunghill whereon England doth cast forth its rubbish. Rogues and whores and such like people are those which are generally brought here. A rogue in England will hardly make a cheater here. A bawd brought over puts on a demure comportment, a whore if handsome makes a wife for some rich planter. But in plain, the island of itself is very delightful and pleasant.[69]

Whistler portrays a social inversion of life in England, with its strict rules. Nevertheless, Caribbean societies were heavily dependent on England. Most necessary goods, foods, and materials were imported from the metropolitan motherland, as well as neighboring English-controlled colonies in North America. Indeed, over the following decades and especially in the eighteenth century, British colonies in North America would become heavily involved in the slave trade that became critical to their development. It would be enslaved Africans who labored on tobacco plantations in Virginia and Maryland, as well as rice plantations in South Carolina and cotton plantations in the southern states.[70] Furthermore, the sugar colonies in the Caribbean were deeply reliant on manufacturing in England to refine sugar. As the fates of England and the Caribbean became increasingly entwined in the seventeenth century, the distance between the two would narrow. As time progressed the two societies would influence each other more, not less. The entangled relationship between England (later Britain) and the Caribbean saw each impinging inevitably on the other. Contrary to the congratulatory narratives that would quarantine enslavement from British history, or revise it as a force of benevolence, racial slavery was the glue that tied Britain to the Caribbean and vice versa.

AFRICAN-CARIBBEAN TRACES IN EARLY MODERN ENGLAND

As the decades wore on, more Africans would come to England. The presence of people of African descent in Britain dates back to the Roman era. While small in number, some arrived as a result of globalizing trends that brought Africans and Europeans into closer contact from the fourteenth century onward. During the Tudor period, some lived in cities and others could be found in rural villages. Some were ambassadors, porters, servants, silk weavers; others were sailors or musicians; and a small number worked as prostitutes.[71] Over the seventeenth century, and after the Glorious Revolution of 1688–89 that saw King James II deposed and replaced by his Protestant daughter Mary and her Dutch husband, William of Orange, their numbers grew.

The physical presence of Africans increased as hereditary racial slavery progressed and planters returned to England with their enslaved property. Some planters gave enslaved people as gifts to friends and family members. Although much is unknown about the lives of people of African descent in England, Scotland, and Wales, it is evident that some were kept in similar states of slavery by their masters. But Africans in England had ambiguous legal status. This ambiguity both aided those who invoked the legal language of property rights to defend keeping enslaved people in their service and also allowed Africans a means to try to escape their bondage.

A litany of newspaper ads calling for the return of runaway servants and enslaved men and women speak to how Africans resisted their treatment. In 1687 one ad reported: "A Negro Boy about 9 years old" as missing.[72] Three years later, in 1690: "A Negro boy, named Toney, aged about 16, was lost from Ratcliff... He has a Brass Collar on, with directions where he liv'd."[73] In the same year, an enslaved woman named Katherine Auker approached the Middlesex Sessions asking for removal from her master, the Barbadian planter Robert Rich, who had brought her to England. Auker had wrongly believed that baptism would afford her freedom and asked to be discharged; in response she had been brutally attacked by her master and mistress. They refused to release her, and even when they returned to Barbados, they did not allow her to enter anyone else's service and had her imprisoned. But the court intervened and granted her permission to serve anyone else until her masters came back to England.[74]

A majority of Africans in England were servants. Having an African servant in the seventeenth and eighteenth centuries elevated one's social status. When King George I arrived in England from Hanover in 1714, he came with Mustapha and Mahomet, two servants of African background.[75] A plethora of portraiture indicate that having a black servant, especially a young male one, symbolized wealth and power. In most images, very dark-skinned black boys stand in a subordinate position next to a white woman or man—the contrasting skin tones conveying a society fascinated with whiteness as well as blackness. In some, their enslavement is made clear with apparatus such as collars hanging around the black person's neck. In other images, black people were visually equated with animals. Depictions of people of African descent in Britain were carefully staged and so cannot be viewed as an exact narrative of their lives.[76] Yet from high art to cheap prints, England in the early modern era was replete with visual representations of people of African descent. In addition to servants, other Africans were barbers, cooks, maids, butlers, footmen, or dockworkers in various cities. They came from various parts of the world—some directly from West Africa, others from the Caribbean or via Europe. The majority were male and young and lived in both urban and rural areas. They came to seventeenth-century England alongside small numbers of South Asians, Turks, East Asians, and indigenous peoples from the Americas.

A Young Girl with an Enslaved Servant and a Dog, oil on canvas by Bartholomew Dandridge, c. 1725.

People of African descent and cultural products from the continent and the Caribbean were also visible within broader English culture. Docks, for instance, were replete with goods from the Caribbean, and white Englishmen and -women consumed products or by-products of enslaved labor. After sugar the most popular products tended to be rum and tobacco, which led to the rise of tobacco shops, coffee shops, and a new wave of consumption. Early modern travel literature, poetry, and visual culture gave white Britons insight into people from Africa and the Caribbean too.[77] Theatrical plays such as William D'Avenant's opera *The Cruelty of the Spaniards in Peru* performed in 1658; Mary Pix's 1697 *The Innocent Mistress*; Thomas Southerne's dramatic version of Aphra Behn's novel *Oroonoko* (1688), first performed in 1696; and the comic opera *Inkle and Yarico*, staged in 1787, provided somewhat stereotypical and negative representations of the Caribbean that shaped attitudes to people of African descent. Furthermore, as scholar Noémie Ndiaye has powerfully argued, sound, images, and dance within wider theater and performance culture across early modern Europe "provided spectators and participants with new ways of thinking about the Afro-diasporic people who lived in their midst... [and] did not passively reflect the intercolonial emergence of blackness as a racial category but actively fostered it."[78]

Yet in most cases, white Britons were not always fully aware of, or informed about, the brutality of hereditary racial slavery. And it is a live question whether they would have cared, even if they had been fully aware, given that during this era violence, in the form of public judicial torture and execution, still occurred in Britain. Slippages between the meanings of "servant" and "slave" were also part of the somewhat vague understandings of racial slavery. The Royal African Company described enslaved people as "perpetual servants," a euphemism for the violence of racial slavery.[79] In the seventeenth and eighteenth centuries, white Britons already had some ideas about interactions with Africa that drew from European engagement with North Africa, and Iberian and Dutch trade with West and Central Africa.[80] Some white Britons knew of a much longer history of the bondage of Africans, dating back to fourteenth- and fifteenth-century use of African slavery in countries in the Mediterranean.[81] The realities of hereditary racial slavery as experienced by Africans in the Caribbean and North America were not widely represented. The relationship between Britain and the enslaved economy of the Caribbean was simultaneously distant (and willfully obfuscated) and proximate, in image, social encounter, stories, objects, and consumption. The physical and visual presence of Africans, the enslaved, and the Caribbean in seventeenth-century England shows that the British Empire was not a faraway, distant entity divorced from the lives of the English. As the seventeenth century gave way to the eighteenth, the empire itself became, in historian Catherine Molineux's words: "a frontier of Britain, but Britain was also a frontier of the emerging Atlantic world."[82]

On that "frontier," back in the Caribbean, as the sugar revolution was intensifying jaggedly across English, French, and Spanish colonies, so too were attacks on indigenous peoples. The English engaged in warfare with indigenous communities in the Eastern Caribbean. In 1681, the governor of the Leeward Islands, Sir William Stapleton, wrote in a letter to colonial officials in London: "I beg your pardon if I am tedious, but I beg you to represent to the King the necessity for destroying these Carib Indians. [. . .] We are now as much on our guard as if we had a Christia[n] enemy."[83] Stapleton was then given permission to mobilize militia for a full-scale attack on indigenous communities. But Kalinagos resisted Spanish, English, and French attempts to decimate their community and take over their land to create more plantations.

In December 1675, merchants in London sent a petition to the Lords of Trade and Plantations in support of Governor Stapleton's

"ONE OF THE RICHEST SPOTS OF GROUND IN THE WORLD"

plans to attack the indigenous communities and called for a commission to be given to Philip Warner, Stapleton's deputy, to send soldiers to Dominica to "destroy those barbarous savages."[84] Stapleton had already sent Warner around three hundred men to attack Kalinago communities in Dominica, and many Kalinagos were executed. But still the Kalinago continued their defense.

European conflict raged simultaneously. The most significant for the Caribbean was the Seven Years' War of 1756–63, between the British and the French and their Spanish allies. British victory cleared the way for its naval supremacy and increased movement into Eastern Caribbean territories. The Treaty of Paris that ended the Seven Years' War saw the British secure new islands, including Dominica, St. Vincent, Tobago, and Grenada. Britain could claim more territories and make further incursions into the lands of the Kalinago, Karifuna, and other indigenous communities. Elsewhere, the British gained Senegal, Florida, and Canada, all of which would contribute to the ever-expanding British Empire. As global sea routes grew in the eighteenth century, sugar, tobacco, and other crops drove a new era of commodities. The luxuries favored by settlers in the Caribbean and other neighboring colonies in North America fueled the rise in intercolonial trade that coexisted with trade to the metropole.

The British quickly supplanted the Spanish (who kept hold of Cuba and Puerto Rico) and came to dominate the Caribbean. And in this era, Britain's slave empire expanded beyond the Caribbean, stretching into North America to include Virginia, Maryland (1632), South Carolina (1629), North Carolina (1712), and Georgia (1733). And in northern states of North America, the enslavement of African people also occurred during this time.

The period from the 1490s to the late seventeenth century galvanized the development of capitalism and hereditary racial slavery. The Caribbean formed the center of these processes. The growth of English and later British colonialism in the region depended on and was made possible by the violent dispossession of indigenous communities that contributed to British wealth. These processes tightly wove together Britain and the Caribbean.

This period presaged the Caribbean becoming Britain's critical periphery. While myths would cast the region as a minor player on the world stage, the Caribbean was never insignificant. Rather, the violence wrought there, the near collapse of indigenous communities, and the beginning of the mass human trafficking in African peoples made it formative to the development of Britain and other European colonial powers. With the emergence of hereditary racial slavery came also the creation of the racial-caste hierarchy and the beginnings of Caribbean people's persistent attempts to dismantle and destroy it.

2

"A dreadful state"
The Making of the Racial-Caste Hierarchy

In September 1661, while Barbados was in the throes of the sugar revolution, trouble was stirring among white servants and enslaved Africans. Both groups were defiantly resisting their inhumane treatment. The 1630s–1650s saw several servant-led rebellions against their masters, and once they arrived in Barbados, enslaved Africans adopted a range of strategies—from flight to planning revolts.[1] The Barbados Legislature, chaired by the Oxford-educated Humphrey Walrond, met in Bridgetown. The "planter-legislators" wanted to ensure that although they were few, they would rule supreme. The two laws they passed would revolutionize the Caribbean.

The first—"An Act for the good governing of servants and ordaining the Rights between Masters and Servants"—increased servants' rights.[2] Although it did not raise white "servants" to legal equality with planters, the act prohibited, for instance, English children under the age of fourteen from serving as indentured laborers (but the law was vague in relation to the rights of Irish or Scottish children) and encouraged married servants to be kept together rather than separated.[3] It also encouraged masters to care for servants when they became ill. Servants still could not marry without consent from their masters, nor could they trade. But overall, the act was designed to enhance the status of servants, in part to prevent further disturbances.[4]

When attention turned to enslaved Africans, the planter-legislators acted in a distinctly different way, passing the act "for the better ordering and governing of Negroes." Better known as the Barbados Slave Code (or Slave Act), it entrenched the status of enslaved Africans as chattel property, formally legalizing hereditary racial slavery, which would last for over two hundred years. While other forms of coerced labor did indeed exist, as well as other rationales for enslavement, this law and others that followed marked the creation of the reification of race—in other words the racial-caste hierarchy.

At the core of hereditary racial slavery were new terms to differentiate people based on their skin color, which became synonymous with the concept of race. In the Barbados Slave Code, *Negro*—a term derived from the Spanish and Portuguese word for the color black—referred to enslaved Africans. While an earlier 1661 act used the term, the Barbados Slave Code of 1661 included additional descriptions of the purported character of said "Negros," calling them a "heathenish brutish and an uncertain dangerous pride of people."[5] These traits justified their enslaved status and contrasted with indentured laborers and servants, referred to as "Christians," who were considered civilized. While the 1661 Barbados Act relating to servants did not use the term *white*, in legislation from 1652 the words *white* and *Negro* were used, and in later adaptations of slave codes and servant acts white would come to be used more often.[6] While debate remains about the first use of the term *white*, it seems that it was used variably and interchangeably with *Christian servant*, before becoming more widespread in the eighteenth century.[7] In this way race became more conflated with skin color.

By creating and assigning specific traits to "Negros," "Christians," and "whites," the acts signify how the Caribbean became a space for a set of ideas and characteristics deemed intrinsic to white Europeans and black Africans as defined by skin color. The acts reinforced these differences by assigning rights to those with lighter skin and stripping them away from those with a darker hue. They enforced further differences between enslaved Africans and indentured laborers through contrasting punishments, the former experiencing more violence for any wrongdoing than the latter.

For any first offense in which an enslaved person had attacked a "Christian," the Barbados Slave Code stipulated that the enslaved would be "severely whipped by the Constable." If more offenses occurred, noses would be slit and faces burned. And if an enslaved person lost their life because of punishment, "no person whatsoever shall be accomptable to any Law therefore."[8] It is worth remembering that in seventeenth-century England, if a convict died while being judicially mutilated there would be legal consequences because, although a convict, they remained a legal person even if inferior. In Barbados, however, killing an enslaved person convicted of a crime had become, legally speaking, like killing vermin. The Barbados Slave Code was and remains a chilling document.

Tactically, the harsher punishments meted out to enslaved people were also designed to prevent white servants from seeing them as potential allies in struggles against planter power. What this shows is how the reification of race also obscures the class aspects of this struggle, keeping white and black people from common cause, or a perception of shared status, even though economics, class exploitation, and the extraction of labor one way or another was still at the heart of this enterprise. Other violent acts buttressed these provisions—whipping, branding, castration, gibbeting, rape, and execution, to name just a few. This violence, along with the greater militarization of colonies equipped via colonial militias (the "arm of the plantocracy")—imperial troops, police officers, the Royal Navy, and freelance bounty hunters who captured runaway enslaved people—speak to the violence that centrally underpinned hereditary racial slavery.[9] That such power was necessary proved that white power existed only because it was attached to brute force.

Fundamentally contradictory processes were occurring simultaneously here. Race was becoming naturalized as an "obvious" natural basis for enslavement, with black people assigned a lower hierarchical position in "nature." Yet it is clear from the raft of laws and the ferocious brutality that white superiority, privilege, and power could exist only when fully supported by cruelty, violence, and the law—making its own "unnatural" basis visible to anyone who cared to observe it.

Other clauses in the Barbados Slave Code limited the freedom of movement of the enslaved, established specific rules regarding runaway enslaved people (including penalties for those who sheltered them and rewards for those who captured them), permitted searches of enslaved residences for weapons, and denied the enslaved a trial by jury.[10] Significantly, the law governing the enslaved made no distinction on the basis of sex, unlike the law governing servants. English law had long distinguished between men and women. But in the Caribbean, it was clear that the legal protections offered to white female servants, who could protest against rape, did not apply to enslaved African women.[11]

The Barbados Slave Code was created in response to the colonial context, but it drew on English legal precedent relating to vagabonds and servants—evidence again of the legal entanglements between England and the Caribbean.[12] Moreover, the Barbados Slave Code traveled across the Americas, influencing the 1664 and 1684 Slave Acts in Jamaica. In South Carolina, where enslaved people labored on rice and indigo plantations, legislators borrowed the Jamaican 1684 Act in their slave code of 1691. And amendments to the Barbados Slave Code in 1676, 1682, and 1688 were later copied by colonists in Dominica, Tobago, St. Lucia, St. Vincent, and Antigua.[13] In the British-controlled Caribbean, these acts buttressed hereditary racial slavery that in turn supported the construction of a racial-caste hierarchy.

Organized as a pyramid, albeit not a stable one, the Caribbean racial-caste hierarchy, which was especially prevalent in sugar-dominated colonies, had a small group of white Europeans at the top; a slightly larger middle group of free people of color—usually the offspring of European men and African women (white men often, but not always, freed their mixed-race children and their enslaved mothers); and formerly enslaved people known as "free blacks," who had purchased or gained their limited freedom from slave owners through a complex and varied legal process known as *manumission*.[14] Enslaved Africans, the largest group within these societies, occupied the bottom of the pyramid. A critical feature of the racial-caste system was that markers of skin color and legal status differentiated one group from another; indeed, the hierarchy was often referred to as a pigmentocracy.

Some degree of mobility existed within the racial-caste hierarchy. For instance, formerly enslaved people who were manumitted could leave the bottom tier and enter the middle as free blacks. Some free people of color whose skin color was very light could try to pass as white and enter the top tier of society, although this was rare. Mixed-race people could also be enslaved. The categories of sex, religion, national origin, and class inflected the racial-caste hierarchy too. Yet what distinguished the Caribbean-born racial-caste order was that those at the very top tier—white elites—rarely ever moved down. And this fact—that once installed there, the white elites remained the white elites at the top of the pyramid—is one of the fundamental reasons for adopting the term "racial-caste hierarchy" for what occurred in the Caribbean. The hierarchy was not one simply based on race or class. Moreover, the order was fortified because hierarchies existed within each group, often created by white elites, which helped prolong their power.

Documenting the different groups in the racial-caste hierarchy remains a challenge, especially when looking at those at the bottom. So much of what historians know about racial slavery comes from white elites who had the time, privilege, freedom, wherewithal, and wealth to write letters, diaries, plays, draw images, publish historical and scientific tomes, and commission works about Caribbean societies. To tell the history of the enslaved, writers and scholars scour the "archival fragments" that mention them in court documents, newspapers, and petitions.[15] They also read sources in varied ways, to glean unintended meanings and consider how official sources can, at times, both shape and limit our knowledge. Only in the late eighteenth and early nineteenth centuries, when narratives by figures like Olaudah Equiano and Bermudian-born Mary Prince began to circulate, often as powerful propaganda for the anti-slavery movement, did enslaved people's voices come to the forefront. Yet even these sources, often mediated through the prominent white people who edited and published them, still provide only a partial view.

Ultimately, however, while the racial-caste order aimed to keep different groups in their place, everyone operated within a complicated web of interdependency in the unstable, chaotic Caribbean. Indeed, the very conditions of the racial-caste hierarchy sowed the seeds of instability and subversion within the system, not only in open resistance but in racial mixing that undercut the clear boundaries of race as a biological construct in the first place.

DEFINING THE RACIAL-CASTE HIERARCHY

At the apex of the racial-caste hierarchy stood white elites. In the early years of Caribbean colonization in the seventeenth century, many planters consisted of royalists, often from the English aristocracy, who had lost their fortunes during the English Civil Wars. These men arrived with an entrepreneurial spirit, driven to recover their losses and regain their financial and social standing. Some were religious, others were not. But religion did not deter enslavement; there is evidence of some planters in the seventeenth century who first came to the region as Irish indentured laborers who shed or downplayed their Catholicism to assimilate into elite planter circles with English and Scottish men.[16] Men like the Somerset-born royalist Walrond not only bought up large parcels of land but also took charge in the governing of colonies. They established assemblies and passed laws that strengthened their power. Indeed, Walrond wore many hats: as slave owner, judge, colonel, and councillor. The wealthiest planters invested in sugar and with their riches built large, lavish residences on plantations, often called "The Great House," like that of Rose Hall in Jamaica, complete with fashionable furnishings, exquisite artwork, and all the finery of England's mansions.

Illustration of Rose Hall, Saint James, from *A Picturesque Tour of the Island of Jamaica* by James Hakewill, London, 1825.

White female planters, although a minority, were just as commercially driven as men.[17] Although she died in 1832, Mary Dehany was listed as an absentee owner with the largest number of enslaved people (205) among white female plantation owners in Barbados in 1834.[18] Some female planters inherited estates from their husbands and others had enough wealth to invest in plantations themselves. Their sex did not modify their participation in racial slavery, nor did it detract from their traditional roles as mothers and wives. They also held influential roles on plantations as investors, invigilators, and managers on estates. As with male planters, white women planters examined the bodies of the enslaved at auctions and sought to purchase only the most physically strong and capable.

Some Britons who inherited plantations wrote about racial slavery and the Caribbean for English audiences, such as English-born Jamaican planters Bryan Edwards and Edward Long. Hailing from Wiltshire, Edwards was sent to live with his uncle in Jamaica in 1759 and inherited his estate of more than a thousand enslaved people. In 1793 he published two volumes of *The History, Civil and Commercial, of the British Colonies in the West Indies*, which conveyed a benign image of planters who came into possession of their plantations "by inheritance, and by accident."[19] Long first came to Jamaica in 1757 to run a plantation called Lucky Valley in the parish of Clarendon, which he inherited from his father, and in 1774 published his widely influential *History of Jamaica*.[20] Following in Walrond's footsteps, Edwards and Long both became leading figures in the Jamaican colonial assembly.

In the heyday of the eighteenth-century sugar boom, the ranks of absentee planters grew. They enjoyed their wealth in the cooler climate of Britain, leaving their estates in the Caribbean in the hands of overseers and attorneys tasked with protecting their economic profits. One of the most famous absentee planters was Gothic writer Matthew Lewis, author of *The Monk* (1796), who owned the Cornwall and Hordley estates in Jamaica. The English wives of Caribbean male planters also often became absentee planters. In 1775, Anna Elizabeth Elletson inherited Hope Plantation from her late husband Roger Hope Elletson, a Jamaican-born slave owner, and managed it from England through letters to attorneys.[21]

Absentee planters, especially those who owned large sugar plantations, were a new phenomenon in Britain, and they ostentatiously displayed their wealth whenever and wherever they could. Scottish author and poet Tobias Smollett's 1771 epistolary novel *The Expedition of Humphry Clinker*, and Jane Austen's 1814 *Mansfield Park*, portrayed absentee-planter wealth fairly accurately. Absentee planters built large estates in important towns and cities such as Bath, Bristol, London, Cheltenham, and Southampton, and "as rich as a West Indian" became a popular adage in the eighteenth century. Many educated their children in the top private schools and spread their wealth and influence by endowing elite institutions. In 1710 Christopher Codrington, for instance, who owned plantations across the Caribbean, endowed All Souls College at Oxford University with the Codrington Library. Absentee planters further entrenched their influence by establishing banks, sitting as MPs, and forming powerful lobbying groups, such as the Society of West Indian Planters and Merchants, which defended their economic interests and property in Parliament. In the profoundly hierarchical society of late seventeenth- and eighteenth-century Britain, where those who owned land and property were considered natural elites, newcomers such as absentee planters were, at times, derided. But their growing presence and power, alongside merchants and bankers—especially during the sugar boom—were just one way in which hereditary racial slavery in the Caribbean profoundly changed Britain's social and economic order. There was no separation between enslavement "over there" in the Caribbean and the transformation of British society and wealth.

As they engineered and reaped the benefits of hereditary racial slavery, absentee planters were joined by merchants, sailors, and manufacturers in investing in the transatlantic slave trade, which fueled economic growth. The argument that British financial wealth rested on the back of racial slavery was made most clearly in the groundbreaking 1944 book *Capitalism and Slavery*, by Eric Williams. Williams was one of the first scholars to emphasize the links between racial slavery, capitalism, the industrial revolution, and abolition. Although it is now assumed that racial slavery did not directly create the industrial revolution, it certainly transformed its scope and pace.[22] And as new research emerges, especially on slave ownership, it becomes all too clear that despite his critics, Williams's arguments still stand.[23] The Caribbean became for Britain a place of wealth extraction that set the region on the path toward underdevelopment. And in one way or another, enslavement in the Caribbean infiltrated and helped shape almost all the economic, political, and social institutions of Britain. It was not solely the extraction of resources generated by enslaved people in the Caribbean, but all the organizations that supported enslavement: shipbuilding, banking, insurance, political representation, religious associations, universities, to list just a few.

Racial slavery shaped economic development in Britain through the 1713 Treaty of Utrecht, which ended the War of the Spanish Succession (1701–13), a conflict that had involved England, Spain, France, Austria, the Netherlands, Prussia, and Portugal. The treaty gave Britain the *asiento*—the right to supply enslaved people to Spain's colonies in the Americas, including the Caribbean, Mexico, and Florida, through the South Sea Company. The *asiento* made Britain a world leader in slave trading.

"A DREADFUL STATE"

For British manufacturers, slave trading offered the opportunity to transport various goods like cotton, muskets, bottles, glass, copper, textiles, guns, spirits, and cutlery on ships built in London, Bristol, and Liverpool. Once in Africa, those goods were used to barter for people. Enslaved Africans were then sent to the Caribbean to produce other commodities such as sugar, rum, ginger, chocolate, and spices, which were then shipped back to Britain. This highly lucrative triangular trade drove Britain's economic boom. It developed too through trade with Britain's North American colonies, as places like Massachusetts sold goods to British and other European Caribbean colonies.[24]

In *The Wealth of Nations* (1776), Scottish economist Adam Smith wrote: "the profits of a sugar-plantation in any of our West Indian colonies, are generally much greater than those of any other cultivation that is known either in Europe or America."[25] In 1775 the value of Caribbean plantations as a whole stood at £50 million (the equivalent of £7.6 billion today).[26] This incredible wealth facilitated the economy of key British cities and helped the spread of industrialization.

London was the financial center of the slave trade—a transnational banking center that mirrored the transnational plantation economy of the Caribbean. The Bank of England, formed in 1694, regulated profits from the transatlantic slave trade and racial slavery that, alongside other forms of economic activity, enriched its directors. Other well-known bankers in the capital were the Quaker brothers Alexander and David Barclay, both listed as slave traders in 1756. London-based insurance companies like the London Assurance and the Royal Exchange Company were leaders in Caribbean dealings, and London merchants provided vital credit that bankrolled the slave trade.

The rise of Bristol was due largely to the slave trade. Merchants there participated in the slave trade before the end of the seventeenth century, which breached the Royal African Company's monopoly.[27] In this way, merchants were flouting mercantilist ideology that was central to the slave trade. Mercantilism was built on various ideas including economic intervention by the state, the importance of gaining national success in foreign relations, the growth of sea power and the shipping industry, the dominance of the metropole at the expense of the colonies, and ensuring that colonies were replete with unskilled cheap labor.[28] Merchants in Bristol were not the only ones infringing on mercantilism, though. Many European empires in the Caribbean pretended to be mercantilist monopolies but traded with each other. Bristol became a vital port city for shipbuilding and home to successful slave-trading companies such as James Rogers and Associates and Isaac Hobhouse and Company.

Liverpool later rivaled Bristol and dominated the slave trade to Jamaica.[29] The city also developed slave-trade-produced cotton, a booming enterprise in Liverpool and throughout northern England. In Glasgow, Scottish merchants traded in sugar, cotton, and tobacco, and the city grew and developed. Elsewhere, slave ships departed from Southampton, Lancaster, Plymouth, Preston, Dartmouth, Poole, Exeter, and Chester, all of whose local economies grew as a result. Yet it was not just large cities and towns that were implicated in the slave trade and slavery. As historian Corinne Fowler has stressed, colonialism more broadly impacted rural and remote parts of Britain too.[30]

Some merchants who profited through racial slavery had close ties to the Church of England, an institution deeply implicated in hereditary racial slavery. It provided theological support for enslavement through selective passages in the Bible and itself owned plantations across the Caribbean. By 1834, more than 120 Anglican clergymen in Britain and Ireland owned enslaved Africans in the Caribbean, according to compensation records.[31]

Edward Long by William Sharp, after John Opie, 1796.

With their energies focused on profit margins, market speculation, and wealth accumulation, white planters—male and female, resident and absentee—saw hereditary racial slavery not as an inhumane institution but an economic necessity and eventually as something "natural." Apologists for racial slavery became the theoretical and intellectual bedrock for white supremacist ideology. Edward Long was a leader within this group and would earn the title "father of English racism."[32] Long described Africans as having a "bestial fleece, instead of hair," "noxious odour," being "void of genius," and "[they] seem almost incapable of making any progress."[33] Long suggested that Africans not only had more in common with animals than humans but also that sexual relations between the two occurred:

> When we reflect on ... their dissimilarity to the rest of mankind, must we not conclude, that they are a different species of the same *genus*? ... Nor (do Orang-utans) ... seem at all inferior in the intellectual faculties to many of the Negroe race; with some of whom, it is credible that they have the most intimate connexion and consanguinity. The amorous intercourse between them may be frequent ... and it is certain, that both races agree perfectly well in lasciviousness of disposition.[34]

Planter William Beckford also spewed racist rhetoric. A creole born in Jamaica, Beckford inherited four sugar plantations when his father died in 1756. In his 1788 pamphlet *Remarks Upon the Situation of Negroes in Jamaica*, he argued that "under a kind owner or a benevolent overseer" enslaved people faced better conditions than "the generality of labouring poor in England."[35] Drawing parallels between the experiences of enslaved Africans and the poor white working classes became a staple argument for racial slavery advocates. Beckford, and some other white planters, believed that removing Africans from the continent and transporting them to the Caribbean was an act of mercy. Beckford saw Africa as a dangerous, uncivilized, warring continent that the enslaved in the Caribbean were lucky to have escaped.[36]

Beckford advocated for the "comforts of protection" that good planters would bestow on the enslaved, but this was more fantasy than reality.[37] While it is certainly true that not all white planters were abusive, many engaged in intense levels of physical and psychological violence. Take the actions of Walrond as just one example. Walrond, who after a group of his enslaved property died by suicide believing that this would return them to their home country, caused one of their heads to be cut off, and set it upon a pole a dozen foot high; and having done that, caused all his Negroes to come forth, and march round about this head, and bid them look on it, whether this were not the head of such an one that hang'd himself. Which they acknowledging, he then then told them, That they were in a main errour, in thinking they went into their own Countreys, after they were dead.[38]

Botanist Hans Sloane, whose collections were among the founding collections of the British Museum and who lived in Jamaica in the late 1680s, vividly described brutal aggression toward the enslaved.[39] In his 1707 *Voyage to the Islands Madera, Barbados, Nieves, S. Christophers and Jamaica*, he wrote:

> The Punishments for Crimes of Slaves, are usually for Rebellions burning them, by nailing them down on the ground with crooked Sticks on every Limb, and then applying the Fire by degrees from the Feet and Hands, burning them gradually up to the Head, whereby their pains are extravagant. For Crimes of a lesser nature Gelding, or chopping off half the Foot with an Ax' were common.[40]

Charles Leslie, a Scot residing in Jamaica, corroborated Sloane's description in his 1740 *A New History of Jamaica*. Leslie witnessed enslaved people

> treated in that cruel manner, for no other reason, but to satisfy the brutish pleasure of an overseer, who has their punishment mostly at his direction. I have seen their bodies all in a gore of blood, the skin torn off their backs with the cruel whip; beaten pepper and salt rubbed in the wounds, and a large stick of sealing-wax dropped leisurely upon them.[41]

White women planters and those in positions of power on estates could be just as violent as their male counterparts. One of the most influential accounts of this came from Bermudian-born Mary Prince.[42] Born into racial slavery in 1788, Prince described her first mistress as a "kind-hearted good woman," but her second was a "fearful woman, and a savage mistress to her slaves." Beaten regularly from a young age, Prince quickly learned "the exact difference between the smart of the rope, the cart-whip, and the cow-skin, when applied to my naked body by her own cruel hand."[43]

Pregnant women were not immune from severe punishment, and often it led to their death and that of their unborn child. Prince remembered the fate of Hetty, an enslaved pregnant woman she toiled alongside. One day their master:

> flew into a terrible passion, and ordered the poor creature to be stripped quite naked, notwithstanding her pregnancy, and to be tied up to a tree in a yard. He then flogged her as hard as he could lick, both with the whip and cow-skin, till she was all over streaming with blood. He rested, and then beat her again and again ... The consequence was that poor Hetty was brought to bed before her time, and was delivered after severe labour of a dead child.[44]

Hetty later died of her injuries. Hetty's vicious experience is a reminder that the experience of racial slavery was not only gendered but also shaped by reproduction.[45] The physical abuse white elites wielded was often coupled with sexual violence, and this was particularly acute for enslaved women. As producers and reproducers, enslaved women's bodies were the bedrock upon which hereditary racial slavery was founded.[46]

Salacious stereotypes of African women as highly fertile, overly sexed, lascivious, and lustful—in contrast to the supposed sober and virtuous white European woman—became staples of writing by European travelers to the African continent and rationalizations for their sexual abuse and enslavement.[47] William Towerson, who ventured to West Africa in the 1550s and helped develop trading links with Britain, described African women's breasts as "very foule and long, hanging downe low like the uddur of a goate."[48] Writing in his journal, planter Lewis stressed: "I really believe that the negresses can produce children at pleasure; and where they are barren, it is just as hens will frequently not lay eggs on shipboard, because they do not like their situation."[49] Although crass and crude, these stereotypes were taken as gospel by many at the top of the racial-caste order.

With these sentiments in mind, and drunk on a lethal mixture of white supremacy, patriarchy, and lust, white male planters frequently wielded sexual violence on enslaved girls and women, with rape being a critical part of everyday white male planter life. One of the most sadistic serial rapists was English-born planter Thomas Thistlewood.[50] He arrived in Jamaica in 1750 and worked first as a surveyor's assistant before climbing the ranks, soon becoming an overseer of a plantation in the parish of St. Elizabeth. He left diaries covering the thirty-seven years of his time in Jamaica, and these highlight that Thistlewood raped with impunity. In his diary he recorded 3,852 sexual encounters with 138 different women and girls.[51]

In various entries Thistlewood writes about Sally. Shipped to Jamaica from the Congo, Sally caused Thistlewood many problems as she frequently absconded from the plantation, for which she was punished, physically and sexually. He records having sex with her thirty-seven times.[52] When Sally was around fifteen or sixteen, Thistlewood chose sexual partners for her. If an enslaved woman got pregnant, this boosted the enslaved population, and the sexual services rendered also provided financial benefits to men like Thistlewood. According to Thistlewood's records, Sally suffered from several forms of venereal disease, and this would have been compounded by decades of sexual abuse. Her diseases had a crippling effect on her body, and she did not bear a child.[53]

Thistlewood formed a thirty-three-year union with another young woman, Phibbah. As his mistress, Phibbah was one among many enslaved women who allied themselves to white planters. By doing so, Phibbah and others could transcend some of racial slavery's limitations for personal advancement, which they could then extend to other enslaved people. While sexual violence was more likely for enslaved women and girls, Thistlewood's diaries recorded an incident of an enslaved man being sodomized by his master.[54] Thistlewood was also famous for the brutal punishment he invented known as "Derby's dose," named after an enslaved man. The punishment entailed forcing another enslaved person to defecate into Derby's mouth, which was then closed with wire for hours.[55]

At times, white women's sexual exploitation of enslaved women also brought them financial gains. John Waller from England, who visited Barbados, discussed the "hiring out" sexual labor system on the island and other colonies in his travel book *A Voyage in the West Indies*. "In the family where I lodge," he wrote, "a respectable lady . . . was regretting to the company at dinner, that a young female slave, whom she had let out for several months, was about to return, as she would lose twelve dollars a month, the price of her hire, and besides, be at the expense of maintaining her."[56] Waller later learned that this enslaved woman "had been let out to an officer in the garrison, with whom she had been living as a mistress, and that her return was occasioned only by his being ordered to another island."[57]

Although white women at the top of the racial-caste hierarchy wielded their power through black women's bodies and sexuality, they remained themselves controlled by white male heteropatriarchy. Within the context of racial slavery, white women were considered physically and emotionally frail and in need of protection from enslaved men. While there is evidence of white women of different classes marrying or having sexual relations with black men and free men of color in the seventeenth century, over time this practice declined as race and gender barriers hardened. White men saw white women's sexuality as critical to ensuring racial difference, and so they punished enslaved African men for having sexual relations with them. Inventing and investing in the stereotypes of the black male rapist and the cult of pure white womanhood helped ensure that mixed-race children would be born into racial slavery. Mores concerning sexuality and race were inseparable in a racial-caste construction; racial hierarchies demanded the policing of sexuality and reproduction. This is another way that the boundaries of the system were all but impossible to patrol: one could "move" from one level to the next through racial mixing. Ultimately without sexual boundaries, the racial boundaries eventually would disappear.

While those at the top of the racial-caste order tended to hold most power and control in the colonies, they had their own intragroup divisions and conflicts. At times, clashes occurred between planters and colonial governors (or the colonial decision-makers in London). In other cases, planters with large estates quarreled with those on smaller plots. Religion also proved to be a dividing line, especially in the seventeenth century when Irish Catholics came into conflict with English Protestants. Within individual families, relations could be fraught too.

Below white elites at the top of the triangle were white people of the middle and lower classes, some of whom were creole. Many were planters with medium-size plantations or yeomen with smaller pockets of land who kept a smaller number of enslaved people. Among this middling group were merchants, professionals, and those involved in the colonial militia or navy. Women held positions such as teachers or owners of brothels and inns. White creole women were considered inferior to white women born in Europe or North America. Lady Maria Nugent, born in New Jersey, was the wife of the governor of Jamaica, Sir George Nugent. In her diaries, Nugent disparaged white creole women. In her opinion:

> The Creole language is not confined to the negroes. Many of the ladies, who have not been educated in England, speak a sort of broken English, with an indolent drawling out of their words, that is very tiresome if not disgusting. I stood next to a lady one night, near a window, and, by way of saying something, remarked that the air was much cooler than usual; to which she answered, "Yes, ma-am, *him rail-ly too fra-ish.*"[58]

Nugent's words speak to the anxieties that white elites had about white creoles. Within this group, many challenged white elite views of the enslaved and of racial slavery. James Ramsay was a former slave owner and naval officer, later turned vicar, surgeon, and abolitionist. Based mainly on St. Kitts, Ramsay wrote essays that challenged planter depictions of enslaved African inferiority. In his 1784 essay he argued:

> Negroes are capable of learning any thing that requires attention and correctness of manner. They have powers of description and mimickry that would not have disgraced the talents of our modern Aristophanes . . . Their slavish employments and condition; their being abandoned to the caprice of any master; the subjection in which it is thought necessary to keep them all; these things depress their minds and subdue whatever is manly, spirited, ingenuous, independent, among them. And these are weights sufficient to crush a first-rate human genius.[59]

Ramsay was writing at a time when the abolitionist movement was gathering steam and revealed fissures between white elite planters and a nascent merchant and professional class that did not see the racial-caste hierarchy as inherent.

"Poor whites" occupied positions below men such as Ramsay. Often descendants of indentured laborers and servants, in Barbados they concerned colonial officials to the extent that they granted them poor relief. They occupied a liminal position in the racial-caste order. Their skin color provided them with privileges, but their status as laborers meant that they might variously fall into the middle of the racial-caste hierarchy—another example of the inherent instability and incoherence of a hierarchy based increasingly on attempts to harden racial distinctions. On plantation estates, poor whites worked as artisans or elsewhere as schoolteachers, but on occasion they faced job competition with skilled enslaved or free people.

Within the racial-caste system, those poor whites who considered themselves above enslaved people nevertheless often came into conflict with them. Indeed, colonial laws codified poor whites' ability to capitalize on white supremacy. In this regard, poor whites were encouraged to invest in the "wages of their whiteness," as scholar David R. Roediger calls it, drawing on the work of Black American scholar and activist W. E. B. Du Bois in his writings on white Southerners in America during Reconstruction. Poor whites shunned class solidarity in order to invest in their racial superiority, to compensate for their economic exploitation at the hands of the white elite.[60]

In many ways, this behavior led to poor whites feeling emboldened to attempt to climb up within the racial-caste order. While a sizable gulf typically separated white elites and poor whites, with the former often casting aspersions on the latter, during times of enslaved rebellion, and by the end of the eighteenth century when racial slavery was increasingly coming under attack, class antagonism could sometimes defer to a unity in defense of the privileges of whiteness.

Free people of color and free blacks also occupied the middle strata of the racial-caste order, although they were small in number compared to the enslaved population. In Jamaica in 1775, there were 4,500 free people compared to 192,800 enslaved and 18,700 white people, while in Barbados in 1786 there were only 838 free people living alongside 16,167 white people and 62,115 enslaved.[61] Visual stereotypes depicted free people of color living lives of esteem and elegance, often adopting European manners, customs, and clothes, as depicted in the paintings of Rome-born artist Agostino Brunias. Brunias lived in the region in the late eighteenth century before his death in 1796 in Dominica. His images of handsome, genteel free people of color were partly encouraged by Sir William Young, then the commissioner of Dominica, St. Vincent and Tobago, to entice European settlers to move to the Caribbean.[62]

In reality, however, the economic condition of free people of color and free blacks varied widely. Some had enough money to participate in the plantation economy, and those who did so tended not to invest in sugar but developed other crops. Other free people of color and free blacks worked as masons, tailors, and carpenters; women could often be found working as shopkeepers, hucksters, and tavern or brothel owners.[63] Rachael Pringle-Polgreen, a former slave owner from Barbados, was the infamous owner of the Royal Naval Hotel, visited by Prince William Henry (later King William IV). She was relatively successful and, on her death, owned around nineteen enslaved people, and in her will she manumitted six.[64] Although Pringle-Polgreen accumulated wealth and power, she should not be seen as a triumph of female agency. Just as she experienced violence through the institution of hereditary racial slavery, she wielded it in turn against other enslaved and free women.[65]

"A DREADFUL STATE"

The Barbadoes Mulatto Girl by Agostino Brunias,
printed in 1810 after a painting c. 1774.

Across the Caribbean, most free people of color and free blacks could not vote, give evidence in court against white people, serve on juries, or hold any political office. Free people could own only a stipulated amount of land and enslaved people. There were some exceptions to these restrictions. In Antigua, located at the southern end of the Leeward Islands chain, free people did have the opportunity to vote, but only if they fulfilled property requirements.[66] Even so, white people did not necessarily honor these legal exceptions. And as the growing wealth of free people of color threatened white people, new laws restricted them further.

In the 1760s a report was published in Jamaica stating that free people owned property worth a total of £200,000–£300,000.[67] Partly in response, the Jamaican Assembly in 1761 passed legislation forbidding white people to leave property worth more than £1,200 to any free people of color or black people, thereby undercutting the growing prominence of the former on the island.[68] In the northeastern extremity of the Greater Antilles lies the British Virgin Islands, and there, after 1783, a law insisted that whites had to serve as patrons for free people.[69]

White elites not only feared that expanding rights for free people of color or free blacks would threaten their economic power—they were also anxious about whether free people's loyalties resided with white people with whom they shared a certain economic status, or with the enslaved, with whom they shared racial status. As it turns out, white elite fears that free people of color or free blacks would inspire the enslaved to revolt were often misplaced. Most free people of color sought mobility within the enslaved society rather than its demolition. Indeed, while some could feel solidarity based on race, others felt more aspiration based on class. Some free people of color stressed their ties to white people and distanced themselves from enslaved people. Many espoused the Euro-creole culture of white people but were not always welcome among white society, or wealthy enough to fully join it.[70] The gulf between free people of color and white people was sometimes bridged by sexual relations.

Relations between free people of color and free blacks and those in the lower echelons of the racial-caste hierarchy were complex too. Some, having friends and family in common, interacted with enslaved people and participated in mixed free and unfree social networks. Often free people would attempt to purchase the freedom of their enslaved family members. But free people were not a united group. Divisions surfaced around sex, as well as hierarchies in skin color—an obsession throughout the Caribbean—with new names created for the different combinations of mixed-race people. *Mulatto*—derived from the Portuguese *mulo*—referred to a cross between a donkey and a horse that cannot reproduce and was used to describe the mixture of a black and white person; *sambo* was the mixture of a black and mulatto person; *quadroon* the mixture of a mulatto and white person; *mustee* the mixture of a quadroon and white person; *musteefino* the mixture of a mustee and white; and *quinteron* the mixture of a *musteefino* and white. In Jamaica, those classed as *quinteron* (the mixture of a *musteefino* and white person) were legally considered white.[71] The fixation on skin color elevated proximity to whiteness in the racial-caste system. While some lighter-skinned free people deemed darker-skinned free people of color as inferior, some darker-skinned free people thought themselves superior to darker-skinned enslaved people. How a free person gained their freedom was another divisive factor. Those who were born free were often treated more favorably within the law than manumitted free blacks. Again, all these differences created some potential for movement within the system, but ultimately strengthened white control.

At the bottom of the racial-caste pyramid, enslaved Africans constituted the largest group. From 1701 to 1800 the British traded in 2,532,300 enslaved Africans.[72] Most enslaved men, women, and children worked within the agricultural sector, often on sugar plantations. While islands like Barbados and Jamaica were heavily dominated by sugar plantations, other crops were important too. In Jamaica, for instance, the enslaved worked to cultivate indigo, cocoa, ginger, and cotton. Elsewhere, enslaved people labored on cotton, coffee, and cocoa plantations in larger numbers and lived in enslaved quarters—often shabby lodgings on the outskirts of plantations.

The majority of enslaved men and women performed intense, strenuous labor in the fields, in what enslaved man Ashton Warner described as "a dreadful state of slavery."[73] On sugar plantations, the enslaved worked in gangs of three or four. The first gang consisted of those deemed the strongest and was tasked with planting and cutting cane; the second gang did minor tasks and included older and pregnant enslaved people; while the third gang, which included children, did the weeding.[74] As a vulnerable group among field enslaved people, enslaved girls and women were often the targets of sexual abuse from other enslaved men as well as white people. Records from Newton Plantation in Barbados show that in 1796, four field girls—Fanny Ann, Little Dolly, Membah Jubah, and Jemenema—aged between thirteen and sixteen had mixed-race children.[75]

Sugar plantation, 1850–90.

"A DREADFUL STATE"

Drivers, usually enslaved men but also sometimes women, took charge of ordering field enslaved people to work, and whipping them if they did not. White planters who selected enslaved people as drivers did so intentionally, often to forge a rift between them and enslaved field-workers. Planters often gave drivers better clothes and food provisions as a way of ensuring their loyal obedience. On some plantations, drivers would use this supposed authority to violently punish those who worked in the fields, which fueled resentment among enslaved communities. Drivers could be both victimizers and victims.

In colonies where sugar was not the dominant crop, the enslaved worked in different ways. On the northeast coast of Central America lay the colony of British Honduras (later Belize). Here the enslaved worked in groups of between ten and twelve, cutting timber, the main exported crop. In the smaller flat island of Barbuda in the Eastern Caribbean, the enslaved grew provisions transported to those working on plantations in neighboring Antigua; whereas in the Bahamas the enslaved labored salvaging shipwrecks.[76] On the tiny islands of Turks and Caicos, southeast of the Bahamas, the enslaved worked in salt ponds. There Mary Prince was given "a half barrel and a shovel, and had to stand up to my knees in the water, from four o'clock in the morning till nine ... Our feet and legs, from standing in the salt water for so many hours, soon became full of dreadful boils, which eat down in some cases to the very bone."[77] In the low-lying Cayman Islands, around 290 kilometers northwest of Jamaica, the small, enslaved population labored on cotton plantations and were involved in logging from the 1730s.

Skilled enslaved people, often mixed-race males, were an important subset among the enslaved. They worked as carpenters or coppersmiths, sawyers, distillers, and boilermen, and could be hired out to other owners on different plantations.[78] Some earned money from their labor, from which they paid planters a sum. They tended to save any remaining earnings, which could be used to purchase their freedom. Just as they did with enslaved drivers, planters elevated as "elite" some skilled enslaved people, especially men and those with lighter skin color, at the expense of others.[79] White planters used promises of promotion or threats of demotion to ensure fidelity. The skilled enslaved in turn sometimes viewed those field-workers as beneath them.

Working in the houses of white masters and mistresses as washerwomen, cooks, and nursemaids, female domestics—some of whom (but by no means all) were mixed-race—were another prominent group among the enslaved. They had a close degree of intimacy that fostered loyalty to white people. As a young girl, Prince described how she was "truly attached" to her first mistress, and "next to my other mother, loved her better than any creature in the world. My obedience to her commands was cheerfully given: it sprung solely from the affection I felt for her, and not from fear of the power which the white people's law had given her over me."[80] Affection and paternalistic ties often saw enslaved people defend their masters from attacks by other enslaved people. Some domestics managed to use their close relationship to white people to gain manumission. But manumitting domestic enslaved women was not always common. A woman named Mulatto Kitty from Worthy Park in Jamaica bore eight children by five men (three white and two black), none of whom gained their freedom.[81] When it came to manumission, many white masters tended to manumit enslaved women after their childbearing age to limit the number of free children born.

In most of the British colonies, the enslaved population did not reproduce itself but was replenished with newly enslaved captives from Africa. The physical toll of racial slavery explains why many enslaved women in the Caribbean did not bear a child in the mid-eighteenth century. Prior to that time, a policy of "buy rather than breed" prevailed among planters, since it was costlier to let the enslaved raise children than to purchase new human labor. Eventually, however, planters realized the value of using childbirth as a way to increase the enslaved population. As historian Sasha Turner has argued, enslaved women's pregnancy, motherhood, and child-rearing practices became a complex fight for control.[82] Nonetheless, the sexual and physical violence they faced translated into high rates of infant mortality and the death of relatively young, enslaved people. Death, especially in the sugar colonies, was central to the experiences not just of the enslaved but of all those involved in hereditary racial slavery, with rampant violence and disease.[83]

The divisions between field, skilled, and domestic enslaved people often fractured the enslaved population and helped strengthen white elite control. Divisions existed too between enslaved people born in Africa and creoles born in the Caribbean. Yet despite divisions, enslaved people defied their status as chattels. Using whatever means at their disposal, they carved out a relative degree of autonomy. "Provision grounds," located on the margins of plantations on land not used for production, were significant spaces where the enslaved developed crops, reared livestock, and created crafts, many of which they sold in markets, a space for trade that allowed the enslaved to earn small amounts of money. Market days that some enslaved people could attend were not just important economically but also functioned as social spaces where they could interact with friends and family members from different parts of the colony. Giving the enslaved provision land, and the time to grow food, was beneficial for planters too: it served to cut the costs they incurred to provide basic staples for the enslaved and kept the enslaved on plantations.[84]

Although under intense pressure (owing to violence and separation), enslaved people worked hard to form families. The narratives of Prince and Warner testify to the powerful bonds within nuclear families, as well as with other kin and friends. Religion, too, became a powerful force among enslaved people that strengthened family and kinship ties. Enslaved people encountered Western religion in varied ways—through, for instance, their contact with Irish Catholic indentured workers in Barbados, or through small traders who were often Quakers, who established meeting houses in Barbados, Jamaica, Antigua, the Virgin Islands, and Nevis.

Christian conversion did not undermine enslavement. When British missionaries increased their presence in the Caribbean, especially in the nineteenth century, they did not denounce the sin of white supremacy or preach the importance of Christian equality, but rather a gospel that sustained hereditary racial slavery. Methodist, Baptist, and Anglican missionaries were to instruct the enslaved that God had willed racial slavery as their punishment for their heathen life, and that they should work hard to rise into the gates of heaven rather than fall deep into the fiery pit of hell. The charter of the "Society for the Conversion and Religious Instruction and Education of the Negro Slaves in the British India Islands" stated, for instance, that missionaries:

> Would not only be an act of true Christian Charity and Benevolence, but . . . a measure of the soundest Policy, by promoting the Prosperity and the Commercial Interests of those Islands . . . [and] would tend more effectually than anything else can do, to check and extinguish those pernicious and destructive vices so prevalent among them [the enslaved].[85]

Yet missionaries converted many enslaved people, including Prince.

RESISTING RACIAL SLAVERY

Resistance to hereditary racial slavery was endemic throughout the Caribbean, although not every enslaved individual resisted. Some collaborated with white planters, informing them of potential revolts, perhaps in the hope that deference would lead to freedom. Some enslaved creole people reported to white people the suspicious behavior of African-born rivals if they were at odds with each other, and vice versa. These practices speak to the complexity of human choices and decisions. They are also a reminder that for many enslaved people, resistance was not always at the forefront of their minds. Instead, their priority was living to see another day.[86] Moreover, the racial-caste system was designed to preempt unrest at the bottom and prevent enslaved unity to ensure white dominance. Therefore, it is remarkable—and testimony to the human longing for freedom—that enslaved people chose to resist, when many knew that they were putting their lives at risk by doing so.

As the decades progressed, flight and *petit marronage* (defined as temporary absence from plantations) became commonplace. Those who ran away were in most cases running to someone—seeking comfort with a lover, friend, or family. Women often practiced *petit marronage* in part perhaps because family bonds attached them more firmly to plantations than men. Some enslaved people ran away after other slave owners enticed them with better conditions, and others ran away to force their owners to improve conditions.[87]

Theft was another common, everyday form of resistance. The enslaved stole food from their masters' houses to avoid starvation, and domestic women sometimes stole their white mistresses' possessions. The resistance of domestic cooks was particularly worrying for white people, who believed that they would try to poison their food, and mistresses and masters recorded incidents of enslaved domestic women being noncooperative, disobedient, and arguing with other enslaved people more often than their male counterparts. Alison Carmichael, owner of plantations in St. Vincent and Trinidad and the wife of an army officer, remarked on enslaved women's brazen behavior in 1833:

> I have frequently seen our female domestic[s] ... when sent to the stocks, make a very low curtsey, and with the most ironical smile of insolence say, "Thank you massa, much obliged to you for let me sit down softly" ... I regret to have it to say, that female negroes are far more unmanageable than males. The little girls are far more wicked than the boys: and I am convinced, were every proprietor to produce the list of his good negroes, there would be, in every instance, an amazing majority in favour of males.[88]

In efforts to resist male planters, enslaved women like Sally Bassett in Bermuda drew on African cultural practices.[89] Many used knowledge of African herbs and medicine to concoct poison, practice contraception, and induce abortion. African resistance strategies were clearly in evidence when it came to religion. In Jamaica, the enslaved drew on West African forms of belief to practice creolized religions that mixed healing with harm, as in the case of Obeah. The Obeah man or woman was known for making potions from plants to fend off ghosts, known as duppies. Planters saw Obeah and other African-syncretic creole religions such as Myal, which linked to the relationship between the living and the dead, as superstitions that, if successful, could undermine their power and potentially instigate rebellion, and so passed laws banning these practices.[90] But the enslaved defiantly continued to practice them. In the very language that they spoke—a creole that blended African and English terms—the enslaved strived to preserve their African history and heritage.

The enslaved often took part in industrial sabotage, committing arson or willfully destroying equipment on plantations. In other instances, they deliberately worked at a slow pace to foil production. They also tried to cultivate tensions between white overseers and owners. Still others took more drastic measures, resorting to suicide or plotting revolts.

The possibility of imminent rebellion was always on the minds of white people, inspiring slave codes and other efforts to limit interaction between enslaved people. On plantations, planters tried to keep certain ethnic groups or enslaved people from the same nation separate. They considered markets dangerous spaces, where rumors and information could spread quickly. Yet from the beginning of racial slavery in the seventeenth century, revolts big and small occurred routinely, often during moments when colonial officials were distracted, such as holidays, Christian festivals, or lavish balls. Extreme forms of reprisal were typical responses to revolt and rebellion. White planters publicly displayed bodies of the enslaved, especially decapitated heads. Many dead bodies were burned or tossed into the sea.

Despite drastic attempts to crush revolt, rebellions continued to occur, the largest of which took the form of warfare in 1760 in Jamaica.[91] The insurrection was spearheaded by enslaved people known as "Coronmantees"—a term used by whites to describe various peoples from the west coast of Africa, stereotyped for their physical strength and perceived military acumen—and led specifically by a man named Tacky, a name that referred to a man with royal connections in the Ga language, who was said to have been a chief in Guinea.[92] Shortly after midnight on April 8, around one hundred Africans marched to Fort Haldane in St. Mary's parish and seized gunpowder and weaponry and later began a series of raids, burnings, and killings throughout the parish.[93]

The rebellion, influenced by Obeah practitioners who played leading roles, soon spread across the island, its ranks swelling to thirty thousand. In the planning of the revolt it became clear to onlookers that those involved shared military experience in Africa, and that women were not absent bystanders but key figures in the uprising alongside men.[94] There were even reports that in Kingston, an enslaved rebel woman known as the "Queen of Kingston" who had been transported to Spanish Cuba had returned to Jamaica during the conflict.[95] She eluded authorities' attempts to capture her for some time before being found and brought to Kingston, where she likely faced a death sentence.[96]

The revolt that extended to 1761 saw not just imperial militia involved in its suppression but also Maroons. Tacky's rebellion occurred when the British were mired in the Seven Years' War against Spain and France (1756–63), which distracted British forces and partly explains why it took over a year to suppress the rebellion. Indeed, historian Vincent Brown has made the case that Tacky's revolt should be seen as a crucial element of the Seven Years' War and viewed also as part of warfare originating in Africa.[97] At its end, deaths stood at sixty white people, approximately sixty free colored and free blacks, and between three and four hundred enslaved people, with one hundred more facing execution. Around five hundred enslaved people were deported from the island, with the suppression of the rebellion costing £100,000.[98]

What occurred in the Caribbean was a dual and countervailing momentum, with a white elite desperately trying to construct and harden a fixed hierarchy based solely on race and the instability of that construct—evidenced in revolts and rebellions that revealed the inherent fragility and contrived nature of the racial-caste hierarchy.

While planters, colonial officials, and imperial militias were dealing with repeated revolts in the Caribbean, they also struggled to control a group slightly on the margins of the racial-caste order. The term *marronage* denotes a wide variety of practices by which enslaved people contested their enslavement throughout the Americas. *Grand marronage* referred to the practice of enslaved people fleeing plantations and establishing independent Maroon communities. Some consisted of indigenous peoples and escaped African enslaved people; others included African and creole-born runaways. Small bands of Maroon groups in St. Kitts comprised runaway Africans and Kalinagos. In Antigua, Maroons lived in the Sherkerley Mountains from around 1685, while others occupied New Providence in the Bahamas in the 1780s. Dominica and Barbados were also home to small but powerful Maroon groups. The two most long-standing Maroon communities existed in Jamaica and the Dutch colony of Suriname.

The Jamaican Maroons threatened not only those at the top of the racial-caste system but also the institution of hereditary racial slavery itself. They shared a long history that dated from the time of Spanish settlement. Their numbers increased in the latter part of the seventeenth century, when more African-born runaways joined their ranks. Jamaica's topography made it ideal for Maroons. Its mountainous limestone terrain, with dense forests, provided plenty of hiding spots. By the 1720s, Jamaican Maroon numbers had swelled from the hundreds to thousands. Led by a man named Cudjoe, the Leeward Maroons lived in the western part of the island. Another group, the Windward Maroons, occupied areas in eastern Jamaica.[99] To survive and thrive, Maroons developed sophisticated methods of agricultural crop production. Maroons became exceptionally skilled in guerrilla warfare against colonial troops. Women were important too within Maroon communities.[100] Some had leadership roles, such as the infamous "Nanny of the Maroons," said to be an Obeah woman, who had a position of authority among the Windward Maroons. Maroon men tended to be in the majority and often raided enslaved communities in search of women for partnership. But enslaved women also fled to join Maroon communities voluntarily.

In the 1730s Maroons accelerated their raids on plantations and more enslaved people sought to join them. Colonial leaders used this time as an opportunity to attack Maroon communities, but as late as 1739 neither side could claim victory. According to Edward Long, the Maroon war of the 1730s cost £250,000, and hundreds on both sides died.[101] The British decided it was better to negotiate with Cudjoe through a peace treaty that equally applied to the Windward Maroons. By signing, the Maroons gained some advantages such as freedom and legal recognition of their unique status and land rights. In exchange, the Maroons agreed to help the British by returning runaway enslaved people or providing evidence that they had killed them. Ultimately, however, the treaty did more harm than good; the presence of white superintendents put in control of the Maroons by the British stifled their autonomy.[102]

Conflicts between the two led to the 1795 Second Maroon War, known also as the Trelawny War, a group of Maroons in Trelawny Town who chafed at their lack of freedom and land. The Jamaican governor's fear that the enslaved there were enticing the Maroons to rebel informed his decision to enter into war. Outnumbered, these Maroons agreed to surrender to the British on the condition that they be allowed to stay in Jamaica. Initially the British decided not to deport them, but then quickly reneged, sending them first to Nova Scotia and later to Sierra Leone.[103]

Maroon communities represented not just military resistance but also cultural resistance to the racial-caste hierarchy—an example being the practices of Nanny or Queen Nanny of the Maroons, who is said to have been a guerrilla leader. While there are few historical written sources that provide an accurate picture of her, she remains a powerful presence in oral history traditions of female resistance in Jamaica (influenced by West African forms of oral storytelling), which would later become critical to post-independence Jamaican nationalism. As a practitioner of Obeah, she was considered a "diviner and exorcist" who had the power to fend off evil.[104] Like enslaved communities, Maroons engaged in various forms of creolized practices through religion and language. Yet it is important to not overly romanticize Maroons, for they still faced severe limitations from the colonial elites.

In between the two Maroon wars in Jamaica, the British spent time fighting off indigenous resistance. As mentioned, the 1763 Treaty of Paris that ended the Seven Years' War sparked the second phase of British colonization in the Caribbean as Britain gained new territories, including Grenada, Dominica, Tobago, and St. Vincent. When Britain landed and took over Dominica and Grenada, they faced resistance from French settlers. In St. Vincent and Dominica, the British also clashed with Kalinagos. In St. Vincent the Kalinago included men and women of mixed African and Kalinago descent, who fought off the invasion of their land by British planters in the 1770s and 1790s. In 1797, however, they were overpowered by the British, and around five thousand were transported to Roatán Island off the coast of Honduras. In Dominica, meanwhile, an agreement was made whereby Kalinagos would be given reserve land in exchange for not harboring runaway enslaved people. Through their interaction with Maroons and indigenous groups, the British subdued those on the margins of the racial-caste order, which helped strengthen white control in the Caribbean.

The development of racial slavery in the Caribbean was not only an economic engine for creating wealth for elites in the Caribbean, Britain, and its expanding empire. It was also an ideological engine for making the racial-caste hierarchy. Moreover, the events in the Caribbean permeated beyond the region and enormously transformed Britain. Although the racial-caste hierarchy in the region was not replicated in exactly the same way in Britain, the 1760s saw a growth in the number of people of African descent in Britain, which in turn increased anti-black racism, a consequence of the racial-caste hierarchy. At the same time, awareness of the horrors of hereditary racial slavery began filtering back to Britain, and this would influence a movement to end it—a movement that would drastically alter the rights of the enslaved, while keeping white supremacy firmly intact.

3

"The sooner all this mass of impolicy, crime and suffering, is got rid of, the better"

Anti-Black Racism in Britain, Abolition, and Emancipation

On September 6, 1781, the Liverpool-registered slave ship *Zong* departed from Accra on the Gold Coast and headed in the direction of the port of Black River in the southwest of Jamaica. *Zong* belonged to a syndicate led by William Gregson, a leading slave trader and former mayor of Liverpool. It was a journey made frequently in the eighteenth century, but what was unusual about this particular trip was the size of the *Zong*'s cargo: 440 Africans, nineteen crew, and one passenger—a ship that would typically carry around 190 enslaved Africans.[1] Like many voyages across the Atlantic, the captain and crew faced challenges throughout their journey. After two months, disease was spreading rapidly among the enslaved and the sailors, and water was in short supply. Due to navigational errors (they thought they were farther from Jamaica than they were), it was believed that there was not enough water for all on board to last until arrival. To deal with the looming crisis, those in positions of authority made a monumental decision.

On November 29, 1781, fifty-four enslaved women and children were pushed overboard. On December 1, forty-two men followed, and a few days after that thirty-eight enslaved Africans were killed; ten others, fearing murder, jumped overboard. In total, around 144 Africans lost their lives. Death, especially of enslaved people, was a common part of the Middle Passage (the journey from West Africa to the Americas), but this case was particularly noticeable because of the large number of Africans who died by design. Confusion abounded about who specifically decided the Africans should be thrown overboard. The captain of the ship, Luke Collingwood, supposedly made the order so that the healthy would survive and there would be adequate supplies for the others. Whatever the case, mass murder had occurred. When the *Zong* arrived in Black River, only 208 Africans were on board.

It took two years for the wider public to learn of the fateful events on the *Zong*. The tragedy came to light during a court case, held at London's Guildhall, in which the Gregson syndicate sought to recoup their losses by claiming insurance for the Africans who died. The trial hinged on a legal question that cut to the heart of racial slavery in the British Empire: Were enslaved people to be considered by law as human beings with legal rights or as movable property? In other words, were the officers of the *Zong* murderers or careless supercargoes? Everyone *knew* enslaved people were people—slaveholders used the humanity of the enslaved against them.[2] Nonetheless, the jury found in favor of the syndicate.

The Morning Chronicle and London Advertiser published news of the syndicate's victory. Included in the report was an anonymous letter, apparently written by someone with access to the trial. "It is hardly possible for a state to thrive," the nameless writer wrote, "where the perpetrator of such complicated guilt, as the present, is not only suffered to go unpunished, but is allowed to glory in the infamy, and carries off the reward of it."[3] While many Britons were aware that enslaved people had died during the voyage, the public of the 1780s was horrified by the actions of white people aboard the *Zong*, leading many to express sympathy for enslaved Africans. These sentiments were part of the broader emotional revolution that occurred in eighteenth-century Britain, when politeness and sensibility became key features of a society shaped not only by the institution of racial slavery but also by Enlightenment ideas about the backwardness of enslavement and Evangelical ideas about God saving the souls of all, regardless of complexion.

The *Zong* case shaped and symbolized changing attitudes toward the slave trade that had been stirring in Britain since the 1780s, galvanizing the anti-slavery activism of prominent former enslaved people who were living in Georgian Britain. These included Ottobah Cugoano, who had been brought to London by a slave owner but who managed to secure his freedom and called the Gregson syndicate "inhuman connivers of robbery, slavery, murder and fraud."[4] Olaudah Equiano hurriedly wrote a letter to abolitionist Granville Sharp to inform him of the *Zong* news.

Sharp involved himself in the next legal case presided over by Chief Justice Mansfield. Playing an advisory role on the insurer's legal team, Sharp made the case about much more than insurance. The underwriters argued that Africans and white people should have had the same amount of water, while the lawyers for the Gregson syndicate focused instead on arguments related to property rights. At the trial's end, Mansfield ruled that the captain and crew were at fault, and the Gregson syndicate did not get compensation. The ruling, however, did little to deter their business or damage their reputation: they continued to prosper in slave trading. Mansfield's ruling also left open the possibility of another trial, a decision that the Gregson syndicate and other slave traders supported.

Although the case transformed British opinion on hereditary racial slavery, it is important not to overstate its significance. While reaction to events on the *Zong* is often used to show the British public in a positive light, it highlights a different side to the growth of abolition of anti-slavery sentiment—namely one that reflects institutional inertia and indifference. Yes, the owners lost, and the public was appalled by stories of what occurred on board the ship—but it still took more than twenty-five years before the slave trade was abolished. Although the *Zong* case helped weave the various strands of abolition and emancipation movements, it is vital to understand that while they helped end hereditary racial slavery, this did not overturn the racial-caste hierarchy.

As political liberalism became more prominent, some white, wealthy, and propertied British abolitionists began to view racial slavery as a backward institution and anathema to individual freedom, free trade, and market liberalization.[5] They envisaged a post-emancipation Caribbean with formerly enslaved peoples transformed into communities of the working classes, who would labor for cheap wages and emulate middle-class European religious and patriarchal norms, all of which would "civilize" them. But this white supremacist narrative of civilization did not mean that formerly enslaved Africans would ever be considered equal to white people. Moreover, when formerly enslaved people failed to respond properly to the market economics that drove liberalism, they were considered to lack civilization, and this in turn helped strengthen white supremacy, thus revealing how liberalism came to have racist undercurrents.[6] Indeed, as racial slavery waned, anti-black racism waxed. This meant that hereditary racial slavery in the Caribbean continued to transform the presence of Africans and African-Caribbean people in Britain and the identity of the nation.

Abolition and emancipation were never intended to abolish the white supremacy that was central to hereditary racial slavery:

white elite pro-slavery advocates (often collectively known as the "West India Interest") and many abolitionists believed in the importance and continuance of white supremacy.[7] To be clear, both pro- and anti-slavery white activists had varied ideological leanings, and their self-interests (whether religious, economic, political, social, or cultural) directed their actions; nor were all white elite anti-slavery advocates or those who spearheaded important organizations inherently racist. However, white supremacy in its various guises seemed utterly self-evident to many on both sides of the debate. A degree of contradiction lay at the heart of anti-slavery activism—it was predominantly (but not comprehensively) elite-driven and did not reflect what enslaved rebels who also played their role in its end wanted. Most importantly, it did not threaten the status quo, leaving white supremacy and the racial-caste hierarchy unscathed in Britain and the Caribbean.

BEING BLACK IN GEORGIAN BRITAIN

The end of the eighteenth century saw increased attempts to fix specific characteristics to different racial groups, while growing numbers of black people in Georgian Britain came to shape the rise in anti-black racism.[8] In the eighteenth century, estimates show a figure of around ten thousand black residents in Britain.[9] The largest number resided in London and Liverpool, with smaller communities in other port cities like Plymouth. As highly mobile figures moving back and forth between Britain and the Caribbean, absentee planters continued to bring their enslaved property, as well as their mixed-race offspring, to Britain. A few notable examples include Francis Barber, an enslaved boy brought from Jamaica by planter Richard Bathurst to England in 1752. In his will, Bathurst freed Barber, who went on to become secretary to writer Samuel Johnson and later a schoolmaster.

There is some suggestion that Barber may have been Bathurst's illegitimate son. William Beckford had several mixed-race children in Jamaica, the island of his birthplace, and one of his sons, Richard, stood as a parliamentary candidate in Wiltshire in 1774.[10] Nathaniel Wells, the son of a plantation owner from St. Kitts, was sent to be schooled in Britain, and after his father died in 1794, he inherited around £200,000 and three sugar estates. Wells freed his enslaved mother and other family members but did not return to the Caribbean. Instead, he bought a home—Piercefield House near the town of Chepstow in Wales—and became high sheriff of Monmouthshire.[11]

Other black people in Britain included African seamen who had replaced white British crew members. Many African sailors worked alongside their Asian counterparts, known as Lascars.[12] Students, usually the sons of prominent West African elites and rulers who played crucial intermediary roles in facilitating racial slavery, were often sent to be educated in Britain.

White Britons could also see black people displayed publicly for entertainment. Amelia Lewsam (or Newsham), dubbed the "White Negro Woman"—and described as having "all the features of an Æthiopian, with a flaxen woolly Head, a Skin and Complexion fair as Alabaster"—came from Jamaica in 1754 at the age of five.[13] Onlookers paid a shilling at exhibition sites such as Charing Cross in London to stare at Lewsam. Saartjie Baartman became one of the most famous African women displayed.[14] Dubbed "the Hottentot Venus," she was brought to Britain in 1810 and baptized in December 1811 in Manchester under the name Sarah Baartman. Following her death in 1815, the French naturalist Georges Cuvier dissected her body, and her brain and skeleton were later preserved with a plaster cast of her body at Musée de l'Homme in Paris until 2002, when Baartman's remains were repatriated to her homeland, the Gamtoos Valley in South Africa.

The central question for black people in Britain who came from the Caribbean was whether they remained enslaved or were free. Slavery did not exist under British law, although many individuals were considered as enslaved people by their masters, and despite legal judgments enslaved Africans could still be bought and sold in Britain.[15] By the eighteenth century the craze for black servants had somewhat subsided. Yet many black people worked in domestic service, and the line between being a servant and being enslaved was often blurred. Black people took on work as pages, cooks, maids, coachmen, laborers, and seamen; some performed as musicians in pageants. Often, black women were laundresses, seamstresses, acted as nurses to children, or were involved in sex work—there's evidence of a black brothel in London in 1774.[16]

The wider presence of black people within Georgian society was visually depicted by the prolific artist William Hogarth.[17] Hogarth included black people in *Marriage A-la-Mode*; *Noon*; *A Rake's Progress*; and *A Harlot's Progress*. His satirical caricatures provoked debate too about the underside of Georgian society. Although there was no single black community in Georgian Britain, dispersed black communities gathered at weddings, christenings, and funerals.

Some black people in Georgian society gained notoriety and fame. Enslaved Black American Phillis Wheatley became widely popular after becoming the first black woman to be published in Britain in 1773, the year in which she was manumitted. At the age of nineteen, Wheatley's *Poems on Various Subjects, Religious and Moral*, which she wrote in New England, was considered a literary success. Traveling to the capital with the Wheatley family, who owned her, she spent a month mingling with the elite, including Benjamin Franklin, who at the time was the European agent to the colonies in North America. Wheatley's fame, however, was short-lived. She died destitute in 1784 at the age of thirty.

Marriage A-la-Mode, Plate IV by Simon Francis Ravenet, the elder, after William Hogarth, 1745.

Born enslaved in St. Kitts, Julius Soubise was another well-known figure. He was brought to Britain in 1764 and came under the control of Catherine Hyde, the Duchess of Queensberry, who paid for his education. Over the years the two developed a close bond, intimated in the diaries of English noblewoman Lady Mary Coke. In 1767 Coke visited the duchess and noticed her

> half dress'd & half undress'd; She was talking to her Black Boy, who indeed seems to have a very extraordinary capacity, something very uncommon; She told me She had taught him everything he had a mind to learn ... but When She told me he learnt to ride & fence, I could not help thinking those exercises too much above his condition to be useful, & wou'd only serve to give him expectations that cou'd not be answer'd.[18]

Coke voiced anxiety about attempts to provide black people with similar opportunities to whites. Soubise gained a reputation within Georgian society for his lavish lifestyle, and he took a liking to equestrian activities, but his standing in elite society came under attack in 1777 when he faced accusations of rape. In response, the duchess played a role in sending him to India, where in Calcutta he established a riding school and married. He died in 1798 after falling from a horse.[19]

James Gronniosaw gained fame following the 1770 publication of his *A Narrative of the Most Remarkable Particulars in life of ... an African Prince*. Born in what is today Nigeria, Gronniosaw was sold at age fifteen to a Dutch captain and then bought by an American in Barbados, who sold him in New York. His owner educated and instructed him in the Christian faith and, following his death, freed Gronniosaw in his will. Gronniosaw continued to care for the remainder of the family, but when they died, he was left destitute and desperate. He went on to work as a cook and later entered the British army, serving in Cuba and Martinique, and traveled to England after being discharged. On his arrival in Plymouth, he "expected to find nothing but goodness, gentleness and meekness in this Christian land."[20] He soon found himself "among bad people, who defrauded me of my money and watch; and that all my promised happiness was blasted."[21]

Ignatius Sancho was born in 1729 aboard a slave ship, and around the age of two his owner brought him to England, where he was given to three sisters. Later he entered the service of the Duchess of Montagu, who encouraged his education. He began writing prose, poetry, and music, became famous among literary circles, and was painted by Thomas Gainsborough in 1768. He married Anne, an African-Caribbean woman, with whom he had six children, and with financial help from the Montagues he established a grocery shop in London. Sancho shared a wide circle of friends, including writers Laurence Sterne and Samuel

Johnson and sculptor Joseph Nollekens. He died in 1780, and two years later his *Letters* were published and quickly became a bestseller.

Other black people in Britain became widely popular due to their involvement in anti-slavery activism, and Equiano was a leader among this group, especially in London. Born around 1745 in Igboland, in what is today southern Nigeria, Equiano was first brought to Barbados, then to Virginia, before being taken to England by a British naval officer, who renamed him Gustavus Vassa. Arriving in approximately 1759, he was educated by relatives of his master and baptized. Equiano was soon sold again, this time to Captain James Doran, who returned him to the Caribbean, where a Quaker merchant, Robert King, purchased him. Through his savings, Equiano managed to pay £40 for his freedom and then worked as a free man for King. He went back to England in around 1767 or 1768 and gained an apprenticeship. Equiano also spent time working as a sailor and officer on merchant ships—including at least one voyage to purchase enslaved people and bring them to the Mosquito Coast.

Equiano returned to Britain in 1777 and worked as a servant. In his aforementioned autobiography, Equiano hoped that it would inspire "a sense of compassion for the miseries which the Slave-Trade has entailed on my unfortunate countrymen."[22] The book became a commercial success, with nine editions published between 1789 and 1794, and it transformed Equiano into a widely known figure, especially in anti-slavery circles.[23] The autobiography revealed to a larger audience the experiences of enslaved people in various parts of the Atlantic world and would come to influence debates about ending the slave trade and later abolition. Equiano also worked alongside other black abolitionists, such as Ottobah Cugoano, helping Cugoano compile a collection of essays, *Thoughts and Sentiments on the Evil, and Wicked Traffic of the Slavery and Commerce of the Human Species*, in 1787. In this work Cugoano demanded both restitution and reparations for the injustices of racial slavery. Calls for reparations were present from the start of resistance against racial slavery and formulated by the enslaved and formerly enslaved themselves, who understood how much substantive freedom relied on landholdings or reparations to build wealth.

Many of these figures are now well-known, but questions remain about ordinary black people. Their lives, as described by historian Gretchen Gerzina, "were an odd mixture of isolation and assimilation, of separation from each other and the larger society while being connected to both."[24] Many lived precariously on the margins of society. Due to their limited family and parish connections, many were not eligible for poor relief through poor laws. They also risked being captured and sold back into slavery. Anti-slavery advocate Hannah More once witnessed the kidnapping of a black woman in Bristol. In a letter to writer Horace Walpole, she described a bellman during "church-time" who:

> was crying the reward of a guinea to any one who would produce a poor negro girl who had run away because she would not return to one of those trafficking islands, whither her master was resolved to send her. To my great grief and indignation, the poor trembling wretch was dragged out from a hole in the top of a house where she had hid herself, and forced on board ship.[25]

For those who managed to settle in Britain, many formed unions and families with white Britons. As the black population in Britain was predominantly male, some married white women, and mixed-race marriages could help black men assimilate into wider British society. But for some, especially those spearheading hereditary racial slavery, this pairing provoked great concern. Once again it was Edward Long who led the way, authoring tracts that rebuked white working-class women who engaged in sexual relationships with black men. "The lower class of women in *England*," he wrote,

> are remarkably fond of the blacks, for reasons too brutal to mention . . . By these ladies they generally have a numerous brood. Thus, in the course of a few generations more, the English blood will become so contaminated with this mixture, and from the chances, the ups and downs of life, this alloy may spread so extensively, as even to reach the middle, and then the higher orders of the people, till the whole nation resembles the Portuguese and Moroccos [sic] in complexion of skin and baseness of mind.[26]

For Long, mixed-raced sexual relations sparked severe anxiety about the maintenance of racial divisions inherent in the racial-caste hierarchy and the role of the state in their responsibility to mixed-race Britons. Army officer and rabid racist Philip Thicknesse, who divided his time between Georgia in North America and Jamaica, went further than Long in the second edition of his 1789 book *A Year's Journey through France and Part of Spain*. He wrote of the need for laws banning interracial relationships: "A mixture of negro blood with the natives of this country is big with great and mighty mischiefs and if they are to live among us, they ought by some very severe law to be compelled to marry only among themselves, and to have no criminal intercourse whatever with people of other complexions."[27] These thoughts reflect how far status was determined by race: the maintenance of racial inequality all but dictated the maintenance of sexual inequality, control, and patriarchy. "Race mixing" was seen as an existential threat to the white supremacist worldview and hierarchy.

An institutional color bar also emerged in the eighteenth century. In London as early as 1731, an employment bar prevented black people from learning a trade.[28] Legal officials voiced deep concerns about the rising number of black servants, arguing that they were depriving white servants of employment. In 1762 magistrate Sir John Fielding commented that slave owners

> bring them to England as cheap servants, having no right to wages; they no sooner arrive here, than they put themselves on a footing with other servants, become intoxicated with liberty, grow refractory, and . . . begin to expect wages according to their own opinion of their merits: and, as there are already a great number of black men who have made themselves so troublesome and dangerous to the families who have brought them over, as to get themselves discharged, these enter into societies, and make it their business to corrupt and dissatisfy the mind of every black servant that comes to England; first, by getting them christened or married, which, they inform them makes them free.[29]

Fielding was not alone in his complaint. In the *London Chronicle* in 1764, someone calling themselves "Anglicanus" wrote of black servants:

> [A]s they fill the places of so many of our own people, we are by this means depriving so many of them of the means of getting their bread, and thereby decreasing our native population in favour of a race, whose mixture with us is disgraceful, and whose uses cannot be so various and essential as those of white people . . . they never can be considered as a part of the people, and therefore their introduction into the community can only serve to elbow as many out of it who are genuine subjects, and in every point preferable.[30]

These comments heralded arguments that black people, whose labor was critical to Britain, were unwanted individuals who deprived white people of their livelihoods, arguments that would persist well into the twenty-first century.

The rise of the Enlightenment also buttressed anti-black racist ideas. In the 1753 reprint of his 1748 essay "Of National Characters," Scottish philosopher David Hume wrote: "I am apt to suspect the negroes . . . to be naturally inferior to the whites. There never was a civilized nation of any other complexion than white, nor even any individual eminent either in action or speculation."[31] In 1764, German philosopher Immanuel Kant said: "The Negroes of Africa have by nature no feeling that rises above the trifling."[32] For Kant, there were "fundamental" differences between white and black people "in regard to mental capacities as in color."[33] These opinions overlapped with the rise of pseudoscientific racism from the 1770s. Some European scientists in the period became obsessed with classifying and categorizing humans. One of the most influential scientists, Swedish naturalist Carl Linnaeus, argued that Europeans were "acute, inventive . . . *Governed* by laws," whereas black people were "crafty, indolent, negligent . . . *Governed* by caprice."[34]

Ideas about race as expressed by planters, pseudoscientists, and Enlightenment thinkers were considered scientific (and by default legitimate and factual). But from the outset, elites in Britain had similar contempt for those they ruled in the colonies and for poor white people in Britain, often drawing comparisons between the two.

Just as these ideas circulated in the 1770s, more legal rulings helped in some measure to protect Britain's black population. But here again, challenges to enslavement did not challenge white supremacy in its familiar or new, pseudoscientific iterations—nor were they intended to. Indeed, increased white supremacy, buttressed by pseudoscience, among other things, was the legacy—or perhaps even the successor system, with the color bar—of racial slavery.

"THE SOONER ALL THIS MASS OF IMPOLICY"

The legality of racial slavery was contested terrain in Britain, but some semblance of clarity on the position of the enslaved came through Granville Sharp. A keen debater, musician, and intellectual, Sharp taught himself ancient Greek and Hebrew while working as an apprentice to a London draper. After completing his apprenticeship in 1757, he accepted the position of clerk in the Ordnance Office at the Tower of London. His involvement in the plight of black people in Britain occurred almost by accident when he met Jonathan Strong, a young enslaved man from Barbados who had been badly beaten by his owner in 1765. When Strong's master tried to recapture him and sell him, Strong solicited the help of Sharp, who came to his defense.

Granville Sharp. Frontispiece from *Memoirs of Granville Sharp, Esq.*, edited by Prince Hoare, London, 1820.

Sharp is best remembered today for his involvement in the case of James Somerset, an enslaved man from Virginia, brought to London by his owner Charles Stewart, a Boston customs official, in November 1769. In February 1771, Somerset was baptized in London and in November escaped from Stewart's household. Attempting to recover his property, Stewart ordered Somerset's retrieval and re-enslavement. After he was captured, Somerset was taken to the *Ann and Mary*, a ship bound for Jamaica. In desperation, Somerset solicited the help of the white godparents he received at his baptism, and they managed to gain a writ of habeas corpus, granted by Chief Justice Lord Mansfield, which meant that the captain of the slave ship had to present Somerset to court. Through requests by Somerset and his allies, Sharp agreed to take the case forward and gathered a team of lawyers, including many with anti-slavery leanings.

The case began in January 1772. Stewart and his lawyers focused their arguments on the property rights of slave owners as supreme and tended to elide debates about the morality of racial slavery. Sharp, Somerset, and their team focused on the lack of laws regarding racial slavery in Britain. If Mansfield agreed with Stewart, he would set a considerable precedent. If he sided with Somerset, he would undermine slave owners' property rights. Mansfield's particular thoughts on racial slavery are unclear, but his family was implicated in its consequences. His nephew, Captain (later Rear Admiral) Sir John Lindsay of the Royal Navy, had a mixed-race daughter, the offspring of an affair with an enslaved woman in the Caribbean known as Maria Belle. In 1765 Lindsay had brought his four-year-old daughter, Dido Elizabeth Belle, to England and entrusted her to Mansfield and his wife, Elizabeth Murray. They raised her as a free woman alongside their great-niece Lady Elizabeth Murray (whose mother had died) in Kenwood House, north London, where she lived for thirty years. Lady Elizabeth and Dido were famously pictured together by Scottish portraitist David Martin in the late 1770s in a rare painting of a white and black woman seemingly as equals. When Mansfield died in 1793, he left Dido an annuity, thereby making her an heiress, which suggests concern for her well-being and independence. It was perhaps Mansfield's complicated involvement in hereditary racial slavery, coupled with the precedent-setting importance of his judgment, that caused him to postpone a final decision in the case.

Finally, on June 22, 1772, Mansfield made his ruling:

> The state of slavery is of such a nature, that it is incapable of being now introduced by courts of justice upon mere reasoning, or inferences from any principle natural or political; it must take its rise from *positive law* ... No master ever was allowed here to take a slave by force to be sold abroad because he deserted from his service, or for any other reason whatever; WE CANNOT SAY, *the cause set forth by this return* IS ALLOWED OR APPROVED OF BY THE LAWS OF THIS KINGDOM, and therefore the man must be discharged.[35]

Then, as now, ambiguity hovered over Mansfield's ruling. To some, Mansfield ruled that racial slavery did not exist in Britain because there were no laws for it. Others interpreted Mansfield's judgment as limited, pertaining only to whether a slave owner had the right to forcibly remove an enslaved person from Britain. But the Somerset ruling gave runaways only minor, not full, protection. Slave servants were fleeing households, evidence shows, even after 1772. And the case hinged not just on the freedom of enslaved Africans in England but also on whether colonial rules would apply in the metropole and the extent to which England would remain a "free land."[36]

Portrait of Dido Elizabeth Belle and Lady Elizabeth Murray by David Martin, c. 1778.

Around the same time, the number of people of African descent in Britain was growing as enslaved and free black men joined the ranks of the British Loyalist camp in the American War for Independence. In 1775, Lord Dunmore, the governor of the British colony of Virginia, offered freedom to Black American enslaved men who left their owners and joined the royalist forces. Proclaimed for practical rather than humanitarian reasons, within months of Dunmore's proclamation thousands of enslaved men absconded and enlisted as black Loyalists. Thousands of enslaved people from the Thirteen Colonies fled to British lines or fought in hastily formed black regiments like Lord Dunmore's Ethiopian Regiment. But these men did not experience equality among segregated British forces. When the war ended in November 1783, the British withdrew around fourteen thousand black men from New York, Charleston, and Savannah. Some were sent to, or escaped to, British-controlled Canada and others to the

Caribbean, where some ended up enslaved once again. Hundreds, however, found their way to Britain's shores.

In 1784, around a hundred black Loyalists arrived in London. A year earlier, the British government had established the Loyalist Claims Commission, tasked with compensating Loyalists who had lost land and property. Around forty-seven black men, most of whom had been free men with property in the US, asked for compensation, but many claimants received less than white Loyalists. With no family and little money, many black Loyalists quickly descended into poverty. Their plight alongside other black people from the Caribbean became a concern for affluent Londoners, MPs, and merchants, who came together to create the "Committee of Gentlemen," which first organized relief for Lascars and later extended help to black people. Soon renamed the "Committee for the Black Poor," they began raising money through publicity and provided food, clothing, and money. The government also provided the committee with money and favored resettlement of the black poor as a solution, with Sierra Leone emerging as the favored destination.

A botanist and frequent exaggerator of the truth, Henry Smeathman, touted the Sierra Leone plan as ideal. He and the London merchants who supported him had a financial stake in the scheme rather than any interest in the fate of the black poor, whereas Sharp, who supported the project, thought Sierra Leone would be a better place for black people to experience more freedom than they had in Britain. The plan was to have the black poor grow crops such as cotton in the colony, and Smeathman persuaded the Treasury to pay him £14 for every black person who went to Sierra Leone. His death in 1786 did not kill the scheme, and soon the committee put pressure on black people to sign up.

While initially the black poor did favor resettlement, their preference was for Nova Scotia, home to other black Loyalists.

They were suspicious of Sierra Leone due to fears of potential re-enslavement. Reluctance in turn provoked coercion. In October 1786 the committee decided to not give any more money to a black person who had not agreed to resettlement. Some black Georgians were deeply skeptical of the plan, including Cugoano. In *Thoughts and Sentiments* he wrote: "can it be readily conceived that government would establish a free colony for them nearly on the spot, while it supports its forts and garrisons, to ensnare, merchandize, and to carry others into captivity and slavery."[37] The committee reached out to Equiano to legitimize the scheme, and in November 1786 he was appointed commissary of provisions for the black poor in Sierra Leone. He was later dismissed when he challenged white leadership.

In 1787 ships sailed from the Thames to Sierra Leone carrying 350 prospective settlers, among them forty-one black women and fifty-nine white women who were the wives of black men. But there were many fatalities before arriving in Africa, and once in Sierra Leone conditions were challenging and disease and death rampant. The scheme was considered a failure. Of the 374 who arrived that year, only sixty remained four years later.[38]

The rise of anti-black racism paralleled the rise of the abolitionist movement. While the *Zong* incident shifted opinion against the slave trade, another critical change originated at the University of Cambridge. In 1785, the twenty-five-year-old devout Anglican Thomas Clarkson entered the university's vice chancellor's Latin essay–writing competition. Participants had to answer the question: "Is it lawful to make slaves of others against their will?" Clarkson was not fully aware of the intricacies of Britain's involvement in the transatlantic slave trade, but he dedicated the next months to speaking to those directly involved, and plowing through books, especially the work of influential French American Quaker abolitionist Anthony Benezet. All his research and writing paid off—his essay won the top prize—and the contents and arguments he made in it would soon profoundly change the trajectory of his life.

Clarkson experienced a transformative spiritual revelation—somewhat of a trope among abolitionist rhetoric—while journeying on horseback from Cambridge to London. The slave trade and racial slavery became for Clarkson not just abstract or academic, but

> the subject of it almost wholly engrossed my thoughts. I became at times very seriously affected while upon the road . . . I sat down disconsolate on the turf by the roadside and held my horse. Here a thought came into my mind, that if the contents of the Essay were true, it was time some person should see these calamities to their end.[39]

A year later, Clarkson realized that he was this person and pledged to "devote myself to the cause of the oppressed Africans."[40]

That same year Clarkson's essay was translated from Latin to English and published in pamphlet form, and it quickly became influential anti-slavery propaganda. In *An Essay on the Slavery and Commerce of the Human Species, particularly the African*, Clarkson argued that continued British involvement in the slave trade would lead to punishment for the British nation. Clarkson's circle widened to include Sharp and James Ramsay; and Quakers, Methodists, and Baptists in Britain and the US. In 1783, the year that news of the *Zong* reached the masses, a group of Quakers presented the first petition to Parliament to end the slave trade.

By May 1787, Clarkson, Sharp, and fellow Anglican Philip Sansom, along with nine Quakers, established the Society for Effecting the Abolition of the Slave Trade. Its committee included the famous potter and industrialist Josiah Wedgwood as well as the popular MP for Hull, William Wilberforce. Wilberforce had been one of the few MPs to support the Quakers' 1783 petition and became the society's leading advocate in Parliament. Humanitarian at its core, the society stressed the brutal nature of the slave trade and argued that Britain's involvement in it constituted a national sin. Over the next twenty years, the society became a prominent abolitionist group in Britain, and events unfolding in the French-speaking Caribbean would directly impact their momentum.

FROM REVOLT TO REVOLUTION

Back in the Caribbean in 1791, a group of enslaved people started a revolt that turned into a revolution. The Haitian revolution was a complex rising shaped by the specificities of racial slavery in the colony and the legacy of the French revolution. It would impact not only the Caribbean but the world.[41]

Eighteenth-century Saint-Domingue was the wealthiest colony in the Caribbean and the most important island for France, providing the motherland with two-fifths of its foreign trade.[42] The origins of the revolt began in August 1791 when a rebellion began around Le Cap, a port city on the northern coast. Spreading across the north in the first few months, enslaved men and women attacked sugar plantations and coffee estates and killed hundreds of white people. In retaliation, white people killed large numbers of the enslaved. In an attempt to stabilize the situation, the National Assembly in April 1792 gave equal rights to free people of color, appointed civil commissioners to the colony (including the lawyer Léger-Félicité Sonthonax), and deployed thousands of troops. When Sonthonax arrived in Saint-Domingue, he dissolved the Colonial Assembly and placed free people of color in positions once held only by white people. French forces tried to subdue the enslaved rebels but ended up angering the white people who revolted against them and their attempts to promote racial equality. In response, Sonthonax armed free people of color and the enslaved against them.[43]

The revolt in Saint-Domingue was not the only violent conflict in the Caribbean at that time. France and Britain were at war in 1793, and in 1794 the British attacked the French colonies of St. Lucia, Martinique, and Guadeloupe (with the plan to also reinstate racial slavery in the latter two). The British were expelled from Guadeloupe but occupied St. Lucia for a year, from 1794. Here forces of the French commissioner, Victor Hugues, led a countermovement against British forces. Hugues's agent in St. Lucia abolished racial slavery on the island, albeit briefly, before the British reinstated it, and their occupation, once more in 1796.[44]

The southernmost island in the Antilles, Grenada, known as the "island of spice" for its production of nutmeg, was another source of conflict between Britain and France. The French ceded Grenada to the British in 1763 after the Seven Years' War, and a French-speaking minority remained on the island in the 1790s. With the help of Hugues and French-speaking mixed-race planter Julien Fédon, free people of color revolted against white people in 1795 for sixteen months until British forces suppressed them. Conflict raged also on the island of St. Vincent, north of Grenada, which came under British control in 1783. There, Kalinagos (also referred to as Black Caribs, descendants of runaway enslaved people and indigenous communities) rebelled against the British with the help of French free people of color on the island, but they were defeated and exiled.[45]

From 1796 to 1802 and again between 1804 and 1808, Spain and Britain were also at war, and the latter used the conflict to expand further their power and spheres of influence in the Caribbean. Marking the third and final phase of British colonial expansion in the region, Britain gained Trinidad from the Spanish in 1797 and again in 1802; gained St. Lucia from the French in

1803; and in 1803 acquired Demerara, Essequibo, and Berbice from the Dutch, which collectively would become British Guiana.

Meanwhile in Saint-Domingue, Britain and Spain tried to take advantage of weakened French control on the island and invaded from the east in 1793. The British wanted to capture the colony and reinstate racial slavery, in part to use it as a valuable bargaining chip in the war with France in Europe. This marked the start of a five-year campaign of occupation, which was met with fierce resistance. The Spanish who ruled in neighboring Santo Domingo tried to invade from the west; together the British and the Spanish aimed to preserve racial slavery in the western province of the island and areas in the south. The Spanish convinced many rebels and, significantly, acquired the support of one of the most influential leaders among the enslaved: Toussaint Louverture.

A creole Catholic, Louverture was born enslaved but stressed that "nature gave me the soul of the free man."[46] Around the age of thirty, he gained his freedom and even purchased enslaved people himself. During the uprising, Louverture became popular due to his military engagements against the French as well as mixed-race communities. He turned against the Spanish because of Sonthonax, who tried to get the enslaved on his side by promising to change plantation conditions. Then, in August 1793, Sonthonax abolished racial slavery in the colony, a decision ratified by the National Assembly in February 1794. Sonthonax did not envisage the end of the plantation economy but instead wanted the enslaved to work as serfs tied to estates with wages and still perform compulsory labor when necessary. Abolition led Louverture to the French side and effected the Spanish withdrawal in 1795. In 1798, the British also withdrew.[47]

By 1800 Louverture had ascended to become governor of Saint-Domingue and a year later introduced a new constitution in which it was stated: "Slaves cannot exist in this territory and servitude is for ever abolished. Here, all men are born, live and die free and French."[48] Yet Louverture's authoritarianism also grew in 1801, and he declared himself governor for life at a point when the island was operating as a de facto independent state.

Louverture tried to recover the plantation-based economy but faced strong opposition from the enslaved, who preferred to work on their own small land plots. His annexation of the French territory of Santo Domingo (which the Spanish had ceded to the French in 1795) enraged Napoléon Bonaparte, the French consul and military leader, who sought to reinstate French metropolitan rule. Louverture's forces were overpowered and Louverture surrendered. He was later kidnapped and deported to France, where he was tortured, dying on April 7, 1803. In death he became a martyr. His most recent biographer, Sudhir Hazareesingh, calls him "the first black superhero of the modern age."[49]

In 1802, the French reimposed racial slavery in all their colonies, sparking opposition from people of color. Senior general Jean-Jacques Dessalines became the leader against the French and successfully forced their withdrawal in November 1803. Dessalines then declared Saint-Domingue's independence on January 1, 1804, and changed the name of the island back to the one used by indigenous peoples: Haiti. In the new nation's declaration of independence, Dessalines roused the citizens with a passionate plea: "Vow before me to live free and independent, and to prefer death to anything that will try to place you back in chains. Swear, finally, to pursue forever the traitors and enemies of your independence."[50] With these words, Haiti joined its US neighbor to become the second post-colonial state in the Americas.

Emerging from the ashes of an enslaved revolt, Haiti faced enormous challenges. The collapse of the sugar industry allowed other colonies like Brazil and Cuba to increase their development of sugar-based plantation economies, which would soon surpass other Caribbean competitors. The country's economy was wrecked by the legacies of racial slavery and the revolution. Yet the significance of the revolution is unquestioned.[51] Hazareesingh concludes: "The age's most comprehensive example of radical change, combining democratic and republican goals with an emphasis on racial equality, and became a just war of national liberation which foreshadowed the anti-colonial struggles of the modern era."[52] But for so many years the politics of the revolution remained what Haitian scholar Michel-Rolph Trouillot called an "unthinkable" act, because it was inconceivable that black rebels could have a political ideology that was not simply focused on violent revenge toward white slaveholders and oppressors, and the legacies of the revolution were subsequently silenced by scholars.[53]

Yet the Haitian revolution reverberated globally, and immediately. News spread among the enslaved across the Americas. In Jamaica, as early as 1791, the enslaved heard songs about it.[54] Planters in the British Caribbean interpreted it as evidence of "black savagery." The collapse of the sugar industry on the island was also seen as a dire warning of economic disaster if enslaved revolts spread within British-controlled islands. In Britain, the Haitian revolution inflected the trajectory of abolition. After 1804, the defeat of the French made it easier to make the case that ending the slave trade would not harm the British sugar industry—since British planters' biggest competitor, Saint-Domingue, had been defeated.

The revolution would also have long-term consequences, evident especially today. To gain acceptance of its status as an independent nation-state and recognition from the international community, France imposed an overwhelming indemnity on Haiti of 150 million francs. To pay this huge sum, Haiti took out various loans with high interest rates that stunted its economic development. Over the course of seven decades, Haiti paid 112 million francs (the equivalent of $560 million today).[55] The indemnity was, as historian Kris Manjapra has written, a type of retroactive emancipation whereby Haiti "had to pay reparations to the former slave-owners and accept a tremendous debt burden."[56] While debate about Haiti's status as a failed state rages on, it can be understood only as a direct consequence of colonialism, the revolution, and this punitive indemnity.

LEGALLY ENDING RACIAL SLAVERY

The growth of the abolitionist movement in the late eighteenth century was part of a wider confluence of religious, social, and economic change. Evangelical Christians rose in prominence and inspired believers from the Church of England, Baptists, Methodists, and Moravians to reevaluate religious support for an inhumane institution. John Wesley, a leading Evangelical and one of the founders of Methodism, published an influential anti-slavery pamphlet, *Thoughts on Slavery* (1774), in which he stated:

> Give Liberty to whom Liberty is due, that is to every child of man, to every partaker of human nature. Let none serve you but by his own act and deed, by his own voluntary choice. Away with all whips, all chains, all compulsion! Be gentle toward all men.[57]

What was central to Evangelicals was the spread of their Evangelical religion in Britain and the wider empire, and these religious motives and objectives shaped their involvement in anti-slavery.[58] It led them to enter political debates about vice and wider debates about moral reform that they used to promote Christianity.[59] Also, evangelicals widely extolled the rhetoric of "civilization" as a way to improve the character of Africans, so that they too could learn European norms and customs.

Political debate fulminated, especially between the 1780s and 1830s. In taverns, pubs, and coffeehouses, the British establishment and the middle and working classes debated weighty concepts such as freedom, liberty, monopolies, repression, and tyranny. Ideas circulated in books, newspapers, pamphlets, and broadsides—a function of the thriving print culture and greater literacy in the general public. Many began to notice a contradiction between admiration for British liberty and freedom on the one hand and a British-dominated slave trade on the other.

New political ideas—especially liberalism—merged with Enlightenment arguments about the natural order, rationality, and efficiency, as well as with economic attacks on racial slavery. None was more influential than economist Adam Smith's 1776 *The Wealth of Nations*, in which he argued from "the experience of all ages and nations, I believe, demonstrates that the work done by slaves, though it appears to cost only their maintenance, is in the end the dearest of any."[60] According to Smith, the enslaved cost more to maintain than free workers and slavery impeded free trade. Anti-slavery advocates began to argue that by abolishing the slave trade, and later racial slavery, low wages offered to formerly enslaved people would incentivize hard work and emulation of middle-class norms. Over the hundred years from 1763, multiple and related revolutions changed commodity markets, as capitalists began to speculate in different economic ventures such as factories, railways, and steamships in Britain and worldwide. This diminished the importance of smaller British-controlled Caribbean colonies in the global economy,[61] and in this context the abolition movement gained more drive.

Abolitionists were a mixed group of predominantly middle-class religious zealots, who included Quakers, Anglican Evangelicals, and humanitarians, as well as former and current enslaved people, some of whom were influenced by anti-slavery movements in the US.[62] Individuals became abolitionists for various reasons, and not always because of their attitudes toward enslaved Africans.[63] Some abolitionists were more concerned with the impact that racial slavery was having on morality in Britain and its empire. Disquiet about morality in Britain's colonies was also deeply shaped by the American revolution. The crisis the revolution wrought in the 1760s and '70s, especially with regards to colonial authority, increased the importance of racial slavery.[64]

The abolitionist movement was not linear, and there was no single movement but many. In Britain, abolitionist groups employed various tactics—from encouraging the boycotting of slave-trade products such as sugar and rum to distributing pamphlets documenting the violence of racial slavery. Petitions calling for the end of the slave trade increased from sixty thousand to four hundred thousand signatures between 1788 and 1791.[65] Across the country, smaller groups committed to abolition emerged, led by men and women from places such as Exeter and Plymouth in the southwest of England; the Midlands cities of Birmingham and Sheffield; Liverpool, Leeds, and Manchester in the north; as well as in London. British women of all classes played crucial roles in the anti-slavery movement, which deepened their involvement within civil society.[66]

Prominent black Georgians were also active. Equiano and Cugoano established the group known as the "Sons of Africa," alongside others including: Jasper Goree, George Robert Mandeville, Thomas Jones, Joseph Almaze, Thomas Oxford, George Wallace, Cojoh Ammere, and Boughwa Gegansmel—described by historian Hakim Adi as the "best-known organization of Africans in Britain in the eighteenth century."[67]

Unitarian minister and socialist Robert Wedderburn was a radical voice in the anti-slavery movement. Born in Jamaica in 1762, Wedderburn was the son of an enslaved mother named Rosanna and a Scottish slaveholder and physician, James Wedderburn. Emancipated by his father in 1765, Wedderburn served in the Royal Navy and arrived in England in 1778 or 1779. He joined Thomas Spence's movement of agrarian socialism and in 1819 opened a chapel in London's Soho, which was a hub for radical politics. Wedderburn authored various tracts on racial slavery including, in 1817, *An Address to the Planters and Negroes of the Island of Jamaica*, in which he implored the enslaved to "keep possession of the land you now possess as slaves; for without that, freedom is not worth possessing; for if you once give up the possession of your lands, your oppressors will have power to starve you to death, through making laws for their own accommodation."[68] Wedderburn's warning about landless freedom would prove prescient in the post-emancipation Caribbean.

Class played an interesting role in abolitionism. Many members of the white British working class expressed opposition to the slave trade and solidarity with enslaved people, while others—especially sailors in port cities like Liverpool—were also actively dependent on the slave trade for employment.[69] Among working-class radicals, many subscribed to white supremacist thinking and attacked middle-class abolitionists for their seeming lack of sympathy toward working-class white people and their plight in contrast to enslaved Africans.[70]

Pro- and anti-slavery figures tended to stereotype those they sought to condemn or liberate. While notorious planters like Long and George Hibbert portrayed racial slavery as a redemptive force for inferior Africans, abolitionists portrayed the enslaved as docile, innocent, and in need of salvation by European Christians, thereby reinforcing racial hierarchies. This sentiment inspired powerful iconography such as the engravings *Am I Not a Man and a Brother?* and *Am I Not a Woman and a Sister?* by Josiah Wedgwood, which bore little resemblance to the lived experience of the enslaved. These images represented the cultural racism of the abolitionist imagery in that while they showed enslaved men and women as being sisters and brothers in Christ, it also showed them as subservient, childlike, and in need of tutelage

"THE SOONER ALL THIS MASS OF IMPOLICY"

"Am I not a man and a brother?", woodcut illustration from the broadside publication of John Greenleaf Whittier's anti-slavery poem, "Our Countrymen in Chains," 1837.

American hard times token: "Am I not a woman & a sister," 1838.

by white Europeans.[71] Wedgwood's fellow Quaker James Phillips contributed anti-slavery art as well with his widely reproduced image of the Brookes ship (1788), which starkly illustrated the reality of overcrowding but also rendered the subjects passive and lacking autonomy.[72]

Abolitionists took a particular interest in portraying a certain image of needy enslaved women. Wilberforce and others used horror stories of the abuse of enslaved women and girls to show the violence and inhumanity of racial slavery, a prerequisite for arguments that only its abolition would advance European gender roles in the Caribbean and provide social stability more broadly.[73]

In this respect and others, white pro- and anti-slavery advocates were not as far apart as one might assume. They both believed in the redemptive qualities of European-led civilization, a value underpinned by white supremacy. In Wilberforce's words: "By ameliorating regulations, and by stopping the influx of uninstructed savages, to advance slowly towards the period when these unhappy beings might exchange their degraded state of slavery for that of a free and industrious peasantry."[74] Both anti- and pro-slavery advocates compared enslaved workers to peasants, and there was a racial aspect to this comparison. According to historian Padraic Scanlan: "The concept applied to colonial laborers of African descent a combination of the idyllic aesthetic of smallholding, an expectation of gratitude and obedience, and the discipline and regimentation of wage labor."[75] In other words, the abolition of racial slavery was not envisioned as the abolition of white supremacy in Britain or elsewhere. Pro- and anti-slavery advocates were drawing from the same well. And because of this, the racial-caste hierarchy and white supremacy would endure and grow stronger in the coming years.

By the late 1780s and early 1790s, the Society for Effecting the Abolition of the Slave Trade had gained enough momentum to try to pass a motion for abolition in Parliament. Although public support for abolition had been growing—by 1792 the society had around four hundred thousand signatures—the mood in Parliament was changing. While the government superficially spoke of abolition, the French revolution, Britain's war with France, and the Haitian revolution would overshadow politics for the next decade. The economic benefits of the slave trade trumped arguments about ending it, exposing the contradictions at the heart of the movement for abolition in these decades. The British government was a serious investor in a slave trade that it was ostensibly keen to end, yet it obscured and downplayed this role. In the 1790s, the British government became the largest purchaser of Africans. Between 1789 and 1807, 767,000 Africans transported into slavery traveled on British ships.[76] Both slave traders and abolitionists knew these numbers but did not make them a significant issue.[77] Thus revealing how the profits from transatlantic slavery trumped the moral weight in arguments against the trade.

By the early nineteenth century, abolitionists had changed tack. They turned pro-slavery arguments into anti-slavery arguments, asserting that the ongoing importation of Africans threatened the stability of the Caribbean and could potentially foster revolt. At this time the Society for Effecting the Abolition of the Slave Trade was changing too. By 1804 its leadership had grown to include more Evangelical Anglicans, known as the Clapham Sect, and included Wilberforce, James Stephen, Zachary Macaulay, Thomas Babington, Henry Thornton, Quaker physician William Allen, and Henry Brougham.

Their arguments began to be heard in a new government led by Lord Grenville after the death of William Pitt the Younger in 1806. With the introduction of new colonies in Trinidad and British Guiana, planters in colonies established in the seventeenth century started to view the abolition of the slave trade slightly more favorably—as a way to limit plantation competition. In 1807 a new bill to end the slave trade was presented and passed by 283 to 16. Taking effect on January 1, 1808, the Act for the Abolition of the Slave Trade banned British ships from holding enslaved people and prohibited slave trading in British ports. Britain was not the first European power to end their involvement in the slave trade—the Danes had done so in 1792. Nevertheless, the 1807 act was a turning point.

The act centrally held that the slave trade was uncivilized and that by ending it Britain was inaugurating a new age of enlightened civilization, driven by liberal political and economic ideas about the necessity of free trade. Moreover, the act increased Britain's involvement in Africa—it led to the Anti-Slavery Squadron and would come to shape the "new imperialism" that marked the Scramble for Africa in the late nineteenth century. A new organization, the African Institution, was formed in 1808 to monitor the civilization of enslaved Africans and to promote to the Royal Navy the new provisions that allowed slave ships to be taken as prizes and for British merchants' "legitimate commerce" in West Africa.[78]

Abolitionists hoped that the end of the slave trade would improve working conditions for the enslaved, encourage their natural growth, and, with the assistance of missionaries, help them conform to European religious and sexual standards of domesticity. Yet while new African captives were not legally permitted to be transported to the Caribbean, hereditary racial slavery continued; for many enslaved people the end of the slave trade meant only more brutal and intense labor. Realizing that hereditary racial slavery would not last forever, planters sought to extract the most profit out of their property, thus forcing more enslaved people to work in the field, including women. Furthermore, abolition did not limit but rather expanded plantations.

When news of these developments reached Britain, and keen to have more information on enslaved working conditions,

"THE SOONER ALL THIS MASS OF IMPOLICY"

abolitionists, led by Wilberforce (who subscribed to a gradual process of emancipation), introduced a new bill in 1815. The Slave Registry Bill planned to have local commissioners sent to colonies to visit estates and collect data on every enslaved person. If a planter could not show the enslaved person was purchased before the end of the slave trade, they might have to forfeit that enslaved person, who would receive manumission. Estates could also be confiscated if it was found that enslaved people were living against the rules of the register. The bill would also help gather data on key metrics such as infant mortality. To many planters, the Registry Bill reeked of unwanted and unnecessary metropolitan encroachment.

Within a year of Wilberforce's presentation of the law, an enslaved revolt, fueled by rumors that the Slave Registry Bill would actually end racial slavery, erupted in "Little England." Around 8:30 p.m. on Easter Sunday 1816, enslaved men and women began setting fire to property in the parish of St. Philip. Within hours hundreds more joined, and soon nearly three-quarters of Barbados was in active revolt. One of the rebellion's leaders was an African-born enslaved man named Bussa, who worked as the head driver on Bailey's Plantation. Bussa collaborated with other enslaved people, including a driver named Jackey and Nanny Grig, a literate domestic, both of whom worked on Simmons Plantation. The plot, later dubbed "Bussa's rebellion," had been long in the making.[79] Leaders began devising a plan at Sunday dances between Christmas and Easter, believing that planters' resistance to the Slave Registration Bill was an indication that they intended to deny the enslaved their freedom, which was to come into effect on Easter Monday 1816. According to Robert, an enslaved man, Grig was

> the first person who told the negroes at Simmons" so: and she said she had read it in the Newspapers . . . That, about a fortnight

after New-year's Day, she said the negroes were to be freed on Easter Monday, and the only way to get it was to fight for it, otherwise they would not get it; and the way they were to do, was to set fire, as that was the way they did in Saint Domingo.[80]

Robert's testimony, given under duress, may not be entirely reliable, but it does speak to the power of rumors of emancipation. News of anti-slavery activity reached the enslaved indirectly. Only a few were literate, and planters tried their best to hide anti-slavery literature. Nonetheless, anti-slavery news spread through printed speeches and newspapers, with literate enslaved people often reading articles aloud to those who could not read or write.

The rebels did not intend to massacre white people. Instead, they focused on attacking property and the militia, but the rebellion was short-lived. By Easter Monday news of the revolt had reached Bridgetown, and martial law was declared. With the combined use of local militia and imperial troops—including enslaved soldiers as part of the 1st West India Regiment, who played critical roles in protecting Britain's interests in the Caribbean—the rebellion ended a few days later. Bussa and others died in the fighting, and those who didn't faced vile and vicious retaliation. Some of the rebels were executed in public, their heads displayed on the estates where they had worked.[81] By September, officials recorded that 144 enslaved participants had been executed under martial law, around seventy sentenced to death.[82] Other figures estimate between one and two thousand enslaved people were killed.[83]

Bussa's rebellion caught planters somewhat by surprise. In a House of Assembly committee report, colonial officials tried to minimize local conditions as factors that led to the revolt. In the report, describing "the most abundant returns" of 1816 and "liberal allowances to the Negroes and abundant supplies in the granaries," it was argued that the "Origin of the Rebellion must be sought for in some other than in any local and peculiar cause."[84]

But this was far from true. By the mid-1810s, the sugar market had slumped, and imported provisions were scarce owing to trade limitations with the US during the War of 1812. This led planters to press the enslaved to work harder to increase sugar production. Desperate, the Barbados assembly asked the colonial government for relief but received none.

Meanwhile, in Britain, debate raged about how the Slave Registry Bill might have influenced Bussa's rebellion. Planters argued that the bill had incited the rebellion, and some missionaries were accused of supporting the rebels, whereas abolitionists pointed fingers at the planters. To gain local autonomy, the Barbadian legislature passed its own Slave Registration Act in 1817. But as part of the 1819 Registry Act that did pass, colonies were to send their own slave registries to London.

Changing course themselves, abolitionists in 1823 established a new group in London. Led by Zachary Macaulay, John Cropper, William Allen, and Thomas Clarkson as well as Buxton and Wilberforce, the London Society for Mitigating and Gradually Abolishing the State of Slavery, also known as the Anti-Slavery Society, believed that the enslaved were not yet ready for freedom as they still needed tutelage, and called for further amelioration. In March 1823 Buxton presented a motion in the House of Commons, calling for gradual abolition.[85] Buxton stressed the need for easier manumission, enforcement of enslaved marriages, the Sabbath as a day for religion and rest, and the admission of enslaved people's testimony in court. George Canning, the foreign secretary, who opposed emancipation, rephrased some of these recommendations (undercutting Buxton in the process) that helped the motion pass. These measures, known as Orders-in-Council, were sent to colonies that did not have legislative assemblies. The orders called for increased time for religious instruction for the enslaved, the prevention of family separation, a prohibition on flogging women, and more accessible routes to manumission.[86]

But soon news that amelioration was having limited effect filtered back to the metropole, especially through missionaries, a greater number of whom were Nonconformist (Protestant dissenters from the Church of England) in the 1820s and '30s. Some preached equality under God and spread democratic principles that threatened the racial-caste hierarchy, while others clashed with planters who placed them in the same group as abolitionists. Many colonies passed restrictive laws to limit missionary activity.[87] Despite these constraints, some missionaries became ardent abolitionists and boosted support for abolition. Unitarian missionary Thomas Cooper, based at Hanover parish in Jamaica, wrote an influential 1824 tract, *Facts illustrative of the condition of the Negro slaves in Jamaica*, that provided evidence that amelioration was failing and that the conditions of the enslaved had not improved. Cooper also revealed the limited influence of magistrates to whom the enslaved were permitted to report about their condition. When two women sought to quit the field due to being pregnant, the overseer refused their request. According to Cooper:

> They went to complain of this refusal to a magistrate, but were stopped in their way by a neighbouring overseer, and by him thrown into the stocks until he sent them back to their own overseer, who put them again into the stocks on their own estate, and had them flogged. Of this proceeding they complained to the attorney. The attorney was of opinion that the overseer had acted with undue severity; but he considered the women to have been highly to blame for attempting to complain to the magistrate; whereas, he said, they ought in the first instance to have complained to him.[88]

"THE SOONER ALL THIS MASS OF IMPOLICY"

With planters resistant to ameliorative measures, rumors began to spread in Demerara, as they had in Barbados, that planters were not passing the "new laws" supposedly emancipating the enslaved—and plans were hatched for a revolt.

The context for the 1823 rebellion in Demerara was a shift away from coffee and cotton and toward sugar production after the formerly Dutch colony came under British control. Because of this shift, plantation owners had to borrow more money. When sugar prices fell in 1815–16, some planters defaulted on mortgages and lost plantations to other British merchants. In the 1820s planters called on Parliament to provide them with loans to offset their losses. While this was happening, the enslaved in Demerara were working harder and had less time for their provision grounds.

Demerara had a large missionary presence, dominated by the Methodist Wesleyan Missionary Society and the Evangelical London Missionary Society (LMS). Established in 1795, the LMS instructed missionaries not to meddle in politics but rather to focus on teaching the enslaved to obey their masters. John Smith was one such missionary. A cabinetmaker from Coventry, Smith came from a modest family. He became attracted to Evangelicalism as a teenager and later trained at a seminary in Gosport, Hampshire. Following his ordination in December 1816, and accompanied by his wife Jane, Smith boarded the *William Nielson* bound for Demerara.

Stationed at Bethel chapel near Plantation Le Ressouvenir, Smith ministered to a growing number of enslaved people. Although the original reason for going to Demerara had been to convert the enslaved, Smith ended up "converted to the slaves' cause."[89] The more success Smith had with the "flock" there, the more it angered colonists and planters.

Within months of his arrival, Smith began noticing that the enslaved were growing restless with their treatment and informed LMS missionaries of this. In a diary entry, Smith anticipated a revolt, noting: "I observed in the slaves a spirit of murmuring and dissatisfaction . . . nor should I wonder if it were to break into open rebellion. However, I hope it may not."[90]

Smith's hopes were dashed in the summer of 1823.[91] At around 6 p.m. on August 18, with the sound of shell horns and drums, a rebellion started on Success Plantation, owned by Scottish politician John Gladstone (father of the future prime minister William Gladstone), and spread to sixty plantations on the east coast. Roughly ten to twelve thousand enslaved people revolted.[92] As in Barbados, rumors of emancipation fueled the revolt. Amelioration dispatches from Earl Bathurst, the colonial secretary—calling for religious instruction, encouraging marriage, and preventing families from separation—had come to Demerara in early July 1823. By early August courts agreed to the proposed reforms but did not make this information public, partly because many planters still opposed them. Enslaved people first heard about what they called the "new laws" and thought they meant emancipation. A cooper around the age of thirty, Jack Gladstone, attended Bethel chapel and knew Smith, as did Jack's father, Quamina, who served as a deacon. Father and son began creating networks among other enslaved people, many of whom were involved with Smith's chapel. The role of religion in the rebellion could not be overlooked. As historian Emília Viotti da Costa writes, the enslaved "appropriated the missionaries' language and symbols, and turned their lessons of love and redemption into promises of freedom."[93]

The rebellion lasted two days. During the period of martial law that Governor John Murray installed, from August 1823 to January 1824, hundreds of enslaved people were tried and brutally killed.[94] The many public executions that occurred were designed to reinforce colonial power and instill fear. Although involved in the plot, Jack Gladstone, who tried to save the lives of some white people during the rebellion, was spared the death sentence and was instead transported to St. Lucia.[95]

Charged with spreading discontent among the enslaved against slaveholders, John Smith was tried in court in October 1823.[96] Although assigned a lawyer, he alone was left to cross-examine witnesses and defend himself. The following month he was found guilty of complicity and sentenced to death by hanging. The colonists sent to Britain for a reprieve: they did not want the cleric executed but rather removed from the colony and returned to England.[97] On February 14, 1824, King George IV signed a reprieve and ordered for Smith to be deported. But it arrived too late. He had died on February 6. Smith's trial and planter attacks on missionaries emboldened abolitionist activity in Britain.

As events in Demerara showed, enslaved people were no longer willing to wait. The direct action they took followed a longer pattern of resistance. The abolitionist movement was never just about the actions of those in the metropole. Acts of self-emancipation paced the abolition movement back in Britain and were critical to the process. Furthermore, events in British Guiana increased metropolitan involvement in ameliorative measures for the enslaved. Additional Orders-in-Council were sent to Crown Colonies in 1824 banning the use of the whip in the fields, introducing recordkeeping of enslaved punishment for those who did not work in the fields, cutting the workweek to six days, adding new manumission rules, and allowing the enslaved to testify in court after sanction by a minister. These measures satisfied some but certainly not all abolitionists. After Demerara, more abolitionists called instead for immediate emancipation, and to some extent that shift occurred because of the acts of self-emancipation by the enslaved.

Leicester Quaker, schoolteacher, and radical Elizabeth Heyrick published in 1823 or 1824 a powerful pamphlet, *Immediate, not*

Gradual Abolition, that criticized figures such as Wilberforce for their gradualism. "An *immediate* emancipation, then, is the object to be aimed at," she wrote,

> it is more wise and rational—more politic and safe, as well as more just and humane, than gradual emancipation . . . the sooner the over-laboured, crouching slave, is converted into a free labourer—his compulsory, unremunerated toil, under the impulse of the cart whip, exchanged for cheerful, well recompensed industry . . . the sooner all this mass of impolicy, crime and suffering, is got rid of, the better.[98]

Heyrick also called for reparations for the enslaved rather than compensation for slave owners: "let compensation be first made to the *slave*, for his long years of uncompensated labour, degradation and suffering."[99] Heyrick's words indicated a crucial change in mood among abolitionists. But she too argued that enslaved people needed to be guided by white tutelage and schooled in civilization.[100]

Steps toward emancipation led by the enslaved themselves soon followed when the largest enslaved revolt in the British Caribbean occurred in Jamaica, the island once dubbed "King Sugar." Again, rumors of emancipation sparked the 1831 rebellion. White Jamaicans fiercely opposed amelioration measures, and the reforms of 1823 proposed by Bathurst were not fully incorporated into acts on the island until 1831, due to fear that the colony might have its right of self-legislation revoked.[101] That year Crown Colonies received new Orders-in-Council that included the introduction of the post of protector of slaves, who was to act as an intermediary between the courts and the enslaved. Based on the colonists' resistance to the 1831 Order-in-Council, many enslaved people thought that it provided for their emancipation. With so many rumors of potential freedom circulating, the colonial secretary had to proclaim that freedom was not imminent. This news arrived in Jamaica on June 3, 1831, but the governor Lord Belmore did not issue it until December 22.[102]

A fire that broke out on Kensington estate on December 27, 1831, in St. James parish began a rebellion that quickly expanded to neighboring western parishes.[103] Enslaved Baptist deacon Sam Sharpe, the purported leader of the rebellion, led ten thousand enslaved people who refused to work without wages. As the rebellion spread, more than sixty thousand enslaved people participated. Martial law was quickly declared and lasted until February 1832. Colonial forces, with the help of the Maroons (who were often used to police enslaved communities in exchange for rights), suppressed the rebellion.[104] During the rebellion two hundred enslaved people and fourteen white people were killed. After it ended, a further 340 enslaved people lost their lives during "judicial murder"—executions, hangings, and decapitations.[105] In addition, "of the 427 persons indicted before the courts-martial, no more than 25 were certainly acquitted."[106] Following a trial in April, Sharpe was hanged on May 23, 1832. With over two hundred properties damaged, the cost of the rebellion amounted then to £1,154,589.[107]

One week after Sharpe died, the British Parliament established a committee "to consider and report upon the Measures which it may be expedient to adopt for the purpose of effecting the Extinction of Slavery, throughout the British Dominions, at the earliest period compatible with the safety of all Classes in the Colonies."[108] Parliament was acting in response to the horror many abolitionists expressed at the attacks on missionaries throughout the rebellion and in its aftermath. Baptist, Wesleyan, and Moravian missionaries dominated the western parishes, and members of the Jamaican assembly recognized the dangers that they posed.

While other denominations could distance themselves from the rebellion, the Baptists could not. Although they voiced surprise at being implicated in the rebellion, many of the enslaved involved were members of the church.[109] Baptists tended to give more independence to black deacons, in part to increase involvement in religious worship, so this encouraged many, including Sharpe, to embrace a spirit of resistance and explains why the rebellion was later dubbed the "Baptist War." White vigilantes attacked those considered religious conspirators, tearing down chapels. Some missionaries were jailed. Many fled the island and returned to Britain.

Rebellion in Jamaica followed rebellion in England and shaped the wider spirit of unrest in the metropole and colonies taking place in the 1830s. An agrarian uprising, known as the Swing Riots of 1830, was shaped by a combination of low wages, poor harvests, inadequate poor relief, and high unemployment in 1829–30. The introduction of new technology such as threshing machines, which displaced workers, also exacerbated problems, as did enclosing fields. Protests started in Kent in August and later spread outward across parts of England. Protesters directed their anger at threshing machines and Irish migrant laborers, who were accused of undercutting wages. Ruling elites, fearing that the rebellion could spread and lead to further chaos, imposed harsh penalties for participants—nineteen faced execution and 481 were transported to Australia.[110] Some of those involved evoked the metaphor of slavery to describe their working conditions.

In November 1830, Whig leader Charles Grey succeeded the anti-reform Duke of Wellington as prime minister and established a government that was decidedly more anti-slavery. That year a splinter group in the Anti-Slavery Society emerged, known as the Agency Committee, which urged parliamentary candidates to pledge themselves to vote for emancipation. The Reform Act of 1832 changed who sat in Parliament: with an increased but still limited electorate, many of the new MPs came from the north of England and were staunchly anti-slavery. It was also part of the broader "Age of Reform" era of the 1830s that saw further changes in British society, including new legislation to regulate factories, social services, education, policing, and prisoning.[111] There was also a wider context that shaped the subsequent Abolition Act. At the end of the Napoleonic Wars in 1815, which weakened French power and increased Britain's, the Caribbean was seen as a less important trading partner, which historian Thomas Holt has argued "made emancipation easier for government officials to contemplate."[112]

In 1833 the Abolition of Slavery Act, which was to come into effect on August 1, 1834, ended racial slavery in the Caribbean colonies, the Cape Colony in South Africa, and the sugar-producing island of Mauritius in the Indian Ocean. But freedom for the enslaved would have to wait. For the act to pass, compromises had to be made. Slave owners' compensation was one such compromise. This in effect kept the proceeds of racial slavery flowing into Britain from persistently unfree labor performed in the Caribbean. Without unraveling the knot of economics at the heart of racial slavery, the post-emancipation world continued to circulate its profits and coerce labor.

As part of this settlement, £20 million was set aside as compensation for the loss of slaveholders' property, a figure equivalent to around £2.3 billion today.[113] To finance this compensation the British state took out loans, and, according to the British Treasury, it took until 2015 for the loan to be redeemed. Three years later, in 2018, the Treasury tweeted, in a somewhat boastful tone:

> Did you know? In 1833, Britain used £20 million, 40 per cent of its national budget, to buy the freedom of all slaves in the Empire. The amount of money borrowed for the Slavery Abolition Act

was so large that it wasn't paid off until 2015. Which means that living British citizens helped pay to end the slave trade.[114]

In effect, this means that generations of Britons, including Caribbean people, have been paying reparations to slave owners—another clear example that the legacies of hereditary racial slavery not only lingered long after its official end but have financially implicated millions of people, in this case indirectly, and for many, unknowingly.[115] A significant amount of this compensation was then reinvested into Britain and its expanding empire, helping fund new investments. For example, many slave owners invested in railways and shipping lines across the Atlantic. Others, like the Gladstones (especially John Gladstone), would invest their funds in other forms of coerced labor, namely, indentured labor.

The second compromise had to do with labor. Racist beliefs that the enslaved were unprepared for freedom and fears that they might revert to "barbarism" and threaten the colonies' economies led to the creation of the apprenticeship system, which did not differ drastically from racial slavery. The formerly enslaved, now called apprentices, received no wages for working forty-five hours a week. If they worked beyond these hours, they would receive payment. For those with a skill, their apprenticeship ended after four years, while those working in the field would have to wait six. However, children under the age of six were to be freed immediately. A new group, special magistrates, were created to ensure that this system was put in place.[116] The Cayman Islands, Bermuda, Barbuda, and Antigua chose not to enter the apprenticeship system, and the enslaved there became free immediately. Most of the enslaved in Bermuda worked in the maritime industry, and planters deemed apprenticeship unnecessary. While in Antigua, planters thought they could control formerly enslaved people without the need for apprenticeship. But the enslaved in Antigua did not experience freedom.[117] Strict limitations were imposed on them, limiting their wages and enforcing hard punishment for vagrancy.

Contestations over the apprenticeship system among apprentices who riled at the restrictions began as soon as it was implemented. In St. Kitts, apprentices refused to work without pay after August 1, 1834. Martial law was declared in response, and apprentices were forced to work.[118] These actions were shaped not only by a lack of wages but also by the fact that many planters changed their attitude toward apprentices, removing some ameliorative measures introduced before the Abolition Act. For example, planters forced women back into working in the field when they had previously been excluded based on age or if they had birthed six children.

Jamaican apprentice James Williams detailed the constant violence he faced. Apprentices, he wrote,

> get a great deal more punishment now than they did when they was slaves; the master take spite, and do all he can to hurt them . . . Apprentices a great deal worse off for provision than before-time; magistrate take away their day, and give to the property; massa give we no salt allowance, and no allowance at Christmas.

"When I was a slave," Williams continued, "I [was] never flogged,—I sometimes was switched, but not badly; but since the new law begin, I have been flogged seven times, and put in the house of correction four times."[119]

Special magistrates also became implicated in, and indicative of, the problems with the apprenticeship system. Planters regarded them similarly to missionaries and sought to undermine and circumvent their power. Indeed, special magistrates sided mostly with planters when it came to disputes and often punished apprentices.

The harsher treatment and violence that apprentices experienced reflected the desperation of white planters who, as they saw their power slightly wane, gave up the pretense of benign treatment and tried to eke as much labor out of apprentices as they could, lashing out when they felt threatened. The apprenticeship system overall illustrated that coercion, violence, and exploitation remained the only approach to life in the Caribbean, and this would continue in the coming years. It reflected a system of labor that rather than preparing apprentices for eventual freedom existed primarily to enrich planters. As news of the injustices of the apprenticeship system proliferated, abolitionists in Britain soon demanded its end.

Quaker abolitionists Joseph Sturge and Thomas Harvey toured the Caribbean on an anti-apprenticeship campaign and published some of their findings. In The West Indies in 1837, they concluded that "nothing less than unfettered freedom can save the colonies; freedom, protected, not circumscribed, by new laws."[120] The Anti-Slavery Society also called for its demise in their January 1838 report, *Negro Apprenticeship in the British Colonies*.[121] The report highlighted how "the hardships of females, aged persons, and children, in most of the Colonies, but especially in the Crown Colonies, have greatly increased," with reductions in provisions, additional labor, and ongoing flogging of women, who were "still subjected to needless and shameful degradation."[122] Calling the apprenticeship system "a complete and manifest failure," they sought immediate freedom for the enslaved as "an act of national justice"[123] and "freedom, in its largest and fullest sense" for the previously enslaved.[124]

Facing growing opposition, the apprenticeship system ended on August 1, 1838, and apprentices were emancipated. The end of racial slavery took longer in other parts of the Caribbean. Sweden abolished slavery in its colony of St. Barthélemy in 1847. The Danish colonies ended slavery in 1848. Meanwhile, it ended in the French Caribbean in 1848, the Dutch Caribbean in 1863, and in the United States in 1865. The Spanish, the first to introduce slavery, ended it in 1886. Two years later in Brazil, racial slavery came to an end.

Those in the middle of the racial-caste hierarchy strived to increase their rights apace with abolition and emancipation campaigns. In Jamaica in 1792 and 1813, free people of color and free blacks had petitioned the local legislature, without success, to complain about prohibitions on giving evidence in court and limitations on how much they could inherit. But by the 1820s, more free people of color and free blacks in the British Caribbean started new campaigns, and by 1833 many had gained more civil rights as a result of pressure from Britain.

After emancipation, free people of color and free blacks improved their standing within society. Many entered politics and other positions previously limited to white people. With many white people in the Caribbean leaving the region for more lucrative areas of the expanding British Empire—the settler colonies of Australia, Canada, and New Zealand, for instance—free people filled the vacuum. And as fewer European laborers came to the Caribbean in the nineteenth century, those white planters who did stay in the Caribbean turned to men of color to hold jobs such as overseers or tradesmen.

The abolition of the slave trade and emancipation did not alter the racial-caste hierarchy—nor were they intended to. White elite anti- and pro-slavery advocates had one major interest in common: the maintenance of white supremacy.[125] And after 1838, both groups had the opportunity to expand white supremacy through the renewed effort to civilize not only African-Caribbean people but also other people of color, as the British Empire expanded throughout Africa and Asia.

The end of racial slavery did not end Britain's interests in the slave trade or racial slavery globally. The British still consumed sugar produced by enslaved people in Brazil, Cuba, Louisiana, and later Queensland, where Pacific Islanders were impressed as indentured laborers; manufacturers still bought cotton grown by enslaved labor from US plantations. Yet these caveats disappeared as histories began to be written and abolition and emancipation began to be commemorated and celebrated.

Soon after, abolition and emancipation falsehoods about how these changes came about began to be spread widely. The 1883 fiftieth-anniversary abolition commemorations, for instance, promulgated the spurious and consequential myth that British anti-slavery was an act of benevolence—a noble, selfless deed, revealing that white Britons and their empire were built on solid foundations of Christianity, liberalism, and civilization. The London-based *Morning Star* declared that emancipation "exalted this nation high above the other civilised nations of the earth."[126] Eric Williams wrote in 1964 of the hero worship of Clarkson and Wilberforce and the tendency to see abolition as a self-fulfilling prophecy: "The British historians wrote almost as if Britain had introduced Negro slavery solely for the satisfaction of abolishing it."[127]

The true nature of abolition and emancipation was quite different. Liberalism drove anti-slavery among white Britons and, in its support for the spread of white supremacy, shared key similarities with pro-slavery ideologies.[128] After emancipation, the self-perception of the British Empire changed. It was now a liberal empire promoting freedom across the world.[129] But it was still a white supremacist empire, the racial-caste ideology persisting beyond the eradication of racial slavery.

The end of hereditary racial slavery posed serious challenges to the formerly enslaved. Their aspirations of working for wages as small farmers, of forming their own families and kinship networks without the threat of white-led violence, of practicing religion freely, and of uninhibited mobility were not what those at the top of the racial-caste system envisaged. No longer enslaved, the formerly enslaved were also not free. In this way, freedom did not act as a rupture between enslavement and emancipation. White supremacist ideas, policies, and practices would only harden during the subsequent centuries as economic decline and the limits of liberalism came sharply into view.

4

"Our freedom can be taken away from us"

Struggles for Economic Justice After Emancipation

In December 1849, just sixteen years after passage of the Abolition of Slavery Act of 1833, an anonymous article appeared in a popular conservative publication, *Fraser's Magazine*. Titled "Occasional Discourse on the Negro Question," the polemic was styled as an imaginary lecture to a philanthropic organization. The author began by painting a desperate picture of Caribbean colonies, all in a "troublous condition . . . sinking wholly into ruin." Worsening economic factors meant that white people in the Caribbean "are far enough from happy . . . [and] the British Whites are rather badly off; several millions of them hanging on the verge of continual famine." White people in the Caribbean and Britain were struggling, but this was not the case for most of those at the bottom of the racial-caste hierarchy. Instead, formerly enslaved Africans were "all very happy and doing well . . . sitting yonder with their beautiful muzzles up to the ears in pumpkins, imbibing sweet pulps and juices . . . while the sugar-crops rot round them uncut."

The author blamed the Caribbean's problems on black people's aversion to work:

[N]o Black man who will not work according to what ability the gods have given him for working, has the smallest right to eat pumpkin, or to any fraction of land that will grow pumpkin, however plentiful such land may be; but has an indisputable and perpetual right to be compelled, by the real proprietors of said land, to do competent work for his living. [1]

If black people refused to work the consequences would be dire. The essayist claimed that they would be made "a slave again (which state will be a little less ugly, than his present one) and . . . be compelled to work," and they "will have to be servants to those that are born wiser than you, that are born lords of you—servants to the whites."[2]

In the 1840s the author's arguments—that the "great experiment" of emancipation had failed and that it was absurd to think that black people could be civilized and emulate white Europeans—were still considered controversial, which partly explains why he used a pseudonym. But by the following decade, opinion had swung. The author revealed his identity and changed the title when his essay was republished in 1853. Scottish writer and philosopher Thomas Carlyle's "Occasional Discourse on the Nigger Question" demonstrates the shift toward an intensification of racist attitudes in the 1850s and '60s.[3] Indeed, a growing number of commentators began to view black people in the post-emancipation Caribbean as lazy, and their alleged refusal to work was deemed the main cause of Britain's and the Caribbean's economic woes. In 1857, for instance, *The Times* published a report on current conditions in Jamaica, Trinidad, St. Kitts, Dominica, and St. Lucia, describing the islands as filled "with towns at once filthy, noisome, and pathless; with mansions, once grand and stately; tottering to decay . . . with a race of negro squatters parading their insolent idleness on lands which they have occupied without purchase, and exhausted without cultivation."[4] Directly attacking abolitionists, the report's author hoped that an Englishman (presumably a white one) would go to the Caribbean islands "and view the negro in all the blazonry of his idleness, his pride, his ingratitude, contemptuously sneering at the industry of that race which made him free, and then come home to teach the memorable lesson of their experience to the fanatics who have perverted him into what he is."[5]

A few years later, writer Anthony Trollope did just that and in his narrative about his travels in the Caribbean surmised that the "negro's idea of emancipation was and is emancipation not from slavery but from work. To lie in the sun and eat breadfruit and yams is his idea of being free."[6] Carlyle's words, *The Times* article, and the writings of figures like Trollope conveyed a starker white supremacist "racial vocabulary of fixed differences," influenced both by the growth of scientific racism and a deep misunderstanding of actual events in the Caribbean.[7]

This rise in anti-black racism was not simply a legacy of hereditary racial slavery. It was tied to the perceived failure of formerly enslaved people to grasp liberalism. In the post-emancipation Caribbean, economic liberal policies imposed on the region by Britain, combined with planters' coercive practices and refusal to pay the formerly enslaved adequate wages, contrasted with black people's ideas about what their freedom should entail. When the formerly enslaved defined their freedom contrary to market forces, white elites blamed them for the economic problems that in turn fueled white supremacist thought.

Although enslaved people achieved freedom, they had not gained economic justice, and the era from 1833 to the end of the century was one marked by a constant low boil of labor strife. The anti-slavery ideal of "civilization" presumed that black free people would work for low wages and accept white supervision; low wages seemed to indicate economic (and thus moral) prudence, and gratitude to white "liberators" seemed to indicate a willingness to accept the bonds of the law. But the labor struggle that occurred was both against the remnants of racial slavery and against the liberal empire. As the economy in some colonies went into free fall, black people took most of the blame, and the Caribbean region, once considered so critical to Britain's wealth, became seen as a colonial backwater.

Caribbean writers, like Jamaican poet and activist Claude McKay, challenged persistent inequality in material and literary forms of protest. Born in 1890, McKay was the youngest son of Baptist farmers. His early poetry gave voice to the suffering in the Caribbean, like his 1912 poem "Hard Times," which documented those men and women whose struggles rooted in racial slavery endured into the twentieth century. In contrast to Carlyle and Trollope, McKay depicted the dire poverty faced by descendants of enslaved Africans that allowed white elites to have time to lounge in the sun while the masses strived. His experiences in Jamaica informed his flight from the region and inspired his political activism. McKay would be joined by other Caribbean men and women who persisted, despite their economic woes, to reject the myths of Caribbean decay and decline and stake a powerful claim to inclusion within the larger imperial family.

Meanwhile, contending with Caribbean economic decline, planters introduced new groups into the region, whom they treated somewhat similarly to formerly enslaved people. The presence of Indian and Chinese indentured laborers continued the region's transformation into multiethnic societies dominated by coercive labor and also helped bolster white supremacy.

Perhaps counterintuitively, during the post-emancipation period and with the end of racial slavery—and perhaps because of the end of racial slavery—the racial-caste hierarchy was strengthened. As the formal institutional, military, and state scaffolding of racial slavery ended, at least nominally, new scaffolding for white supremacy came—and had to come—into existence for white elites who wanted to maintain their status.

DECLINING FORTUNES AND PERSISTENT PROTEST

After racial slavery ended, many African-Caribbean people wanted to become smallholders, farming plots of land they owned—with the understanding that access to land gave them more autonomy—while also working some of the time on plantations. But they were thwarted in this endeavor by various coercive measures used to force them to work just as they had during hereditary racial slavery. The tenancy-at-will system, which linked rents to wages, was one tactic to curtail free people's autonomy. With rents of houses and lands often exceeding wages, many were in debt to plantation owners. Added to this, the act of stopping wages, whereby planters would deduct wages for supposed poor work or minor infractions, meant that laborers occasionally effectively worked for nothing.[8]

These conditions inspired formerly enslaved people to flee plantations. Flight from estates after 1838 varied across the Caribbean. It depended on different factors, not least the laws in the colony, the availability of land, and topography. But even those who wanted to leave estates and establish freeholds and villages were often prevented from doing so. Colonial officials limited the land available for black people and punished them for squatting on unused land. Planters presented the myth that black people were rejecting fair working conditions and thereby free-market logic making them irrational individuals. In reality, it was the planters' own unwillingness to pay adequate wages and provide suitable working conditions that influenced formerly enslaved people's desire to leave plantation work.

The difficulties facing black people in the Caribbean were exacerbated by liberal economic and free trade policies in the form of the Sugar Duties Act in 1846 and the Sugar Equalization Act of 1854, which equalized duties on foreign and British colonial products and meant that Caribbean-based crops were in competition with those sold cheaper and produced by enslaved labor in Brazil and Cuba.[9] The American Civil War (1861–65) also undermined the sugar industry, reducing the price of sugar because Cuban sugar was temporarily diverted from US markets to Britain.[10] Jamaica bore the brunt of the sugar trade's economic woes. Jamaican sugar exports decreased, halving in the years 1838–70,[11] which in turn contributed to shrinking numbers of sugar plantations: in 1770 there had been one thousand, but by 1870 there were only around three hundred.[12] The sugar crisis increased poverty on the island overall, and from the 1850s and '60s so too did the spread of cholera and periodic droughts and flooding that devastated crops and sent unemployment and underemployment to new heights. Barbados, Antigua, St. Kitts, Trinidad, and British Guiana managed better the changes within the sugar industry. Yet even in places where sugar survived, workers struggled to find employment, forcing many to search for work in other colonies.

In the 1860s thousands of workers in Barbados began migrating to other parts of the Caribbean.[13] This intraregional migration pattern would become a mainstay of the late nineteenth century, which saw thousands of African-Caribbean men and women seek work elsewhere in the region because of economic depression, especially in the 1890s. British officials were aware of but did little to address conditions, leading many to venture to agricultural employment opportunities derived from the growth of US imperialism in the region, which quickened after Spain's loss in the 1898 Spanish–American War. Following US victory, the 1898 Treaty of Paris enabled the Americans to temporarily gain control of Cuba, while Spain ceded to them Guam, the Philippines, and, in 1900, Puerto Rico. The US occupation of Cuba lasted until the island gained its independence in 1902. In 1901 the US imposed the Platt Amendment on Cuba's first constitution, meaning that America had the right to intervene in Cuban affairs if political order or American property was threatened. In the late nineteenth and early twentieth centuries, more US businessmen and investors took control of the economy—running sugar plantations, buying land, and investing in the financial industry.[14] These types of activities expanded to Costa Rica with the rise of US-owned banana plantations and the US construction of the Panama Canal that became a vital access point to both the Pacific and Atlantic Oceans.

The rise of the US in the Caribbean drastically curtailed black people's desire to become independent peasants, especially in Jamaica. Between the 1870s and '80s, some peasants in Jamaica with small land plots took to growing traditional staples such as yams, sweet potatoes, and cassava and expanded into other crops such as plantains, callaloo, bananas, and other fruits.[15] The expansion into cultivating fruit led to the rise of the banana industry, which altered the relationship between Jamaica and the US. In 1865 Jamaican exports to Britain amounted to 79 percent and the island purchased 61 percent of British imports. At this time the US received just 8 percent of the island's exports, and 26 percent of US imports were sold there. In 1876–81, however, British imports from Jamaica fell from 54 percent to 46 percent. During these years the reverse happened for US imports, which increased from 29 percent to 39 percent.[16] Most of this change was driven by the growth of the fruit trade and geographical proximity that saw the US become the island's primary trading partner in exports and imports by the close of the nineteenth century.[17]

In the early era of the banana trade, production rested with peasant growers. But soon the industry was dominated by larger American traders who, in the early 1870s, started to purchase fruit from peasant producers and export it. The industry drastically changed with the monopoly created by the United Fruit Company. The company had its origins with Lorenzo D. Baker, owner of Boston Fruit. Baker began visiting Jamaica in 1872 and fourteen years later shipped 42 percent of Jamaica's bananas on ships he owned through his fishing fleet on Cape Cod.[18] During the 1880s and '90s, Baker's business developed into the multinational United Fruit Company, which had as an affiliate another American business, Minor Cooper Keith's banana business in Central America. Baker's purchase of large sugar properties in northeastern Jamaica, which he converted to banana plantations, squeezed out Jamaican peasant production along with most other competitors and exacerbated poverty among Jamaican peasants.

News of economic problems in the Caribbean overlapped with debates about racial slavery in the US. In the Victorian period, prominent Black Americans visited Britain seeking support for their anti-slavery cause. In 1845–47, and again in 1859, the famous former enslaved-man-turned-abolitionist Frederick Douglass denounced racial slavery in hundreds of speeches across Britain that propelled his celebrity. Born free in Massachusetts, Sarah Parker Remond also became an influential abolitionist and women's suffrage activist who championed anti-slavery in Britain in 1859–61. Even after racial slavery was abolished in the US in 1865, Black American activists continued to venture to Britain to gain transatlantic support for their cause. British audiences heard from journalist and anti-lynching campaigner Ida B. Wells, who toured Britain in 1893 and 1894 on an invitation from Somerset-based Catherine Impey, an influential Quaker and editor of *Anti-Caste*, Britain's first anti-racist journal.[19]

The black British population in the Victorian era was small and diverse, as it had been in the eighteenth century. Some navigated key institutions, like universities and churches, while others remained poor and marginalized. A few members of black Victorian Britain gained notoriety, including Jamaican Mary Seacole, who provided medical support and provisions to British troops in Crimea in 1853, or West African-born Sarah Forbes Bonetta, taken into captivity by the king of Dahomey and later gifted to a British naval captain who presented her to Queen Victoria, who in turn accepted her as a protégée.[20] Another prominent Victorian was classical composer and musician Samuel Coleridge-Taylor, the son of a doctor from Sierra Leone living in Britain and a white English mother. Black Victorians continued to intermarry with white people, leading to growing mixed-race communities across Britain. But just as black Georgians lived amid a rise in anti-black racism, so too did black Victorians live amid a rise in scientific racism, especially from the 1870s onward.

Scientific racist ideas were circulating long before this period. Figures such as Edinburgh-born ethnologist and anatomist Robert Knox used pseudoscientific ideas to argue for biological differences and hierarchy between white and black people, as evidenced in his study *The Races of Men* (1850). Knox was a key advocate of polygenesis—the theory of separate origins of races that was favored among many other scientific racists. This theory contrasted with those who subscribed to monogenesis, the theory of common human origin. Monogenism was still a popular belief. Charles Darwin's theory of evolution subscribed to the monogenesis perspective but the application of his ideas to society—social Darwinism—came to provide justification for racial superiority because scientists assumed they were examining natural racial characteristics.[21] Herbert Spencer's use of the term *survival of the fittest* was adapted from Darwin in 1869 and came to influence the idea that the survival and competition of some racial and national groups was "natural" rather than shaped by human actions.[22]

Such ideas did not exist in a vacuum but rather became inextricably linked to the project of imperial expansion, especially within North America, Africa, Australia, New Zealand, and Asia that developed from the last decades of the nineteenth century. As white Britons were considered innately superior to people of color, this buttressed imperial expansionist and civilizational narratives of the necessity of imperial tutelage to develop other backward nations and races. Whereas in the aftermath of the 1830s there was still the notion that other racial groups could assimilate with white Britons, by the 1870s there was increasing support for the concept that some groups were intrinsically on a different developmental path.[23] As historian Douglas Lorimer has argued, scientific racism "offered one such narrative incorporating hierarchies of race and culture, promoting science in the project of empire, and presenting an apartheid vision of the world critical to humanitarian initiatives of the past and premised on strategies of separate development in the future."[24]

The spread of scientific racist ideas took many forms, whether in commercial exhibitions of supposed "savages" or in children's adventure stories of the "dark continent." Many of these cultural forms drew on perceived objective science to support racist representations.[25] In an era that saw the expansion of the reading public and a decrease in the cost of publications aimed at middle- and working-class audiences, figures like Irish linguist Augustus Keane and Scottish journalist and botanist Robert Brown helped popularize scientific racism from the 1880s. They wrote prolifically for a public audience about their travels throughout the world, including the Caribbean, and coupled descriptions of racial groups with attendant personality traits in ways that ended up reinforcing racism and imperialism. The professionalization of science also helped spread scientific racist ideas—in particular through the emergence of the discipline of anthropology—and would go on to inspire the growth of eugenics in the twentieth and twenty-first centuries.[26] It bolstered white supremacist ideology, transposing it to a new discourse. White supremacy was endlessly adaptable—but so too was resistance to it.

Figures like Catherine Impey and her journal played important roles in challenging racist ideas, and by the final decades of the nineteenth century so too did the emergence of the pan-African movement that sought to link black people from the continent and diaspora to collectively combat racist and colonial abuse. The movement thrived on the mobility of African-descended people, often of middle- and sometimes working-class backgrounds, who had the financial and social means to travel. Key advocates included Black American Martin Robison Delany, who spent time in Britain in 1860. As a Black nationalist, abolitionist, radical, and novelist (among other things) Delany was one of the first to use the phrase "Africa for Africans." Another important pan-Africanist was Edward Wilmot Blyden. Born on the Danish-controlled Caribbean island of St. Thomas, Blyden later emigrated to Liberia in 1850, where he was active in spreading pan-Africanism in West Africa. He also served as Liberian commissioner to Britain in 1861–62 and Liberian ambassador in Britain in 1877–79 and in 1892.

Other pan-African leaders included Sierra Leonean James Africanus Beale Horton, a student at King's College London and the University of Edinburgh; Egyptian nationalist and journalist Dusé Mohamed Ali, who established the *African Times and Orient Review*; and Trinidadian barrister Henry Sylvester Williams. In 1896 Williams moved to London and a year later established the African Association alongside South African activist Alice Kinloch and Thomas John Thompson from Sierra Leone, a group dedicated to promoting the interests of black citizens in the British Empire. The African Association played a critical role in organizing the first Pan-African Conference, held in Westminster Town Hall, July 23–25, 1900. Delegates from the Caribbean, US, Africa, and Britain, including prominent black feminist American Anna Julia Cooper, pledged to challenge white supremacy, and it was here that W. E. B. Du Bois famously declared "the problem of the twentieth century is the problem of the color line."[27] The inequalities these figures faced in their countries of birth and their encounters with racism in Britain and elsewhere as they traversed the West inspired other pan-African groups, and individuals including women, that grew in the early twentieth century.

Back in the Caribbean, in the aftermath of emancipation, black people continued in their efforts to eke out independence, sometimes with the support of well-intentioned white people. Baptist and Methodist missionaries and British philanthropists helped black people establish free villages, which were often named after key abolitionists. The construction of many of these villages started during the apprenticeship period. The first independent villages in Antigua were established around 1835, and by 1842 there were twenty-seven village groups. In November 1839, sixty-three former enslaved people, mostly headmen on plantations, paid $10,000 for Northbrook Estate in British Guiana.[28] They purchased land, known as family land, which was passed down from generation to generation and became an essential part of formerly enslaved people's visions for freedom. And they were correct: access to land allowed black people a chance to forge more independent lives and presented one pathway to political agency, since small landowners could exercise their right to vote.

In Jamaica, mixed-race and black male representatives, often those from the middle of the racial-caste hierarchy whose wealth derived from land or family, or both, joined together to create the Town Party, which opposed the planter-dominated Country Party. In 1849–54 there were thirteen mixed-race and three black assemblymen out of forty-seven.[29] Although a minority, they tried to thwart planter plans to limit the franchise.

The growing power of these representatives worried white people on the island, especially when they did not vote in the majority-white sugar planters' favor. Sensing that their power was waning, some white sugar planters opted to sell their estates and leave the region. But white power remained dominant. In the Bahamas (derived from the term Bahama used by the Taíno), a chain of islands in the Atlantic Ocean west of Turks and Caicos, white creole elites, most of whom were merchants in the import-export trade and who participated in shipwrecking and salt extraction, used their supremacy to usher in "the most rigid racial segregation in the British Caribbean."[30] The "Bay Street Boys," named after Nassau's main commercial street, almost entirely controlled politics. The exclusion of black and mixed-race people from social and cultural life in hotels, restaurants, and clubs endured well into the mid-twentieth century.[31]

As white people left the region, some black and mixed-race men and women were in instances able to exercise a relative degree of social mobility. Some worked in medicine, law, and education, as well as clerks, nurses, and teachers in rural schools, and were able to move upwards within the racial-caste hierarchy to the middling strata. In Jamaica, middle-strata black and mixed-race men like Robert Osborn, George William Gordon, and Edward Jordan played influential political roles—all were members of the House of Assembly between 1831 and 1865.[32]

While coalitions among those in the middle strata of society was one tactic, those at the bottom took direct action against the elusiveness of their freedom. In 1844 the "Guerre Negre" rocked Dominica, an island in the Eastern Caribbean that is largely covered in rainforest. The disturbances came in response to free people's opposition to the census. It began when freewomen and -men attacked census-takers trying to collect names, and as the protest grew, others damaged property. The militia quelled the disturbances, killing four and arresting three thousand. Some believed that the census was part of an attempt to re-enslave free people. One freeman named Saint Louis believed that re-enslavement was imminent, stating: "I think that our freedom can be taken away from us . . . it is only for the Queen to send a Gazette, and say 'make them slaves again,' and they will be all made slaves."[33] Rumors of re-enslavement—and that the US planned to annex Jamaica and control it as a slave state—also spurred protests in Jamaica in 1848. Such swirling speculation—that black people would soon be back in chains—illustrates awareness of their tenuous position, especially in economically struggling colonies. Over the next few years, riots and labor strikes would erupt elsewhere—in Antigua in 1858, Jamaica again in 1860, and St. Vincent in 1862.

The largest and most significant protest that sparked a larger rebellion took place in 1865 in Morant Bay, the main town in Jamaica's St. Thomas-in-the-East parish. That year the island experienced a combination of floods, drought, cholera, and smallpox. Furthermore, tensions between white and black people grew. White people entrenched their power politically, setting high court fees so that many laborers could not access justice against their employers, who in any event often judged cases themselves. Arguments over land were another issue. Many free people believed that certain smallholdings belonged to them and consequently did not think they should have to pay rent for those lands.

Land quarrels were also a problem for those in the nearby parish of St. Ann. In April 1865 laborers there drafted a petition addressed to Queen Victoria. They asked for access to Crown lands on which to build free communities and sought to "put our hands and heart to work, and cultivate coffee, corn, canes, cotton and tobacco, and other produce," profits from which they intended to use to pay for their land. They planned to "repay our Sovereign Lady by instalments of such produce as we may cultivate."[34] The petitioners received a blunt reply from the Colonial Office that ignored most of what was requested and the context

"OUR FREEDOM CAN BE TAKEN AWAY FROM US"

in which they lived and instead reinforced the pervasive myth that black workers were too lazy to work. They were told to return to the plantation, and throughout 1865 those accused of squatting on abandoned estates and farms faced eviction. But black people's demands for access to Crown lands was part of their desire to belong to the wider imperial project rather than languishing on its margins. This demand for inclusion would become more commonplace in the next decades.

Paul Bogle, detail from a Jamaican banknote.

Edward John Eyre, c. 1860.

Some turned to petition while others turned to violence. On October 11, 1865, hundreds of men and women marched into the town of Morant Bay. Their march was related to events earlier that month, when a court case about a man's eviction had led to a small disturbance outside the courthouse. Charges had been issued to arrest Baptist deacon and farmer Paul Bogle, but when the police arrived at his residence in Stony Gut village, locals confronted them. Led by Bogle, the crowd attacked a police station and then came face-to-face with the militia and other parish authorities at the courthouse, where the parish vestry was supposed to meet. The militia and police went back into the courthouse, and the crowd set fire to the building to force those inside out. As in previous disturbances, women were actively involved: they encouraged the men to attack, and when some withdrew they were goaded: "Now, you men, this is not what you said in the mountain. You said you come to the Bay and do so and so, and now you leave all this work to the women."[35] The confrontation at Morant Bay propelled a rebellion that quickly spread throughout the east, west, and north of the island, with numbers growing to fifteen hundred to two thousand people.

The elites responded quickly. When the violence started, the Jamaican governor, Bedfordshire-born Edward Eyre, declared martial law and soldiers were sent on ships from Kingston to evacuate white people from areas under attack. Eyre, who harbored racist views of African-Caribbeans, was convinced of a looming race war. He also feared that Jamaica would be the next Haiti. Jamaican forces and British troops, helped by Maroons—some of whom had pledged loyalty to colonial forces—suppressed the rebellion over three days, with over five hundred people killed.

During the monthlong period of martial law from October 13, around one thousand men and women involved in the rebellion were imprisoned. From this group, two hundred were executed and two hundred flogged.[36] Some of those imprisoned faced torture to extract confessions, and around eight hundred rebels died during the uprising. Eyre also took the opportunity to attack his enemies, namely George William Gordon. A mixed-race member of St. Thomas assembly, Gordon clashed frequently with the white elite and especially Eyre. Their animosity reflected growing tensions between rising mixed-race politicians and landholders and white elites, the latter fearing loss of dominance and control in the colony. Gordon also had a close relationship with Bogle and other black Baptists. Although Gordon denied involvement in the revolt, Eyre ordered him to be arrested and transported from Kingston to Morant Bay so he could be tried by a military tribunal. With scant evidence, Gordon was charged with high treason and sedition, and on October 23 he was found guilty and hanged.

Eyre ordered that the rebellion be dealt with severely, based on his fears that black people were trying to take over the colony and expel white people. He also used events as an excuse to force constitutional change. First, he engineered plans to abolish the increasingly black and mixed-race House of Assembly and proposed that Jamaica become a Crown Colony from 1866. Crown Colony government meant that a governor ruled with the support of a nominated council, comprising six officials and three unofficial members, all under the direct control of the Colonial Office in London. Other legislative colonies in the Caribbean had opted for Crown Colony status, which became more or less the norm in the region from the mid-1870s onward.

When news about the rebellion in Jamaica reached Britain, Eyre was praised for his quick response. However, as more details emerged opinions changed. The high death toll and Gordon's execution raised eyebrows, and the Colonial Office recognized the need for an inquiry, relieving Eyre of his duties during the investigation. While the commissioners' final report commended the rebellion's swift suppression, it expressed concern about the violent retribution and long period of martial law, stating: "That the punishment of death was unnecessarily frequent . . . That the floggings were reckless . . . that the burning of 1,000 homes was wanton and cruel."[37] Investigators also found little evidence that the rebellion was part of an island-wide conspiracy.

The Morant Bay rebellion and its aftermath provoked widespread debate in Britain. For some, it symbolized the failure of emancipation. In November 1865, *The Times* compared the revolt to the recent 1857 Indian Uprising, where Indians had challenged the British East India Company's rule. This had led to the creation in 1858 of the Raj, whereby British Crown rule was established in India. The article stated that events in Jamaica were

> Though a fleabite compared with the Indian Mutiny, it touches our pride more and is more in the nature of a disappointment... [because] Jamaica is our pet institution and its inhabitants are our spoilt children... It seemed to be proved in Jamaica that the negro could be fit for self-government; that he could be a planter, a magistrate, a member of the Legislative Assembly; that he could preach and pray with unction and even decorum; that he could behave like a gentleman, and even pay taxes.[38]

The writers echoed the opinions of planters who had warned that "the negro was... incapable of either self-control or gentle management." For them, the rebellion cast a blow to those, especially abolitionists and missionaries, who preached "grand triumph of humanity, and the improvement of races, and the removal of primeval curses."[39]

For others, like leading liberal John Stuart Mill, Eyre's actions were excessive and criminal. In 1865, Mill, who was active in Nonconformist circles, along with Herbert Spencer, Thomas Huxley, and Charles Buxton MP (son of abolitionist Thomas Fowell Buxton), organized the Jamaica Committee. After the publication of a Royal Commission report that seemingly absolved Eyre, the committee called for him to be tried for Gordon's murder.[40] In response Thomas Carlyle, Charles Dickens; priest, professor, and historian Charles Kingsley; Carlyle protégé, writer, and historian James Anthony Froude, and Alfred Lord Tennyson, among many others, rallied to Eyre's defense, establishing the Eyre Defence Committee, which called for him to receive a seat in the House of Lords. The Defence Committee proved popular, raising £10,000 to pay for Eyre's legal fees. But although Eyre was ordered back to London, he was never brought to trial.

The events at Morant Bay showed the extent to which, as in the time of racial slavery, excessive violence persisted as a mainstay of white elite power. Gordon's execution also speaks to the enormous trepidation white elites had about the growing presence and political power of mixed-race people and the extreme lengths the elites would take to suppress them. Ultimately, Morant Bay symbolized the failure of emancipation. For the formerly enslaved, it represented a failure of the post-slavery visions of their future life.

Meanwhile, a slew of late nineteenth-century publications in Britain blamed the plight of the tropics on black people. In 1888, the year of the "Emancipation Jubilee," Froude published *The English in the West Indies* where he, as Carlyle had done, described black people in the Caribbean as leading happy, carefree lives. "In no other part of the globe," Froude noted, "is there any peasantry whose every want is so completely satisfied as Her Majesty's black subject in these West Indian islands . . . In their own country they would have remained slaves to more warlike races . . . the 'nigger' who now basks among the ruins of the West Indian plantations is the supremest specimen of present humanity."[41] Froude upheld the myth that racial slavery, abolition, and post-emancipation liberalism had somehow improved their lives.

Froude thought it vitally important to maintain white rule in the Caribbean. He warned against the British colonial government losing interest in the Caribbean, arguing that it would undermine the struggles their ancestors had fought to gain the territories in the first place.[42] The region was no longer economically important, but nonetheless, it critically projected an image of the British Empire as one that civilized supposed backward peoples and endowed them with rights. It allowed them to dress racial hierarchy and white supremacy in the garb of civilization and benevolent enlightenment. This civilizing ideal was central to the expansion of the British Empire in the period after the Berlin Conference (1884–85), at which major European powers convened to negotiate and agree claims for territory in Africa.

Morant Bay was highly symbolic but by no means the last of the uprisings in the Caribbean. In 1876, instability erupted in Tobago over problems with wages and that same year, disturbances arose in Barbados. In the 1890s workers protested against low wages and difficult working conditions in St. Vincent (1891), Dominica (1893), Grenada (1895), St. Kitts, and in British Guiana (both 1896). In Montego Bay, Jamaica, riots broke out in 1902 over high taxes and three years later workers rioted again in British Guiana. Realizing that their employers were in no hurry to address their grievances, workers banded together to create organizations that represented their interests, such as the Trinidad Workingmen's Association and the Artisans' Union, founded in Jamaica in 1898.

Black-led protest also took literary form. *Jamaica's Jubilee; Or What We Are and What We Hope to Be* (1888) addressed a white British audience. Its Jamaican authors—Rev. R. Gordon, W. F. Bailey, Rev. S. J. Washington, J. H. Reid, and R. Dingwall—challenged the likes of Froude and Carlyle, insisting on the progress that those in the Caribbean, and specifically Jamaica, had made in the fifty years since emancipation. "No other people could," the authors argued, "under similar circumstances, have reached a greater height on the ladder of social advancement within the same period of time," as Jamaicans.[43] They highlighted the improvement in society, evidenced in the rise of elementary schools and civil society, and praised Nonconformist missionaries for playing a key role in developing Jamaica. However, they blamed the British colonial government for abandoning the formerly enslaved, adding that, as British subjects, they should have "the interest, sympathy, and protection of those who were instrumental in effecting the expiration of (their) ancestors."[44]

This bold statement, pointing out that Britain remained responsible for Jamaica's current condition because of its treatment of their ancestors during hereditary racial slavery, was a harbinger of a reparations discourse that would only grow in the coming century.

At each turn, the formerly enslaved and their descendants understood that the core basis of their enslavement was labor extraction and coerced labor for profit—even if these issues were obfuscated in the abolitionist movement and discourse about liberalism. As the authors of Jamaica's Jubilee wrote, they were also "the subjects of a common king, the servants of a common Master; possessing the same rights, entitled to the same privileges, claiming the same regard and affection, and having the same destiny" as those in Britain.[45] Such claims directly challenged white supremacy and joined the black nationalist rhetoric that asserted: "We form the bulk by far of Jamaica's people" and "Jamaica is emphatically ours."[46] A year later Froude was further discredited with Trinidadian school teacher John Jacob Thomas's 1889 rebuttal, *Froudacity: West Indian Fables*. Here he described Froude's book as a "negrophobic political hobgoblin," unattuned to the "actual facts of West Indian life in particular."[47]

As both publications suggest, by the late nineteenth century more mixed-race and black members of the middle strata in society were asserting their equal citizenship rights in Britain's racially diverse empire. They occupied a key position in the racial-caste hierarchy, as they exercised some mobility, based on class, that potentially undercut the racial-caste hierarchy. In an age of retrenchment along pseudoscientific lines of fixed racism and racial boundaries, these figures publicly and explicitly challenged such ideas.

A broader pan-African consciousness was also growing in the region, associated with figures such as Bahamian doctor, clergyman journalist, and politician Joseph Robert Love. Love, who lived in Jamaica, stressed the significance of race pride and racial unity and founded *Jamaica Advocate*, a newspaper catering to black Jamaicans. This consciousness developed simultaneously with movement in the racial-caste hierarchy. A small group of darker-skinned black men and women entered the middle class in the late nineteenth century. Many of these individuals had attended schools and ascended into professions within education or the Church or had acquired land and become successful peasants to the extent that they were able to earn sufficient incomes to climb up the economic ladder. Many middle-class black people stressed the need for respectability, a view linked to the Church's influence over Caribbean people's behavior and traits. They also believed in meritocracy rather than skin color as the determining factor in social mobility.

They were also influenced in this era by a more overt spread of British colonial nationalism. In various cultural arenas in the Caribbean—whether it be schools, the Church, or in newspapers, Empire Day was held annually on May 24, when the British Empire was celebrated in Britain and across the colonies—the message of British cultural superiority was spread to colonial subjects who were taught to identify always with Britain as the colonial motherland and to have a deep sense of reverence and respect for all things British. Caribbean colonial subjects were taught to especially have admiration for the British monarchy, which became closely aligned with the project of empire during Queen Victoria's reign. Queen Victoria symbolized virtue, duty, and sacrifice, and as more and more imperial imagery became linked to the monarchy, especially evident during the 1897 Diamond Jubilee, her image conjured deference and awe from her millions of colonial subjects. Caribbean members of the middle class were schooled in various ways to see themselves as belonging to Queen Victoria's global empire. When, however, many of them traveled to the imperial motherland in the Edwardian period, they soon found this belonging wanting. Although the growth of the black middle class and the actions of the black working class did not fundamentally alter the power of white elites, it did intimate change.

Even as this was happening, however, white people were devising new ways to both save the flailing economy and strengthen racial divisions to maintain their power.

REMAKING THE MULTIRACIAL CARIBBEAN

Beginning in 1835, Portuguese men and women from Madeira, the Portuguese colony off the northwest coast of Africa, began arriving in British Guiana. Many came to the colony with their families on five-year working contracts, intended in part to increase the white population. Historian Brinsley Samaroo writes that the Portuguese became "a useful social buffer between the dominant white population and the subordinate non-white majority."[48] Many received attractive and favorable credit rates, allowing them eventual entry into the lucrative retail industry.[49] Tensions between Portuguese and black people in the Caribbean arose when the former were offered higher wages than the latter. Their whiteness also enabled them to climb up the racial-caste hierarchy, thereby kindling resentment among those at the bottom, which often led to violent skirmishes.

Although state-subsidized Portuguese immigration to British Guiana ended in 1882, many more Portuguese followed.[50] Outside British Guiana, smaller numbers of Portuguese communities lived in Antigua, Jamaica, Trinidad, and St. Vincent, and from these places tended eventually to migrate farther, to the US.[51] As Portuguese men and women climbed into business and trade, they likewise climbed closer to the top strata within different colonies. But in Trinidad, some Portuguese of working-class backgrounds blended with their counterparts in the creole community.[52]

"OUR FREEDOM CAN BE TAKEN AWAY FROM US"

From the 1890s, immigrant communities made up of Syrians and Lebanese joined the Portuguese in the middle strata. Often owning property and businesses they also clashed with creole African-Caribbean communities. However, the largest demographic change in the Caribbean resulted from the tensions between planters and the formerly enslaved. The crisis in labor shortage shaped by many free black people who opted to leave plantation work led planters to set their sights on bringing in new laborers. Around 39,332 Africans "liberated" from slavery in West Africa were sent to the Caribbean after emancipation between 1834 and 1867.[53] But planters needed still more workers and secured them from India and China.

Newly arrived Indian indentured laborers, Trinidad, c. 1897.

Plans to import easily exploited and nominally free laborers began in the era of racial slavery. In 1806, a small group of sugar workers were imported into Trinidad from Penang in Malaya, Macau in China, and Calcutta. This experiment failed, with most returning to Asia after only a couple of years.[54] But in 1838, ships filled with indentured Indians arrived in British Guiana. Privately organized, this venture ran into many problems. Indians became sick during the long voyage and high mortality rates were common. These complications forced a temporary halt in 1839. But by 1843 the prohibition was lifted, and starting in 1845 more Indians accepted contracts to emigrate to the Caribbean. Between 1838 and 1917, British Guiana received 238,909, Trinidad 143,939, Jamaica 36,412, and the Windward Islands 10,026 Indians.[55] Indian laborers were targeted not only because India was part of the British Empire but also because many Indians were struggling to find work at home, and there was a long history of Indians laboring in other parts of the world, from East and South Africa to Mauritius and Southeast Asia. The turn toward indentureship shows the generational shifts in coerced labor—with racial slavery, followed by apprenticeship, then indentureship—and while racism became more explicit in some ways, its incoherence and flexibility as a concept expanded to embrace other people of color.

The majority of Indian indentured laborers came from varied castes across northern India. Some were craftsmen, but most were general laborers. Hindus were in the majority, while around 15 percent were Muslim.[56] Most laborers were male, and debate ensued about what kind of woman should be encouraged to participate in the scheme: officials did not want to entice pregnant women. If a woman was visibly pregnant, it was unlikely she would have qualified for migration. Investigations conducted by magistrates into single women's lives and families were designed to prevent known prostitutes or those from lower castes from boarding ships.[57] In the early phase of indentureship, planters focused on male laborers and thought that women would be a financial liability, if they needed to cover the costs of children. Also, women were considered naturally physically weak.[58] But planters' needs for low-cost labor clashed with Indian men's desires for wives. By 1855, the Indian government called for a minimum of thirty-three women to one hundred men, but this was increased to forty women in 1868 to address the unequal sex ratio.[59] Government officers or emigration agents located in Madras and Calcutta were tasked with extolling and promoting indentureship. Yet some recruiters stationed near major railways, markets, and temples deliberately spread misinformation, disguising the harsh realities of indentureship, to encourage more people to sign up, and there is some evidence of kidnappings as well. Nonetheless, employment opportunities encouraged thousands of poor and landless Indians to venture to the Caribbean.

The voyage from India to the Caribbean took from three to three and a half months. Conditions on board were still dangerous and sometimes lethal, but changes in maritime technology had made sea passage more comfortable. Nineteenth-century ships were better ventilated and could carry more passengers.[60] Women and men were accommodated separately. Evidence from the 1850s and '60s shows that measles, dysentery, and cholera spread rapidly on board, contributing to high mortality rates. As the indentured laborers scheme continued in the 1870s and beyond, conditions did improve in some respects. Yet because they were in the minority, Indian women who decided to migrate tended to be single women, not wives or mothers, and were often targets of severe sexual and physical violence. Historian Verene Shepherd has painstakingly pieced together the fate of one Indian woman named Maharani whose experience illustrates the dangers women faced.

On July 24, 1885, Maharani, aged between sixteen and twenty, was one of 660 laborers who sailed aboard the *Allanshaw* from Calcutta to British Guiana.[61] On September 27, she died, one of seventeen who did not survive the journey. While the deaths of the other sixteen were "recorded without question, Maharani's death was the subject of intense controversy, uncertainty and speculation," because before she died, she confided to friends that she had been sexually assaulted by two sailors.[62]

After her death, the *Allanshaw*'s surgeon-superintendent Dr. Edward A. Hardwicke examined Maharani's body. Although he heard testimony from Moorti and Mohadaya, two friends Maharani had confided in about her assault, Hardwicke's report stated that the cause of death was not rape. He concluded:

> There was no evidence of injury from recent assault on the private parts . . . I consider in the case of an assault on a small Coolie woman, that the shock might persist and be sufficiently great to cause death even five or six days after . . . By shock I mean nervous shock. In a European I would expect the shock to be severe at first and become less severe as time passed; but I ascribe the shock in this case, to a considerable extent to mental depression as the result of shame.[63]

Despite Hardwicke's opinion of Maharani having a "very good character," he held fast to the scientific racism.[64] Hardwicke assumed thus despite reports that Robert Ipson, a black man, had raped Maharani, an accusation Ipson denied.

When the *Allanshaw* docked in British Guiana, Ipson was taken to trial, where he was acquitted due to insufficient evidence. Yet the governor of the colony was convinced Ipson was guilty and wanted another commission to find out more information. The chairman of this commission concluded that evidence provided was hearsay, adding that Ipson could not have raped Maharani without someone hearing the attack. Later, the government secretary Charles Bruce made a recommendation to the governor, based on all the commission and independent reports undertaken, that Maharani's death was due to a "sexual connection" with one or more members of the crew, but that no one should face prosecution.[65]

While the evidence suggests Maharani was raped, how she died remains unknown. According to Shepherd: "The most possible scenario was that as a result of the rape, a virulent infection such as streptococcus or gram negative bacterial infection was introduced into the vagina and from there, to the cervix and uterus."[66] Maharani's fate exposes the reality that for many Indian women, ships were dangerous and sometimes deadly "spaces of (s)exploitation."[67]

Derogatorily described as "coolies," the Indian laborers who came to Jamaica, Trinidad, and British Guiana, and also to smaller islands in the Caribbean, were contracted to work for one employer for five years, mainly on sugar plantations, although some labored on cocoa and coconut estates. When their period of indentureship was over, laborers could move to another employer. After ten years in the colony, Indians received a free return passage to India. Contracts guaranteed fundamental rights such as wages, accommodation, and medical care, but conditions for the workers were far from satisfactory. Laborers had to work nine hours a day, and many worked for up to fifteen. From 1862, workers on five-year contracts received daily wages of one shilling in British Guiana and one shilling half pence in Trinidad.[68] Indentured laborers faced harsh punishments too. Their employers had the right to prosecute them for minor offenses, such as using foul language or not paying enough attention at work. If a worker was missing from the plantation without a pass, this was considered a criminal offense.[69]

Indentured men, women, and their children lived in dismal housing conditions. Englishman Robert Lechmere Guppy, mayor of San Fernando in Trinidad, vividly described their homes. "A family has a single room in which to bring up their boys and girls if they have children," he wrote. "There are no places for cooking, no latrines. The men and women, boys and girls, go together into the canes or bush when nature requires. Comfort, privacy and decency are impossible under such conditions."[70] Poor housing exacerbated health problems, with malaria and hookworm all too common, often compounded by inadequate medical care.

East Indian women, men, and children, Trinidad, c. 1890–96.

Unsurprisingly, indentured laborers protested against their treatment and conditions. Strikes and riots frequently erupted in British Guiana in 1869 and 1870 and Trinidad in 1882.[71] Indentured laborers also used covert resistance methods such as sabotage of machinery and buildings. Conditions were so bad that some took their own lives. Violence itself was endemic to indentureship. Overseers on plantations physically abused laborers.

Female indentured laborers contended with physical and sexual violence. The sexual exploitation that women experienced in transit only increased once they arrived in the Caribbean, as both white and Indian men used violence as a means of control. British Guiana, especially, had high numbers of "wife murders."[72] Rising incidences of wife murders led to the introduction of marriage laws in the 1880s, which were thought to help protect women by placing them under the patriarchal protection of husbands. These laws arose due to concern that critics of indentureship would use wife murders to attack the system.

With growing unrest among indentured laborers, skeptics, such as some members of the Anti-Slavery Society, began to compare the labor system to the enslaved system it had replaced. Colonial officials also noted the comparison. Joseph Beaumont, the chief justice of British Guiana from 1863 to 1868, published *The New Slavery: an account of Indian and Chinese immigrants in British Guiana* in 1871, in which he described indentureship as a new form of slavery.[73] He also outlined the effects of indentureship on black free workers, understanding that the scheme was "contrived in order to substitute and control the labour of the freedmen, when they had become thoroughly alienated from the planters by the course pursued after the emancipation of the slaves, and which, after various experiments, has for some twenty years been settled upon a tolerably uniform system."[74] According to Beaumont, indentureship was "a monstrous, rotten system, rooted upon slavery, grown in its stale soil, emulating its worst abuses, and only the more dangerous because it presents itself under false colours, whereas slavery bore the brand of infamy upon its forehead."[75] Beaumont also spoke out against the abuse of Indian women.[76]

Many who argued that indentureship was a new form of slavery were part of the continuation of anti-slavery activism that largely fizzled out by the 1870s as indentureship became institutionalized.[77] Hereditary racial slavery and indentureship were not the same thing. But what they underscore is how planters in the post-emancipation period could not escape from labor models rooted in coercion and violence. Planters considered Indian laborers inferior, but because they could be more easily controlled than black people through laws mandating the terms and conditions of their indentureship, and because they helped revive the sugar economy, they viewed them more favorably than the formerly enslaved and their descendants. For planters, stereotypes of Indians as unruly, disruptive, vengeful, and violent coexisted with contradictory notions of their docility. But while white people saw Indians as inferior to them, they also considered them superior to black people, and this played into tensions between the two communities.

Conflict between African-Caribbean communities and indentured Indians shaped by the colonial-driven "politics of difference" had a lot to do with economic competition that benefited white people. The former looked down upon the latter because they had the least lucrative positions on plantations. African-Caribbeans also blamed Indians for driving down the cost of labor by accepting lower wages.[78] Furthermore, by 1890 many realized that one-third of the cost of Indian immigration came from the colonies' revenue, meaning that black people "were subsidising those who were replacing them."[79] Indians also cast aspersions on African-Caribbeans. The white-elite-led strategy of pitting people of color against each other kept black people and Indians from seeing themselves as a larger unified collective or class of exploited laborers, and thus bolstered white minority power. Yet Indians themselves were not a wholly united group. There existed long-standing strains between Bengalis and Tamil-speaking groups from the Madras. Caste differences among Indians created divisions as well.[80] But interactions among those of African and Asian descent were not always contentions. They both worked side by side, and forms of intimacy leading to African-Asian families challenged divisions.

The majority of Indian indentured laborers chose to remain in the Caribbean after their contracts ended. As free laborers, they became a significant group among the peasantry, producing rice and other essential food crops. As their dominance in these sectors grew, some Indians climbed their way into the middle strata of society.

Alongside Indians, the British also brought Chinese indentured laborers to the Caribbean.[81] Chinese laborers tended to be skilled artisans, and more commonly male than female. Commercial agencies ran recruitment drives from China and sometimes used threats of violence. Up to 1866, 17,804 Chinese laborers were in the British Caribbean—13,533 in British Guiana, 2,645 in Trinidad, 1,152 in Jamaica, and 474 in British Honduras.[82] Chinese laborers were stereotyped as more commercially driven, and after their indentureship, many left plantations and entered the retail industry.[83]

Although indentureship did help alleviate economic crises in the Caribbean, opposition to the scheme gathered momentum in the late nineteenth century. Opponents argued that it was causing unemployment, leading to unwanted demographical change in the region, and that conditions remained unfavorable for laborers themselves. The plight of women was central to this opposition. After complaints that Indian indentured laborers in Natal in South Africa faced racist discrimination after their contracts ended, opposition also came from India. Mohandas K. Gandhi led activism against indentureship, and in 1911 the Indian National Congress campaigned for a ban on emigration to Natal, which then contributed to a broader attack on Indian indentureship "as wrong in principle because it used criminal sanctions to enforce a civil contract for labour."[84]

Opposition to indentureship among Indian nationalists became part of the wider twentieth-century critique of the colonial system. In 1917 the government of India suspended indentured labor schemes because they would disrupt recruitment for the First World War, and between 1918 and 1920 indentureship ended. The fight against indentureship saw Indian nationalists, as writer Gaiutra Bahadur observes, "kill off indenture without firing a shot, or taking a single bullet, in the first major success of their anti-imperial struggle."[85] In 1917, toward the end of indenture, around eighteen thousand Chinese and 450,000 Indians had been shipped to the British Caribbean.[86]

Those indentured laborers who remained in the Caribbean contributed to religious, social, and cultural changes in the region. Many Christian missionaries worked to convert Indians, and some succeeded, especially the Canadian Presbyterian Mission to the Indians of the Caribbean, which started missions in Trinidad in 1868 and spread to Grenada, Jamaica, St. Lucia, and British Guiana.[87] Christian conversion was an opportunity to climb up the social ladder, and Chinese men who tried to enter wider society in the nineteenth century did so through Christianity, which paved the way for some to gain education and pursue trade and shopkeeping activities. But indentured laborers still practiced Hinduism and Islam. While the success of many wealthy Indians and Chinese continued to feed tensions with African-Caribbeans, relations between the groups were not always acrimonious—this, despite the fact that the system of indentureship was designed to strengthen stratification in the racial-caste hierarchy.

The end of hereditary racial slavery did not provide the benefits that anti-slavery liberals envisaged. This was true in part because the demise of enslavement did not similarly demolish white supremacy and the racial-caste hierarchy; to the contrary, it reinforced those ideologies and applied them to successor systems of forced labor by other names, such as indentureship. Planters' ideas about what the post-emancipation era would look like contrasted starkly with those of black people, and this

"OUR FREEDOM CAN BE TAKEN AWAY FROM US"

increased conflict, with the former seeking to retain their place at the top of the racial-caste hierarchy and the latter contesting the status quo. But in 1914, when Britain and the empire entered the First World War, it would be African-Caribbeans who saw new opportunities to continue to assert their rights as citizens and continue to challenge the racial-caste hierarchy.

5

"Fighting to prove that we are no longer merely subjects, but citizens"
War, Anti-Colonialism, and Rebellion

Six months after the Caribbean received permission to raise a battalion for the First World War, the *Federalist*, a Grenadian newspaper, published a bold statement: "As Coloured people we will be fighting for something more, something inestimable to ourselves. We will be fighting to prove to Great Britain that we are not so vastly inferior to the whites that we should not be put on a level, at least, of political equality with them." The brave men who would volunteer in the thousands would be "fighting to prove that we are no longer merely subjects, but citizens—citizens of a world empire whose watch-word should be Liberty, Equality and Brotherhood."[1]

For the writers and readers of the *Federalist* and the growing group of African-Caribbean men and women who continued to challenge anti-black racism, the First World War meant something distinct and different for these subjects. It was a transformative moment, a crucible for inclusion in empire, and a potential equalizer.

By proving themselves on the battlefield, African-Caribbean men could both defy white supremacist stereotypes of them as brutish, backward, lazy, and uncivilized, and display both traditional tropes of masculine valor, duty, and strength and their loyalty to the British Empire. Many held passionate feelings of imperial belonging that had increased in the post-emancipation era, as myths that Britain's empire was founded on liberty and equal justice were spread widely within colonial culture. Empire Day, school curricula, and the cult of the benevolent monarchy entrenched this myth and eclipsed the reality that Britain's liberal empire remained grounded in white supremacy. Nevertheless, its influence came to shape the strong bonds of Britishness that Caribbean people identified with and helped change over time.

This colonial identity was heavily invested in middle-class respectability, Christianity, and domesticity. Empire loyalty was, however, uneven across Caribbean society. An individual's class, racial identity, skin color, and status in society shaped whether or to what extent they embraced or rejected their British colonial identity. Working-class African-Caribbeans tended to be less likely to adopt a British sense of identity compared to white-collar individuals.[2] In addition to loyalty (a sentiment shaped by other colonial subjects across the British Empire), further factors encouraged the involvement of Caribbean men in the war. With regional economic decline, the military offered wages that in some cases were significantly higher than local wages, and many working-class men volunteered as a result.

Nonetheless, a range of Caribbean voices spoke out in opposition to the war. Some took pacifist stances, while others argued that black and mixed-race men should not fight for an inherently unequal empire.[3] But overall, the Caribbean overwhelmingly supported the First World War. People from the Caribbean donated large sums to the war effort, in the form of cash, charitable donations, and war-related taxes, amounting to around £2 million.[4] This was a substantial total, given the region's economic woes, but black Caribbean communities would soon realize that while they thought the war could shatter the racial-caste hierarchy, white elites in Britain and the Caribbean believed otherwise.

For white elites in the Caribbean and Britain, the global nature of the war defied racially specific geographical boundaries and could potentially undermine racial separatism, while black men's desires to be included as equals potentially challenged white supremacy. Elites in Britain, then, were waging two wars: one against a foreign enemy and another to maintain racial hierarchies. Over the course of the conflict, anti-black racism fed into specific policies, proposals, and practices designed to uphold the racial-caste hierarchy.

At the end of the war, anti-black racism imposed by white elites influenced working-class white people, who in the context of economic competition turned their anger and frustration toward small communities of black men and women residing in Britain. White-led racist violence on the streets of Britain further influenced anti-black, racist legislative policies. The British state took racist violence as a rationale to implement policies that stripped black people of their citizenship in the 1920s, in an attempt both to resolve economic competition and maintain Britain's demographic whiteness. The continued existence of a covert but nevertheless powerful color bar on British soil served as a more structural replication of the Caribbean-derived racial-caste hierarchy. It was evidence too of the racialized nature of citizenship in Britain.[5]

This color bar, however, did not go uncontested. In the ongoing push and pull between those who challenged and those who tried to uphold the racial-caste hierarchy, the color bar, another iteration and reinvention of that hierarchy, facilitated the growth of anti-racist activism led generally by middle-class black African-Caribbean and West African men and women in the interwar years. Resistance was both constant and inventive. Among this group, radicals went further, denouncing not just the color bar but colonialism. Their activism—calling for the fall of empire—planted the seeds of a burgeoning global anti-colonial movement. Meanwhile, back in the Caribbean, labor disturbances that swept the region in the 1930s revealed the growing political power of workers who continued to agitate against their persistent inequality. These disturbances were part of the labor agitation taking place across the industrialized world, and in the case of the Caribbean reflected the interplay of movements against racism and capitalist exploitation. The first three decades of the twentieth century, then, were critical to the racial-caste hierarchy, which, although not shattered, was beginning to crack.

SERVING KING AND EMPIRE

Many white British officials saw the First World War as a white man's war, to be fought by white men from Britain and the Dominions, especially on the Western front. Hence they had a litany of racist justifications for why African-Caribbean men should not serve, including suggestions that black men would not be able to withstand the European climate.

Many argued that the image of black men fighting white men would undermine white racial prestige, even if, at the same time, it would increase the ranks defending Britain and the empire. The two wars white elites were fighting had conflicting agendas in this respect. Black men were seen simultaneously as inferior to white men and yet physically stronger, with the potential to make white soldiers look frail or meek. There were also fears that armed black men could attack those who oppressed white elites, including white settlers in various parts of the British Empire.

Yet there was also concern within the Colonial Office that excluding black troops from the Caribbean would damage empire loyalty and spur retaliation. Indeed, as debates within the War

Office and Colonial Office continued into 1915, Caribbean commentators voiced outrage at the idea of black Caribbean men's exclusion. Writers in the *Federalist* realized that such exclusion would be based on "the nasty cowardly skin prejudice characteristic of the empire."[6]

Some Caribbean men decided not to wait for officials to make up their minds. A few were so desperate to be involved that they made their own way to Britain to enlist. In 1915, nine men from Barbados who intended to volunteer for the army arrived on board the SS *Danube*. Insisting that "They had come to fight, and they were going to fight," the men refused to return to Barbados.[7] But there remained no official stance on black recruitment. Some black British men were conscripted into the army following the 1916 Military Service Act, but recruitment officers dismissed others based on race.[8] The skin color of the Caribbean men concerned some officials. They recorded that lighter-skinned men had been accepted but those of a darker hue faced more difficulty.[9] W. A. Moore, a manager of one of the departments of a store in Trinidad, paid £25 to travel to England to enlist in the army, but military personnel refused to sign him up because of his complexion.[10] When he was asked why he had not been recruited, Moore replied: "Well I have a suspicion it is a colour question, but when I paid £25 for my passage I had not the least idea there was any colour question in England."[11]

In May 1915, King George V, sympathetic to the Caribbean commitment to the war effort, called on the War Office to "gratify the wish of the West Indies to send a Regiment to the Front" and a recruitment drive led by churches, government, press, and local committees coordinated male enlistment.[12] Men of varied racial and class backgrounds rushed to volunteer to serve in the British West Indies Regiment (BWIR) after its formation in September 1915. Praised for their martial traits, the small but significant communities of Maroons and Kalinagos were also encouraged to enlist. Caribbean women actively aided recruitment, calling on their husbands, partners, brothers, uncles, and sons to enlist. Some gave speeches at rallies, challenging men to prove their masculinity. This encouragement was often economically motivated: BWIR men were provided with separation allowances to partially pay for any dependants, including wives and children.[13]

> **YOUNG MEN OF THE BAHAMAS**
>
> The British Empire is engaged in a Life and Death Struggle. Never in the History of England, never since the Misty Distant Past of 2,000 years ago, has our beloved Country been engaged in such a conflict as she is engaged in to-day.
>
> To bring to nothing this mighty attack by an unscrupulous and well prepared foe, HIS MOST GRACIOUS MAJESTY KING GEORGE has called on the men of his Empire, MEN OF EVERY CLASS, CREED AND COLOUR, to
>
> **COME FORWARD TO FIGHT**
>
> that the Empire may be saved and the foe may be well beaten.
>
> This call is to YOU, young man; not your neighbour, not your brother, not your cousin, but just YOU. SEVERAL HUNDREDS OF YOUR MATES HAVE COME UP, HAVE BEEN MEDICALLY EXAMINED AND HAVE BEEN PASSED AS "FIT."
>
> **What is the matter with YOU?**
>
> Put yourself right with your King; put yourself right with your fellowmen; put yourself right with yourself and your conscience.
>
> **ENLIST TO-DAY**

"Young men of the Bahamas ... Enlist to-day,"
poster printed in Kingston, Jamaica, 1915.

Initially, recruitment to the BWIR did not extend to African-Caribbean people outside the region, such as those in Panama, home to the largest population of British Caribbean migrants, because of the country's neutral stance in the war. Between 1904 and 1913, in the early years of US involvement in the construction of the Panama Canal, twenty-three thousand British Caribbean people were hired to construct the canal, and thousands more came to Panama without contracts and ended up working in the banana industry. African-Caribbean men in Panama lived racially segregated lives imposed on them by the Jim Crow policies of the US. Yet they were as keen as those who remained in the Caribbean to join the war effort.[14] One Jamaican wrote a letter to the British Caribbean community in Panama calling for volunteers, saying: "Don't forget that England was the first country in the world that set our fathers and mothers free and that everywhere that grand old Union Jack flies, there are real courts of justice, where everybody gets a square deal, no matter what his color, his sex, his nationality or his religion."[15]

Such erroneous words encouraged many to enlist, as did economic factors: the opening of the canal in August 1914 displaced British Caribbean laborers, and those working on banana plantations faced reduced wages and job losses. Participation in the war came to be seen as a way to earn money. Before Panama entered the war, African-Caribbean men raised money to send volunteers to Jamaica to enlist in the BWIR. Fifty-one went to Jamaica from Bocas del Toro, and Panama City sent forty-eight Jamaican-born men.[16] When Panama entered the war on April 7, 1917, a day after the US, British officials began a recruitment drive that led to around 2,100 men enlisting in the BWIR.[17]

The BWIR welcomed all Caribbean men regardless of race, which proved contentious to some white men who did not want to serve alongside those with darker skin. In Trinidad and Barbados, white planters and merchants organized separately to establish contingents made up of light-skinned and white men.[18] Writer and activist C. L. R. James, born in the town of Tunapuna in Trinidad, tried to enlist in one of these contingents but in his autobiography recalled that the recruitment official "took one look at me, saw my dark skin and, shaking his head vigorously, motioned me violently away."[19]

Around twenty thousand Caribbean men participated in the First World War. This estimate includes Caribbean men who ventured to Britain to enlist, some of whom were accepted; the 15,601 who were part of the BWIR, inclusive of black British men who entered voluntarily or who joined following unsuccessful attempts to enter the British army; and the two thousand who served in the West India Regiments (WIR).[20] The WIR were some of the first military contingents to include black Caribbean men, and their origins date to the 1790s. Caribbean men also served in other units of the British army, the Royal Navy, the Royal Air Force, Canadian regiments, and the British merchant navy. From 1915 to 1918 Caribbean men in the BWIR would serve in Egypt, Palestine, East Africa, Mesopotamia, Italy, France, England, and Belgium. Caribbean women also played important roles in the conflict. Alongside encouraging men to enlist, women participated in war fundraising, aided in donating war materials, such as clothing, which was used for local contingents and forces abroad, and a group of twenty-four elite women from Jamaica served in England as nurses in the Red Cross.[21] Furthermore, some Jamaican women worked as drivers in local ambulance corps.[22]

A color bar remained in place in the BWIR, nevertheless, whereby only white men were allowed to be officers. The highest position a Caribbean man of color could hold was that of a noncommissioned officer. What's more, BWIR soldiers regularly experienced racist discrimination. In March 1916, 1,140 Jamaican men heading to Britain on the SS *Verdala* were diverted from the usual route by German U-boats and ended up in Halifax, Nova

Scotia. The ship was not properly heated, and the soldiers were not given warm clothing. Wearing mostly light tropical uniforms, the Jamaicans ended up freezing. By the time they reached Halifax, five had died due to hypothermia and six hundred suffered from frostbite and exposure. All told, 106 of the men had to stay in Halifax to undergo amputations,[23] and two hundred were sent to Bermuda to recover. The incident was not widely reported in the British press, but it appeared in the Canadian papers that circulated in the Caribbean.[24]

The British West Indies Regiment in camp on the Albert-Amiens Road, Western Front, September 1916.

If white elites were fighting a war within the war to preserve racial boundaries and hierarchy, then by the same logic black men were fighting a war within the war against racism and its deadly consequences.

Moreover, while many men who left the Caribbean for military training thought they would be fighting alongside other British

Empire men, racism underlay the decision that most BWIR troops, especially those sent to Europe, would serve as a labor battalion rather than fight in active combat—information that was not made available to recruits during the formation of the BWIR.

Indeed, when news of the BWIR's formation spread in 1915, Caribbean people recognized the historical significance of black men fighting alongside white men. In the Grenadian newspaper the *West Indian*, editors proudly proclaimed: "This is history . . . West Indians, most of whom are descendants of slaves, fighting for human liberty together with immediate sons of the Motherland in Europe's classic fields of war . . . The bones of Clarkson and Wilberforce rattle in their graves to-day."[25] Yet most BWIR men did not come close to military conflict. On the Western front, BWIR battalions contributed to a range of noncombatant roles— from loading ships and transporting ammunition for the British artillery in Belgium and France to digging trenches to building roads. BWIR men often complained about overcrowding, poor food, and a lack of sanitation leading to diarrhea, indigestion, malnutrition, measles, pneumonia, and influenza, which only compounded the psychological impact of the conflict.

Harry M. Brown, a chaplain in 10th Battalion BWIR, stirred controversy in the Caribbean and London when he wrote to the West Indian Contingent Committee (a committee tasked with looking after the regiment's welfare) complaining that German prisoners of war were treated better than black members of the BWIR in northern Flanders. He wrote of barracks with "German prisoners <u>warm</u> and <u>comfortable</u>," and in contrast "West India boys . . . without warming apparatus <u>of any kind</u>, cold and suffering . . . The Officer who took me round described the rooms as the ghastliest and a perfect abomination."[26] The head of the Baptist Theological College in Kingston, Welshman Rev. Ernest Price, received a copy of Brown's letter and wrote to the governor of Jamaica: "our Jamaica men are being treated in a very cruel way ... when they are in hospitals they are kept <u>unwarmed</u> and insufficiently fed, at the same time that they see German prisoners kept in comparative luxury."[27] An investigation later blamed these conditions on the actions of white senior commanding officers.[28] Whatever the cause, these experiences stoked bitterness among BWIR that persisted long after the war.

Although most BWIR men in Europe did not see active combat, a minority of those from the Caribbean in the British army fought on the Western Front, including Jamaican Norman Manley. Manley's parents shared African and Irish ancestry. At the start of the war, he was a Rhodes scholar at Oxford University. In 1915 he and his brother, Roy, were refused entry into the Royal Flying Corps because of their skin color. The brothers were later allowed to join the Royal Field Artillery, and Norman rose up the ranks to become a lance corporal and was sent to the front in France.

Beyond Europe, BWIR troops participated in limited operations in Egypt.[29] Men serving in the WIR were also involved in combat. At the start of the war, Sierra Leone was the base of 1st Battalion WIR. In June 1915 the battalion moved to Jamaica for the rest of the war and was replaced in Sierra Leone by the 2nd Battalion. In April 1916, the 2nd Battalion moved to East Africa and saw limited action.

Racial prejudice, recounted in testimonies, was a constant regardless of where black or mixed-race Caribbean men were stationed. When Norman Manley became a corporal and was in training before being sent to the front in France, he remembered: "Here I came up against violent colour prejudice. The rank and file disliked taking orders from a coloured N.C.O. and their attitude was mild by comparison with that of my fellow N.C.Os. Corporals and Sergeants resented my sharing status with them."[30] Due to his experiences, Manley gave up his rank and transferred to a different unit. But his skin color did not prevent him from being recognized for his contribution: in 1919 he received a military medal for bravery (sadly, his brother did not return to Jamaica—Roy Manley died near Ypres in 1917).

Caribbean men not only experienced racism but saw it wielded against other men of color. When Etienne Dupuch, a middle-class Bahamian of mixed African and French heritage, saw an Indian sergeant abused by a British private, he realized "the lowest, dirtiest, scrubbiest Englishman was considered superior to the finest Indian."[31] Witnessing racist treatment of other men of color kindled a sense of solidarity and empathy among some Caribbean men, but they were not immune to racial prejudices, some of which reveal they had internalized white supremacist ideas. Some African-Caribbeans saw themselves as superior to Indian, Chinese, and West African labor units and objected to sharing accommodations with them.

Rivalries existed among Caribbean men as well. One Jamaican soldier wrote:

> contrary to the accredited belief that the Westies love each other dearly, I soon discovered that Trinidadians look down their noses at Barbadians and all the other inhabitants of the various islands of the Caribbean, and they all look with considerable disfavour on the products of Jamaica . . . [O]ne soon discovers that as much jealously and pride of race exists in the inhabitants of the microscopic little islands dotting the Westian waters as there is amongst Irish, Scotch, Welsh and English folk.[32]

Although Caribbean colonies belonged to the British Empire, the colonial infrastructure did not promote a broader Caribbean collective consciousness. Instead, very strong colony-specific identities prevailed, often described as "islandism." Divisions between neighboring colonies, despite their shared geography and colonial connection, was often blamed on Caribbean people themselves, but it was fostered by the British Empire too.

Historian Gordon K. Lewis describes: "the basic responsibility is that of the English themselves who kept the islands unnaturally apart from each other for three centuries or more."[33] But the war could inspire a more unified Caribbean identity. An English journalist at the BWIR training camp in Seaford, Sussex, noted: "All local jealousies have vanished, and the men no longer say I am a Jamaican, Barbadian, Trinidadian, or Honduranean, but always, I am a West Indian."[34] As this comment suggests, Caribbean nationalism was often created outside the Caribbean, in the diaspora, where in the face of a hostile larger white population African-Caribbeans shed some of their island rivalries in favor of solidarity. And as racism hardened in Britain, it incidentally forged a greater sense of solidarity among Caribbean people.

Despite prejudices, Caribbean men still managed to form important friendships across the color line. Writing about his fellow British soldiers in East Deptford, Manley reflected:

> I suppose because we liked each other, and soon found out that I did not like being called "Darkie" as came natural to them, and I have heard a real tough guy get hold of a new arrival, a casualty replacement, who automatically called me "Darkie," and take him aside and say "Don't call him that—he doesn't like it. We call him Bill and we like him!"[35]

While training in England, some BWIR men remarked on how white British civilians welcomed them. Private Alexander King noted: "One thing that strikes me is the manner in which we are appreciated and respected by the English people. You can just imagine how it makes us darkies feel at ease in our minds."[36] However, white people who forged friendships with black soldiers did not always shed racist ideas. The individual exceptions, while diluting racist structures, did not fully destroy them.

Interracial friendships were more easily tolerated than relations between black Caribbean men and white European women. Indeed, the War Office and Colonial Office also worried about sending black Caribbean troops to Europe due to the potential for interracial sexual relationships, which would inevitably threaten the contrived yet relevantly reified racial boundaries of the racial-caste hierarchy. In 1914, the black British population numbered in the thousands. Resident black British men and women, and African- and Caribbean-born sailors whose numbers increased from the 1870s, lived in scattered communities across cities like London, Liverpool, and Cardiff, forming unions with white women and raising their mixed-race families. But in many parts of Britain, black people remained a novelty. When the first BWIR soldiers arrived in Seaford in October 1915, many white women expressed interest in them. One BWIR man in Seaford remembered seeing: "Plenty of girls. They love the boys in Khaki . . . They love the darkies."[37]

As they traveled throughout continental Europe, black Caribbean men formed short- and long-term relationships with white women. These relationships reduced male social isolation, and in some cases, white women defended men against racist abuse. After the war, some ex-servicemen returned home to the Caribbean with wives from Britain, which many perceived as a threat to white colonial power because it transgressed strict racial boundaries. The white wife of seaman C. Robinson from St. Vincent traveled with him to the island but experienced harassment and due to limited employment opportunities was sent home to Britain.[38]

Back in the Caribbean during the war, the region's economic problems worsened. The *Federalist* lamented: "Grenada is in a state of siege. Food prices are rising every day. Wages continue stationary or are a diminishing quantity. Everybody is complaining and everybody is suffering ... Government must do something."[39]

The colonial government did not, however, do enough, which led to worker disturbances, strikes, and riots throughout the wider region. Many middle-class Caribbean men and women migrated, with numbers peaking in the war years. In particular, migration to the US began to climb.[40] For those left behind, especially the working classes, the postwar era would bring further economic decline and unemployment.

In December 1918, one month after the end of the First World War, groups of BWIR soldiers stationed in Italy surprised white military commanders by challenging their discriminatory treatment. The origins of this "mutiny" began earlier in the year when the British army had decided to increase soldiers' wages, but the War Office excluded the BWIR because they were not regarded as British soldiers but rather as "natives."[41] BWIR soldiers protested, sending letters to colonial officials in the Caribbean, who passed them on to officials in London. A petition began to circulate from NCOs and others in 1st and 2nd Battalions BWIR, which stated: "We feel that this discrimination is not only an insult to us who have volunteered to fight for the Empire but also an insult to the whole of the West Indies."[42] The Colonial Office also voiced opposition to the Caribbeans' exclusion from the pay raise, fearing that it could undermine loyalty in the region. Yet the calls went unheeded.

After Armistice Day, eight BWIR battalions across Italy and France were relocated to the coastal base of Taranto at the Cimino camp, in southern Italy. They were later joined by three BWIR battalions from Egypt and men formerly based in Mesopotamia. Many were still disillusioned that they had not had the chance to fight and angry at not receiving the pay raise, and they quickly confronted more racism. Black troops were not allowed to use canteens frequented by white soldiers, and hospital facilities were also racially segregated. In December 1918, those from the Caribbean were forced to do the laundry for white troops.

Command of the camp fell to Brigadier General Carey Bernard, a white South African and a well-known white supremacist. He declared that African-Caribbeans "were only niggers and that no such treatment should ever have been promised to them, that they were better fed and treated than any nigger had the right to expect, that he would order them to do whatever work he pleased, and if they objected he would force them to do it."[43] Some were so outraged at the unabashed racism and the conditions at Taranto that they refused orders. Others took a more confrontational stance.

On December 6, 1918, a group of men from 9th Battalion BWIR gathered at the tent of their commanding officer, Lieutenant Colonel R. E. Willis, and slashed it with their bayonets. Some credited the attack to Willis's order that a group of BWIR men clean Italian labor corps' latrines.[44] On the same day, a petition signed by 180 BWIR sergeants circulated calling for black soldiers to be given the same pay and opportunities as white troops.[45] A few days later a group of BWIR soldiers refused to work, a decision that spread to other units, including the 10th Battalion, and during the four-day disturbance one black NCO killed a mutineer in self-defense.[46] To restore order, the Worcestershire Regiment was deployed, and 9th Battalion BWIR was disbanded and its men disarmed. Later, sixty BWIR soldiers were tried for mutiny. Of those who were convicted, sentences varied: some faced imprisonment for three to five years, one man was sentenced to twenty years, and another was executed by firing squad.[47]

Resentment ran high among the regiment. On December 17, 1918, sixty NCOs from the BWIR held a meeting that led to the creation of the Caribbean League, which sought to promote "all matters conducive to the General Welfare of the islands constituting the British West Indies and the British Territories adjacent thereto."[48] At a subsequent gathering, one man stated that "the black man should have freedom and govern himself in the West Indies."[49] While these words were greeted enthusiastically, not all in the Caribbean League considered violence necessary. Details of the meeting were shared with army commanders, who feared the Caribbean League might provoke revolution. The Colonial Office was also worried about the new organization but warned against attacking it for fear that it would cause further trouble in the Caribbean.[50] Ultimately, interisland rivalries and disputes about the direction of the group led to its demise. Nonetheless, the events at Taranto demonstrated the very potent frustration and deep disappointment that many BWIR soldiers felt.[51]

By the end of the war, nearly 1,200 BWIR servicemen had died;[52] around ninety WIR soldiers had been killed, and other white Caribbean men died serving in other regiments.[53] Yet the sacrifices these men made, especially black Caribbean men, were overlooked. During the Victory Parade on July 19, 1919, in London, no black men marched. By choosing not to recognize the contribution of black men in the war, the loyalty to empire many had felt so ardently on the eve of the war started to waiver.

When BWIR troops returned home, it was not easy for them to simply put aside resentment and disillusionment, and when confronted also by the poor economic conditions facing their home colonies, some turned to violence. One major disturbance took place in Belize Town, the capital of British Honduras. In July 1919, while thousands gathered to cheer the return of the BWIR contingent, groups of BWIR soldiers in uniform brandishing clubs led crowds, including civilians, through the streets calling for an end to white domination and attacking white men, looting, and targeting shops.

As its numbers grew, the group soon gained control of the city center. The British warship HMS Constance responded to Governor Eyre Hutson's radio appeal for help. Those BWIR soldiers who did not take part in the riots helped police and the defense force maintain order until the *Constance* arrived. Martial law was declared, and the navy rounded up leaders of the violence, with some BWIR soldiers acting as special constables. An inquiry organized to investigate the disturbances heard various testimony about the racist abuse BWIR soldiers from British Honduras had experienced in Mesopotamia. Yet overall, the inquiry said there was no justification for the actions of the soldiers. It was also recommended that a detachment of around a hundred white troops should be stationed in Belize Town to restore order, showing again how in response to anti-black racism, white men were considered crucial to reinforcing unequal hierarchies.[54]

Although postwar confrontations did not directly threaten colonial power, they did signal a growing confidence in African-Caribbean people to explicitly challenge racism, and this would only grow in the next decades. The blatant anti-black racism that underpinned their involvement in the war could no longer be overlooked or excused. Meanwhile, back in Britain, elite-driven racism had combined with economic challenges to stoke white working-class racial animosity toward fellow British citizens.

RIOTS AND REPATRIATION

Between January and August 1919, a series of disturbances ranging from riots to skirmishes erupted, with thousands of white men attacking black men and women as well as those described as "colored" (a group that in some instances included black people but also referred to Arabs and those from South Asia, like Indians and Burmese, and Chinese communities). This violence occurred in Glasgow, South Shields, Salford, London, Hull, Liverpool, Newport, Cardiff, and Barry. Sporadic rioting continued into 1920 and 1921, and in total five people died, 250 were arrested, and many injured. The riots were caused by a combination of factors, including postwar competition for jobs in naval industries, housing shortages, and racial antagonism that exposed conflicts over the very definition of British national identity.

During the First World War, larger numbers of African, Arab, South Asian, and Caribbean men had come to Britain to work within the manufacturing and naval industries. They were not the only new arrivals in the country. Other male laborers came to Britain from Poland, Russia, Sweden, and Denmark. After the war, calls grew for the dismissal of specifically black and other men-of-color workers and their replacement by demobilized white soldiers. Some white former soldiers accused men-of-color workers of driving down wages, objected to working alongside them, and blamed them for housing shortages. On the whole, employers and union leaders sided with white workers. Black men faced accusations of stealing British jobs, even though many were British-born, and those who were colonial subjects were eligible to work in Britain.

Aside from employment, black men also became targets for abuse because many had formed relationships with local white British women. The informal "policing" of sexual mixing arguably became even more visible and important to white supremacists after the end of racial slavery.

The riots began in Glasgow. Fighting broke out between black and white sailors. Later, Arab sailors, mainly from Yemen and Somalia, also faced attacks in South Shields. Many black voices spoke out against the violence and the racist reporting of the riots. Glasgow was home to a small but significant black population of students, workers, and professionals. Some of them formed the African Races Association of Glasgow (ARAG) and wrote a letter protesting against the riots to Scottish newspapers, including the liberal *Daily Record and Mail*. In the letter the ARAG asked: Are ex-service men of color "not British subjects the same as the white men, and consequently deserve the same consideration? Did not some of these same men fight on the same battle fields with white men to defeat the enemy and make secure the British Empire? Why can't they work now in the same factories with white men?"[55] The white Glaswegian wife of a black man defended her husband in the newspaper: "I think as the white wife of a British coloured man I have a right to speak . . . we, the white wives, know better than anyone what they are. We, the white wives, have been married for years and find the British coloured man—I don't say all, but I say most—make us very good husbands."[56]

Black men and women called on the government to prevent further violence. In June 1919, the *South Wales Echo* reported: "A meeting was held at Cardiff docks yesterday of Arabs, Somalis, Egyptians, West Indians and other coloured races, to protest against the treatment to which they are being subjected . . . They claim that as British subjects they are entitled to protection, and a resolution was adopted calling upon the Government to take measures with this end."[57]

The riots in Britain mirrored those taking place in the US. The summer of 1919 in the US was dubbed the "Red Summer" by Black American activist and writer James Weldon Johnson, on account of the twenty-six race riots and eighty-three lynchings targeting Black American veterans who were attacked on the streets, especially in the North.

In Britain, those in power ignored calls to defend black subjects and instead proposed repatriation (especially for colonial workers) as a solution. On June 23, 1919, Colonial Secretary Lord Milner issued a "Memorandum on Repatriation of Coloured Men," in which he surmised that the disturbances in Britain's seaports were

> even more serious in regard to their possible effect in the Colonies . . . when these men get back to their own Colonies they may be tempted to revenge themselves on the white minorities there, unless we can do something to show that His Majesty's

Government is not insensible to their complaints... I am convinced that, if we wish to get rid of the Coloured population whose presence here is causing so much trouble we must pay the expense of doing so ourselves.[58]

By the end of 1921, the government had repatriated to various colonies around two thousand British colonial sailors, although this figure may have been higher.[59] Unemployed men who rejected repatriation were denied maintenance payments used for general subsistence.[60] Hundreds refused as they considered Britain their home and did not want to face poorer job prospects in the colonies.[61]

Four years later, in 1925, the British government took further steps not only to repatriate black seamen but also to strip some of their British nationality. The Special Restriction (Colored Alien Seamen) Order forced undocumented black seamen to register as aliens in Britain and allowed police to stop black seamen when they landed in British ports and check their documents in order to prove their national or colonial status. But in many instances, sailors did not carry passports. Those who could not show that they were British subjects or those whose documents the police deemed unsatisfactory had to register as aliens, which made deportation easier and hindered the seamen's ability to find work. This act, devised by the Home Office Aliens Department, has been described by historian Laura Tabili as "the first instance of state-sanctioned race discrimination inside Britain to come to widespread notice."[62] Black seamen did resist the 1925 order, with the help of the Colonial Office and the India Office (which structured British colonialism in India), who feared that the order would offend elites in the colonies.[63]

In protests, seamen invoked their rights as British subjects and in some cases drew on their wartime service to challenge their designation as aliens. Many did resolve to get passports to abide by the law, but then the Home Office had devised new plans to subjugate them. In the early 1930s, the Home Office designed the Special Certificate of Nationality and Identity, a passport that restricted travel within the British Empire on the grounds of class, occupation, and race.[64] Though the Colored Alien Seamen Order was finally revoked in 1942, it set a high-water mark at the time for state-driven racism.

BLACK INTERNATIONALISM

Along with this state-defined racism, the unofficial color bar in the interwar era placed racist restrictions on black people in Britain, and as more African-Caribbean people moved to Britain they developed multiple organizations committed to vigorous anti-racist activism.[65] Harold Moody was one of the leaders of this movement. Born in Kingston, Jamaica, in 1882, Moody was the son of a pharmacist, and the family found a place in the middle class. At the prestigious Wolmer's Free School he was

> educated away from my heritage. My desire then was to have as little as possible to do with my own people and upon Africans I looked down as a species too low in the rank of human development for me in any way to associate with. I was black indeed but I was not African... At heart I really believed I was English.[66]

When Moody won a competitive "island scholarship" to study abroad, he made the intrepid journey to London, where he planned "to become as much English as I could and discard everything Jamaican."[67]

In the autumn of 1904, Moody disembarked at Avonmouth in Bristol. Once the center of the transatlantic slave trade, the city also shattered Moody's confidence in his Englishness. He may not have seen himself as black, but the majority of white

Bristolians did, making it difficult for him to find lodgings. Even after he completed his studies in medicine at King's College London, Moody, keen to stay in England to help support one of his younger brothers who was also a student, looked hard for a job, but regularly received rejections because of his race. When he wanted to marry white English nurse Olive Tranter, some family members accused her of letting the family down, but eventually they gave their blessing. Realizing that his skin color would prevent him from gaining employment, Moody had limited options and decided to establish his own practice in the home he and Olive shared in Peckham. Yet even after years of medical experience and with his established reputation as a respected doctor, the Camberwell Board of Guardians refused him entry to the post of medical officer because "the poor people would not have 'a nigger to attend them.'"[68]

Confronting the color bar became a common rite of passage for the hundreds of predominantly middle-class black and mixed-race colonial students, professionals, activists, and artists from the Caribbean, Africa, and the US who came to call Britain home between the wars. They drew on a legacy of black and pan-African political activism in Britain dating from the late Victorian era. Daily confrontations with racism ignited transformative change and made African-Caribbean people in Britain rethink their racial identity. As black people from different parts of the world began to interact and learn more about each other's culture and history, they came to reject the anti-black and anti-African stereotypes that they had been indoctrinated with, forging instead a racial consciousness of pride. By 1933, Moody began admitting: "I am proud of my British citizenship, but I am still more proud of my colour, and I do not want to feel that my colour is going to rob me of any of the privileges to which I am entitled as a British citizen."[69]

Moody paved the way for the establishment of black-led anti-racist organizations that instilled race pride. In 1931 he formed the League of Coloured Peoples (LCP), one of the first organizations in Britain led by people of African descent that campaigned for the equal rights of people of color. At its core, the LCP aimed to "promote and protect the Social, Educational, Economic and Political Interests of its members; to interest members in the welfare of Coloured Peoples in all parts of the world; to improve relations between the Races; to co-operate and affiliate with organisations sympathetic to Coloured people."[70] It existed alongside other groups such as the West African Students' Union (WASU), the Negro Welfare Association (NWA)—established in 1931 by Arnold Ward, a Barbados-born communist—and the International African Friends of Ethiopia (IAFE), which later developed into the International African Service Bureau (IASB). As the titles here suggest, activism against Britain's color bar was only one item on the agendas. Groups also adopted "black internationalism," creating ties within and beyond the Black Atlantic with black people worldwide. They challenged global inequalities—specifically, racism, colonialism, and fascism—through their organizations and affiliated newspapers that helped disseminate their ideas transnationally. Anti-fascism was an especially important part of these groups' work, especially following Italian leader Benito Mussolini's 1935 invasion of Ethiopia, then one of only two remaining non-European-colonized African states, which galvanized activism across the African diaspora as Ethiopia represented for many the birthplace of African civilization.

African- and African-Caribbean-led organizations and activists used a variety of methods to achieve their aims in Britain. Members delivered fiery speeches to large crowds in Hyde Park and Trafalgar Square or sent letters of protest to MPs and officials at the Colonial Office. Their activism also inspired new novels, plays, and poetry. While the LCP, IAFE, and IASB focused their energies on London, the capital was by no means the only place in Britain where black-led activism thrived. Students and activists collaborated in the universities of Oxford, Cambridge, Edinburgh, and Glasgow, and in cities including Liverpool and Manchester. Organizations in Britain interacted with counterparts in interwar Paris, New York, Chicago, and elsewhere. Furthermore, African-Caribbean people, especially those who shared a radical anti-colonial vision, collaborated with white-led leftist organizations in Britain to challenge not just the color bar but also colonialism, in collaborations that presented both opportunities and challenges.

Dr. Harold Moody, 1930.

One of the leading black nationalist groups of this era was created in Jamaica. In 1914, Jamaicans Amy Ashwood and Marcus Garvey established the Universal Negro Improvement Association and African Communities League (UNIA-ACL), which quickly became one of the largest pan-African organizations of the twentieth century. Established to challenge racism and unite black people living in the diaspora, the UNIA preached the importance of black self-help and race pride and wanted to return black people in the diaspora "Back to Africa." Garvey was born in 1887, and during the 1890s his working-class family faced significant economic hardship. Searching for employment, Garvey worked as a printer's apprentice in Saint Ann before moving to the capital. There, he began to learn more about the burgeoning race consciousness movement espoused by figures such as Robert Love. After a period in Costa Rica and Panama, he ventured to England in 1912, where he collaborated with Dusé Mohamed Ali on the *African Times and Orient Review*. On his return to Jamaica in 1914, Garvey met Amy Ashwood. Born in Port Antonio, Jamaica, Ashwood had also spent some of her upbringing in Panama and was heavily influenced by pan-African ideas. Two years after establishing the UNIA, Garvey decided to relocate to Harlem in New York, where the organization blossomed.

Harlem in the 1920s was fast becoming home to thousands of African-Caribbean migrants. Many developed a new sense of racial consciousness similar to that experienced by African-Caribbean people in Britain, whereby race pride and solidarity with other black people became an important element of defiance against Jim Crow racism.

With the US as its base, the UNIA shaped the growing New Negro movement and the Harlem Renaissance—a vibrant political and cultural response to global anti-black racism. UNIA membership grew to over 6 million, with branches throughout America as well as in Canada, the Caribbean, and Africa. In the

US, leaders wanted to put into motion the "Back to Africa" plan and established the Black Star Line shipping company designed to transport black people back to Africa, although this venture had limited success. It was Ashwood and, later, Garvey's second wife, Jamaican Amy Jacques Garvey, who critically boosted the UNIA's popularity through their involvement with its newspaper, *Negro World*, which shared important stories about black global politics in English, French, and Spanish. Given the UNIA's radicalism, colonial officials were wary of the influence of the publication and went to great lengths to ban its circulation in the Caribbean and Africa.

Although the UNIA sought to liberate and lead those of African descent, the group often fell into the trap of reinforcing Western stereotypes of Africa. For instance, one of the group's aims was "to assist in civilizing the backward tribes of Africa . . . to establish a central nation for the race."[71] UNIA members saw themselves as more civilized than Africans because of their closer contact with the West and Europeans, and in their plans for returning "Back to Africa" they failed to consider the rights of Africans already living on the continent. Other problematic views related to segregation. When Garvey met with Ku Klux Klan leaders who like him supported racial separatism but also openly advocated violence toward black Americans, his followers became disenchanted. US authorities closely monitored Garvey's activities, fearing his subversive tendencies would lead to more racial tensions. A convenient pretext to silence him came in 1925, when Garvey was jailed following his conviction for mail fraud related to shares of the Black Star Line. When he was released in 1927, US authorities hastily deported him back to Jamaica. In 1929 (after another spell in jail, this time for contempt of court), Garvey again tried to spread his message through the press by establishing the *The Black Man: A Monthly Magazine of Negro Thought and Opinion*. In 1935 Garvey, still facing financial troubles, relocated to London. In 1940 he died of a cerebral hemorrhage, but his influence endured.

Garveyite ideas about racial pride and the New Negro movement's emphasis on resistance to racism boldly inspired attacks on Britain's color bar. In the autumn of 1919, Claude McKay arrived in London from New York. He migrated to the US in 1912, the year in which his first poetry collection, *Songs of Jamaica*, was published, to study agriculture at the famous Tuskegee Institute, one of the first educational establishments for Black Americans, led by Black American Booker T. Washington. By 1914 he had moved to New York, where he joined the Industrial Workers of the World (IWW), an inclusive and radical group that brought black, white, male, and female workers together. After the 1919 race riots, McKay took inspiration from the Russian revolution, increasing his defiance against working-class oppression and racism, and gravitated toward pan-Africanism. Seeking refuge from Jim Crow segregation, McKay ventured to Britain. Like Moody, McKay had long dreamed of visiting the motherland and in his 1912 poem "Old England" provided some insight into his hopes and expectations of visiting the capital city's monuments, from St. Paul's Cathedral to Westminster Abbey.[72]

But like Moody, McKay struggled to find housing and was assaulted on the streets. He quickly came to realize that "prejudice against Negroes had become almost congenital."[73] In order to combat British racism, McKay forged links with various figures. He socialized with members of the Bloomsbury set and Fabians at the 1917 Club in Soho; he worked alongside radical feminist suffragette and socialist Sylvia Pankhurst and her party, the Workers' Socialist Federation (WSF), serving as a journalist in its anti-racist newspaper, *Workers' Dreadnought*; and he interacted with other leftists in the International Club, a group he described as "full of excitement, with its dogmatists and doctrinaires of radical left ideas: Socialists, Communists, anarchists, syndicalists, one-big-unionists and trade unionists, soap-boxers, poetasters, scribblers, editors of little radical sheets which flourish in London."[74] McKay remembered being the only African member of the International Club, but later he introduced "a mulatto sailor from Limehouse, a West Indian student from Oxford, a young black minister of the Anglican Church ... a young West Indian doctor from Dulwich ... and a couple of boxers" to the club.[75]

In fact, McKay saw much potential in collaborating with left-wing working-class movements to challenge racism and undermine the racial-caste hierarchy. In December 1919 he wrote a letter to Marcus Garvey: "As I have said before in your paper, radical Negroes should be more interested in the white radical movements. They are supporting our cause, at least in principle. To me they are the great destructive forces *within*, while the subject races are fighting without." McKay was also aware that white radicals could usurp the struggle for racial equality and qualified his argument by admitting: "I don't mean that we should accept them unreservedly and put our cause into their hands ... but at present we meet on common ground against the common enemy. We have a great wall to batter down and while we are working on one side we should hail those who are working on the other."[76]

If joining forces with white radicals was one useful, albeit difficult, approach to combating Britain's color bar, another was Harold Moody's emphasis on a color-blind society and collaboration with white moderates. Moody also became active in interracial organizations committed to improving race relations, such as the Joint Council to Promote Understanding between White and Coloured People in Great Britain. Quaker John Fletcher led the charitable group and Moody acted as vice-chairman. But it was the League of Coloured Peoples to which Moody dedicated the majority of his time and energy. The LCP and its journal, *The*

Keys, came to play a leading role in championing black people's causes in Britain. It supported black British-born residents as well as black colonials from the Caribbean and Africa. The LCP also worked alongside South Asians and Black Americans. Its members spoke out too against the injustices facing the indigenous communities in Australia. Although membership numbered only in the hundreds, the LCP had branches in London, Liverpool, Cardiff, and British Guiana. With his middle-class background, Moody was often welcomed into white liberal spaces and used his influence to lobby the Colonial Office and sympathetic MPs. He also became an important figure for visiting African-Caribbean and African people in London. Moody's Peckham home quickly became a hub for those seeking respite from racism, and he often welcomed lodgers who had struggled to find accommodation, including his fellow Jamaican Una Marson.

Before moving to Britain in 1932, Marson was well-known as a rising poet, playwright, and writer within Kingston's burgeoning literary scene. In 1928 she established *The Cosmopolitan*, a monthly journal that made her the island's first female editor-publisher. When she arrived in London, hoping to advance her literary career, she had a rude awakening. "Once I tried to register for work as a stenographer," Marson recollected, but "one agent told me she didn't register black women because they would have to work in offices with white women. Another agent tried to find me a position and he told me that though my references were excellent firms did not want to employ a black stenographer."[77] Through Moody, Marson became an active member of the LCP, serving as its secretary in 1933 and organizing social and political events. She also wrote in *The Keys*, which published her powerful poetry and editorials.

Through her involvement with the LCP, Marson was also able to develop her playwriting credentials. In November 1933 she directed her play, *At What a Price*, first performed in Kingston at the YMCA Central Club with an all-black and mixed-race cast of LCP members. It received rave reviews and was later shown in the Scala Theatre in the West End, becoming one of the first times that a play written and performed by black and mixed-race colonial people was staged in the capital.[78]

Yet despite the sense of community Marson felt within the LCP, she sometimes felt isolated due to the small number of black Caribbean women in Britain. Marson expressed her feelings of loneliness and isolation in another iconic poem written during her time in Britain, titled "Little Brown Girl." The poem depicts a series of questions that Marson poses to herself about her sense of belonging in England, and a set of questions by a white English observer about why she is in the motherland while conveying British colonial ignorance of the Caribbean's geography and culture. The poem gives voice also to the growth of racial consciousness in the protagonist's apparent pride in her identity that was shaped by the discrimination she experienced. Marson experienced this too. According to her biographer, in London Marson no longer straightened her hair and began to embrace her natural Afro-styled hair.[79] Following the Italian invasion of Ethiopia, Marson became actively involved in anti-fascist activism, serving as secretary to Haile Selassie while he was in exile in London. She returned to Jamaica in 1936 but found herself back in London in late 1938, and in March 1941 was appointed full-time assistant on the "Calling the West Indies" series on BBC radio, becoming one of the first black women to work for the organization.

Amy Ashwood was also politically active in London at this time. Following her split from Garvey, Ashwood moved to the capital and forged ties with West African student groups while also traveling throughout Europe and the Caribbean. She returned to London in the mid-1930s and in 1935 opened the International Afro Restaurant on New Oxford Street and later, with her partner, the Trinidadian actor Sam Manning, the Florence Mills Social Parlour, a nightclub and restaurant named after the famous Black American singer and dancer, which became a social hub for black people in London and an important meeting space for political groups.

Like Marson, events in Ethiopia propelled Ashwood's antifascist activism. Ashwood played a leading role in cofounding the International African Friends of Abyssinia (IAFA, also known as the International African Friends of Ethiopia, IAFE), which aimed "to assist by all means in [its] power, in the maintenance of the territorial integrity and the political independence of Abyssinia."[80] The IAFA had a broad membership. Trinidadian C. L. R. James was chair, Ashwood the treasurer, Peter Milliard from British Guiana and Grenada's T. Marryshow were the vice chairs, and Kenyan student Jomo Kenyatta was honorary secretary. IAFA members compiled pamphlets and gave speeches at Speakers' Corner in Hyde Park to raise public awareness of Ethiopia. Through her role in the group, Ashwood delivered talks to the British Labour Party and the League Against Imperialism (LAI); her activism brought her into contact with Pankhurst, with whom she collaborated.[81]

In 1938, Ashwood closed the Florence Mills club and the following year left London to resume her travels throughout the Caribbean, Europe, and the US. In the summer of 1945, she returned to Britain and chaired a session at the fifth Pan-African Congress in Manchester. It was here that she famously declared: "Very much has been written and spoken of the Negro, but for some reason very little has been said about the black woman. She has been shunted into the social background to be a childbearer. This has been principally her lot."[82]

Another leading male pan-Africanist Ashwood worked alongside was Trinidadian George Padmore.[83] Born in 1902 or 1903 as Malcolm Nurse, he began writing articles for the communist *Daily Worker* under the name George Padmore in 1928. The following year, he journeyed to Moscow and was appointed to lead the Negro Bureau of the Red International of Labour Unions and organized the first International Conference of Negro Workers in 1930 in Hamburg. Hitler's rise to power shaped Padmore's desire to leave the northern port city, and after voicing criticism of German colonialism in its African colonies, Padmore was deported to Britain. Around this time Padmore had grown disillusioned with what he saw as the lack of interest in African liberation shown by the Comintern (an international organization created in 1919 and led by the Communist Party of the Soviet Union that was committed to advancing world communism), and in 1933 he resigned from his role in communist activism. By 1935 Padmore had made London his home and become involved in black radical politics.

George Padmore.

In 1935 Padmore joined the IAFA and, like others involved in the group, began to identify the direct link between fascism and colonialism, once observing that "the fight against fascism cannot be separated from the right of all colonial peoples and subject races to Self-Determination."[84] A prolific writer who described the British Empire as "the worse racket yet invented by man," Padmore authored numerous works, including *The Life and Struggles of Negro Toilers* (1931), *How Britain Rules Africa* (1936), and *Africa and World Peace* (1937).[85] When the IAFA expanded in 1937, he took the helm of its new organization, the International African Service Bureau (IASB), which supported "the demands of Africans and other colonial people for democratic rights, civil liberties and self-determination."[86]

Padmore's close friend C. L. R. James was also involved with the IASB and arrived in London in 1932. James, like Moody and McKay before him, had long held excitement about what life would be like in the imperial metropolis. In his early remarks about life in London he too observed the nuances of the color bar, noting:

> The average Englishman in London, is, on the surface, quite polite. Furthermore, you will make friends with certain people or even certain families and they will stick by the average coloured man and even quarrel with some of their friends who treat him in any out-of-the-way manner, and generally prove themselves staunch with a staunchness that is particularly English. But nevertheless the average man in London is eaten up with colour prejudice.[87]

His experiences led him to collaborate with others from the Caribbean.

Having Britain as their base provided these Caribbean-born activists and their organizations with a relative degree of freedom with which to directly challenge anti-black racism and colonialism.

Back in the Caribbean colonies, the authorities were more wary of activists who might cause unrest than those in Britain, where colonial structures were more intact and instances of resistance relatively small in number. At the same time, in the Caribbean, laborers adopted different tactics to challenge racist economic inequality than their middle-class compatriots in Britain. In some colonies the labor rebellions spawned island-wide nationalism, the leaders of which would soon replace white elites and thereby reconfigure the racial-caste order. Their actions would not go unnoticed by middle-class Caribbean activists in Britain, showing again the close entanglements with Caribbean-led resistance.

WORKERS' REVOLT

In the 1930s, protests and riots swept across various British Caribbean colonies.[88] Workers' plights deepened with the Great Depression. Unemployment and underemployment reached new depths, exacerbated by the return of African-Caribbean migrants from Latin America following anti-immigrant legislation that excluded them from jobs. Urbanization was on the rise too, as workers from rural areas moved to capital cities searching for employment. Slums emerged, with overcrowded housing and poor sanitation causing additional public health problems. Critic of colonial rule William Macmillan published *Warning from the West Indies* in 1936, in which he astutely described conditions in the Caribbean that "tell a tale of poverty so profound as to give little warrant for the assumption that colonies are a source of great profit to the possessing country."[89]

Resentment of economic oppression and racist discrimination flourished in this context. Garvey's race-conscious message of self-help and pan-Africanism motivated many Caribbean people to see their predicament as linked to struggles facing people of

African descent across the world. Events in Ethiopia, especially, helped inspire new religious ideas in Jamaica. When Ras Tafari was made emperor of Ethiopia and took the name Haile Selassie in November 1930, some in Jamaica saw him as a messiah. In the struggling areas of Kingston, many began preaching about the physical and spiritual return to Africa and opposed slave-like conditions for the poor, which shaped the movement of Rastafarianism.

The first disturbances, strikes, and petitions of the interwar period began in British Honduras in 1934, where the colony's economy centred on the export of forest products such as logwood and mahogany. In 1935 labor rebellion and riots erupted elsewhere, in St. Kitts, St. Vincent, St. Lucia, Trinidad, Barbados, British Guiana, and Antigua. These actions in the Caribbean reveal how working-class laborers were the leading edge of protest in the Caribbean but not necessarily in Britain, which had a stronger black middle-class dimension. It is evidence, again, of how different the racial-caste hierarchy looked and was experienced in Britain and the Caribbean.

Jamaica—which, given its larger size, and although economically waning in its significance to Britain, was still seen as an important Caribbean colony—saw some of the largest strikes in the region. In 1935 they began with banana workers and soon spread to dockworkers and other laborers. By June 1936, the unemployed were leading hunger marches in Kingston. Nascent nationalism shaped worker unrest, with one newspaper sympathetic to Garveyism in 1936 arguing that: "the whites today [are] . . . now fully aware of the mistake of their ancestors but are now powerless. The Blacks are not so powerless, for they are in the majority . . . Arise Jamaicans from your slumber and let your slogan be, 'Jamaica for Jamaicans.'"[90]

In the spring of 1938, unrest started at the Frome estate in western Jamaica following disputes over workers' wages.

Feeling frustrated, workers attacked the pay officer's windows, and clerks responded by "bolting" them—firing warning shots. Over the next days, more violence erupted. *The Daily Gleaner*, the island's leading newspaper, noted: "widespread violence stalked the little square at Frome, the crowd hurling missiles, breaking windows, and doors, wielding dangerous weapons, causing officials of the estate to take cover, and even injuring a policeman."[91] The police opened fire on the crowd, and casualties, at that point, were four dead, seventeen wounded; over ninety were arrested.[92]

In Kingston on May 11, around a hundred unemployed workers marched to the legislature headquarters asking for work. Days later, workers at the United Fruit Company's wharf in Kingston walked out. Others were inspired to act, with sanitation workers striking for higher wages. Soon after, tramcar operators, city cleaners, bus workers, and shirt manufacturers were also protesting.[93] On Empire Day, crowds gathered and once again faced a large police presence. The police opened fire, killing a mother and her son.[94]

During the disturbances, Norman Manley entered the fray, agreeing to mediate between employers and employees. After the First World War, Manley had completed his studies, returned home, and become a prominent barrister on the island. Members of the political elites, such as the governor Edward Denham, hoped Manley could help restore calm. Manley called for the creation of a labor committee to represent workers and for the release of jailed agitators.

After consultation with workers the strikes ended, and one of the most prominent agitators and labor leaders, William Alexander Bustamante (a cousin of Manley's), led efforts to bring workers together. In 1939 several unions he was involved in united as part of the Bustamante Industrial Trade Union (BITU). Meanwhile, Manley's exposure to the crisis on the island spurred his political ambitions, and in September 1938 he established the left-leaning People's National Party (PNP), which spearheaded calls for self-government. Bustamante used the BITU to create the PNP's opposition, the center-right Jamaica Labour Party (JLP), inaugurating party politics in Jamaica.

Labor disturbances did not occur in every Caribbean colony, but where they did, it shook the colonial edifice and displayed the galvanizing impact of workers' power. The unrest increased calls for the creation of trade unions, but events in Jamaica, especially, prompted calls for a Royal Commission to investigate conditions in the region.

The commission, led by Lord Moyne, was intended to show people in the Caribbean that Britain did care about the crises. Instead, its all-white composition led to protests by the International African Service Bureau, which argued that the commission's slant toward conservatives and lack of Africans or members of African descent "can inspire no initial confidence in the success of its efforts."[95] The IASB went further, declaring:

> The Royal Commission is a bluff. The Government knows the condition of the people. Commissions, Royal or otherwise, have reported it over and over again. Why is nothing done? Because the white officials are the friends of the white capitalists; by means of dividends and large salaries, golf, tennis and whisky, bravely bearing the white man's burden.[96]

The IASB also called out the ways in which colonial elites captured black "intelligentsia": by "giving them jobs, O.B.Es and even knighthoods, and inviting them to dinner the whites create some local support for themselves and continue to oppress the people."[97] The IASB's fears about the commissioners' narrow mindsets proved prescient. When testimony was given by

Caribbean people, especially those who were mixed-race or black, the commissioners often misunderstood or simply ignored them, revealing the lack of interest many had in understanding the complexity of the Caribbean.

Following testimony from Caribbean people in Britain and in the colonies during their tour in 1938 and 1939, the commissioners' report showed, in the words of Colonial Secretary Malcolm MacDonald, that the region faced "deplorable standards of health and housing, and in social conditions generally, among the working population in the West Indies."[98] But rather than coming to terms with the role of colonialism in creating these dire problems, the report of the West India Royal Commission blamed poor conditions on Caribbean people and culture. In the commissioners' view, the root causes of social problems were high rates of illegitimacy, widespread promiscuity, and unstable family formations, with absent fathers and female-headed households. Blaming family structures rather than colonialism and anti-black racism for problems soon became a popular trope and introduced narratives of the unstable black family and culture that circulated widely in the Caribbean, US, Europe, and Britain. It is evidence, too, of how significant the Caribbean was in the inauguration of this pernicious, ubiquitous narrative of blaming racism on those that experience it the most; of arguing that personal pathologies rather than historical injustice and economic inequalities are the most powerful force behind racism.

Although completed in 1939, the report's negative findings were not made public until the end of the Second World War. Prime Minister Neville Chamberlain was deeply concerned that the report could "inflict serious damage on our war effort."[99] Before the full report was made public, a summary of its recommendations for change was dispatched—which included improvements in social welfare, the creation of trade unions, increased self-government, and universal suffrage—and this summary gradually wended its way through the Caribbean in the 1940s and '50s.

Despite these recommendations and the provision of financial assistance, albeit meager, those at the bottom of the racial-caste hierarchy were not vastly better-off; however, in the aftermath of the 1930s disturbances, attitudes were different: workers realized the power they had to challenge colonial inequalities. And white elites were beginning to glean the shift in power relations. With workers voicing more nationalist sentiment and turning to Caribbean-born leaders to represent their material and political interests, a radical transfer of power would commence, as black and mixed-race middle-class Caribbean men replaced white elites at the top of the region's racial-caste hierarchy.

The First World War and its aftermaths revealed the fractures within the empire forged by the racial-caste hierarchy. Many, but by no means all, people in the Caribbean saw the conflict as an opportunity to display their loyalty to empire and share in the supposed equality and justice that they had been schooled to believe lay at the heart of colonialism. But serving alongside British soldiers and in British units exposed Caribbean men to combined personal and structural racism, revealing in sharp relief the distance between the ostensible ideals of the British Empire and the reality. After the war, white workers in Britain, equal in status to their Caribbean counterparts, would riot at black men and women's exercise of their colonial rights to live and work in the metropole. These events would mobilize Caribbean activists, who increasingly linked their struggles against the racial-caste hierarchy with other people of African descent across the globe, and to other political movements such as anti-fascism. This period revealed not just the false promises of empire but also the class dimensions of colonialism.

"FIGHTING TO PROVE"

After 1939, the hypocrisies of empire would become more visible and make the empire far more vulnerable to challenges from Caribbean people in Britain as well as workers who stayed in the region. As unrest in the Caribbean simmered in 1939, global war was again on the horizon.

6

"One united family"
The Second World War

As news spread that Britain was at war, twenty-two-year-old Charles Arundel "Joe" Moody made his way to Whitehall's recruitment office hoping to enlist. To his dismay, Moody found he was ineligible. The color bar that his father, Harold Moody, was campaigning against was a crucial aspect of the British army's recruitment policy. In 1938, the Army Council restricted "all army recruitment to men of pure European descent," and a similar color bar operated in the RAF and Royal Navy.[1]

Angry and frustrated at his son's treatment, Harold Moody mobilized the League of Coloured Peoples, International African Service Bureau, and West African Students' Union for support. Taking his complaint directly to the Colonial Office, Moody and his allies pressured for policy change. On October 19, 1939, the Colonial Office's response was to issue new rules granting commissions in the armed forces for men of non-European descent from the colonies.[2] Although Joe Moody was accepted into the ranks, serving in the Queen's Own Royal West Kent Regiment from April 1940, and would later receive a commission, his father remained unsatisfied. This right only applied in emergency conditions, for example during war.[3] In a letter to Colonial Secretary Malcolm MacDonald in December 1939, Harold Moody had forcefully argued:

> We are merely seeking to establish our spiritual, cultural and mental equality, as members of the British Empire, with every other member of the Empire and to embody the term "British Citizen" with some meaning and some reality . . . and that no discrimination whatsoever should be made against us, except on the grounds of character and qualification.[4]

In the Second World War, as in the First, black Britons and other people of color who were colonial subjects continued to struggle against an imperial state that refused to abandon racist policies. Although radical organizations and activists in Britain, the US, and the Caribbean opposed Caribbean involvement in the war on the grounds of ongoing colonial inequalities, many in the region wanted to defend Britain and its colonies. The desire of black Caribbean citizens to fight for the British Empire was answered with humiliating reminders of the racial-caste hierarchy. Even when black Britons and colonial subjects were admitted into the armed forces, many were met with racist abuse. Black American soldiers stationed at British bases had similar experiences. Imperial service did not blunt anti-black policies or public sentiments.

Within official circles scientific racism and eugenics—at the heart of the Aryan supremacy underpinning Germany's National Socialism—became unpopular. Yet racism remained and was made compatible with denunciations of racism elsewhere. With Britain's growing black population, white Britons could in the same breath deplore racism and project particularly hostile attitudes toward black people—voicing, for instance, an aversion to interracial relationships, particularly the pairing of white women with black men, which became a central issue during the war. Worries about mixed-race children—"Brown Babies," as they were called—illustrates just how much the war racialized white women's bodies, in particular. Their ability to reproduce whiteness became critical to ensuring that Britain did not become a "mongrel" nation, especially in the wake of a world war that would leave the country on the brink of economic collapse and spark real fears for the future of Britain's empire and global influence. But attempts to prevent interracial relationships would once again prove futile, and when Britain passed a Nationality Act in 1948, it unintentionally started the country down a path to becoming even more multiracial.

During the Second World War, American influence over the Anglophone Caribbean increased, due to the region's strategic importance; its vital sea routes linked the Atlantic to the Pacific via the Panama Canal, and its reservoirs of oil and bauxite were critical to US economic and political interests. The US negotiated deals with Britain that extended its military presence in the Caribbean, which had long been part of American imperialism. US forces had previously occupied Haiti (during the years 1915–34) and the Dominican Republic (1916–24) when both countries' political and economic instabilities threatened the US. In addition to their control in Puerto Rico, the US also gained more territory in the region through their purchase of the Virgin Islands from Denmark in 1917, which became the United States Virgin Islands (USVI). The presence of white US troops in the British Caribbean would come to play an important role in undermining white supremacy, because when black locals saw white Americans in drunken brawls or performing manual labor usually assigned to dark-skinned members on the bottom rung of the racial-caste hierarchy, "a revolution in sentiment and mentality" ensued that weakened white prestige.[5] At the same time, the presence of Black American troops in the Caribbean exposed as hypocritical white elite assertions that their policies and attitudes toward people of color had nothing to do with race. The larger US influence in the British Caribbean precipitated by the war would only increase in the coming decades and even grow to supplant Britain's.

The Second World War shaped concurrent attempts to reassert and undo the racial-caste hierarchy. The British government, along with white colonial leaders in the Caribbean, condemned racism in public while continuing to assert anti-black racism in private. For African-Caribbean men and women, their participation in the war effort continued to challenge their perceived inferiority and provoked reconsiderations of their attitude toward colonialism and their relationship to the motherland.

In the aftermath of the war, worsening economic conditions in the Caribbean and changes to colonial legislation in Britain would increase Caribbean migration to the metropole. The powerful combination of both Caribbean migration to Britain and the war would thoroughly transform the formal end of empire.

BLACK TROOPS IN BRITAIN

Even as the Caribbean was reeling from the 1930s disturbances, they loudly expressed patriotic loyalty at the news that Britain was at war again. Once more the Caribbean gifted funds, raising upward of £2 million to support the motherland.[5] Even those calling on the colonial government for reform briefly set aside their demands and fully backed Britain and the empire. As in 1914, many reasons stirred people to want to serve. For many, like Jamaican Dudley Thompson, Hitler's explicit racism inspired them to enlist. Thompson remembered flipping through *Mein Kampf* and becoming "angry and stung into activity."[7] Others joined due to patriotism, or to earn a better wage. Some black Caribbean men, like those in 1914, were so eager to fight that they made their way directly to Britain to enlist. Thompson, for instance, traveled to Britain as a civilian and applied to join the Royal Air Force. "One of the questions on the form which I had to fill out," Thompson remembered, "was 'Are you of pure European descent?' I answered 'yes.' When the recruiting officer queried me—thinking I hadn't understood the question—I challenged him to prove otherwise by a blood test. I think he gave up in disgust or frustration."[8]

The War Office was reluctant to include African-Caribbean men and argued with those in the Colonial Office who knew that continued exclusion would only inflame unrest in the already unruly colonies and give credence to accusations of racism when a war was being fought ostensibly against fascism and racism. They were right. Thompson remembered that in Trinidad demonstrations erupted due to Britain's "hesitation . . . to let Black men enlist in numbers to fight the war."[9]

Usually, African-Caribbean men were admitted only in response to protests such as those started in Trinidad or by Harold Moody, or when manpower reached critically low levels and there were heavy losses. When they were eventually allowed entry, a small but significant number moved to Britain. Around one thousand African-Caribbean men worked in munitions factories in the north of England, and 1,200 British Honduran foresters labored in Scotland.[10] By around 1944, there were ten thousand Caribbean men in the RAF, 1,100 in the British army, and two thousand in the Royal Navy with men serving in noncombat and a minority in combat roles. In addition, some men joined the merchant navy, and there were Caribbean men serving in the Royal West African Frontier Force and the Indian army as well as some in Canadian forces.[11]

Although included in the war effort, Caribbean men, especially those in Britain, experienced unequal treatment. One Caribbean veteran quipped: "Show me a black serviceman who claimed not to have encountered any prejudice in the UK during the War and I'll show you a liar!"[12] Meanwhile, Cy Grant from British Guiana, who served in the RAF, "discovered through a friend that there were problems with the English aircrew not wanting to fly with black pilots."[13] While Grant remembered that the British civilians he encountered "were generally friendly," he "occasionally heard a child say, 'Look, Mummy, a black man!' That always brought me up sharp. Before coming to England I didn't think of myself as black—a quite salutary shock! I was to realize that I was defined in a certain way 'at home' and another in the 'mother country.'"[14] Growing up in British Guiana, Grant's middle-class, mixed-race identity derived from his parents' African, Asian, and European heritage, and in school he remembered that although he sat next to "boys of African, Chinese, Indian or Portuguese descent, the education we received implied that everything black was inferior."[15] In Britain, Grant, like African-Caribbean people of the interwar era, developed a racial consciousness that led him to embrace his blackness. Meanwhile another RAF serviceman, who joined from Barbados, commented on the "silent, subtle and obviously racial prejudice and indecent display of superiority from people of British nationality."[16]

Those from the Caribbean were being allowed entry into war work and the RAF, but there remained a desire for a Caribbean contingent to experience action on the battlefield. Since the outbreak of the conflict, the War Office had remained steadfastly opposed to including African-Caribbean soldiers on the ground, though the Colonial Office persistently made a case for the inclusion of a Caribbean regiment.

Despite lingering opposition, in December 1943 the War Cabinet approved the creation of a new unit. The 1st Battalion of the Caribbean Regiment comprised fifty-four officers and 1,159 other ranks. Senior officers were white while junior officers could be mixed-race.[17] The regiment trained first in Virginia in the US, where officials worked hard to ensure they did not flout Jim Crow segregation, advising Caribbean men that "on no account must there be any attempt at friendship with a white woman whether she is willing or not."[18] Once they had completed their training in the US, debates raged about where the regiment should go next. It was sent to Naples in July 1944, though only to continue its training, as resistance lingered over the men's involvement in combat, and for further training in Gaza, before being transferred to Egypt.[19]

Besides the British army, RAF, and the Caribbean Regiment, Caribbean men served in other capacities in the war effort. They worked as agricultural laborers overseas, with thousands sent to the US and six thousand sent to Panama.[20]

West Indian troops Sapper Hibbert (*left*) and Corporal Simmons, both from Jamaica, serving with the Royal Engineers at Clitheroe, Lancashire, 1941.

For many Caribbean men, involvement in the war had fundamental political consequences. In Cy Grant's case it inspired anti-colonialism. During a bombing mission to Germany's Ruhr, Grant's plane was shot down over the Netherlands and, following capture and interrogation, he was sent to a German POW camp for two years. While imprisoned, Grant reflected on his future.

His wartime experiences led him to want to contribute to change in the Caribbean: "I decided then, that I would study law, because I wanted to go back to the Caribbean. My ambition was to help get the British out of the West Indies."[21]

Likewise, for Thompson, the war increased his determination to push for Caribbean self-government. During the war, he wrote:

> I was coming into contact for the first time with West Indian, African, and Black American soldiers, and with students, writers and blue-collar workers from the British colonies . . . Being in England, fighting and suffering with her during the war, had truly opened the eye of the colonials . . . we felt we had more than proved our equality and had earned the chance for self-government.[22]

These political goals fostered an expansive sense of Caribbean nationalism, which undermined colonialism and shaped postwar political reforms in the Caribbean.

Caribbean women joined their male counterparts in contributing to the war effort and faced both anti-black racism and sexism. Women's organizations in Jamaica and elsewhere across the region played important roles in helping fundraise and organize supplies.[23] Labor shortages and female unemployment led to their acceptance in 1943, with some serving in the Women's Auxiliary Air Force (WAAF), but the majority participated in the Auxiliary Territorial Service (ATS). Including women in ATS units at a local level in the Caribbean proved unproblematic, and many of the women involved thought the opportunity valuable. Around three hundred women in the ATS remained based in the Caribbean.[24] But the situation for Caribbean women in overseas ATS branches was different. Bermudian Lobelia Curtis applied to join the ATS in Britain, and her acceptance was based on the

"ONE UNITED FAMILY"

false assumption that she was white. When it emerged that Curtis was black, the War Office tried but failed to exclude her.[25]

A group of West Indian women recruited to join the ATS (Auxiliary Territorial Service) on the way to training camp, UK, 1943.

In late October 1943, Curtis and twenty-nine other women arrived in Guildford, Surrey, for training. This group of thirty were the first out of one hundred recruits who would enter the ATS.[26] Most came from the middle classes and were selected due to their professional backgrounds and training in administrative roles. Odessa Gittens from Barbados, who came to Britain as part of the first recruits, spoke fondly of her time in the ATS, remembering the sense of being "one united family behind Britain."[27] Although small numbers of black Caribbean women were allowed to go to Britain, not one was permitted to serve in the ATS branch in Washington DC. The two hundred Caribbean women who did go were all white—a decision designed to not offend American authorities who insisted on racial segregation and further evidence of the entangled ties of the racial-caste hierarchy and Jim Crow.[28]

The anti-black racism that underpinned Caribbean involvement in the war, especially for those based in Britain, was linked closely to anxieties about interracial relationships. In the context of war, the patrolling of social and sexual boundaries to maintain deeply held yet unstable and contrived boundaries between white and black became all the more "vital" to the preservation of the order—showing again how enforcement of the racial-caste hierarchy seeped into intimate spaces. For instance, in 1941 around nine hundred men from British Honduras went to Scotland as part of the forestry unit, where they met challenging conditions. Sharing accommodation in meager huts, some fell ill and when they could not work were refused pay. Others, however, received a warm welcome from locals. Logger Theo Lambey remembered that "The people [were] friendly and accommodating. In the public houses, we were treated like special guests. They were really good to us."[29] White women were among the welcoming locals, and some developed relationships with the Hondurans—alarming a local landowner, the Duke of Buccleuch, especially, who had allowed the Hondurans to work on his land only because their accommodation was well away from the locals. The duke was so troubled by the idea of interracial relationships that he wrote to the government asking to bring in measures to prevent them. Harold Macmillan, then undersecretary of state for the colonies, replied that, although the Hondurans' presence could have "some undesirable results ... All we can do is to mitigate the evil."[30] By 1943, there were four marriages between Hondurans and white British women.[31] That year, the government decided to disband the unit and gave the Hondurans two options: return home or find work in Britain. Half voted to stay, intending to find jobs and earn good wages, but many struggled to find employment.

Apprehension about interracial relationships intensified with the arrival of Black American soldiers, who were part of the larger US presence of GIs in Britain during the war. The government feared that they would consort with white women and that their presence would exacerbate racial tensions and tried, unsuccessfully, to limit the number of arrivals. War officials in Britain and the US were so concerned that they designed a guidance document approved by the home secretary and secretary of state for war. The document encouraged serving Britons to "be friendly and sympathetic towards coloured American troops—but remember that they are not accustomed in their own country to close and intimate relationships with white people."[32] It addressed the largest official concern: "for a white woman to go about in the company of a Negro American is likely to lead to controversy and ill-feeling"—advising: "This does not mean that friendly hospitality in the home or in social gatherings need be ruled out, though in such cases care should be taken not to invite white and coloured American troops at the same time."[33]

White Britons considered Black Americans a novelty, especially when they were stationed in areas that did not have a visible black British population, and warmly accepted them—on occasion even fostering close friendships. When Black American GIs faced confrontation from their white compatriots, white Britons sometimes sided with them. Yet when it came to interracial relationships, they could be just as racist as white Americans. And when black men and white women came together in social venues likes bars, pubs, and dance halls, some white Americans objected. Sexual competition between black and white Americans was rife. Writing in the *Tribune*, George Orwell remarked that some white GIs were unhappy with the British because, as one put it, "the girls here walk out with niggers."[34]

Mass Observation, established in 1937, conducted academic social research among a white, liberal, and middle-class demographic, and in 1939 and 1943 organized what were called Race Directives. These monthly questionnaires asked respondents for their views on different national and racial groups. The directives did not necessarily influence policy but offered insights into the persistent belief in essential differences between black and white people that underpinned hostility toward interracial sex.[35] One observer remarked:

> I consider negroes on the whole to be at an earlier stage of civilisation than white races, and because of that, I consider that except in the cases of exceptionally advanced negroes, association between the negro and white races cannot be on an exactly level footing but rather that of a schoolmaster and middle school or senior boy.[36]

Others made frequent comparisons between black people and animals, with one respondent remarking: "Would I willingly share a bedroom, a dinner-table, or a change of clothes with a negro? No, no more than I would admit my dog to such intimacy."[37] For some, their antipathy toward interracial relationships called them to action. One frankly stated: "I could cheerfully clout coloured men I see about with white women."[38]

White women also voiced opposition to interracial relationships. A letter to the editor of the *Huddersfield Daily Examiner*, written by a white woman, revealed another level of repulsion toward interracial romance, with the author admitting:

> I am thoroughly disgusted with my own sex. It is no use . . . [making] excuses for our girls . . . my girls three of them workers, shrink with horror and disgust over this subject, and they aren't prudes, either. They will have a bit of fun anytime, but I don't call that kind of pleasure "fun." I call it degradation of the worst type.[39]

Such views speak to what historian Wendy Webster has called "sexual patriotism," which inspired "censure of women's relationships with white enemies and white and black allies" by women themselves, men, and the larger state.[40]

Most of the opposition to interracial relationships related to the union of white women and black men. When asked about the pairing of white men and black women, Mass Observation reported that it was "hardly ever mentioned and aroused no strong feeling," which serves as a reflection of the importance surrounding white women reproducing whiteness that underpinned hostile attitudes toward interracial sex.[41] It also shows the patriarchal racist standard that white men should have unrestrained (including forced) access to all women, built on centuries of sexual racial hierarchy.

Black men who engaged in sexual relations with white women not only often brushed shoulders with violent opposition but in some instances came close to death. This was the case with a thirty-year-old Black American GI, Corporal Leroy Henry. Tried and found guilty by a US army court martial in Wiltshire of raping a married white woman, Irene Maude Lilley, in May 1944 Henry was sentenced to death by hanging.[42] During the trial, Henry claimed that they had previously had consensual paid-for sex. On the night of the alleged rape, Henry stated that Lilley had asked him to come to her house and then had tried to solicit more money from him for sex that he did not have.[43] When Henry refused to pay, she threatened to get revenge. During the trial, Lilley stereotyped Henry in racist and sexist terms, conjuring up the image of the hypersexual and brute black man. The knife that Lilley said was used against her was never found, nor were there bruises consistent with the alleged crime on her body.

The severity of the sentence, the scarce evidence, and Lilley's sullied reputation elevated the case to the national and international spotlight. Many were sympathetic to Henry given the conditions under which his "guilt" had been ascertained. Following his arrest, Henry was interrogated and forced to sign a confession, even though he had limited education, could not read adequately, and lacked any legal representation. Henry later wrote a second statement professing his innocence.[44] Broad British opinion objected to the verdict and the harsh punishment, and civilians started a petition that garnered thirty-three thousand signatures calling for Henry's acquittal.[45] The case galvanized the LCP, who came to Henry's defense, as did the US civil rights organization, the National Association for the Advancement of Colored People, which had been fighting legal battles against racism for three decades by this point. After a second review of the case, Henry was acquitted. He was not the only Black American man found guilty of rape with scant evidence. It was widely known that black men faced harsher punishments for sexual abuse than their white counterparts.

Although actively discouraged, small numbers of black American men and white British women did form relationships, resulting in the birth of mixed-race children. The LCP estimated in 1946 that there were 553 "Brown Babies," offspring of black GIs and white British women. By 1948 the number had risen to 775.[46] Mixed-race children and their white mothers often faced the stigma of illegitimacy as well as racial prejudice.[47] Some women were ostracized by their families and local communities. Others faced barriers to marrying their black partners, due to US anti-miscegenation laws. Some of these children lived with their mothers or other family relations, in cases where women had committed infidelity; others were placed in children's homes or put up for adoption.

US GIS IN THE CARIBBEAN

As racial divisions were widening in Britain, they were as well in the Caribbean, especially in places with a visible US presence, where racial-caste hierarchy and Jim Crow policies worked together to further entrench white supremacy in the colonies.

In September 1940, Britain and the US struck the Anglo-American "destroyers for bases" deal, by which the US provided Britain with fifty destroyers in exchange for the right to establish bases on ninety-nine-year rent-free leases in St. Lucia, British Guiana, Bermuda, Antigua, Jamaica, the Bahamas, and Trinidad, all of which were manned by US troops. American garrisons were also present in US-controlled Puerto Rico, the US Virgin Islands, Guantánamo Bay in Cuba, and the Dutch Antilles, with US personnel increased in the Caribbean when they formally entered the war in December 1941. Further US encroachment in the Caribbean came with the formation of the Anglo-American Commission of March 1942, an advisory body established to improve social and economic cooperation and research. Nonetheless, the presence of US soldiers increased the number of violent clashes between white and black American troops and black Caribbean people in the British colonies. Again, fears about interracial relationships caused major problems for colonial officials who found themselves in a complicated position. As they maintained the racial-caste order, they had little ground to defend colonial citizens against Jim Crow racism and feared that even if they tried to, they could alienate their important ally.

US troops numbered the most in Trinidad—somewhere in the region of twenty thousand.[48] Trinidad was strategically important due to its location and because it was home to a large oil refinery. While most US troops were white, in May 1942 the 99th Coastal Artillery Regiment, comprising 2,484 Black American soldiers, landed on the island.[49]

Fears that Black Americans and African-Trinidadians would realize the shared hierarchical system they lived under and rebel together—or compare themselves and in response resent each other and clash—worried those who had already spent the last few years trying to quell unrest in the colony. A sense of British unease about Black Americans in Trinidad is evident in a US War Department memo: "The local authorities try to keep the native populations contented with a low standard of living. Obviously, a situation will be created which will result in an unfavourable comparison which is bound to cause local disturbances."[50]

Colonial officials were right to be anxious. In some parts of the Caribbean, the creation of US bases led to eviction notices for local residents, which caused understandable bitterness. Although the bases provided Caribbean people with the opportunity for employment, discord occurred with US soldiers on racial grounds. From October 1941 to January 1942, the War Cabinet heard reports of fights, some of which had led to fatalities.[51] Wary of offending the US and knowing full well the racism inherent in colonialism, colonial officials did little to defend colonial subjects.

REDEFINING MULTIRACIAL BRITAIN

In the aftermath of the demands of total war and imperial mobilization, anti-black racism remained a powerful force beyond 1945. In July of that year the Labour Party won the election and encouraged Europeans to join Britons in the herculean task of rebuilding the nation. Irish immigrants also came to Britain in search of work. African-Caribbean men and women were drawn to migration due to economic conditions in the Caribbean that had only worsened during the war, with the cost of living having doubled. In Jamaica, unemployment crept above 25 percent of the working population.[52] Many knew about labor shortages in Britain, and this pushed them to make the journey to the motherland. In 1947, the SS *Almanzora* and the SS *Ormonde* brought hundreds of people from the Caribbean to Britain (arriving at

Southampton and Liverpool respectively). Then on June 22, 1948, the *Empire Windrush* docked at Tilbury in Essex.

This caught the British government somewhat by surprise. As early as March 1948, the Colonial Office had proposed a scheme to recruit colonials similar to European migrant-worker schemes. They envisaged a small group of Caribbean workers who would be put to work in specific sectors, under the control of the Colonial Office. But before a decision had been made, around five hundred people from the Caribbean came to Britain of their own volition. The *Empire Windrush* included men and women from Jamaica, Trinidad, Burma, Mexico, Gibraltar, and elsewhere.[53] Around half of the Caribbean men on board had been in Britain during the war. Indo-Caribbean people were on board too. Some of the ship's famous passengers included singer Lord Kitchener and his fellow calypsonians Lord Woodbine and Lord Beginner (calypso being a creolized form of popular music originating in Trinidad), as well as singer Mona Baptiste.

The *Empire Windrush* arriving at Tilbury docks, having sailed from Australia via Jamaica, June 21, 1948.

The Labour government reacted to the *Empire Windrush* as mentioned earlier—with ambivalence. From the outset those on board were seen principally as unemployed people who intended to leech off the British state. However unwanted, the government did recognize that those from the Caribbean had the right to reside in Britain. "They are British subjects (some, at any rate, ex-servicemen)," commented Lord Listowel, minister of state for colonial affairs, "and we can neither prevent their landing nor compel their departure. We must therefore see that the smoothest possible arrangements are made to minimise the risk of any undesirable incidents or complaints that the Mother Country does not bother to look after coloured Colonial British Subjects."[54] Initially, those in the Ministry of Labour argued that as many had come to Britain at their own expense they should not expect assistance, but the Colonial Office disagreed, and eventually the labor ministry helped secure temporary accommodation and employment for them. Some in government hoped that no more would follow in their footsteps. In fact, the government had tried in vain to prevent the ship from coming. But rather than an end to Caribbean migration, the *Empire Windrush* was the leading edge of Caribbean migration, abetted by the passing of the British Nationality Act in 1948.

The act's origins stemmed from Canadian legislation, namely the Canadian Citizenship Act of 1946. This piece of legislation made British subjecthood secondary to Canadian national status, which concerned British colonial and government officials who felt that British subject status was being demoted. When Australia expressed its intention to pass similar legislation, the British government realized that unless British nationality was reinstated, those in the predominantly white settler Dominions, who had long been considered part of "Greater Britain," might forge their own distinct national identities, and thus weaken British global dominance. The 1948 Nationality Act equalized British subjects in the metropole, the Dominions, and the colonies, through the creation of the new category of "Citizen of the United Kingdom and Colonies" (CUKC).

After the act came into effect on January 1, 1949, all CUKCs had the right to live and work in Britain. The act fortified imperial citizenship as part of an effort to shore up the empire and maintain British global supremacy—deemed essential not just because of the actions taken by the Dominions, but also by increasing anti-colonial nationalism in Asia and Africa and the US's emergence as a superpower.

Although ministers were aware of the migratory consequences of the act, they envisioned, as Conservative MP Quintin Hogg put it, "free trade in citizens, that people would come and go."[55] Thousands of Caribbean, South Asian, and African colonial subjects who fell under the CUKC category did come to Britain, and the majority chose not to leave.

While the 1948 act conferred universal imperial citizenship and was legally inclusive, the larger migration of black and Asian colonial citizens had the unintended consequence of increasing Britain's identity as a multiracial country. And this provoked widespread outcry among politicians. As one group of MPs put it, "an influx of coloured people domiciled here is likely to impair the harmony, strength and cohesion of our public and social life and to cause discord and unhappiness among all concerned."[56]

Unrest did in fact follow. In late July and early August 1948 in Liverpool, a group of white Britons attacked an Indian restaurant and the homes and social spaces frequented by colonial men and women, many of whom had been involved in the war effort. The racist violence reprised the 1919 race riots. When white mobs attacked hostels where black sailors lived, the police raided them and arrested the black men. As this violence suggests, Liverpool was becoming a hotbed of racial antagonism, ignited by postwar competition for jobs and housing between white and black people. The racist violence would not be a discrete event but a recurring pattern. If the years 1939–48 saw official attempts to maintain racial divisions at any cost, the subsequent postwar years would see renewed efforts to ensure that as the numbers of people of color in Britain rose, the country would always remain, above all, a white nation.

Back in the Caribbean, the Second World War had the direct consequence of more calls for leaders there to have a greater say in politics and for the region to become more unified. These sentiments would shape emerging nationalist leaders, often from the middle class, who vied to replace white elites at the top of the racial-caste hierarchy. They voiced a range of political ideas, but against the backdrop of the Cold War, the emergence of left-wing views in the region raised alarm in Britain and the US and set the stage for the violent transfer of power in British Guiana.

7

"Still colonial at heart"

Constitutional Decolonization and the Global Cold War

On October 9, 1953, the chief secretary of British Guiana, John Gutch, read a statement on behalf of the British government on the colony's main radio station. According to Gutch, the Progressive People's Party (PPP) had shown that they were "prepared to go to any lengths, including violence, to turn British Guiana into a Communist State. The Governor has therefore been given emergency powers and has removed the portfolios of the Party Ministers. Armed forces have landed to support the police and to prevent any public disorder."[1]

The suspension of British Guiana's constitution, just 133 days after the PPP had won the colony's inaugural election under universal suffrage, was the first forced removal from office of a democratically elected government in the British Caribbean. The colonial government also arrested and imprisoned many of the PPP's leaders for spreading dissension, including poet Martin Carter, whose poignant collection *Poems of Resistance from British Guiana* (1954) expressed the spirit of protest in the colony. Born in 1927 into a middle-class family of mixed African and European ancestry, Carter was a founding member of the PPP. While in prison he participated in a monthlong hunger strike at the injustice of his internment and also linked his plight to other colonial peoples who had taken up armed struggle to wrench control away from the British, like the Mau Mau in Kenya. His urgent poetry, reflecting his steadfast unwavering resolve to resist British colonial encroachment, would inspire a generation of Guianese radicals who longed to see the end of empire. Ultimately, the 1953 coup was a crucial moment in the untethering of Caribbean colonies from the British Empire, revealing the strong-arm tactics used to constrain leaders opposed by Britain and the US.

The crisis that engulfed British Guiana occurred during the early years of the global Cold War. The communist confrontation reached a crescendo in Cuba's revolution in 1959. But the 1950s and '60s saw calls for self-government and independence grow elsewhere, including among Caribbean-born anti-colonial nationalist leaders, who sought to wrest political control from the British. Many leading this charge drew inspiration from their colonial counterparts in Asia and Africa. The postwar era witnessed the formal end of British colonialism in parts of Asia, with the violent partition of India in 1947 that displaced between 10 and 20 million people and the creation of the independent states of India and Pakistan, and later Bangladesh. The following January and February, Burma and Ceylon (later Sri Lanka), respectively, gained independence. Colonial officials in Britain and middle-class nationalist leaders in the Caribbean widely agreed that independence was fast becoming a political reality, but the communist threat raised fears in Britain about how much control officials were willing to relinquish. Indeed, the perceived communist risk in the Cold War context coexisted with decolonization and consequentially defined how it would unfold. If the Caribbean fell under the Soviet orbit, it would undo the centuries-long colonial experiment.

The British and the Americans also worried that communism could undermine stability in the area and threaten their political and economic interests. However, many anti-colonial nationalists—drawn by the purported anti-racism of communism and the Soviet Union, and the latter's criticism of colonialism and Jim Crow segregation—were sympathetic to the cause, which also worried Britain and the US. For these reasons, the British and the US spearheaded an anti-communist campaign in British Guiana, which fueled political instability. This episode in Anglo-American Cold War politics demonstrates how communism as well as the racial-caste hierarchy were variously exploited by the British, Americans, and Guianese leaders to ensure continued Western dominance, in ways that led to deadly racist violence. It also reflects how this moment, especially, saw the rise of US dominance in the Anglophone Caribbean. The US's rising global power status grew after the Second World War and began to compete with the British-controlled Caribbean for political, economic, and cultural reasons, a trend that would only increase in the coming years.

While British Guiana was the target for covert and overt anti-communist activity, in other parts of the Caribbean moves toward independence did gain ground as anti-colonial nationalism merged with economic reality. In 1948, the cost of running colonies exceeded revenue in various Caribbean colonies. Although some colonial officials wanted to eliminate these costs quickly, the small size of some Caribbean territories and their long-standing, entrenched economic dependency on Britain meant that independence was not yet a viable political option. Alternative political unions thought to be more conducive to eventual independence were debated, a reminder that self-government did not always necessarily mean the creation of a nation-state.[2]

The process of constitutional decolonization—by which dependent colonies obtain constitutional independence from their former colonial power and become a sovereign state—led to a range of political structures that saw some colonies gain sovereignty and others not. Even with the diversity of constitutional arrangements, there was never a decisive break with British colonialism. And even when some colonies, such as British Guiana, tried to reverse the negative effects of colonialism through the efforts by progressives, they were robustly challenged. British power and prestige endured, and it did so due to the actions of both British and Caribbean leaders. While praise has been heaped on populist middle-class male leaders for the purported nonviolence of Caribbean constitutional decolonization (with the exception of British Guiana), they have also taken blame for its limitations. But blame needs to fall too on British policymakers who encouraged a British-centered decolonization that ensured the longevity of colonial traditions, especially within independent states.[3] Although formally and constitutionally decolonized, colonial structures, inequalities, power relations, hierarchies, and mindsets persisted, making the post-colonial Caribbean, as English leftist writer and journalist Katrin Norris put it in 1962, "still colonial at heart."[4]

Furthermore, while British and Caribbean leaders focused on reforming politics, the elimination of the racial-caste hierarchy was not a priority or even a goal. Indeed, in some colonies, white creole elites in this era further entrenched it, while in other parts of the region, the transfer of power saw members of the black and mixed-race middle class rise to the top of the racial-caste hierarchy and, in some cases, join with or replace white elites. But with their focus on wresting control of power from the British, many leaders neglected the elimination of colonial-derived racist inequalities that festered long after the lowering of the Union Jack.

COLD WAR CONFLICT IN BRITISH GUIANA

Anti-communist activity took numerous forms in the Anglophone Caribbean. Paralleling the concurrent Red Scare in the

US, colonial officials tried to ban and confiscate what they considered communist, radical, or subversive literature. Fearing that nationalist politicians could exploit the Cold War for personal and political gains, the British pressured leaders to prove their anti-communist credentials.

But it was in British Guiana that Anglo-American anti-communism took on a starker, more sinister form—and it was one that came to influence how constitutional decolonization was managed and ultimately undermined the future post-colonial state. From the late 1940s, two men, Cheddi Jagan and Linden Forbes Burnham, steered political changes in British Guiana.

Born on a sugar plantation in Berbice, Jagan, whose parents had been indentured laborers, was the eldest of eleven children. At the age of fifteen, he attended the prestigious Queen's College in Georgetown and in 1936, with $500 of his family's savings, ventured to the US to study at the historically Black Howard University in Washington, DC. He later transferred to Northwestern University, graduating with a degree in dentistry. In Chicago, Jagan took classes in politics and history and soon began to learn more about left-wing politics, Marxism, and the anti-colonialism of the Indian National Congress. This shaped his emerging political identity as a left-wing socialist. It was in Chicago that Jagan met Janet Rosenberg. Raised in a middle-class Jewish family on the South Side of Chicago, Rosenberg became involved in left-wing politics as a member of the Young Communist League. Rosenberg and Jagan quickly became a couple, but her family objected to their marriage on the grounds of race and religion—her father even threatened to shoot Jagan.[5] Undeterred, the couple married and returned to British Guiana in 1943.

Since the 1930s protests led by workers, conditions in the colony had worsened, especially among sugar workers, who were predominantly of Indian descent. Booker Brothers, McConnell & Co., a London-based limited company, dominated the sugar industry. The company's near-total control led many to comment that British Guiana should be referred to more accurately as "Booker's Guiana."[6] Workers frequently complained about the company's notoriously poor working conditions. The colony's other main industry was bauxite, which was dominated by large US and Canadian companies and had a mainly African-Guianese workforce. African-Guianese men and women also worked in the civil service, education, and police sectors, while urban mercantile jobs tended to be held by the Chinese and Portuguese.[7] With employment closely linked to racial and ethnic identity in British Guiana, unemployment and poor working conditions became a flash point for racial conflict.

Cheddi and Janet Jagan quickly became dismayed by the deteriorating conditions in the colony and sought to challenge colonialism and calm racial tensions. In 1946, the Jagans, alongside Ashton Chase, an African-Guianese trade unionist, and J. M. Hubbard, a white Marxist, established the Political Affairs Committee (PAC), which aimed to forge a progressive movement in British Guiana. The group focused their efforts on gaining representation on the legislative council during the 1947 elections. At twenty-nine, Cheddi Jagan became the youngest member of the legislative council, on which he served until 1953. Soon after, the PAC moved to form a political party.

While Cheddi and Janet Jagan were mobilizing forces against colonialism, so too was Linden Forbes Burnham.[8] Burnham came from the colony's black middle class. Like Jagan, he attended Queen's College and, like Harold Moody, won an island scholarship that took him to the London School of Economics and Political Science in the 1940s, where he graduated with a law degree before being called to the Bar at Gray's Inn. In London, Burnham was active within the Caribbean student community and attended events organized by the British Communist Party. When he returned home, he started his practice as a barrister and entered politics, leading the British Guiana Labour Party (BGLP) in 1949. The PAC and BGLP would merge in 1950 and, in turn, take on a new name, the Progressive People's Party.

The socialist and anti-colonialist PPP was the first mass political party in British Guiana. It called for increased rights for workers and changes to land ownership. While these policies raised eyebrows in Britain and the US, the party, although sympathetic to communism, was more focused on reform. But the union between Jagan and Burnham, while certainly symbolic in undermining the colonial strategies that often pitted African-Guianese and Indian-Guianese communities against each other, was one of convenience rather than ideological affinity. Burnham was more of a moderate socialist than Jagan, who supported Marxism, and the two often clashed. When the PPP was established, Jagan acted as a leader while Burnham served as chairman. Janet Jagan took on the role of general secretary and editor of *Thunder*, the party's paper. Others involved in the party included Chase, Clinton Wong, of Chinese heritage, who served as vice chairman, poet Martin Carter, and Sydney King (later Eusi Kwayana).

Following the PPP's founding, the British government formed a new commission, chaired by Sir E. J. Waddington, the former governor of Barbados, to review the colony's constitution and franchise. The Waddington Commission's findings led to the introduction of universal adult suffrage from the age of twenty-one, and a new constitution allowed for a ministerial form of government, taking effect from 1953. In April of that year, the first elections took place.

The PPP campaigned on a reformist platform of land reform, higher wages, increased trade union representation, and improvements in housing and education. They also called stridently for independence. The PPP manifesto linked independence in British Guiana to the larger anti-colonial movement: "All over the world the people of the colonies are fighting for independence. In Malaya, in Africa, in Indo China, the fire burns brightly. We who live in the West Indies and British Guiana must consider ourselves one unit in the international colonial liberation movement."[9] The *Daily Argosy*, a newspaper that represented planter interests, for instance, labeled and discredited the PPP as unabashed communists. The Anglican and Roman Catholic churches also voiced opposition to the PPP, as did the influential union of sugar workers, the Manpower Citizens' Association (MPCA). The PPP's closest political party rivals during the election were the National Democratic Party (NDP), which garnered support from the colony's black middle class and shared links with the MPCA. Yet on election day, the PPP cruised to victory, winning eighteen seats; the NDP took two, and independents secured the remaining four.[10]

The PPP's overwhelming triumph alarmed colonial officials. After the election, the secretary of state for the colonies, Oliver Lyttelton, wrote to Prime Minister Winston Churchill, admitting that "the situation gives me cause for anxiety," but conveyed that the newly arrived governor, Sir Alfred Savage, was not unduly pessimistic, provided that they "are prepared to work within the framework of the Constitution and to see reason on financial and economic matters." The PPP plan, Lyttelton said, had "none of the usual communist aims and it advocates industrial development through the encouragement of foreign capital." He likened the PPP to Britain's Labour Party, but did warn that colonial officials needed to "keep a close watch on the leaders" and prevent them if they "use their position to further the communist cause."[11] Savage acquiesced to this request and, after the election, met with Burnham and Jagan and asked them to release a statement disavowing any PPP ties to communism. Jagan and Burnham both refused and stressed that Savage had been duped by media accusations that the PPP were communists. Attempts to smear the PPP as communists reeked of paternalism and colonial leaders' skepticism about these leaders' competency.[12] Whatever the case, the US began to monitor PPP movements closely.

When the PPP took office, they sought to undermine colonial hierarchies and improve conditions for the working classes. Their actions worried the white minority and, importantly, potential foreign investors wary of doing business in a colony that looked unstable. As the months passed in 1953, strikes by sugar industry workers worsened economic conditions in the colony.

One of the most influential bodies in the colony was the Guiana Industrial Workers' Union (GIWU), which was formed in 1948 partly in response to allegations of corruption within the MPCA. Although the GIWU shared close ties with the PPP, it was not recognized officially as a union. For this to happen, it needed to gain support from the British Guiana Sugar Producers' Association (SPA), the collective voice of the sugar planters.

The situation in late August 1953 deteriorated when GIWU leaders called for a strike. Violence erupted, and some PPP leaders voiced support for strikers. As the strike dragged on, elites and those who opposed the PPP argued that the GIWU action was part of a communist plot. The Colonial Office shared this view and accused PPP ministers of stoking labor unrest to win political points. But weeks later the GIWU called on strikers to return to work, without GIWU gaining recognition from the SPA. After the strike ended, the House of Assembly met to debate the Labour Relations Ordinance, which would require the recognition of a union if it had the support of the majority of workers.

Around this time, the Colonial Office began to make plans to thwart the PPP. On September 25, Colonial Secretary Lyttelton sent a memo to the British Cabinet, stating: "we must take away the Ministers' powers, imprison the extremists and suspend the Constitution at the earliest possible moment."[13] He later attached a document titled "Evidence of a Communist conspiracy in British Guiana" to support his recommendation. Subsequently, he wrote another memo to the British Cabinet informing them that "the Communists had been the moving force behind the strike which had paralysed the sugar industry, and they were evidently seeking to establish a totalitarian dominance over the territory by penetrating the trade unions and local government."[14] After further discussions, the Cabinet agreed to security forces in Jamaica heading to British Guiana.

The House of Assembly passed the Labour Relations Bill, which required employers to negotiate with trade unions that had a majority of workers' support, and on the same day, October 8, British troops entered British Guiana: "Armed to the teeth. And, with bayonets fixed on their rifles and armoured cars patrolling the streets of Georgetown," PPP minister Jai Narine Singh remembered, "the British soldiers generated an air of hostility towards the inhabitants."[15]

With minimal evidence, the coup and suspension of the constitution were justified on the spurious grounds that the PPP "were completely under the control of a communist clique," who were using their power "not to further the interest of the whole community, but to pervert the constitution and secure totalitarian control over all aspects of the social, cultural and economic life of British Guiana."[16] In fact, the mobilization of troops to British Guiana spoke to British fears about the dominance of Caribbean nationalist leaders who sought to challenge British interests in the colony. It clearly demonstrated that self-government in the Caribbean would be allowed only at the behest of the British, who sought by any means necessary to install Caribbean leaders who would ultimately enforce and broaden British economic and political influence, rather than threaten it. In other words, the logic of colonialism persisted on Cold War, anti-communist terms.

Meanwhile, the Colonial Office drafted an interim constitution that excluded all PPP members from the new government, which Governor Savage filled with elites. Savage also declared a state of emergency, under which the police raided the residences of PPP members; arrested, detained, and restricted the movements of many; and seized documents in an attempt to find a communist conspiracy. Many PPP stalwarts flouted these limitations.

By 1954, the economic situation in British Guiana was grim. Savage asked the Colonial Office for $10 million in aid, but they could provide only half that amount in 1954–55.[17] With elites arguing that Savage was not adequately punishing PPP members, he retired in 1955 and was replaced by Sir Patrick Muir Renison, previously the governor of British Honduras.

By 1955, Burnham and Jagan's relationship had also deteriorated, shaped in part by colonial forces who tried to drive a wedge between the ostensibly respectable socialism of Burnham and the radical communism of Jagan.[18] Burnham challenged Jagan's leadership again, which split the PPP into two factions. In February 1957, the Colonial Office permitted the governor to allow the partial return of elected government and new elections. During the 1957 election, the Jaganite faction of the PPP appealed to Indian-Guianese communities with "Apaan Jhaat," a Hindu expression loosely translated as "vote your own race."[19] Burnham used a similar appeal to African-Guianese voters. In effect, they ended up manipulating racial divisions between those of Indian and African descent for personal and political goals. In the 1957 elections, the Jaganite section of the PPP won nine out of the fourteen seats, in contrast to the Burnhamites, who won three, and Jagan became chief minister.[20] By 1958, the split between Jagan and Burnham was more formalized when the latter created a new political party, the People's National Congress (PNC). But after the election the economy was still struggling.

Ousted British Guiana Cabinet members, 1953.
Left to right: Dr J. P. Latchmansingh, minister of health and housing; Sydney King, minister of communications and works; L. F. S. Burnham, minister of education; Mrs. Jagan, secretary of the People's Progressive Party; Cheddi Jagan, leader of the House Assembly and minister of culture; Janarine Singh, minister of local government and social welfare; and Anton Chase, minister of labor and industry.

At this point, changes in British colonial thinking influenced moves toward independence for British Guiana. In the Suez Crisis of 1956–57, Egyptian forces defeated Israeli, French, and British troops after Egyptian president Gamal Abdel Nasser nationalized the Suez Canal, through which passed the majority of western Europe's oil supplies. This led to the resignation of Prime Minister Anthony Eden. His successor, Harold Macmillan, argued that Britain could no longer afford its colonies. His 1960 "Wind of Change" speech signaled the acceptance of nationalist independence in Africa. During his time as prime minister, Britain granted independence to Ghana (1957), Malaya (1957), Nigeria

(1960), and Kenya (1963). After 1960 the British government had agreed to independence in theory for British Guiana, but the debate continued about how it would be achieved, since fears about Jagan lingered.

In March 1960, at a constitutional conference regarding British Guiana's future, leaders decided that the next elections would take place in 1961. Following the conference, Cheddi and Janet Jagan traveled to Cuba, where they met Communist leader and revolutionary Fidel Castro, secured $5 million for hydroelectric development, and negotiated a deal for Cuba to purchase Guianese rice. The US viewed any funds British Guiana received from Cuba as emanating from the Soviet Union, and so after US president John F. Kennedy took office in January 1961, the US began to intervene more directly in British Guiana. They did not want Jagan to be head of an independent country with ties to Cuba, located close to the US. The Americans favored Burnham to lead British Guiana into independence, believing that he would secure US interests.

Back in 1951, the Americans had pressed for Britain to interfere in the elections in the colony, but the British responded that if the PPP found out, it would only bolster the party's support. Under President Kennedy, US covert anti-communist intervention in British Guiana included stoking racial animosity between Indian- and African-Guianese communities, arson attacks, and bombings. US anti-communist groups also tried to infiltrate labor unions in British Guiana to defeat Jagan. During the August 1961 elections, the US met with supporters of the PNC and United Force (UF), a conservative party established in October 1960 by businessman Peter D'Aguiar that drew support from the MPCA and indigenous and Portuguese communities.[21] Even so, in 1961, the PPP won the elections again, taking twenty out of thirty-five legislative seats; the PNC won eleven and the UF four.[22] As in 1957, divisions among voters rested on racial identity. This election also saw a rise in violence, some instigated by the US influence, and this caused many residents to leave British Guiana for the US or Britain.

After Jagan's reelection, the US increased its covert operations. In 1962, the CIA orchestrated protests to destabilize the government and country, and by the end of the year Britain acquiesced to Washington's demands, and Macmillan agreed to Kennedy's scheme to support opposition parties in British Guiana.[23] That year the Colonial Office sought to rid itself of British Guiana, with Commonwealth Secretary Duncan Sandys telling Macmillan: "the sooner we get these people out of our hair the better."[24] From September 1963, Sandys attempted to defeat Jagan by changing electoral rules. Another constitutional conference occurred in October 1963, but because Guianese leaders could not agree on how to move forward, they relinquished control to Britain, which decided to implement proportional representation, angering Jagan. By this point, the US had promised additional funds to British Guiana if a PNC-UF coalition won the election.

In April 1964 more racially based violence gripped the colony, shaped by tensions between Jagan, Burnham, and other politicians, who ended up advancing divisions further once they realized how crucial it was in their respective quests for political power. It was of course also shaped by centuries of colonial rule and the politics of difference that divided African- and Indian-Guianese communities—pitting them against each other—and the role of the US in actively destabilizing politics that made British Guiana ungovernable under Jagan.

Bloodshed ensued when the PPP introduced a bill to get the PPP-supported Guiana Sugar Workers' Union (GSWU) recognized as a trade union to replace the MPCA. Those in the anti-Jagan Trade Union Congress (TUC) feared the GSWU would dominate the sugar industry, so they called for a strike. Violence, beatings, and murders on both sides increased when

African-Guianese strike workers moved from Georgetown to Demerara. By late July, order had been restored, but 166 people had been killed, with around eight hundred wounded and 1,400 buildings destroyed.[25] A combination of forces had shaped these days of violence, including the PPP, PNC, and covert activities by America's CIA.

The next decisive elections took place in December 1964. Although the PPP won the highest percentage of votes compared to the PNC and UF, they did not secure a winning majority. With the help of proportional representation, Burnham created a coalition with the UF and became premier on December 14, 1964. Although he promised that as head of the government, racial divisions would end, his words would soon ring hollow. Under Burnham's rule, the colony gained independence and changed its name to Guyana in 1966, but it was riddled with racist violence, corruption, and poverty. Although favored by the British and the US, Burnham caused them more problems than they anticipated, especially when he nationalized the bauxite mines and sugar industry and developed relations with the Soviet Union. A series of undemocratic elections kept him in power until he died in 1985. The PPP finally took office in 1992, and Cheddi Jagan ruled until his death in 1997, when Janet Jagan took over as leader.

The crisis that unraveled in British Guiana saw both the manipulation of the communist threat and the reckless, bold, and brazen exploitation of the racial-caste hierarchy. Under the ruse of anti-communism, Britain and the US effectively and deliberately undermined democracy in British Guiana to ensure decolonization would be only to their best interests. Of course, British Guiana's political leaders' actions, shaped indelibly by an inherited colonial hierarchy, influenced events too. Ultimately, the devastation and destruction that occurred in British Guiana reveal the self-serving economic and political interests of colonial powers that, alongside power struggles between local leaders, set the stage for authoritarianism and racial tensions that would endure beyond 1966.

TO STAY OR GO?

Amid the machinations in British Guiana, leaders in Britain and the Caribbean were taking steps toward federation, which again would shape a policy of constitutional decolonization driven by British interests that did little to undermine the racial-caste hierarchy.

Calls for a wider Caribbean federation had gained renewed resonance following the release of the Stanley Despatch of 1945. Named after Oliver Stanley, the secretary of state for the colonies, the despatch outlined that the future aim of colonial policy was to accelerate moves towards self-government. In September 1947, delegates from Britain and the Caribbean—leaders such as Alexander Bustamante, Norman Manley, Grantley Adams, Antigua's V. C. Bird, and Trinidad's Albert Gomes—met in Montego Bay on the northern coast of Jamaica. At the Closer Association of the British West Indian Colonies conference, delegates discussed Caribbean federation as an expedient path toward self-government. Barbados's Grantley Adams was deeply enthusiastic about the federation, a feeling shared by Grenadian journalist and politician T. A. Marryshow, dubbed the "father of the federation." For Adams and Marryshow, the federation was significant in fostering Caribbean unity, but it meant different things to different groups. Radicals in the Caribbean Labour Congress (CLC), established in 1945 to organize workers, considered federation a critical first step toward self-government and eventual independence. But for the British, the federation was valuable as an administrative convenience. As one Colonial Office official described, the federation intended "to make these scattered legislatures into one compact body in order that the Colonial Office could more expeditiously deal with them in matters relating to the British Government."[26]

At the conference, attendees discussed the pros and cons of a federation. British Guiana and the Bahamas did not see the benefits for them. Some from British Guiana feared that a federation dominated by people of African descent would limit the perspectives of those of Indian descent, while some Bahamians did not believe the island shared close enough ties to other Caribbean colonies. Racism played a decisive role in the Bahamian decision to remain outside a federation, too, as the white Bay Street elites feared the rise of black migrants from other colonies, which could undermine their authority. Leaders in Jamaica were divided on federation in the Caribbean. Bustamante opposed it, arguing that it would provide little benefit to Jamaica, whereas Manley supported it. Indeed, the unresolved debates at the conference would lead ultimately to the federation's unraveling, although a consensus did emerge that plans for a federation should continue.[27]

The Standing Closer Association Committee (SCAC), created after the Montego Bay conference, was tasked with reporting on the federation's structure. In March 1950, the SCAC released the Rance Report that proposed a weak federation with a colonial status, which departed from the desires of many of the scheme's supporters who wanted a self-governing federation.[28] Although most states agreed with the SCAC report, British Honduras argued that it was too early for a federation, and British Guiana and the British Virgin Islands (BVI) both rejected the report. Jagan opposed the federation because of its weak powers, arguing that it "would merely be a glorified Crown Colony, [which] will not solve our problems."[29] The BVI opted out of the federation on the basis that they shared closer ties to the neighboring US Virgin Islands than with the rest of the British Caribbean.[30]

Aside from the Bahamas, British Honduras, British Guiana, and the BVI, the remaining colonies forged ahead with the federation. Various federation conferences occurred in the 1950s, dominated by interisland contentions about major issues. For instance, arguments raged about the location of the capital for the federation and currency and customs unions in the economic realm. Conflict grew also about freedom of movement, which was welcomed by small states and feared by large states, such as Trinidad and Jamaica, who were concerned about how immigration would impact unemployment. Meanwhile, smaller islands in the Eastern Caribbean did not want to be subsumed by the larger islands. At the same time, large colonies worried that small states would become too economically reliant on them. During debates many called for at least £100 million in aid from the British government and the same amount for the "second five years" of the federation—all told,[31] around £200 million as part of a development grant.[32] But these calls went unheard and, despite unresolved problems, plans for the federation forged ahead.

On August 2, 1956, the British Parliament passed the British Caribbean Federation Act, which established the West Indies Federation (WIF) in Antigua, Barbados, Dominica, Grenada, Jamaica, Montserrat, St. Kitts–Nevis–Anguilla (since 1871 the three territories had been governed together), St. Lucia, St. Vincent, and Trinidad and Tobago. The West Indies Federation galvanized support and criticism from Caribbean people in and outside the region. For some, the WIF mirrored the first exciting steps toward nationhood taken by people of African and Asian descent, but others viewed it cautiously, inferring that Britain wanted to withdraw from the Caribbean as quickly and cheaply as possible. The Colonial Office understood this could cause much reputational damage and chose not to put undue pressure on reluctant territories to join the WIF. Cold War geopolitics shaped the WIF as well. From the British and American point of view, the WIF had the potential to keep radical or recalcitrant Caribbean leaders in check. The final version of the WIF constitution upset many nationalists because it did not provide the Caribbean with dominion status, meaning that it remained subordinate to Britain. Yet there was a provision to review constitutional arrangements within five years, which alleviated some fears. The WIF formally came into being in January 1958.

Although constitutional and financial issues remained undecided, many were optimistic that the WIF would help the Caribbean achieve a collective regional identity. For political leader Eric Williams from Trinidad and Tobago, federation in the Caribbean could make the region stronger, as he feared that if colonial dominance was still present with independence, it could lead to limited sovereignty.[33] The WIF was important not just for Caribbean unity but as a template for larger struggles against colonialism and racism. Barbados-born Richard B. Moore, active in left-wing political circles in New York starting in the 1920s, commented that the federation would "hasten the day of full equality and self-determination for the millions of African descent in the United States, for the African and all other colonial peoples, and for all working and oppressed people everywhere regardless of race, color or creed."[34] This diasporic expression reflected the broader spirit of the April 1955 Bandung Conference in Indonesia, the first gathering of newly independent African and Asian states, which signified the rising tide of these countries in global politics.

Yet in 1958 independence for the Caribbean remained a ways off. There was no date set for independence, the WIF had only a small civil service, and the governor general, former Conservative MP Lord Hailes, had key powers over defense and foreign relations. The obvious, and deliberate, limitations of the WIF led Alan Lennox-Boyd, then Conservative secretary of state for the colonies, to remark that the "Federal Government is hardly worth the name."[35] These limitations caused problems from the start. Internal debates over customs unions, tariff rates, taxation, the movement of people and goods, and federal representation persisted.

In 1959, Jamaica gained internal self-government, allowing for the creation of a formal cabinet government, which quickened the desire for independence. Manley also began to have reservations about federation and made inquiries in Britain about the potential consequences if Jamaica left the WIF. In January 1960, Manley visited London to talk with Colonial Secretary Iain Macleod about Jamaican independence. Although the Colonial Office wanted Jamaica to stay in the WIF, Macleod told Manley that if Jamaica became independent, the British government would still pay the remaining balance of the colonial development and welfare fund and the current five-year block grant-in-aid. But a draft Colonial Office memo stressed that the British would need to "avoid any situation which results in our being left with any of the present federated territories on our hands for which we can see no obvious future except as colonies."[36]

In May 1961, Bustamante and the Jamaica Labour Party formally announced their opposition to the WIF, and Manley responded by calling for a referendum on Jamaica's continued membership in the WIF. On September 19, 54 percent voted for Jamaica to leave. There were many reasons for this: political elites failed to adequately articulate the benefits of the WIF, for one thing, and Jamaican national identity tended (like other colonies in the region) to be insular, for another. The Jamaican referendum sounded the death knell for the WIF. Macleod described it as the "most grievous blow to the Federal ideal" and admitted that "it is certain that the Federation cannot continue in its present form and must be doubtful whether it can survive at all."[37]

After the referendum, Manley played a leading role in constitutional negotiations with Britain about Jamaican independence. During these talks, Jamaican leaders borrowed the Westminster model for the new nation. In other words, Manley and other nationalist leaders sought independence within the framework of the British Empire.[38] The Caribbean, colonized by Britain for significantly longer than other colonies, opted to continue using colonial modes of government that also reflected the fact that, although nationalists might have been opposed to colonial rule, they did not object necessarily to maintaining a colonial connection. And by adopting the Westminster model in Jamaica—and later, elsewhere in the Caribbean—colonial political frameworks became embedded and enshrined in newly independent sovereign states. Manley defended the model in a speech about the draft Jamaican constitution in 1962, arguing: "I make no apology for the fact that we did not embark upon any original or novel exercise in constitutional building . . . Let us not make the mistake of describing as colonial, institutions which are part and parcel of the heritage of this country."[39]

Caribbean leaders remained loyal to the British Empire and the Crown, with Jamaica keeping the Queen as the head of state, represented by a governor general. This decision symbolically came to be seen as a strong invocation of colonial ties and dependency on the motherland. Jamaica would also retain use of the British Judicial Committee of the Privy Council (JCPC) as the final court of appeal. These choices demonstrate the complexity of constitutional decolonization as undertaken by leaders who identified, sometimes uneasily, as empire loyalists and Caribbean nationalists simultaneously.[40] Unlike many of Britain's former African colonies that, following independence, transitioned from monarchies to republics, like Ghana in 1960, Nigeria in 1963, and Kenya in 1964, the Caribbean did not always follow that path.[41] They modeled themselves instead on the Dominions, such as Canada, Australia, and New Zealand, that remained constitutional monarchies.

After calling for new elections in April 1962, Manley's PNP lost. In August, Bustamante led the country to independence as its first prime minister. But as Katrin Norris, who lived in Jamaica in the 1960s, noted that year: Jamaica was still "drawing her values from foreign sources," which, she argued, "is the greatest wrong colonialism has done her."[42] Norris decried Jamaican nationalists because they had "no impetus, no inspiration to build a new society based on the endowments, achievements and abilities which are his own. He tends to despise everything which is most characteristic of himself, and to place his nationalism in the confidence that Jamaica can successfully build a miniature Britain, America, or a European-type state."[43]

Left to right: Sir William Alexander Bustamante, head of the Jamaican opposition party; Hugh Fraser of the colonial office; Colonial Secretary Reginald Maudlin; and premier of Jamaica Norman Manley, after the final session of the Jamaica Independence Conference held at Lancaster House, London, February 9, 1962.

Once Jamaica left the WIF, Trinidad and Tobago soon followed, gaining independence in August 1962, similarly adopting the Westminster model and retaining the Queen as head of state. With the two largest states out, in 1962, the British government passed the West Indies Act, which formally dissolved the WIF.

Debate continues about the failure of the WIF. Responsibility cannot fall just on those from the Caribbean and their leaders. It has to lie with the British, who designed a deliberately weak federation and provided meager financial support. In the 1970s, Sir Kenneth Blackburne, the last governor of Jamaica, admitted in hindsight British responsibility. "Our mistake," he wrote, "was that we acted too fast in the establishment of the Federation, animated in part by the vapourings of the United Nations, in part by the desire of the British Treasury to rid itself of financial responsibilities overseas, and in part by the natural desire of West Indian leaders to control their own destinies."[44]

Given the self-congratulatory narratives in Britain about the benevolence of the British Empire and the steady, teleological march toward greater equality and progress that it purportedly conveyed, it is important to note the seeming largesse of decolonization, such as it is, had more to do with the exigencies of economics—ridding Britain of regions that had become economically useless or a drain—and much less to do with any liberal or progressive sensibility toward autonomy.

But the failure of the WIF speaks more broadly to somewhat paradoxical colonial control of constitutional decolonization in the Caribbean. Constitutional decolonization did not redress the reality of economic colonial exploitation. Although Bustamante asked for £14.5 million in loans and grants, the British government offered Jamaica a development loan of £1.25 million.[45]

Trinidad and Tobago also received insufficient payments from the British government after independence. In November 1962, speaking at the LSE while on a visit to London, Eric Williams stated: "The West Indies are in the position of an orange. The

British have sucked it dry, and their sole concern today is that they should not slip and get damaged on the peel."[46] Trinidad's representative to the UN subcommittee of the Committee on Colonialism expressed the country's frustration eloquently: a colonial power "is not entitled to extract for centuries all that can be got out of a colony and when that has been done to relieve itself of its obligations by the conferment of a formal but meaningless—meaningless because it cannot possibly be supported—political independence." Speaking further, they remarked that "Justice requires that reparation be made to the country that has suffered the ravages of colonialism before that country is expected to face up to the problems and difficulties that will inevitably beset it upon independence."[47]

That the issue of reparations and the legacy of colonialism was not fully debated during constitutional decolonisation points to one of the process's central problems: it left colonialism intact in the region.

Talks ensued about the creation of another federation among remaining islands, including Barbados, Grenada, Dominica, St. Lucia, St. Vincent and the Grenadines, St. Kitts–Nevis–Anguilla, and Antigua, twinned with Barbuda and Montserrat. But talks collapsed when it became quickly evident that Barbados wanted independence rather than membership in another federation. In 1966, Barbados gained independence under the leadership of Errol Barrow of the Democratic Labour Party (who had served in the RAF during the Second World War) and, following Jamaica and Trinidad and Tobago, adopted the Westminster model and retained the Queen as head of state. The following year the remaining islands, apart from Montserrat, became "Associated States."[48] Under this arrangement the islands had internal self-government, but control of security and finance rested with Britain. Associated statehood was understood as a useful way of gradually ending colonialism while still allowing metropolitan control to ensure stability and order.

But not all territories agreed with this model, and events in Anguilla came to reveal the downsides of associated statehood. Located in the Eastern Caribbean, the territory consists of the flat island of Anguilla alongside a series of smaller cays and islands. The crisis in the twenty-six kilometers long Anguilla, an island with around six thousand residents and scarce electricity and other resources, had its origins at a beauty contest. Held as part of celebrations of the islands' new status, a Miss Statehood competition was organized, with St. Kitts, Nevis, and Anguilla each tasked to select a contestant.[49] In February 1967, during the Anguilla contest, protesters threw stones at the police, who responded with tear gas.[50]

Unhappiness with associated statehood predated these protests. But with associated statehood, Anguillans resented St. Kitts's leader, Robert Bradshaw. Elections had been held for the three islands in July 1966, and Bradshaw's Labour Party won all seats in St. Kitts. Peter Adams of the People's Action Movement was the only elected Anguillan representative. Notably, Ronald Webster, fearing that Anguilla would lose its autonomy under Bradshaw and that he would ignore their calls for development, created a new opposition movement against the union with St. Kitts.

Weeks later, more disturbances occurred when the house of the warden, Vincent Byron, was set ablaze, prompting him to leave Anguilla. Anguillans also attacked police, who were controlled by St. Kitts, and they decided to evacuate Anguilla in May. In June 1967, Anguillans attacked St. Kitts's capital, Basseterre. Following a referendum held the next month, Anguillans autonomously declared independence. Fearing an escalation of violence, Bradshaw asked Britain and other Caribbean states for help. The British grew increasingly concerned about the deteriorating situation, foreseeing that the demise of the St. Kitts link to Anguilla could set a dangerous precedent for Nevis to leave St. Kitts. But although Whitehall expressed sympathy for Bradshaw, it and other Caribbean governments did not consider armed intervention.

Various attempts to resolve tensions between St. Kitts and Anguilla failed to have an impact.[51] Webster declared Anguillan independence for a second time and began forging links with dubious American businessmen, which again worried the British. In March 1969, Undersecretary of State for Foreign and Commonwealth Affairs William Whitlock was sent to Anguilla to try to solve the situation. It was reported that soon after landing, he was approached by gunmen, leading him to flee before negotiations had started.[52] On March 19, a small group of British policemen and paratroopers was deployed to Anguilla, in a "show of force" named "Operation Sheepskin." But on arrival, they faced little opposition, and fears about potential links between Anguilla and the US mafia were found to be somewhat exaggerated.

British paratroopers searching civilians during the British occupation of Anguilla, 1969.

"STILL COLONIAL AT HEART"

The "Anguillan invasion," as it was dubbed, was embarrassing for the Harold Wilson government, and the incident was widely ridiculed in the press. The brash decision to invade was shaped not only by events on the ground in Anguilla but also by the sense that British prestige would be lost if action was not taken and by a lack of confidence in other Caribbean political leaders to intervene. This prestige was even more important given how much the US was encroaching on the Anglophone region and flexing its military might, and was indicative of the Anglo-American relationship in the Caribbean as one of competition sometimes and collaboration in other instances. In subsequent years British rule was restored on the island through the 1971 Anguilla Act, and in 1980 the island became a British dependent territory. Meanwhile, in 1983, St. Kitts and Nevis gained independence from Britain. As events in Anguilla show, lines between internal and external affairs blurred, and some of the island-wide coalitions in the Caribbean were imposed rather than organic. The case of Anguilla shows too that constitutional change was also related to the colonial legacies of isolation that created distrust among neighboring territories, highlighting how local and colonial factors were at play. Constitutional change in the Caribbean within the context of Cold War politics was haphazard and could certainly inspire and support accusations that the British were rushing to rid themselves of Caribbean colonies, while appearing to do nothing of the sort.

During the 1970s, associated states began renegotiating their relationship with Britain, with many opting to embark upon independence. Under the 1967 West Indies Act that implemented associated statehood, a colony could gain its independence either through a referendum of a two-thirds majority, or through a request by the legislature of the associated state, to be voted on by those in the British House of Commons and House of Lords.

From 1969, Eric Gairy, head of the Grenada United Labour Party (GULP), began asking for Grenada to transition toward independence. In 1971, Britain informed Gairy that if he won the next general election in which independence was the main issue, the island would be granted independence. The February 1972 election saw GULP win against the opposition Grenada National Party (GNP). But some accused Gairy and his supporters of tampering with the votes and intimidating voters. Moreover, during the election, the GULP manifesto had not made independence a central issue. By this point, many in Grenada were wary of Gairy's authoritarianism. As premier, Gairy started to use more violence, such as creating a special police force personally loyal to him known as the Mongoose Gang, whose tactics were compared to those used by the ruthless Haitian dictator Papa Doc Duvalier. Opposition forces in Grenada feared that if Gairy led the colony to independence, he would resort to dictatorial tactics to maintain power. In March 1973, the socialist-led New JEWEL (Joint Endeavour for Welfare, Education and Liberation) Movement (NJM), led by lawyer Maurice Bishop, was established, which joined the GNP in criticizing Gairy.

Bishop was born on the Dutch island of Aruba in May 1944 to Grenadian parents. He studied at the University of London, graduating with a law degree before being called to the Bar at Gray's Inn, and was active in the Caribbean community in London. With growing opposition to Gairy, the NJM gained a large following, attracting support from the working classes, the business sector, and the island's influential Catholic Church. The NJM's manifesto, released in 1973, critiqued independence negotiations, arguing that the "move towards independence is an insincere, opportunist move, designed to strengthen the grip of tyranny and corruption. It is bound to result in a sham, bogus, meaningless independence."[53] Well aware of the financial difficulties facing newly independent Caribbean states, leaders in the

NJM demanded that the British pay "at least one hundred million dollars as partial reparation to make up for some of the money stolen from us and the exploitation, human misery, suffering and degradation we have endured at their hands over the last 400 years." But they knew these demands were quixotic, and all they would get was "a visit by some member of the 'Royal' Family to pull down the old flag, put up a new one and make a speech congratulating us on our 'achievement.'"[54]

Increased violence in Grenada made some MPs in Britain wary of independence. Conservative backbencher Sir Bernard Braine argued: "There is no question of anyone here clinging on to old-fashioned notions of empire. But independence must be true independence for all the people concerned and not a carte blanche for a brutal regime which happens to occupy the seat of power for the moment to do what it will."[55]

In more protests against independence under Gairy, Grenadians and NJM leaders took to the streets in large numbers in 1973 and 1974. On November 18, 1973, later known as Bloody Sunday, the Mongoose Gang assaulted NJM members, including Bishop. British leaders were aware of Gairy's corrupt and violent leadership and the widespread unpopularity of the prospect of independence under him. They were also aware that some in the NJM had called for reparations at independence (as others had elsewhere in the Caribbean). The British hastily agreed to independence under Gairy because of their fears of the NJM and their socialist politics. Recently declassified documents show that Grenada's independence was aided by Edward Heath's Conservative government (1970–74), to ensure that Gairy would deal with the NJM in his own way.[56] The British were wary of accusations of colonial overreach if they were to intervene in the associated state.

MI5, Britain's internal intelligence agency, was also concerned that the NJM were planning to assassinate Gairy on the forthcoming independence day.[57] Sources show that Britain planned to send troops to Grenada in 1974, with the Ministry of Defence preparing a secret invasion plan to restore colonial rule if Gairy lost control. MI5 even had informants in the NJM.[58]

Eventually, Britain agreed to independence, to begin on February 7, 1974. The path to independence in Grenada reveals once again how constitutional decolonization was ultimately a managed process—managed first and foremost to protect Britain's political and economic interests. Braine's warning came to fruition soon after independence day, as Gairy's continued involvement in violence, financial wrongdoings, and rigged elections would contribute to the 1979 revolution.

The transition from associated statehood to sovereign nation reveals how many states were rushed toward independence, especially in Grenada and Dominica, where there was vocal opposition to the authoritarian leaders in charge. After gaining independence, both states would experience instability. Except for Dominica, all formerly associated states adopted constitutional monarchical status, which ensured the persistence of colonial political structures. Dominica opted to become a republic at independence, a decision shaped by the opposition leader Eugenia Charles, who did not want the premier Patrick John to have excessive, unchecked power.

But even in Dominica, and in fact, within most Caribbean colonies that underwent the process of constitutional decolonization, independence did not prompt a major break with Britain. Nor did the transition toward independence address fully the legacies of colonialism or grapple with the complexity of the racial-caste hierarchy, which paved the way for neocolonialism and persistent anti-black racism. Yet while most associated states sought constitutional decolonization, other areas in the Caribbean—similar to the case of Anguilla—pursued a closer relationship to Britain, which entrenched colonial links even more profoundly.

LOYAL TO EMPIRE

Montserrat in the Lesser Antilles, a pear-shaped island nicknamed the "Emerald Isle of the Caribbean" due to its resemblance to Ireland and for the Irish descendants on the island, opted to remain a British colony rather than become an associated state. As chief minister and head of the Montserrat Labour Party (MLP) from 1960 to 1970, W. H. Bramble did not advocate independence. In 1970, his son, Austin Bramble, won the election representing the Progressive Democratic Party, but in 1978, the People's Liberation Movement (PLM) under John Osborne came to power. The PLM voiced support for independence once the island had gained economic sufficiency, but merchants opposed the move, arguing that the colony benefited more from their connections with Britain.

After the West Indies Federation ended in 1962, the Cayman Islands and Turks and Caicos, both dependencies of Jamaica, opted to also deepen their ties with Britain. The Cayman Islands were unique in the context of the Caribbean. Cayman society was not demographically dominated by people of African descent. From the eighteenth century, the Cayman Islands had a large white and mixed-race population. With a sizable light-skinned populace and strong links to the maritime industry, many in the Cayman Islands saw themselves as distinct from the other colonies in the Anglophone Caribbean. During and after the Second World War, the Cayman Islands forged closer ties with the US through tourism and employment, as Caymanians found work with American shipping companies, and the US government agreed to a visa waiver that allowed Caymanians with passports and no criminal records the right to work and live in America. Like Bermuda and the Bahamas, merchant elites dominated politics in the Cayman Islands, and they were determined to keep control of Cayman politics and economy by the exclusion of people of color.

Although many white or near-white members of the elite, such as Ducan Merren and Roy McTaggart, also delegates of the Cayman Assembly, opposed the WIF, the Cayman Islands joined it with Jamaica in 1958.[59] In 1959 the Cayman Islands received its first written constitution and implemented universal suffrage. Around this time, political parties began to emerge, one of which was the National Democratic Party (NDP), headed by Ormond Panton. NDP members were predominantly merchants or civil service workers from the black middle class and supported maintaining ties with Jamaica. In response to the NDP, merchant politicians created the Christian Democratic Party, which opposed internal self-government and tax reform and expressed loyalty to the British monarchy.

When in August 1962 Jamaica gained independence, debates started about the status of the Cayman Islands. In the elections of November that year, the NDP won seven seats. But Jack Rose, an administrator who opposed internal self-government and disliked Panton, did not allow the NDP to gain power in the executive council, nominating three members to the legislative assembly without consulting Panton. With Rose's power to fill the legislative assembly with supporters, the NDP was largely ineffective in promoting full internal self-government. Rose limited the chance for Caymanians to thoroughly debate independence, instead offering Caymanians only two options: internal self-government under independent Jamaica or Crown Colony status with Britain. When Jamaica left the WIF, some Caymanians feared being marginalized in a black-majority sovereign state, and the territory opted in favor of Crown Colony status.

Like the Caymans, the Turks and Caicos Islands chose to secede from Jamaica in 1962 and become a Crown Colony of Britain. Independence was unpopular on the small islands, with a population of just above 5,500.[60]

Not having joined the WIF, the British Virgin Islands, Bermuda, and the Bahamas chose to forge ahead with a revised relationship with Britain too. Crown Colony status allowed the BVI the advantage of receiving aid directly from Britain and retaining its ties with the US Virgin Islands. As in the Cayman Islands, debates about independence were somewhat stifled by the BVI administrator who, in the 1960s and '70s, refused calls for greater autonomy.[61] Although Britain said it was happy to arrange self-government for any territory that sought it, officials undermined this policy.[62] Britain diminished the incentive for self-government by declaring that the BVI would need to commit to independence within two years.[63] Many working-class men and women were somewhat detached from the issue of BVI's Crown Colony status. Administrator Martin Staveley tried to tackle BVI's "cynicism and disillusionment" with British rule by fostering loyalty to Britain and the monarchy with, for example, Queen Elizabeth II's visit to the islands in 1966.[64] Nevertheless, elites were more preoccupied with strengthening ties to the British than ordinary people in the BVI, which suggests that the islands had a complex and somewhat tenuous relationship with Britain, one that had to be continually buttressed and reinforced rather than taken for granted.

Considering itself distinct from the other Caribbean colonies, Bermuda decided not to be a part of the WIF. Often described as the South Africa of the Caribbean, Bermuda was well-known for its strict segregationist policies. By 1948, the island's population was overwhelmingly of African descent. Yet the white Bermudian elite dominated society. Legislation reinforced the daily reality of racial segregation on the island. In 1930, the Hotel Keepers' Protection Act was passed, giving hotel and restaurant owners the right to refuse people on their premises for any reasons and leading to a policy of racial segregation that excluded black, Asian, and Jewish people from hotels and restaurants. With the island fast becoming a tourist haven, many argued that white US tourists would not want to visit Bermuda without racial segregation. But black Bermudians resisted these impositions, lobbying the British colonial government to redress their plight, although this resistance did not produce any immediate change to the electoral system.

Then, in the 1960s, Bermudian activist Pauulu Kamarakafego (born Roosevelt Brown) took an active role in challenging inequality in Bermuda, taking his case in 1961 to the UN and arguing for independence. Two years later, the Progressive Labour Party (PLP), seen as a party of the black working classes, was founded. As part of their platform, the PLP made strident calls for independence and changes to the electoral system. A year later, white elites established the United Bermuda Party (UBP), which wanted to strengthen ties with Britain.

Henry Tucker, chairman of the Bank of Bermuda, led the UBP. In the 1930s, Tucker opposed universal suffrage and supported racial segregation. Yet Tucker knew that neither he nor the UBP could ignore the urgent problem of racism in Bermuda, and although the party predominantly catered to the white elites, they used the language of multiracialism and appealed to members of Bermuda's black middle class, some of whom stood as candidates for the party. British governor John Roland Robinson, known as Baron Martonmere, stepped into his new position in June 1964 and bolstered the UBP's power and control in Bermuda.

In November 1966, the Bermuda Constitutional Conference was held at Marlborough House, London, and cemented the island's colonial links with Britain. The Queen retained the power to appoint the Bermudian governor. The governor controlled Bermuda's executive government and had responsibility for the island's defense and internal security and could veto any laws passed by the local government. Members of the PLP objected to the conference's resolutions regarding Bermuda's colonial status and constitutional gerrymandering that skewed more power to white areas with small populations rather than larger, black-dominated areas of the island.

In 1968 the British government ceded domestic control to local ministers and introduced universal suffrage in Bermuda. The first elections occurred in May, with the UBP winning a majority of seats in the House of Assembly. British colonial figures considered Bermuda economically stable, and so in principle, the island could gain independence, but they deferred to Tucker, who did not support independence. The British supported the UBP because of the importance placed on stability and racial harmony, despite the blatant racism in society, as reinforced in the constitution.[65]

The overwhelming dominance of a white elite that sought to limit moves toward self-government or independence also existed in the Bahamas, but by the 1960s, the island had forged a different path than Bermuda. Formed in 1953, the socially liberal Progressive Liberal Party (PLP) opposed the Bay Street elites. When the party was first established, most of its leaders were white or near-white, but they wanted the PLP to be multiracial, and in 1955 the black lawyer Lynden Pindling, educated at King's College London, emerged as its leader. Like Bermuda's UBP, white Bahamian elites recognized the need to form a stronger union and, in March 1958, created the United Bahamian Party (UBP).

By 1962 the PLP and UBP had become polarized on racial grounds. After a UBP victory in the elections that year, the PLP argued that they had fewer votes because of gerrymandered constituencies and black voters' lack of trust in black Bahamian political leadership. Although the PLP lost the election, they regrouped and, using populist tactics, increased their attack on the UBP, especially around issues such as racial discrimination, constituency boundaries, and immigration. Although Britain continued to control foreign affairs, internal security, and defense, the governor's powers were curtailed. In 1964, increased power was given instead to the premier and cabinet ministers, which initiated the process of self-government. Changes were also made to constituency distribution, but the UBP was still accused of gerrymandering.

The following year, the PLP dramatically increased its opposition to the UBP.[66] On April 27, 1965, PLP member Milo Butler refused to listen to the Speaker of the House and limit his speech to fifteen minutes in a debate over gerrymandering. Butler was subsequently forcibly removed from the House of Assembly by police officers. Next, the deputy leader of the PLP, Arthur Hanna, did the same and was also removed. Butler and Hanna were quickly reinstated, but many PLP supporters began to gather outside the house and booed UBP members as they entered. During the session, Pindling forwarded a motion asking to defer decisions made by a committee on the issue of constituency boundaries but was defeated. Pindling then accused the UBP of being a dictatorship. Walking over to the ceremonial mace in front of the Speaker's chair, Pindling boldly declared, "This is the symbol of authority, and authority in this island belongs to the people," and threw the mace out of the window.[67] Pindling and the PLP members then addressed the crowd outside, asking them to join in a demonstration. The PLP's dramatic action was followed by a boycott of the House of Assembly, which convinced some black voters that the PLP could bring about substantial change in the Bahamas. Furthermore, the PLP accused UBP ministers of having a conflict of interest, as many took advantage of their office to support their own business interests.

Due to growing allegations of corruption within the gambling industry and the announcement of a Royal Commission to investigate the UBP, in January 1967 party leaders called for early elections under universal suffrage. The PLP won narrowly. Once in power, the PLP and Premier Pindling committed themselves to supporting free enterprise, developing tourism, and promoting fairer immigration practices. After a conference held in London in September 1968, powers for the ruling party increased. Although the colonial governor retained control of foreign affairs and defense, he had to consult with the premier before making decisions. But the honeymoon period for the PLP was short. The global recession of the 1970s hurt the tourist industry, and the PLP grew more authoritarian.

Although the PLP had not loudly demanded independence since gaining power, to distract from pressing domestic problems, Pindling announced that he would ask for independence after the September 1972 elections. Opposition, however, came from the Abaco Islands, located in the northern Bahamas, which expressed loyalty to the British Crown. There, black UBP ally Errington Watkins and white property developer Leonard Thompson established the Greater Abaco Council and despatched a petition to the Queen reportedly signed by three-quarters of the adult Abaco population, asking for the Abaco Islands and Grand Bahama to remain a British possession if the Bahamas gained independence.[68] The British government refused the petition, saying they would accept petitions only from the Bahamian government.

Despite the 1972 elections, when the PLP won and gained a mandate for independence, the Greater Abaco Council intensified their separatist efforts to keep the Abaco Islands a part of the British Empire. A multiracial delegation from Abaco attended the conferences held in London to negotiate and arrange independence.[69] The separatists renamed themselves the Council for a Free Abaco and compiled a second petition.[70] Within this group, passionate separatists including Arnold Albury and Chuck Hall began negotiations with the Conservative MP (for Aberdeenshire West) Colonel Colin "Mad Mitch" Mitchell, American arms supplier Mitchell WerBell III, and US millionaire Michael Oliver, who led the libertarian group Phoenix Foundation and wanted Abaco to become a free-market, independent island.[71] But things did not go well for the separatists in London. Lord Balniel, the minister who led negotiations, voiced the general attitude among British officials to the Bahamian separatists when he said: "We just want to get rid of you . . . we'd like to get rid of the colonies."[72]

When the independence bill was debated in the House of Commons, Mitchell and other MPs tried to pass an amendment removing the "colony of Greater Abaco" from the rest of the Bahamas, but their amendment was defeated. The Bahamas was granted independence in July 1973. The Queen remained as head of state, represented by a governor general who was supposed to be a Bahamian appointed on advice from the ruling party. Nonetheless, the Abaco independence movement continued, with little success, into the 1970s.

Like the Bahamas, British Honduras took steps toward sovereignty. In 1954 the People's United Party, led by devout Catholic George Price, won the first election under universal suffrage. In 1961, British Honduras received internal self-government, and Price won the election again and called for independence, but neighboring Guatemala threatened to use force to claim the territory, which they argued belonged to them. The territorial dispute between Guatemala and British Honduras dated back to the early colonization of the region. Following Price's calls for independence, other Commonwealth members used their influence in the UN to support British Honduran sovereignty. In 1973, British Honduras changed its name to the Mayan-derived Belize. In November 1980, the UN General Assembly recommended that Belize become independent by the end of 1981, and when the colony did it retained the Queen as the head of state.

"STILL COLONIAL AT HEART"

Bahamas prime minister Lynden O. Pindling holds the constitutional papers symbolizing freedom from three centuries of British colonial rule, Nassau, July 10, 1973. Pindling received the papers from Britain's Prince Charles, seen lower left.

The fate of Montserrat, the Cayman Islands, Turks and Caicos, the British Virgin Islands, Bermuda, the Bahamas, and Belize reveal that although the pathway to constitutional decolonization in the Caribbean varied, British colonial traditions and links endured. And, with them, so did the racial-caste hierarchy. Debate continues about the persistence of British traditions throughout the process of decolonization in the Caribbean. Caribbean leaders had various reasons for holding on to colonial-derived political traditions, some for their own personal and political gain, others because of their genuine loyalty to the British Empire. Many reasons were tied to political, economic, and social factors—linked to the deep embeddedness that colonial traditions had in the Anglophone Caribbean.

Amid the Cold War context, and on the precipice of real meaningful change (or so some thought), decolonization in the Anglophone Caribbean was a process that many Caribbean leaders thought would evolve and adapt over time. Collectively, the states that gained independence experienced the peculiarities of the "post-colony" state, defined by historian Richard Drayton as "the persistence of a colonial order after the acquisition of constitutional sovereignty."[73] In the late 1960s and '70s across the Caribbean, the post-colony state led to Black Power uprisings that rocked the ruling black, mixed-race, and white elites, who were accused of failing to redress the racial-caste hierarchy. But before Black Power shook the Caribbean, African-Caribbean people in Britain were confronting the realities of an upsurge in racist violence. They, too, would turn to Black Power.

8

"Colonization in Reverse"
Caribbean Migration, State Racism, and Black Radicalism

In her 1966 satirical poem "Colonization in Reverse," Louise Bennett depicted a world turned upside down.[1] Rather than the British colonizing far-flung regions of the globe, mass postwar Caribbean migration to Britain saw the colonized act as colonizers. Using the patwa vernacular of the working classes, Bennett, adopting the public persona of Miss Lou, voiced the irony and complex consequences of Caribbean migration.

After 1945, thousands from the Caribbean made their way to Britain's shores in the hope of finding employment. Many sought succor from the continued economic ravages of colonialism and rising neocolonialism in the region. Population growth in the Caribbean exerted further pressure on already scarce resources, which led to unemployment and underemployment. Environmental damage exacerbated economic and social crises. In 1951, category four Hurricane Charlie hit Jamaica, killing 150 people, leaving thousands homeless, and spurring on migration.

Like Bennett, many others came to Britain to advance their education. After studying social work in Jamaica, Bennett arrived in England in 1945, becoming one of the first black students to enroll in the Royal Academy of Dramatic Art on a scholarship from the British Council. During this time, she followed in fellow Jamaican Una Marson's footsteps and worked for BBC radio. Those from the Caribbean also came to Britain due to genuine deep bonds and a sincere sense of belonging and loyalty with the motherland fostered by colonial culture, especially those who served during the Second World War.

In the last stanza of Bennett's poem, Miss Lou ponders how Britain will react to reverse colonialism. The answer to that question was increased competition, between white Britons and black Britons and those born in the colonies, which shaped the rise of racist violence and later influenced instances of policy-driven state racism—another desperate attempt to maintain the color bar as Britain's whiteness eroded.

In response to rising racism, African-Caribbean men and women in Britain followed their predecessors in the interwar era. They established organizations and created multiracial coalitions. Black activism in the postwar era remained transnational, linking struggles black people in Britain faced with those in the Caribbean, Africa, Asia, and the US. In the era of constitutional decolonization, Caribbean activists in Britain engaged in the process of decolonizing Britain. One definition of decolonization is the transfer of power from a colonized territory to a sovereign state. But this overlooks the complexities of such a transfer. Decolonization was not just a political or economic act, it also profoundly impacted people's personal lives and fundamentally reformed ideas about identity and citizenship.[2]

As part of decolonizing Britain, African-Caribbean people adopted a much more radical political agenda, a vital part of which was the creation of new definitions of Britishness that embedded new understandings of blackness. Shunning the label "colored," many began to embrace the term "black," an inclusive political category shared by those in the Caribbean, South Asia, the US, and Africa. Political blackness and radicalism were at the heart of the turn to Black Power in Britain.

Erupting in the tumultuous decades of the 1960s and '70s, marked by global unrest and upheaval, Black Power in Britain was part of a worldwide movement that sought to challenge anti-black racism and linked class divisions, as well as colonialism. In effect, it tried to address and redress what constitutional decolonization had avoided: namely, economic exploitation through the racial hierarchy. In the US in 1966, Trinidadian-born but New York–raised Stokely Carmichael (later Kwame Ture) popularized the phrase "Black Power," partly in response to the legislative limits of the civil rights movement. After leaving the Student Nonviolent Coordinating Committee, Carmichael joined the Black Panther Party, established in 1966 by Huey P. Newton and Bobby G. Seale in Oakland, California, which championed a radical vision of black political agency and rights that influenced Black Power movements across the world, from Australia to India, Israel, Britain, and Bermuda.[3] As a manifestation of struggles waged by those subjugated by racism and colonialism, Black Power was shaped by, and in turn shaped, the Cuban revolution and anti-apartheid activism in South Africa, as well as feminist, student, gay, anti-colonial, and pacifist protests.

Britain after 1945 was characterized on the one hand by increased anti-black state-led racism, especially in employment and housing, that took the form of racist violence and immigration restrictions, and on the other hand by a vibrant anti-racist and radical movement that decolonized Britain itself by shaping new notions of black British identity. This was an intensification of the ongoing struggle between those who wanted to maintain and those who wanted to destroy the racial-caste hierarchy. What was unique about this period was the denial of anti-black racism at the official level and the repetition that Britain was a color-blind liberal society even in the face of explicitly racist policies and racist violence. Furthermore, this period saw contrasts with the US, as black activists drew connections with their struggles and those taking place by their counterparts across the Black Atlantic. British politicians, too, engaged in comparing Britain's purported color-blind liberalism with racist violence in the US, at a time when Britain's power and empire was waning and that of its rival and collaborator was growing. This all took place amid the broader decline (but not demise) of the British Empire in the wake of the economic crises following the Second World War, the growing tide of self-determination in colonies in Africa and Asia, and the rise of US economic and political influence in the Caribbean.

LOOKING FOR WORK AND SEARCHING FOR HOME

Caribbean migration in the postwar years was part of broader migratory change in Britain. After the war thousands of Europeans, including Latvians, Poles, Irish, Italians, Ukrainians, Lithuanians, Maltese, and Cypriots, arrived in Britain. Some belonged to the European Voluntary Workers scheme, established to help fill vacancies in key labor sectors when the postwar economy was struggling with high domestic costs and a large war debt to the US. Others were refugees affected by the fallout from the war.

Irish migrants were the largest group to come to Britain in these years—forty thousand arrived annually in the 1950s.[4] Following passage of the 1948 British Nationality Act, two thousand people from the Caribbean ventured to the motherland each year from 1948 to 1953, increasing the extant, small black British population.[5] From the 1950s onward, Caribbean numbers grew. When the US Congress passed the 1952 Immigration and Nationality Act (McCarran–Walter Act), which limited Caribbean migration, many more turned to Britain. In 1954 more than nine thousand additional people came from the Caribbean, in 1955 more than twenty-seven thousand and in 1956 over twenty-nine thousand, before numbers dipped. Figures picked up again in 1960 to around fifty thousand per year, and in 1961 to above sixty thousand.[6]

Jamaican migrants (sisters Mrs. Louisa and Mrs. Violet Johnston) arrive at Waterloo Station, London, September 1954.

Between 1948 and 1973, 550,000 people born in the Caribbean moved to Britain.[7] This group comprised a diverse range and included those of African, indigenous, Indian, and Chinese descent, those of Jewish background, as well as those considered mixed-race. In 1956 and 1957, migrants from India and Pakistan, both Commonwealth countries since gaining independence, began coming in larger numbers: in 1956 they formed a quarter of the forty-thousand growth in the people-of-color population.[8]

The Commonwealth of Nations (most often referred to simply as the Commonwealth) was first established in 1931 as an association of Britain and other parts of the empire that had gained some measure of autonomy as self-governing states, namely the old Dominions. The Commonwealth viewed these states as autonomous territories within the British Empire that was united by common allegiance to the Crown, who was the head of the association. When India and Pakistan gained independence in 1947, they joined the Commonwealth, and as more colonies followed in their path this saw the Commonwealth's membership grow. The Commonwealth also included dependent territories within the British Empire. Taken together, the larger numbers of Europeans, Irish, Caribbean, South Asian, and West Africans arriving in Britain hastened Britain's transformation into a more multilingual, multiracial country. Britain had long been both, but this new migratory wave was a significant inflection, because it took place when white Britons were migrating too.

White British migration to the old Dominions of South Africa, Australia, New Zealand, and Canada began in the nineteenth century. Around 20 million people left Britain between 1815 and 1914—4 million to Canada, 2 million to New Zealand and Australia, and 750,000 to southern Africa, with 13.5 million going to the US.[9] But the postwar era saw renewed anxieties about the waning white population of the Dominions, renewing efforts to encourage white Britons to migrate, hoping that this would fortify British imperial prestige. In total, the old Dominions received 1.5 million British residents between 1945 and 1960.[10] The departure of those considered "good"—meaning "white British stock"—exacerbated anxieties about those left behind. The white working-class communities, elites feared, were reproducing too much. *The Times* in 1943, for instance, had reported that "poorer and less successful sections of the community" were having more children than "the more prosperous and more successful sections."[11] These class concerns meshed with racial anxieties. The anxiety surrounding mixed-race children and interracial relationships that arose during both world wars became more pronounced in the postwar period, as the larger presence of people of color called into question the maintenance of Britain's white population.[12]

The diverse group of new- and old-comers to Britain did not see each other the same way. Unlike Europeans, those from the Caribbean did not all consider themselves as migrants. Barbados-born writer George Lamming, who traveled on the same ship to England as fellow writer Trinidadian Sam Selvon—author of the iconic story of Caribbean postwar experiences *The Lonely Londoners* (1956)—observed: "Migration was not a word I would have used to describe what I was doing when I sailed with other West Indians to England in 1950. We simply thought we were going to an England which had been planted in our childhood consciousness as a heritage and a place of welcome."[13] Yet their migration saw them designated as immigrants—a term that marked Caribbean people as foreign other, rather than integrally a part of the British world.[14] All British Caribbean people were colonial subjects (and with the 1948 act were considered "citizens of the United Kingdom and Colonies"). Indeed, from the seventeenth century onward, anyone with evidence of birth within the empire was a British subject. For many Caribbean people, their Britishness was inseparable from their Caribbean identity.

Newcomers did not view each other the same way, nor were they treated the same. European Voluntary Workers were welcomed and aided in their integration into Britain (although they were closely controlled, for instance in the work they could do), but those from the Caribbean were negatively stereotyped as causing harm and disorder to the nation. Initially, from the mid-1940s to the mid-1950s, Caribbean people in Britain were predominantly male, and hackneyed stereotypes of them as lazy, work-shy, and violent shaped negative attitudes toward them. By the late 1950s the number of Caribbean women increased, which worried white British officials for different reasons. As the population of black women grew, stereotypes of them as irresponsible reproducers with their alleged high fertility fed concerns of a potential population crisis and their overdependence on services, which would increase pressure on the emerging welfare state.[15]

In moving to Britain, Caribbean people relied on a range of formal networks, such as local travel agencies and government— and employment-sponsored schemes. The British Caribbean Welfare Service, later known as the Migrant Services Division of the West Indies Commission after the creation of the WIF, helped support new arrivals. But most workers arrived in Britain looking for employment. Caribbean people also depended on informal networks among friends and family. As Whitfield Jones from Barbados, who left the island in 1956, explained: "Coming to England in those days was kind of a fashion. John Brown gone, your other friend gone and you found out, well, you hadn't got many friends home now, so then you come too."[16] Often following people they already knew back in the Caribbean, many new arrivals in Britain ended up residing in London, but significant numbers left the capital for other major cities such as Liverpool, Leeds, Leicester, Nottingham, Bradford, Bristol, Birmingham, Cardiff, Manchester, and Wolverhampton, as well as smaller cities and towns.

Upon arrival most African-Caribbean people expected to gain employment. As writer Donald Hinds, who journeyed to Britain following his mother from Jamaica in 1955, said: "When a migrant makes up his mind that he is going to Britain, he hardly expects to find an earthly paradise. He expects to work for his living, and doubtless do royally well, too."[17] Most of those from the Caribbean who arrived in the immediate postwar era to the end of the 1950s tended to be skilled workers, and racist discrimination became a constant of their working lives. The *Empire Windrush*, for instance, carried mechanics, journalists, masons, and students.[18] Between 1948 and 1955 most Caribbean people hailed from an urban setting, moving to Britain to increase their middle-class status. But after 1955, many more were semiskilled or unskilled and came from rural areas.[19] Those who were unskilled found manual work. But skilled workers who expected to find jobs equivalent to their qualifications faced disappointment. Many found that their Caribbean training was regarded as useless in Britain. They often faced accusations that they diluted skills by taking jobs that they were unqualified for, an argument based on the assumption that their skills were inferior. Some were considered either overqualified, underqualified, or, surprisingly, sometimes both. This led to the super-exploitation of Caribbean workers, as those with skills were often downgraded and shunted into unskilled work. Former RAF pilot Jamaican Baron Baker remembered that despite skills learned during the war: "When I left the Air Force I started to find that the English were racist. Trying to get a job on a bus as a conductor was unheard of. They never dreamed of giving a black man a job there."[20]

Statistics instantiate this downgrading of Caribbean workers. Of those who arrived in the 1950s, 22 percent had unskilled or semiskilled jobs in the Caribbean, but in Britain, that figure amounted to 63 percent.[21] In research conducted by sociologists Ruth Glass and Harold Pollins, 86 percent of skilled Caribbean male workers in London could only find manual jobs.[22] Outside manual labor, the color bar remained in various occupations. Cy Grant from British Guiana, despite being a former RAF officer with a distinguished war record, was unable to pursue a legal career even after qualifying at the Bar. He struggled to find a legal chambers that would employ him and instead turned to a career in entertainment.

For those who did find a job, discrimination in the workplace was the norm. On factory floors, white workers resented their new black coworkers. Trinidadian-born cricketer, later lawyer, and politician Learie Constantine remembered: "Most British people would be quite unwilling for a black man to enter their homes, nor would they wish to work with one as a colleague, nor to stand shoulder to shoulder with one at a factory bench."[23] Some white Britons protested against the employment of Caribbean workers. In September 1955, a group of white bus workers in Wolverhampton started a three-week overtime ban in opposition to the employment of black staff.[24]

Hostility extended to the trade unions themselves. In terms of labor membership, Caribbean people found themselves in a double bind: they were blamed for undermining unions by refusing to join, but many did not participate because they were not welcome in them. By alienating black workers, unions undermined their own efforts, as this left a group of workers employers could easily manipulate by, for example, paying them a lower wage that would limit the bargaining powers of unions and create further tensions among workers.

Despite the color bar in many industries, some sectors with vacancies sought out those from the Caribbean. The British Hotels and Restaurants Association and London Transport actively recruited Caribbean workers. In 1956, the British Transport Commission and London Transport looked for workers in Barbados. The National Health Service, established in 1948, reached out to recruit nurses from Barbados in the 1950s and later from other parts of the Caribbean and Africa. These jobs saw them also confront individual and institutional racism from patients and coworkers that restricted their promotion prospects. Brie from Trinidad, who trained as a nurse in Britain in 1967 when nineteen years old, commented: "To this present day, I find the doctors have no respect, as a black nurse. Absolutely none. They would bypass you and maybe talk to somebody else who's more junior to you than actually speak to you. And I just had to learn to live with it."[25]

The blatant racism that Caribbean men and women faced at work left them more vulnerable to losing their jobs. Britain experienced an economic downturn from the mid-1950s and increasing unemployment. White workers began to voice their anger at workers from the Caribbean, who were often the last to be hired and the first to be fired. One employer admitted as much: "I sack the coloured ones first. I must. There would be a riot if I did anything else. The trouble is that whenever you dismiss West Indians they make such a fuss. They say you have done it because of colour prejudice, and that makes you feel a rotter."[26]

Racism in the workplace paralleled racism in housing. When Caribbean people tried to rent accommodation, they faced well-known signs that read: "No coloureds, no dogs, Irish not required."[27] Landlords had legal licence to discriminate against those from the Caribbean as no laws prohibited it. "I am not prejudiced," claimed one landlady. "Only Jews, I don't like them. And blacks, of course, I don't like blacks. I am sorry for the darkies, that I am, but I know what my neighbours would say: 'Look at her, she really has come down in the world.'"[28] Another landlady who was reluctant at first to accept Caribbean tenants later changed her mind, describing them as "very nice, much more like English people than I had expected."[29]

For those fortunate enough to secure rented accommodation, homes were often in shabby, cramped condition. The housing color bar meant that many Caribbean people often pooled resources together and shared accommodation, which led to accusations that they were taking over specific streets or neighborhoods. Landlords who were willing to rent to Caribbean individuals and families exploited their plight by charging higher rents and then threatening them with violence if they asked for a rent reduction. Peter Rachman, one of the most notorious London landlords, charged Caribbean men and women high rents to live in multioccupational spaces in Notting Hill, an area fast becoming home to the growing Caribbean community. Many Caribbean people had an ambivalent attitude toward Rachman, disliking his practices yet having little choice but to seek his services. Trinidadian-born activist Michael de Freitas explained: "The real villain was not Peter Rachman. It was, and still is, all those who put up notices saying: 'no coloured' . . . They're the ones who made it possible for Rachman to provide his particular kind of service. They and the well-meaning people who condemn him but do nothing about the situation that created him."[30] Those from the Caribbean who could afford their own properties faced discrimination as well, struggling to secure quality housing or reasonable mortgages.

The challenges Caribbean people faced in finding accommodation were exacerbated by the national housing crisis. Half a million properties had been destroyed during the Second World War. As London's suburban housing grew, Harold Macmillan's government transferred resources from the public to the private sector, with local authorities encouraged to use funds for the construction of private homes rather than council houses. By the late 1950s this contributed to a decrease in the available stock of council housing and increased competition between Britain's residents for homes that fuelled overcrowding, especially in large cities.[31] As historian Kathleen Paul points out, government decisions like cutting £25–30 million in the budget for "social investment" limited housing, health, and educational provisions and exacerbated problems.[32] Pressure for housing and on other parts of the welfare state increased competition between white British-born and CUKCs (Citizen of the United Kingdom and Colonies) for access to already depleted resources, especially in areas such as Notting Hill. Competition soon turned to harassment.

The Colville area sat a few streets away from Notting Hill Gate and had become a center for colonial and migrant groups. In the 1920s, it was known as "Little India" because of the many South Asians living there while studying for the Indian Civil Service exams. In the 1950s it was home to Cypriots, Maltese, Irish, and a growing Eastern European community. When Caribbean people began arriving in larger numbers, they also moved there. When white residents began seeing more Caribbean men and women move in, some felt uncomfortable and moved out. Many were unaware of the government's housing policy or landlords like Rachman and were quick to accuse those from the Caribbean of contributing to the housing crisis. As these sentiments spread, the area became home to far-right fascist groups who promoted their rallying cry of "Keep Britain White" and demanded Caribbean repatriation. Active groups included the anti-Semitic National Labour Party, which stressed that "Coloured immigration must be stopped. Not only does it aggravate the housing problem and constitutes a serious threat to workers' living standards in view of increasing unemployment but, most importantly, it will turn our nation into a race of mongrels."[33] Prominent also was the White Defence League (WDL). The largest fascist group in Britain was Oswald Mosley's Union Movement, which grew out of his British Union of Fascists. It led attacks on the Jewish community in London's East End and also had a presence throughout different parts of the capital. Other white nationalist groups active in West London and Britain more widely were the Ku Klux Klan and the League of Empire Loyalists.

In the face of a flourishing fascist movement, the British government remained silent and complicit. They refused to pass legislation against racist discrimination. Rather, in the 1950s, Conservative MPs argued that the best way to challenge racism was not through the law but education. Yet the government did little to change public opinion about Caribbean newcomers or racism. Politicians also argued that any legislation against racist discrimination would infringe on the liberties of individual landlords and businesses and stressed that the state should not be involved in disputes between employers and employees. But for the most part, reticence toward racial discrimination legislation was based on the false assumption, shared by many politicians, that despite overwhelming and blatant evidence to the contrary, racism did not exist in Britain. This relied, again, on the idea of Britain as a liberal land that spread its liberalism to its overseas empire. At the same time, some in both the Labour and Conservative parties continued to lament Britain's racially changing demographics and devise ways to stop it. By attempting to restrict Caribbean people coming to Britain, politicians blamed them rather than white racists for causing racial divisions and followed fascist calls to prevent further migration from people of color.

Plans to prevent large-scale Caribbean movement gained momentum in the 1950s. Following his return to office as prime minister in 1951, Winston Churchill voiced his concern about immigration.[34] His Cabinet and policy officials were well aware that any new law had to be worded delicately so that it would not appear explicitly racist. Yet a committee of ministers established a group to devise new ways to limit migration from Commonwealth citizens. In 1951 they agreed that limits on migration were not appropriate because Britain "has a special status as the mother country, and freedom to enter and remain in the United Kingdom at will is one of the main practical benefits enjoyed by British subjects."[35] This response was explicitly based on worries that any restrictions targeting people of color would also impact the movement of white people from the old Dominions. But the Colonial Office took further steps to limit the movement of people of color by, for example, spreading advertisements in the

Caribbean warning potential newcomers of the difficulties they would face in trying to find accommodation or jobs in Britain. The Home Office also tried to limit the number of passports given to those from the Caribbean, but colonial and later newly independent governments resisted this tactic. From their perspective, Caribbean movement to Britain was a positive way to relieve the region of the ongoing population pressure and economic challenges. Also, remittances sent from Caribbean people in Britain to their families in the region were immensely important in aiding Caribbean economies. However, wary of the growing negative image of the Caribbean, some colonial governments became stricter. In the mid-1950s, for instance, Jamaica stopped giving passports to those convicted of crimes, pregnant women, individuals over the age of fifty, and children without guardians.[36]

The British state's response to rising white racism against Caribbean people was to double down on racism and pursue exclusionary tactics. This was aided by the mainstream popular press, which whipped up anti-Caribbean sentiment by carrying stories of Caribbean people as lazy and sponging off the state reminiscent of Thomas Carlyle's nineteenth-century views. The response of the state and the media ensured that there was little outrage against the color bar, which stalked Caribbean people's working and leisure activities. Racist intimidation became a common part of Caribbean men's and women's everyday experiences, many of whom confronted Teddy boys, a postwar youth subculture of mainly white working-class male youths, some of whom were racist. Rita Sinclair, who arrived in England from Jamaica in the 1950s, remembered that walking the streets of London was "very very dangerous in those days . . . because of all these Teddy boys and especially at night if they go out they do attack you. They beat you up or killed you. But we fight them off . . . (I take my shoes off and whack them into their heads [laughter] . . . that was our experience)."[37]

The 1950s saw a growth of Caribbean novels depicting life in Britain: Lamming's *The Emigrants* (1954), Trinidadian V. S. Naipaul's *The Mimic Men* (1967), and Selvon's *The Lonely Londoners* (1956) all documented the commonplace aspects of life for Caribbean communities in postwar Britain, delving into themes such as interracial relationships, racist violence, and discrimination. Some also detailed the bonds of solidarity those from the Caribbean began to share. Many of these writers gained mass appeal through their involvement with the weekly BBC radio program *Caribbean Voices*, which enabled their work to reach a much larger audience. Nonetheless, racial animosity continued to rise and, unsurprisingly, violence again spilled out onto the streets. In August 1954 clashes broke out between black and white people in London's Camden Town. Four years later, Britain witnessed more white-led riots.

RIOTS AND MURDER

On August 23, 1958, in Nottingham, a riot broke out after a pub brawl instigated by the innocent act of a black man talking to a white woman led to a fight between a black man and a white man. Soon after, a crowd of over one thousand white men and a few white women attacked Caribbean people and left eight (black and white) hospitalized.[38] The day after the riots, white working-class Teddy boys prowled the streets looking for further fights, and black people were advised by police to remain indoors. With no black people to attack, they turned on each other and the police. More than fifty were arrested and twenty-four men and teenagers charged under the Public Order Act.[39] The disturbances clearly originated in animosity to interracial interaction, but the police tried to downplay this. The chief constable adamantly argued that "This was not a racial riot. The coloured people behaved in a most exemplary way by keeping out of the way . . . The people primarily concerned were irresponsible Teddy boys and persons who had had a lot to drink."[40]

This kind of color-blind racism, ignoring or denying the reality of racism as a provocation for violence, marked a distinct phase in the color bar—contrasting starkly with the earlier iterations of the racial-caste hierarchy, which focused on disseminating notions of racial inferiority. But ultimately both ended up enforcing the same goals: the maintenance of white supremacy. While the police tried to ignore the role of race in the violence, this was not so easy a week later, when white mobs attacked black people, their homes, and businesses, in Notting Hill.

Trouble began after a Swedish woman, Majbritt Morrison, argued with her Jamaican husband, Raymond Morrison, in Notting Dale, a council ward within Notting Hill. As their argument grew louder, crowds began to congregate. A man launched racial slurs at Raymond. Majbritt quickly came to her husband's defense. When the Morrisons' Caribbean friends joined them, a fight erupted, and as Majbritt was walking home she came face-to-face with rowdy crowds of white men who taunted her with words such as "nigger lover."[41] This sparked what would become Britain's largest white-led race riots. Crowds of white working-class youths descended on Notting Hill armed with iron bars, table legs, pieces of wood, and knives; black people were chased and beaten and their homes firebombed. Some of their white neighbors defended them and were themselves attacked. Most of the white youths involved were Teddy boys from underprivileged areas, such as Elephant and Castle, and fascists were, of course, quick to appear as well.[42] Violent confrontation between white and black people in West London continued into mid-September, and it was only after black people began to fight back that the police decided to intervene.

Police arrest a white man and woman during race riots in Notting Hill, London, August 1958.

The events in Notting Hill drew on the long tradition of anti-black racism, but they were also directly related to a web of short-term factors, including unfair housing and employment practices, government failure to develop infrastructure commensurate with population growth, government indifference to informing the public that those from the Caribbean had equal citizenship status with white Britons, and the prevailing tendency to deny the existence of racism. The Spectator blamed black people for the violence, warning that they "flood into a few slum and near-slum areas, creating antagonism among the poor whites already installed there, and providing the kind of community where crime and gangsterism can easily breed."[43]

Politicians likewise mourned the demise of law and order and indicted the growing black presence in Britain as the central problem. Conservative MP Cyril Osborne warned: "We are sowing the seeds of another 'Little Rock' and it is tragic. To bring the problem into this country with our eyes open is doing the gravest disservice to our grandchildren, who will curse us for our lack of courage."[44] The reference to events at Little Rock a year earlier showed that US race relations were already deeply influencing debate in Britain. In September 1957, nine Black American students enrolled at the all-white Little Rock Central High School, Arkansas, following the 1954 Supreme Court decision that segregation in public schools was unconstitutional. On the first day of school, Governor Orval Faubus called on the Arkansas National Guard to block the students' entry. Later that month, US president Dwight Eisenhower sent in federal troops to escort the nine students into school. Osborne was adamant that the same efforts to integrate black people into society should not happen in Britain, declaring it is "a white man's country, and I want it to remain so."[45] Pronouncements such as Osborne's stimulated the fascist movement, which gained ground after the riots. In 1960 the White Defence League and the National Labour Party merged to form the British National Party. Osborne's words also reveal how fascist ideas seeped into Westminster and would later directly influence policymaking.

Many Caribbean people were shocked and surprised about the riots. The lack of police intervention and the subsequent blame placed on black people contributed to growing disillusionment with the state for its indifference to protecting its citizens. Lamming echoed many others when he reflected:

> The West Indian, until then, had an implicit faith in the Law, and some ancient certainty that the police would be on his side . . . I recall a feeling of utter stupefaction; for I had argued in America—a year before—that it was difficult to draw parallels in spite of the prejudice, for Georgia or Alabama just could not happen anywhere in England.[46]

Police search a black man during race riots in
Notting Hill, London, September 1958.

Caribbean political leaders were so concerned about the riots that they sent a delegation to London to investigate, including the Jamaican premier Norman Manley, who rejected the proposal to decrease racist violence by no longer issuing passports. For him, the riots had little to do with competition over employment, housing, and women. Manley pointed to racial hostility as the central cause.[47] He thought Britain should intervene against racism with educational training and legislation to ban race discrimination. In remarks in the *New Statesman*, he maintained faith in the principles of British liberalism and justice, stressing the importance of mobilizing the "solid traditional and powerful British opinion which sets its face against colour prejudice and all forms of intolerance."[48] He also encouraged Caribbean men and women to continue to demand their equal rights in Britain. While Caribbean politicians visited black communities in the capital, no senior British politician accompanied them on the relatively short distance from Westminster or Whitehall to Notting Hill.[49]

In public comments, Macmillan blamed the race riots on hooliganism. The prime minister's strategy after the riots was to indirectly blame black people for the violence by arguing that the only way to stop it would be to restrict the migration of people of color.[50] In many ways, the riots were a boon for the government: with more people endorsing immigration control, they no longer had to worry about the appearance of racism. By opting to deal with racism by preventing people of color from entering the country, the government toed the fascist line of trying to keep Britain white. This shows again how deeply saturated and internalized racial hierarchy was in British culture—the assumption being that black and white people living among each other in Britain was fundamentally unnatural and undesirable, so black people must simply be excluded.

While some politicians used the riots to devise new immigration laws, others such as Labour MP Fenner Brockway collaborated with Caribbean activists to promote interracial solidarity. Brockway served as chairman of the anti-colonial lobby group the Movement for Colonial Freedom (MCF) and organized a "Mass Demonstration of Interracial Friendship" in Trafalgar Square. The prominent Trinidadian-born journalist Claudia Jones participated in MCF events. Having served as head of the Young Communist League in New York and edited the *Daily Worker* for the US Communist Party at the height of McCarthyism, she was arrested and charged under the Smith Act with advocating or being a member of a group that advocated the violent overthrow of the US government. In 1955, she was deported to Britain and quickly became a leading radical activist, founding in 1958 the influential *West Indian Gazette and Afro-Asian Caribbean News*.[51] Far-right white nationalists often targeted the newspaper, whose offices were based in Brixton, home to a growing number of people from the Caribbean. Jones was also involved in cultural activism, helping establish the first "Caribbean Carnival," held in St. Pancras Town Hall in January 1959.

Claudia Jones, 1948.

The first Notting Hill carnival, 1959, created by Claudia Jones in response to the previous year's race riots.

Other Caribbean groups were galvanized into action following racist violence. Jones was active in the Association for the Advancement of Coloured People (AACP). Established by Amy Ashwood Garvey, the organization was modeled on the National Association for the Advancement of Colored People in the US. Ashwood Garvey's residence in Notting Hill served as the headquarters of the AACP and a hostel for women of African descent. The AACP formed a legal fund to help black defendants sentenced with crimes following the violence in London and Nottingham.[52] The fund was aided by the West Indian Students' Union, an important organization that brought together Caribbean students, many of whom were politically active in Britain and on their return home, and the Committee of African Organisations

(CAO), an umbrella political organization of African student groups.[53] Key Caribbean activists were involved in the AACP, including Ashwood Garvey, Jones, and Grenada-born physician David Pitt, who was trying to become the Labour Party candidate in Hampstead. The Coloured People's Progressive Association, founded by actor Frances Ezzrecco, was also established after the riots, along with the West Indian Standing Conference, which brought together the High Commission of the WIF and the Migrant Services Division. As demonstrated by this mobilization of Caribbean activism after 1958, white violence precipitated a vigorous response.

The racist attacks continued. On May 16, 1959, Antiguan carpenter Kelso Benjamin Cochrane was stabbed to death by a gang of white teenagers in the Notting Hill area. Again, the police downplayed the role of race in Cochrane's murder, insisting that above all it was a robbery that had "absolutely nothing to do with racial conflict"[54] and made no arrests, despite the fact that recently released documents show that the police were aware of a suspect who had previously declared his intention to murder a black man on his release from prison.[55] In this iteration of the racial-caste system, the goal by the 1950s was to hide and eclipse the reality of racism, even as the efforts to enforce racial privilege became more extreme in some respects and intensified. Like the violence in Nottingham and Notting Hill, it catalyzed Caribbean activism.[56]

The day after the attack, members of the CAO and representatives of Caribbean and African groups met and drafted an open letter to Macmillan. In it, they boldly claimed that "Kelso Cochrane was murdered because he was coloured" and called on the prime minister and other political figures to openly condemn Cochrane's murder as "a sign that at topmost levels, the rights of Commonwealth citizens, irrespective of colour are held sacred." They asked: "Are we to be mauled down just because we are black?"[57] Activists banded together to create a burial committee for Cochrane, and from this collective, the Interracial Friendship Coordinating Council (IRFCC) was born, members of which met with Home Office officials and, afterward, organized a "We Mourn Cochrane" memorial service at St Pancras Town Hall. On the day of Cochrane's funeral, more than one thousand people attended the procession along Ladbroke Grove.[58] Caribbean activists and politicians used Cochrane's death to move the debate about racism away from white hooliganism toward the state's failure to protect its citizens.[59] But even as this was occurring, the government was busy preparing new legislation to maintain Britain's whiteness.

LEGISLATING RACISM

When in the 1959 general election the Conservatives were once more returned to government, calls for immigration restrictions intensified. The solution to limiting black migration without explicitly imposing a color bar came from the Ministry of Labour, which proposed dividing workers into three groups: skilled workers; those with job contracts in hand; and unskilled workers. Those who wanted to move to Britain would need to apply for a permit to enter the country, but only unskilled workers would face a quota.[60] Many believed that this plan would not penalize those from the old Dominions, as the majority would have work plans already in place. In contrast, people of color would be the majority in the third category.[61]

 This idea would later influence the 1962 Commonwealth Immigrants Act. The act divided Commonwealth citizens into three groups: those with employment already secured; those with skills considered advantageous to Britain; and unskilled laborers looking for work. Each group was eligible for A, B, and C vouchers, respectively, but those in the last group were subject to numerical control. This voucher system reduced migration to Britain. The act also gave the home secretary the power to deport individuals who had lived in Britain for less than five years if convicted of a criminal offense that led to a prison sentence.[62] Furthermore, it created a group of British subjects defined as "belonging" to the UK who were not subject to immigration control. This category included those born in Britain or whose passports had been issued on behalf of Britain. The effect was to exclude from the act CUKC residents in colonies whose passports were given by and on behalf of the colonial government.[63] To deflect criticism, the act allowed unrestricted entry for dependants of CUKCs who were already in Britain or who were later admitted.[64]

The object of the 1962 act was to keep black people out of Britain. The act's "restrictive effect," as mentioned in a government memo, "is intended to, and would in fact, operate on coloured people almost exclusively."[65] In the act, British colonial subjects and Commonwealth citizens were referred to as "coloured immigrants." Describing British subjects as immigrants and immigrants as "coloured" reflected how the Act further racialized men, women, and children who had as much right to be in Britain as their white counterparts.[66] The act laid bare the glaring hypocrisy and racism of the government. When the public heard that immigration needed controlling or else social problems would increase, they struggled to distinguish between people of color who were already resident from those trying to come in.[67] The immigrant label marked those from the Caribbean and other Commonwealth citizens of non-white countries as alien outsiders rather than integral long-standing insiders in Britain.

Before the act came into force in the spring of 1962, the proposed bill was met with significant opposition. In late 1961, Fenner Brockway organized public meetings and a conference through the MCF ahead of a parliamentary debate on the topic of

Commonwealth immigration. The MCF also led a public march on January 14, 1962, attended by around two thousand demonstrators. Through the conference and rally, the MCF aimed to create a broader anti-colonial grassroots movement against the proposed bill. The result was the creation of the Afro-Asian-Caribbean Conference (AACC),[68] which included prominent Caribbean activists such as Pitt, Jones, Trinidadian-born Pearl Connor, a literary agent and cultural activist, and Ezzrecco. They also worked alongside other groups like the West Indian Students' Union, Indian Workers' Association, and the CAO to hold a Commonwealth solidarity protest on February 13, 1962. For this event the AACC reached out to members of the High Commissions in the Caribbean, India, Malaya, Ghana, and Nigeria, asking for public statements against the proposed bill.[69] They called on "nurses and medical staff from hospitals in their uniforms, bus, train and transport personnel, factory, canteen and municipal workers in overalls or uniforms" in Britain to join the protest at the House of Commons in February 1962, where they demanded the withdrawal of the bill.[70]

Conservative MP Nigel Fisher, a member of the British Caribbean Association, a parliamentary lobby group created to promote interracial cooperation and shape public policy, also opposed the bill. Fisher pointed out the obvious contradiction between it and "our whole concept of a multi-racial Commonwealth"[71] and its barefaced hypocrisy, given widespread opposition to racial segregation in parts of Africa. "It seems strange to me," he noted, "that in Africa we attack *apartheid* and preach partnership, but in the United Kingdom we are today taking powers to exclude coloured British citizens, which is really a form of *apartheid* . . . Our words to Africa are inconsistent with our action."[72] Fisher's comments were poignant given that in May 1961 South Africa had withdrawn from the Commonwealth due to pressure from members to change its apartheid policy.

The bill ignited fierce debate among Caribbean politicians. The high commissioner for the West Indies Federation, Garnet Gordon, critiqued not only the proposed content of the bill but also its timing. In August 1961 Britain sought membership in the European Economic Community (EEC), which, established under the terms of the 1957 Treaty of Rome, fostered greater economic cooperation among member states. As EEC member states were allowed to have imperial possessions, Britain's application represented its attempt to remain a global power as more Asian, African, and Caribbean colonies edged toward independence. Although Britain's application was unsuccessful, it would have given European workers in member states the right to free migration, and Gordon wryly noted that "the possibility of non-British Europeans, exercising rights permitted to citizens of the Commonwealth restrictively, calls for much explanation."[73]

Meanwhile, in November 1961, Grantley Adams, then serving as prime minister of the West Indies Federation, expressed his views on the bill forcefully in a dispatch to Macmillan, describing it as a "flagrant disregard of every liberal principle on which Britain has based its customs and traditions since Lord Mansfield's famous judgement of 1772. West Indians are firmly convinced that by this action Britain has begun to take steps which are no different in kind to the basis on which the system of apartheid in South Africa is based." Britain, he insisted, had a "historic responsibility" due to the "rich (slave) trade in bodies and goods on which much of Britain's prosperity has been founded."[74]

Despite opposition, the bill received royal assent in April 1962. In June, Part II of the Commonwealth Immigrants Act came into effect, granting the home secretary the right to deport any Commonwealth citizen convicted of a serious crime who had resided in Britain for less than five years. Ministers hoped for smaller numbers of colonial and Commonwealth citizens, but instead many from the Caribbean, aware of upcoming restrictions, informed family members and friends that they should migrate before the doors shut. Caribbean arrivals rose sharply in 1960 between January and October, when 43,500 entered the country in comparison to 16,400 in 1959 and 29,800 in 1956.[75] Between July 1962 and June 1963 the intake of colonial subjects was 34,500, and within the next year the number increased to sixty-eight thousand.[76] Indeed, migration from newly independent members of the Commonwealth to Britain in 1960–62 was more than the number of all postwar colonial migration before.[77] The act, inherently racist, cemented state-led anti-black racism in immigration legislation, which would shape future laws. But for each action there is a reaction: brazen state racism fueled a vibrant radical wave of Caribbean-led anti-racist and Black Power activism.

BRITAIN'S BLACK POWER

Caribbean activist groups increased in the 1960s. Alongside the formation in London of the AACP and the ACCA, other parts of the country such as Manchester saw the creation of the British Coloured Association, the British Society for Coloured Welfare, the Leeward Islands People's Association, the West Indian National Association, among many others.[78] Black newspapers also thrived, including *Flamingo*, edited by Dominican Edward Scobie from 1961 to 1963; and *Magnet*, edited by Guyanese writer Jan Carew. Both shared national news about black life and culture in Britain and other parts of the African diaspora.

Caribbean activism in this era drew inspiration from black direct protest in other parts of the world, an indication of the global dimensions of anti-racism. In 1963, for instance, a group participated in the Bristol Bus Boycott. The city was home to around three thousand people from the Caribbean, and the Bristol Omnibus Company refused to employ Asian or black bus crews. Youth worker Paul Stephenson, the British-born son of a West African and a mixed-race woman, led the bus boycott, along with the West Indian Development Council, an action group created by Roy Hackett, Owen Henry, Prince Brown, and Audley Evans. The boycott lasted for four months and resulted in the company reversing the color bar. It borrowed tactics from the US civil rights movement, especially the Montgomery Bus Boycott of 1955, during which Rosa Parks's defiant courage drew international coverage.

Indeed, the concurrent civil rights movement in the US profoundly shaped British activism, as both movements drew connections and strength from each other.

Key US leaders ventured to Britain to share their message, which often inspired the formation of new anti-racist organizations. On December 5, 1964, Martin Luther King Jr. visited London on his way to Stockholm to receive the Nobel Peace Prize for leadership in the civil rights movement. King came with his friend and fellow activist Bayard Rustin, who worked with Trinidadian activist and LSE student Marion Glean to arrange a meeting between King and other anti-racist and anti-colonial organizers. With members of Multiracial Britain, a group of leftists committed to interracial cooperation, King met members of different African, Caribbean, and South Asian organizations after a historic speech at St. Paul's Cathedral. This meeting helped inspire a new umbrella group, the Campaign Against Racial Discrimination (CARD), which united Caribbean, West African, and South Asian anti-racist leaders that would later influence the government plans for anti-discrimination legislation, a tactic that would also reveal inner tensions within the group.[79] Nonetheless, CARD was part of the emerging urgency among Caribbean activists who realized they needed to create larger coalitions beyond sympathetic white people to enact meaningful change. As Glean described this militant turn: "It is time that we coloured people of Britain stop this nauseating begging for crumbs and behave like men. We have a right to share in the prosperity the three centuries of our labour has helped to build. We have a right to be ordinary citizens of Britain."[80]

Nebraska-born Malcolm X's visits to Britain also shaped Caribbean activism. He was no stranger to Caribbean history or politics. His mother, Louise Little, was born in Grenada and was an early supporter of Marcus Garvey. In December 1964, Malcolm X spoke at the University of Sheffield, the Oxford Union, and the University of Manchester, and on February 11, 1965, at the Africa Society at the LSE, and later visited Smethwick in the West Midlands. His trip to this industrial town was linked to events a year earlier, when Smethwick had become a hotbed in the election for white working-class and anti-immigrant hostility. During the election, Conservative candidate Peter Griffiths had used the explicitly racist campaign slogan: "If you want a nigger for a neighbour, vote Labour." His Labour opponent, Patrick Gordon Walker, had opposed the 1962 Commonwealth Immigrants Act, leading Griffiths to label him as anti–white working class and pro-immigrant. Griffiths's views were not exceptional—they embodied many of his constituents' views. The election was one of the first instances that racism had been so explicit in a mainstream political party. Again, it is a reminder of the visibility and invisibility of anti-black racism at the time; the simultaneous efforts to whitewash racism and insist that it is a nonissue, say, in the case of anti-black violence, while using explicit racism to whip up hysteria and win elections. Griffith won 47.6 percent of the vote in contrast to Walker's 42.6 percent. Labour won the election overall. Its response to the result and the changing tide of public opinion was in the years to come to alter their views on immigration restriction.

In Smethwick, Malcolm X met with BBC television crews who hoped to arrange a meeting between him and Peter Griffiths. When Griffiths withdrew, it left Malcolm X with time to walk around the town. During an interview, he explained why he had come, saying he "had been disturbed by reports that coloured people in Smethwick were being treated like those in Alabama . . . 'like the Jews under Hitler in the war.'"[81] On February 21, 1965, nine days after his visit to Smethwick, Malcolm X was murdered while preparing an address at the Organization of Afro-American Unity in New York.

After Malcolm X's inspiring visit, the Racial Adjustment Action Society (RAAS)—committed to combatting white racism—was created by Jan Carew; Roy Sawh, also from Guyana, who had worked as a street vendor selling the *West Indian Gazette*; and Michael de Freitas, who changed his name to Michael X.[82] These emerging groups would challenge legislative plans to impose further restrictions on the migratory movements of people of color.

Following the Labour Party's narrow victory in the December 1964 election, Prime Minister Harold Wilson set about making additional changes to immigration legislation. The government's plan for stricter immigration controls sat alongside the Race Relations Act 1965, which, they argued, aided black Britons in their social integration. The act outlawed discrimination in public spaces on the grounds of ethnicity, race, color, or nationality and treated as a criminal offense attempts to incite racial hatred. But it did not tackle racist discrimination in housing or employment because of fears of infringing too heavily on individuals' rights.

The act enforced penalties of up to £1,000 in fines and two years' imprisonment for any person convicted of inciting racial hatred. A Race Relations Board was created to oversee local conciliation committees that would mediate cases within the confines of the legislation. Prosecutions remained low. In the years 1965–69, only fifteen people faced prosecution for instigating racial hatred,[83] and the ineffectiveness of the act increased calls for its reform. In July 1967, Home Secretary Roy Jenkins announced his intention to amend the Race Relations Act to include housing and employment.[84] These emendations were designed to prevent further divisive racial conflict. Yet on the same day, he banned Stokely Carmichael from reentering Britain. For the past two weeks, Carmichael had been on a speaking tour in London. Carmichael's visit influenced Britain's burgeoning Black Power movement, which again highlighted the strong transnational dimensions fueling black activism.

Carmichael's trip coincided with a wave of black-led rebellion in the US against racism, police brutality, and inequality. In the summer of 1967, rebellions in Newark, New Jersey, would influence other areas, including Detroit, New York, Pontiac, and Toledo.[85] In London, Carmichael delivered talks at the West Indian Students' Centre in Earls Court, Africa House, and Speakers' Corner. He met with activists like C. L. R. James and spoke at the Marxist International Congress on the "Dialectics of Liberation" conference, where Black American communist Angela Davis was also in attendance. The government was apprehensive about Carmichael's potential impact on unrest, given the troubles in the US. Carmichael left Britain before the home secretary could put in place the ban prohibiting his return. By leaving Britain early, Carmichael was unable to speak at Michael X's RAAS meeting in Reading. Instead, Michael X decided to give the talk and was arrested under the Race Relations Act for inciting racial hatred.[86]

Although Black Power had been developing in Britain before 1967, Carmichael's trip energized it further. Black Power embraced the unifying label of black and sought to raise black consciousness through rejecting colonial-derived racist ideas and tropes about black people and challenging class oppression. After the dialectics conference, Obi Egbuna, a Nigerian-born writer and activist, and others in the Universal Coloured People's Association (UCPA) penned the pamphlet *Black Power in Britain: A Special Statement*, which drew heavily on Carmichael's speech and grounded the ideology of Black Power in the British context.[87]

Through the Committee of African Organisations he had helped organize Malcolm X's visit to Britain in 1965.[88] On April 19, 1968, at the UCPA general meeting, Egbuna resigned and established the British Black Panther Movement (BBPM) and became editor of its journal, *Black Power Speaks*. He left the UCPA in part because of ongoing debates about the meaning of Black Power.

Egbuna envisioned the BBPM as a secretive vanguardist revolutionary movement, distant from the larger community, that worked to shape an anti-capitalist revolution and supporting anti-colonial movements worldwide.[89] In Egbuna's words: "We do not dream for one moment that the Black people in Britain can organise themselves as a unit totally separate from other Black forces in the world. Black Power is an international concept."[90] But when Egbuna was imprisoned and held on remand for six months for conspiracy to murder police officers after publishing a 1968 pamphlet, *What to do when cops lay their hands on a Black Man at the Speaker's Corner*, he lost control of the group.[91] The BBPM remained a secretive organization, which makes their activities difficult to piece together, but among other changes the organization had new leadership, which fell first to David Udah. Udah was replaced in 1970 by Trinidad-born PhD student Altheia Jones-Lecointe, who was studying biochemistry at University College London. Jones-Lecointe came from a politically radical family: her mother, Viola Jones, served as a member of the Women's League of the ruling People's National Movement (PNM), and her two sisters would be involved in Black Power activism in Trinidad.[92]

With Jones-Lecointe as leader, the BBPM became involved in a range of activities. They aided the legal defense of black people, visited them in prison, led book groups, and held cultural and community activities.[93] In 1970 the center of the BBPM moved from Notting Hill to Brixton, and they created other branches in Finsbury Park and Acton, which increased their community outreach.[94] Under Jones-Lecointe, the BBPM turned to more orthodox Marxism.[95] It also joined in multiracial class struggles, forming alliances with white radicals and progressives. They had a youth group that dub poet and activist Linton Kwesi Johnson participated in. Like their US counterpart the Black Panther Party, BBPM members carried weapons, usually knives, as part of their self-defense. Their direct protests often led to conflicts with the police, and they campaigned against police brutality. Between 1970 and 1972 the director of public prosecutions gathered files on the group. The Metropolitan Police also monitored the group. From the 1960s, the police became more aggressive in their attitude toward black activists, youths, and those on the margins of society.

The trial of the Mangrove Nine was momentous in the history of targeting activists, especially those in the BBPM. The Mangrove Nine were seven black men and two black women who in 1971 faced charges after a clash with police at a demonstration against police harassment of the Mangrove restaurant, an informal center for the black community in Notting Hill, which was raided several times by the police, who suspected drug use there, with little evidence. The Mangrove Nine included the owner of the Mangrove, Trinidad-born Frank Crichlow, Jones-Lecointe, Rhodan Gordan, Darcus Howe, Godfrey Millet, Rupert Glasgow Boyce, Barbara Beese, Rothwell Kentish, and Anthony Carlisle Innis. Many but not all were members of the BBPM. Activist Darcus Howe (C. L. R. James's great-nephew) challenged repeated police harassment by organizing a protest march with the BBPM in August 1970. During the march, the police clashed with protesters, and Howe, Critchlow, Jones-Lecointe, and six others were tried for various offenses, including affray and riot, bodily harm to police officers, and carrying offensive weapons. The BBPM mobilized grassroots support for the trial and, through Howe, placed police racism under a national media spotlight.

Eight members of the black British activists' group Mangrove Nine, December 16, 1971. Left to right, front: Rothwell Kentish, Rhodan Gordon, Altheia Jones-Lecointe, and Barbara Beese. Left to right, back: Frank Crichlow, Godfrey Millet, Rupert Boyce, and Darcus Howe. The ninth member, Anthony Innis, is not pictured.

The trial began in early October 1971 and lasted for eleven weeks. Throughout, the defendants used the trial to highlight British state racism. They asked for but were denied an all-black jury, invoking the right to a trial by a jury of one's peers as they argued white jurors were divorced from the reality of racist discrimination that they faced in their daily lives.[96] Jones-Lecointe and Howe decided to defend themselves, as did Rhodan Gordon. In their speeches, they criticized state authoritarianism and police brutality. They linked their contemporary fight to past injustices and to similar struggles that faced black people in other parts of the diaspora. By the end of the trial, the jury found the defendants not guilty of the most serious charge of conspiracy to incite a riot. Meanwhile, Gordon, Boyce, Innis, and Jones-Lecointe received suspended sentences for lesser crimes. The Mangrove

Nine trial encapsulated so much of what made this era unique in the struggle against the racial-caste hierarchy: the growth of radical black activism and police harassment under the guise of color-blind liberalism.

South Asians played an important role within radical black political circles. The movement embraced a broader political definition of blackness that sought to create coalitions among other people of color. Ambalavanar Sivanandan was one such figure. A Sri Lankan Tamil, Sivanandan moved to Britain in 1958 around the time of the Notting Hill riots. He found solidarity in political blackness. In his own words: "Black Power, in particular, spoke to me very directly because it was about race and class both at once."[97] After leaving his career in banking, he became director of the Institute of Race Relations (IRR), an independent educational charity based in London, and wrote articles for the IRR's journal *Race & Class*, established in 1974. Similar to Sivanandan, Bob Ramdhanie, from Trinidad, came to Britain in his late teens in 1965 and spoke about his identification as black, remembering: "We were really strong Caribbean Black people. All of us were Black in those days. We never spoke about Indians or South Asians . . . In those days, when I was growing up . . . we were all Black people."[98]

While many black radical groups were male-dominated, especially with regard to leadership, black women often played critical roles within them. Alongside Jones-Lecointe, figures like Olive Morris and Barbara Beese were active in Black Power. Leila Hassan and Gerlin Bean played important roles in the Black Unity and Freedom Party.[99] Zainab Abbas served as international secretary in the Black Liberation Front formed in 1971. Some of these women would also play a leading role in the growing black British feminist and women's movement. Bean, alongside Stella Dadzie, Abbas, Morris, Beverley Bryan, and Liz Obi, cofounded the Brixton Black Women's Group, which sought to dismantle racism and sexism, and was inherently internationalist.[100] In 1978, Susanne Scafe, Gail Lewis, Bean, Dadzie, Morris, Beverley Bryan, and others cofounded the Organisation of Women of African and Asian Descent (OWAAD), a national umbrella group for women of color in Britain. OWAAD specifically sought unity among women of Asian and African descent and challenged both male patriarchy and white feminism, spreading its message through its journal FOWAAD! OWAAD's activism was broad. They campaigned on behalf of nurses, and protested against the use of Depo-Provera, a form of contraception disproportionately given to African and Asian women, which had a long-term negative impact on fertility. Alongside OWAAD, the black feminist group Southall Black Sisters (SBS) campaigned against "virginity testing" at airports for South Asian women who were entering Britain. Gynecological examinations known as "virginity tests" were conducted by doctors and immigration staff based on racist and sexist assumptions that South Asian women were abusing immigration rules in the 1970s. These examinations were seen as "proof" that the women were unmarried and did not already have children. OWAAD split in 1982 due in part to internal conflicts. But their influence continued, as did black British feminism more broadly, which is evident in the 1985 landmark publication *The Heart of the Race: Black Women's Lives in Britain*, by Dadzie, Beverley Bryan, and Suzanne Scafe.

Developments in publishing and literature helped disseminate black radical politics. Guyanese activists Jessica and Eric Huntley moved to Britain in the 1950s and established the Bogle-L'Ouverture publishing house, which became a key activist and cultural space. The Huntleys also worked with Andrew Salkey, a Panamanian-born Jamaican. He moved to Britain in the 1950s and was an important figure for the BBC's *Caribbean Voices*. Alongside Barbadian (Edward) Kamau Brathwaite and Trinidadian John La Rose, Salkey formed the Caribbean Artists Movement around

December 1966, which played a leading role in creating links between black political and cultural expression. New Beacon Books was another important vehicle for black radical politics. Established by Trinidadian John La Rose alongside Sarah White, New Beacon Books followed in a long tradition of Caribbean publishing in Britain and became its first black publishing house in 1966, selling major texts by black activists.

The rise of Black Power in Britain was critical to bringing the consequences of decolonization abroad home to Britain, through the insistence that black people be included as insiders rather than outsiders in Britain, and in expansive new definitions of blackness that critiqued the logics of racial competition imposed by anti-black racism. Black Power activists saw their struggles connected to wider battles waged against ongoing racism, class inequalities, and the legacies of colonialism in other parts of the world. This is because they were aware that due to the way the racial-caste hierarchy operated, it was always in dialogue with other liberation global struggles against oppression waged by, in the main, white elites at the top of the caste structure. The transnational connections made by black activists in Britain in the 1960s would continue well into the 1980s and overlap with struggles against colonialism in parts of southern Africa, as well as apartheid.[101]

During the 1960s and '70s, Black Power politics would also come to shape Caribbean activism within education. A raft of new educational policy changes in the 1960s negatively impacted black children, especially those with a Caribbean background. Fearing that white children were becoming a minority in classrooms in areas with high migration figures, government policies from 1964 recommended that some local education authorities disperse "immigrant children" in order to prevent too many attending local schools. They recommended the "busing" of immigrant children to schools outside their neighborhood. These decisions followed a report by the Commonwealth Immigration Advisory Council in 1964, which noted:

> The presence of a high proportion of immigrant children in one class slows down the general routine of working and hampers the work of the whole class, especially where the immigrants do not speak or write English fluently. This is clearly in itself undesirable and unfair to all children in the class ... The evidence we have received strongly suggests that if a school has more than a certain percentage of immigrant children among its pupils the whole character and ethos of the school is altered.[102]

Busing as a potential solution was used also, more widely, in the US on black and white children and proved another way in which racial policies in Britain mirrored those across the Atlantic.

Often black children who were bused continued to face racist treatment, and for this and other varied reasons black parents in both Britain and the US protested against the policy. In 1968, Caribbean parents in the London borough of Haringey realized that along with busing, as more schools turned into comprehensives (nonselective high schools), there was a policy of moving black children between schools and funnelling them into lower-ability bands (due to stereotypes of Caribbean children as intellectually inferior to white children) as part of a policy of grouping pupils based on their ability. For many Caribbean parents, education provided one of the only means for their children to strive for equality with their white peers and was critical to social mobility. Moving black children to lower-ability bands, where teachers often had and acted upon prejudicial views of the child's ability to progress, proved another way of enforcing racist practices that drew on notions of black intellectual inferiority while trying to make racism invisible. These parents, however, were aware of the racism behind the policy and created the North London West Indian Association (NLWIA) and led a campaign against "banding." They also raised issues with the number of black children placed in Educationally Subnormal (ESN) schools, established as an alternative to mainstream schools. Statistics indicated that in 1972 Caribbean students accounted for 4.9 percent of those in ESN schools while making up only 1.1 percent of children in state primary and secondary schools.[103]

In 1971 New Beacon Books published Grenadian scholar and activist Bernard Coard's pamphlet *How the West Indian Child is Made Educationally Sub-Normal in the British School System*. Coard found that figures from the Inner London Education Authority report titled *The Education of Immigrant Pupils in Special Schools for Educationally Subnormal Children* noted that five of their secondary ESN schools had over 30 percent "immigrant" pupils in 1967.[104] In 1970 figures showed that although "immigrant" children made up around 17 percent of the school population, around 34 percent of the ESN school population were "immigrants," and four out of five in these ESN schools came from a Caribbean background.[105]

Coard's study documented the devastating impact of ESN schools on children with a Caribbean background. He argued that, as a consequence of being placed into an ESN school, a pupil would be eligible only for "simple, repetitive jobs of a menial kind, which involve little use of intelligence . . . In turn, through his getting poor wages, poor housing, and having no motivation to better himself, his children can look forward to a similar educational experience and similar career prospects!"[106] Coard pointed out that teachers played a role in recommending that Caribbean children go to ESN schools, by assuming that these children were less intelligent. He observed too that many middle-class teachers acted on their bias against those with different cultural practices and language abilities. Of course, some teachers were also openly prejudiced.

To combat educational racism, Coard encouraged the establishment of supplementary schools, and around 150 were created, spearheaded by Caribbean parents.[107] They became important for fighting racism in education: students learned the national curriculum but also took classes on black history, deemed critical in anti-racist circles as a means to correct ignorant understandings of the black past and to improve children's self-esteem. Black studies grew in the 1970s and expanded in higher education, but its integration into school curricula was controversial. The group Teachers against Racism, created in 1971, led a campaign for black studies to be part of school curricula. But even as some aspects of black studies found their way into mainstream schools, educational activists voiced concerns about how the radical politics of anti-racism, which had the potential to both expose young people to the realities of the racial-caste hierarchy and prepare them to challenge it, was getting eclipsed in the narrative by liberal multiculturalism that sometimes overlooked institutionalized racism and instead presented a much more sanitized, often color-blind view of Britain's racist past and present.

Yet new legislative efforts to restrict people of color from entering Britain flourished apace with Black Power and Caribbean education activism.

RACIST BACKLASH

In late February 1968, the Commonwealth Immigrants Act passed as an emergency piece of legislation. It amended the 1962 act and further limited the rights of Commonwealth citizens. The act removed the rights of CUKCs, allowing only those born in Britain or who had one parent or grandparent born in Britain the right to work and live in Britain. The act passed amid fears that two hundred thousand Kenyan Asians would pursue their right to move to Britain as Kenya was undergoing an Africanization policy that targeted Asians. The act also imposed a quota system of entry vouchers.[108] To counterbalance this explicitly racist act, the Labour government passed a Race Relations Act, which amended the 1965 version and made it illegal to refuse employment, housing, or public services due to a person's race, skin color, ethnicity, or nationality.

But the government's efforts to appear balanced in its approach to immigration remained racist at their core. Moreover, many on the right railed loudly against the Race Relations Act, arguing that equality for people of color would lead to inequality for white people. For instance, in a 1968 article in the Wolverhampton newspaper *Express and Star*, a spokesman for the West Midland Engineering Employers' Association (who stated he was not speaking on their behalf) remarked: "I think it is highly probable that people will bend over backwards to show they are not being discriminatory, perhaps, even, to the extent of discriminating against white workers."[109] Others, such as Conservative MP for Wolverhampton South West, Enoch Powell, argued that the act infringed on individual liberties, denying a person the right "to discriminate in the management of his own affairs between one fellow citizen and another."[110] Following a Cambridge classics degree, Powell embarked on an academic career in Australia, later serving in India during the Second World War. As minister for health from 1960 to 1963, Powell had overseen the recruitment of Caribbean nurses in Britain but had grown more troubled by Commonwealth migration by the late 1960s. As a staunch empire loyalist, he saw colonialism as historian Shirin Hirsch has described as "a world system deeply enshrined in his very being, interwoven into what it meant to be an Englishman."[111] As former colonies became sovereign states, Powell feared greatly that white British dominance was diminishing. And as more Commonwealth citizens moved to Britain, he feared even more that their presence would not only diminish but ultimately destroy Britain.

In April 1968, in front of an audience of around eighty-five Tories in the Midland Hotel in Birmingham, Powell delivered his infamous "Rivers of Blood" speech. Although Powell addressed a small audience, he wanted his speech to get national attention, sending transcripts to the national and local press. An ATV television crew broadcast the speech live. In his remarks, Powell warned his audience that if the current rate of Commonwealth migration continued, "In fifteen or twenty years, on present trends, there will be in this country three and a half million Commonwealth immigrants and their descendants." According to Powell: "Whole areas, towns and parts of towns across England will be occupied by different sections of the immigrant and immigrant-descended population."[112] For Powell, white Britons were the victims of Commonwealth migration, for they "found themselves made strangers in their own country. They found their wives unable to obtain hospital beds in childbirth, their children unable to obtain school places, their homes and neighbourhoods changed beyond recognition."[113] Speaking of the Race Relations Act, Powell remarked that white Britons "now learn that a one-way privilege is to be established by Act of Parliament: a law, which cannot, and is not intended to, operate to protect them or redress their grievances, is to be enacted to give the stranger, the disgruntled and the *agent provocateur* the power to pillory them for their private actions."[114]

Pointing across the Atlantic, Powell prophesied that the racial unrest in the US, "that tragic and intractable phenomenon," would soon be commonplace in Britain.[115] Powell's speech was noteworthy for his specific animosity toward children. He described black children born in Britain as "wide-grinning piccaninnies."[116] And he famously predicted "the River Tiber foaming with much blood." [117]

After the speech, Conservative leader Edward Heath swiftly sacked Powell from his Shadow Cabinet, describing "Rivers of Blood" as "racialist in tone."[118] But Powell's speech simply echoed the words of Edward Long from the eighteenth century, as well as fascists of the day who were keen to claim their influence. After Powell's speech, a National Front spokesman told the Guardian: "We have been saying for donkeys' years, what Powell has at last belatedly come out with, but he has given it an air of respectability."[119] Although in the letters section of *The Times* it noted that the speech was "the first time that a serious British politician has appealed to racial hatred, in this direct way, in our postwar history,"[120] Powell was not doing anything that prime ministers Attlee, Churchill, Eden, Macmillan, Home, and Wilson hadn't also been trying to do since 1948: namely, maintaining the white British domestic nation at the cost of its black and Asian citizens.

And Powell garnered a considerable amount of support, especially among kindred fascists and white working-class racists. Days after his speech, hundreds of London dockworkers marched to Westminster alongside meat porters from Smithfield to protest against Powell's dismissal.

Powell's actions serve, again, as a reminder that Britain has never been on some sort of liberal march forward—from a time when racism was a lamentable aberration on Britain's liberal ideals to a post-colonial time when the country became even more non-racist. On the contrary, the trajectory is a jagged, rough, and uneven road, and it's more the case that the racial-caste hierarchy gets reiterated and metamorphoses into new forms than that it gets increasingly diminished.

African-Caribbean people were profoundly impacted by Powell's speech. Jamaican-born Rhodes Scholar and later influential scholar Stuart Hall, who traveled to Britain in the 1950s, remembered "the sudden, shared feeling of fear, the sense of hostility, the huddling together against the impending violence, the unspoken aggression in the streets as little groups of black men and women came together to discuss how to respond to the violence it seemed calculated to unleash."[121]

Hall's and other Caribbean people's fears of violence were soon realized. Indian journalist Dilip Hiro recounted twelve incidents of racist violence occurring in Wolverhampton in just the first two weeks after the speech.[122] But in a reprise of events after the racist violence in Nottingham and Notting Hill, people of color collaborated to defend themselves and challenge racism. After the speech, Caribbean, Indian, and Pakistani labor groups formed the Black People's Alliance and in 1969 led the "March for Dignity" against racism and the 1968 Commonwealth Immigrants Act. The march, comprising thousands of protesters, who converged on Downing Street, became one of the largest demonstrations against racist discrimination.[123]

It was evident that broader political coalitions had gathered force in the 1960s to counter anti-black racism. At the same time, racism intensified. Powell's speech became the first of many utterances by politicians on both the left and the right that encouraged white Britons to target blame not at political policies but at individuals—in this case, citizens scapegoated as "immigrants." Politicians would use this scapegoating as an effective tactic for years to come, and it would influence another racially exclusionary piece of amended legislation, the 1971 Immigration Act.

Passed by the new Conservative government, the act explicitly centred whiteness as the primary basis of British national identity. It defined British nationality on the basis of ancestral ties to Britain and did so by introducing the term "patrial." The act allowed only patrials, those born in Britain or a citizen of a Commonwealth state with a parent born in Britain, the right to enter and stay in Britain. The act ended the right of CUKCs to enter Britain but gave the right to abide (to live, work, and enter Britain) to those who had lived in Britain for at least five years.

Essentially, the act codified whiteness with Britishness.[124] Yet the irony of the act was soon evident when on the same day that it came into effect, January 1, 1973, Britain entered the EEC, giving European member-state citizens the right to enter and settle in Britain.

State-led racism—in the form of policies that exacerbated competition among Britons, nonexistent or weak racist discrimination laws, and above all explicitly racially exclusionary legislation—marked British efforts to entrench anti-black racism and racial division, and precipitated a wave of racist violence. All these tactics were essential to the maintenance of the racial-caste hierarchy in the three decades after the war. But these efforts to entrench were never uncontested. Instead, they incited a vigorous response by Caribbean people and their allies, who forcefully demanded their rights to enjoy the spoils of their ancestors' labor, in the motherland. This entrenchment sat alongside a broader decline in the British Empire in the wake of the Second World War, the humiliation of the Suez Canal crisis, and the rise of US influence in the Caribbean. These decades saw a dual decline of the British Empire with a larger rise, through Caribbean migration, of the British Empire coming home to Britain. The response to these issues on the part of Caribbean people was political radicalism, and their actions were matched by the radicalism and revolutionary activism of those who stayed in the Caribbean.

9

"Flag independence"

Caribbean Black Power and the Rise of Neocolonialism, Neoliberalism, and US Imperialism

"Today, in spite of our 'independence' real power is still in the hands of foreign white people who own our basic resources. The social structure is still white on top, brown in the middle and black at the bottom. Black people still have no economic power. White culture still reigns supreme."[1] These words, written by George Beckford, a Jamaican student-activist and later a political theorist, appeared in the February 1969 edition of the radical newspaper *Abeng*. Formed in the aftermath of the "Rodney riots"—sparked after the Jamaican government prevented the Guyanese scholar-activist Walter Rodney from reentering the country—Abeng became an influential mouthpiece for Black Power protest and ideas that swept throughout the Caribbean in the late 1960s to mid-1970s, which represented the first major political challenge in the Anglophone region in the late twentieth century.

The initial enthusiastic optimism that followed independence was soon replaced with a sense of déjà vu, as the limits of constitutional decolonization came starkly into view. Black Power activists loudly criticized Caribbean "flag independence," the notion that nothing had changed after independence except for new national flags. And they criticized middle-class leaders, dubbed Afro-Saxons—"the educated, colored English gentleman who imitates European models"— for continuing colonial-derived economic, social, and cultural policies.[2] They were not the only ones to notice the persistence of colonialism in sovereign states: in 1970, a CIA report noted that "political independence in Guyana, Trinidad-Tobago, Jamaica and Barbados . . . has (not) significantly altered their socioeconomic structures. In many ways, the social patterns that developed in the plantation economies during the days of colonialism persist today."[3] In attacking the limits of constitutional decolonization, Black Power advocates questioned who had power in the Caribbean. In many cases, the answer was Britain, Canada, and the US. Black Power was not limited to those areas that had recently become independent. In non-sovereign states, Black Power became a vibrant movement that revealed the fragility of ongoing colonial control.

Caribbean Black Power took aim at white supremacy, colonialism, and class inequality. One of its key proponents, Walter Rodney, defined Black Power as "(1) the break with imperialism which is historically white racist; (2) the assumption of power by the black masses in the islands; (3) the cultural reconstruction of the society in the image of the blacks."[4] Black Power activists called for economic, political, and cultural change and tried to subvert the persistent denigration of all things black and African. Changing the psychological mindset of African-Caribbean people was crucial too. Powerful phrases that circulated across the Black Atlantic like "Black is Beautiful" and the wearing of dashikis and African hairstyles were all challenges to European beauty standards. Yet, as historian Kate Quinn notes, "Caribbean Black Power was not a singular ideology but a heterogeneous movement that encompassed a range of convergent and divergent political positions and concerns."[5]

Global and regional forces shaped Caribbean Black Power. Caribbean students based at colleges and universities in Canada and the US became inspired by Black Power protest movements in these locations, identifying similarities to struggles in the Caribbean. At home the burgeoning Rastafarian movement in islands like Jamaica emphasized that post-independence freedom had proven elusive—a theme Bob Marley and the Wailers often sang about, in hits like "Get Up, Stand Up" and "Redemption Song," as well as a host of other reggae and calypso artists.

Although widely popular, Black Power in the Caribbean was far from uncontested. Within the movement, there were debates regarding political blackness and the inclusion of others, such as Asians, within the category. The movement also debated whether African culture should be privileged above creole Caribbean culture. Issues relating to gender sometimes caused tensions, with black men occasionally overlooking how sexism affected the challenges faced by black women.[6]

Across the region, Black Power protests distinguished between primary and secondary decolonization. If primary constitutional decolonization is understood as the transfer of political power from white men to black and mixed-race men, then Black Power marked a more radical form of secondary decolonization led by the masses, whose goal was to attack the lingering presence of the racial-caste hierarchy.[7] A closer look at this secondary decolonization in Jamaica and Trinidad and Tobago reveals the various methods Black Power activists used in their quest to transform the Caribbean. Meanwhile, in Bermuda, Black Power activities focused on challenging the island's colonial status.

In the aftermath of Black Power movements in sovereign Caribbean states, a new political and economic transformation was taking place that would enshrine the racial-caste hierarchy further through neocolonialism and neoliberalism. Neocolonialism—"the indirect domination of a society which, very likely but not necessarily, once held the status of a colony"—and neoliberalism—"an entire structure of beliefs founded on right-wing, but not conservative, ideas about individual freedom, political democracy, self-regulating markets and entrepreneurship"—ravaged sovereign states.[8] Neoliberalism, a capacious concept, applies not just to the economy but also to intellectual ideas, political policies, and social and cultural practices.[9] According to historian Daniel Rodgers, at an economic level, neoliberalism

> inscribes on politics and culture the needs of a global capitalism that sustains itself on the free flow of capital, goods, disembedded labor, and market-friendly state policies. It does not rely on the state in the same way that the 'embedded' corporate capitalism of the mid twentieth century did, but it is not a creature of the minimal state either. It depends, rather, on complex structures of institutional supports, business-friendly regulations, and free-range investment opportunities arrayed in different ways across the globe.[10]

At its core it has been described as "the restoration or reconstitution of naked class power," and the spread of inequality.[11]

Neocolonialism and neoliberalism were features of a late twentieth-century new world order that came to ensure the continuance of the British Empire, albeit in a different form from earlier periods, in sovereign and non-sovereign territories that remained tied to Britain. But it was simultaneously a time when British political influence in the independent Caribbean was waning, as the region came under the US's sphere of influence. Taken together, they all shaped the persistence of racial capitalism that was critical to the racial-caste hierarchy.

This shift unfolded in different ways in the Caribbean. In 1970s Jamaica, it took the form of political contestations with the US and economic collapse caused by local and global factors. In Grenada, it was shaped by a revolution that was soon followed by a US-led invasion. Meanwhile, in the Cayman Islands it was evident in the growth of the offshore financial industry, which ensured the hoarding of wealth in the hands of the few at the expense of the many, contributing to waxing global inequality. Throughout the Caribbean, these developments also informed the expansion of tourism, crime, and violence—all of which became hallmarks of the final decades of late twentieth-century and early twenty-first-century Caribbean life.

POST-INDEPENDENCE DÉJÀ VU

The early years of Jamaican independence looked promising. Known as the "golden era," the 1960s saw the island's economy grow in part because of the ongoing success of the bauxite and tourist industries. Due to an array of favorable policies, including tax incentives—which it was hoped would see post-colonial states borrow economic models from the US and Europe in the promise that it would modernize the Caribbean—foreign businesses continued to flock to the island, with American and Canadian companies holding monopolies in those industries.[12]

Foreign control of the tourist industry increased racial tensions. Wealthy white tourists were largely cut off from the black majority, mingling instead in the somewhat artificial world of US-style hotels, some of which imposed a color bar that stoked resentment between residents and vacationers. Furthermore, most of the profits from tourism went to the foreign companies that owned the luxury resorts. Evan X. Hyde, a British Honduran graduate from Dartmouth College, summed up Black Power activists' views of the industry with a quip: "Tourism is whorism."[13] US and Canadian imperialism in the Caribbean came also through their control of finance. By the mid-twentieth century, US private investment in the Anglophone Caribbean amounted to $2.5 billion.[14] Canada, too, had a substantial financial stake in the region, controlling 60–70 percent of its banks in the early 1970s.[15]

Although the manufacturing industry saw more local Jamaican ownership, the economic model created vast class and color hierarchies, as the capitalist class predominantly comprised white, Jewish, Chinese, Syrian, and Lebanese individuals.[16] Black and mixed-race members of the educated middle class took advantage of the increase in professional jobs, but dark-skinned working-class black people remained overwhelmingly poor and unemployed. By the late 1960s, 150,000 Jamaicans were unemployed.[17] In urban areas, telephone, light, and power services had continued to deteriorate since independence, and the rural regions still struggled. After years of drought, water supplies were also scarce. Migration to Britain or the US was seen as the only escape. But with doors to these countries closing, many were left to piece together lives on the margins of society.

Poor, overcrowded housing triggered the rise of deprived areas in Kingston like Tivoli Gardens and Trench Town, which soon became a space for "garrison politics" as the Jamaican Labour Party (JLP) and People's National Party (PNP) armed rival gangs to drum up party support, which in turn amplified violence. Famously, Trench Town was home to Bob Marley, whose music with the Wailers, described the proliferating Rastafarianism (which had its roots amid rising poverty in the 1930s) fashioned by everyday life in garrison areas. Rastafarians believed that Africans were the Israelites of the Old Testament and saw life in Jamaica as a type of temporary forced exile in Babylon. Their vision of one day returning to the spiritual and physical homeland of Africa influenced Rastafarian reggae musicians who created the soundtrack to the Black Power movement.

Rastafarian critiques of Jamaican society and especially the persistence of white superiority led some to wage war on the state. In 1960, Rev. Claudius Henry launched an armed attack and even reached out to Fidel Castro, expressing support and solidarity for Cuba's revolutionary struggle. Henry's Rastafarian group of around a hundred worked with the First Africa Corps, a militant New York–based group, to oust the Jamaican government, but to no avail.[18] Recognizing that Rastafarian ideas posed a serious threat to the state, the Jamaican government intensified attacks on the community. In 1963, the killing of a gas station owner, allegedly by Rastafarians in Coral Gardens near Montego Bay, led to the arrest, detention, and torture of hundreds.[19] Confrontations between the state and Rastafarians were part of the growth of police violence in the post-independence era that, in many ways, mirrored the colonial use of force to quash disturbances before 1962. From August 1967 to April 1968, police shot around thirty-one people, sixteen of whom died.[20]

The next instability to rock the island was anti-Chinese disturbances in 1965. Conflict between African-Jamaicans and Chinese (many of the latter being descendants of Chinese indentured labor from the nineteenth century) had flared up at different times across the decades, often shaped by the economic tensions and class inequalities of the two communities. While many Chinese-Jamaicans were wealthy and sat comfortably within the middle rungs of the racial-caste hierarchy, this was not the case for all. The crisis started when a female employee of a store in Kingston alleged that her Chinese employers had beaten her following a disagreement. Subsequently, an angry crowd of hundreds attacked Chinese businesses over the course of a week, which left eight people shot and ninety arrested.[21] The 1965 disturbances indicated worsening racial and economic tensions on the island, and the next year saw further, politically motivated violence between supporters of the PNP and JLP and the police in areas in West Kingston from February 1966 until the election ended in 1967.

The state was trying to quell disturbances as it was simultaneously attempting to engender a sense of collective national identity. After independence, Jamaica selected a new national motto,

"Out of Many, One People," its leaders keen to stress the island's multiracial demographics. But the island's population was overwhelmingly made up of people of African descent (91.4 percent in 1967), which led many to argue that the government actually wanted to avoid labeling the nation as a black country to appeal to white tourists and, in turn, continue the colonial-derived denigration of black African culture.[22] Katrin Norris poignantly portrayed how blackness was viewed in the post-independence era, writing: "Racial equality exists in Jamaica, but it is an equality on the white man's terms, based on the presupposition that the white man has agreed to tolerate the black man, rather than on a belief in the black man's equal rights."[23] In an attempt to silence this criticism, in 1964 the Jamaican government repatriated Marcus Garvey's body from London to Kingston and designated him, along with the enslaved leader in the 1831 rebellion Sam Sharpe and the female leader "Nanny of the Maroons," all official national heroes.

But these symbolic acts did little to address racial, color, and class hierarchies on the island that would explode in 1968. That year, Rodney took a position as lecturer at the Mona campus of the University of the West Indies (UWI), where his teaching of African and Caribbean history and his critique of colonialism and neocolonialism garnered him a large student following. He also taught among the youth and Rastafarians in poor urban areas. With these "groundings," as they were called, Rodney connected history with politics to argue that the Jamaican government was serving "the interests of a foreign, white capitalist system, and at home they uphold a social structure which ensures that the black man resides at the bottom of the social ladder."[24] Rodney construed "black" to include Africans and Indians. In his opinion,

> the moment that power is equitably distributed among several ethnic groups, the very relevance of making the distinction

between groups will be lost. What we must object to is the current image of a multiracial society living in harmony—that is a myth designed to justify the exploitation suffered by the blackest of our population, at the hands of the lighter-skinned groups.[25]

According to Rodney, "Black Power must proclaim that Jamaica is a black society . . . we will treat all other groups in the society on that understanding—they can have the *basic rights of all individuals* but *no privileges to exploit Africans* as has been the pattern during slavery and ever since."[26] Students at Mona were deeply influenced by Rodney's groundings, and Black Power groups emerged among them.

Wary of another rebellion from below, the Jamaican government—headed by former Jamaican leader Alexander Bustamante's protégé, cousin, and trade unionist Hugh Shearer, who became prime minister in April 1967—increased police surveillance of Rodney and other Black Power activists. The government also repressed radical black and revolutionary literature, banning works penned by Carmichael, Malcolm X, and Che Guevara. Repression soon led to riots. In October the following year the Shearer government made the decision to ban Rodney from reentering Jamaica, following his attendance at the Black Writers Conference in Montreal. According to Shearer, Rodney posed an ominous threat to national security due to his alleged "plots and plans to promote a Castro-type revolution in Jamaica."[27] Shearer's government used Rodney's trips to Cuba and his attendance at a student congress in Leningrad as evidence of his communist affiliation, although Rodney was not a member of any communist party.[28]

When news of Rodney's ban reached Mona campus, UWI students met with Ralph Gonsalves, the St. Vincent–born president of the UWI students' guild, and organized a protest. The next day, a group set off to deliver petitions to the offices of the prime minister and the minister of home affairs, Roy McNeil. On their way, students marched past the headquarters of the Bustamante Industrial Trade Union (BITU), which was still linked to the JLP, and here a clash occurred between rival unions, which was broken up by police using batons and tear gas. The march ignited other larger protests involving nonstudent groups in downtown Kingston.[29] As Gonsalves remembered: the "unemployed youths and workers gave the events a new turn. For them the protest was not so much about a lecturer who was banned—however influential he might have been—but about the inequalities stemming from the class and racial oppression in the country."[30] Gonsalves also noted that: "More than likely, criminal elements also took advantage of the commotion to loot and plunder... Big businesses, both foreign and local, were attacked. They included Canadian Imperial Bank of Commerce, Bank of London and Montreal, Pan-American, Air Jamaica."[31] During the protests two people died, twenty-three were arrested, and several police officers injured;[32] damage to property amounted to around £1 million.[33]

McNeil reacted by banning all marches and meetings, but the protests galvanized students and radical activists. They banded together to create the *Abeng* newspaper, named after the horn that Maroons used to communicate (partly in attempt to draw energy from the example of the Maroons in the formation of new political ideas that challenged the status quo), and Abeng, the political group that became a vector for "the Black Power movement, socialists, the independent trade union movement, Rastafarians, supporters of the opposition People's National Party, and others disaffected with the two main political parties."[34] The New World Group of radical social scientists also joined with these groups, and soon leftists and Black Power activists gravitated toward Michael Manley, the second son of Norman Manley and white artist Edna Manley, who became leader of the PNP in 1969. The PNP's left turn would topple the JLP in 1972. But before then, events in Jamaica would influence protests in Trinidad.

In February 1969, a group of Caribbean students attending Sir George Williams University in Montreal occupied and were accused of setting fire to the university's computer center (although this was highly contested) in protest over a biology professor's suspected discriminatory grading.[35] By January 1970, of those protesters who faced charges—including arson, which carried a potential sentence of life imprisonment—ten were from Trinidad.[36] Undergraduate students at the St. Augustine campus of UWI created a support group for the students in Canada known as the National Joint Action Committee (NJAC). NJAC consisted of various groups, including students (mainly African-Trinidadians, although they did reach out to those of Indian descent too), trade unions, and cultural, social, and youth associations. NJAC was ideologically diverse, welcoming Black Power supporters as well as those more attuned to left-wing socialism. It was deliberately heterogeneous to challenge the political status quo and use the masses to reform traditional politics.

From February 1970, NJAC organized more protests that, similar to the Rodney-influenced disturbances in Jamaica, became about much more than just the fate of the students in Canada. Black Power and other leftist groups highlighted the persistence of racist discrimination, especially in employment practices and foreign economic dominance. The February revolution, as it became known, lasted for more than three months and spread throughout Trinidad and Tobago.

While many protest groups and other black youths were committed to Black Power ideals, Trinidadians of Indian descent responded ambivalently to their activism. Some struggled to identify with the concept of political blackness. However, Black Power's attention to celebrating culture and identity shaped

Indian-Trinbagonians' assertion of their own cultural, religious, and ethnic identity.[37]

Prime minister of Trinidad and Tobago Eric Williams's responses to the February revolution were complex and at times contradictory. On the one hand, he felt that he had already addressed the colonial economic legacy through his government's policies. On March 23, 1970, in his first public address regarding the demonstrations, Williams defended his government's actions, arguing:

> We have consciously sought to promote Black economic power. We have in five years created 1,523 Black small farmers over the country; we have encouraged small businesses in manufacturing and tourism . . . Our Public Service, at all levels, is staffed almost entirely by nationals mainly Black . . . We have created no fewer than 68,200 new jobs between 1956 and 1969.[38]

On the other hand, Williams saw advocacy for black consciousness as "perfectly legitimate and . . . entirely in the interest of the community as a whole. If this is Black Power, then I am for Black Power."[39]

Yet he still sought to discredit the broader grievances that had led to the February revolution. On May 3, Williams made another national broadcast, contrasting the supposed legitimate problems expressed by the youth and the illegitimate grievances voiced by politicians, academics, students, and trade unionists, who he alleged worked by "unconstitutional means and armed revolution" to take down the government.[40] He outlined plans, following Black Power ideas, to create cooperatives to address economic inequalities and reform of the civil service.[41] On May 10, he outlined further political changes. He added new departments, including the ministry of national security. He also took on the role of minister of external affairs and Tobago affairs—using the

February revolution to increase his own power base.[42] In his independence day address on August 31, 1970, he promised yet more changes in "our relations with foreign capital" and remedies for "the insidious penetration of North American materialist values."[43]

Yet Williams's reforms after the February revolution only increased accusations of one-manism—the undemocratic concentration of political power in the hands of one male leader—that became more dominant when the People's National Movement won all seats in parliament in the 1971 elections. Although victorious, the PNM's success was shaped by the boycott of the elections by opposition parties and saw a low turnout of 34 percent in contrast to 66 percent in 1966.[44]

In the aftermath of Black Power activism, constitutional change came to Trinidad and Tobago. In 1976, the nation became a republic, receiving a new constitution and removing Queen Elizabeth II as the head of state. However, the nation still retained the use of the Privy Council.

As the examples of Jamaica and Trinidad and Tobago demonstrate, although activists were unable to destroy the racial-caste hierarchy, they did force political leaders to enact change, albeit in some cases not to the extent that they wanted. Among the non-independent Caribbean territories, however, Black Power would see violent expression in Bermuda.

Bermuda was well-known for its strict segregationist policies. But in June 1959, black Bermudians adopted strategies from the US civil rights movement and launched a peaceful boycott of the white-owned Island Theatre, which contributed to the desegregation of the island's restaurants and hotels. The boycott occurred simultaneously with a significant strike among dockworkers, leading to the deployment of the overwhelmingly white police force to quell the disturbance. These two events emboldened black Bermudians, giving them increased confidence that they could spearhead change and in turn transform society.[45]

In the late 1960s, many black Bermudian youths who had attended university in the US were influenced by the civil rights and Black Power movements. Direct Black Power protest and anti-colonial agitation mainly led by youth groups began in 1968. In April, a group of youths from Back-a-Town, in the capital Hamilton, were racially discriminated against and subsequently clashed with the police force. This incident extended over three days, as riots in Hamilton spread to Devonshire and Warwick parishes, leading to a state of emergency and the urgent deployment of a detachment of 180 Royal Inniskilling Fusiliers from Britain to end it.[46] Damages due to the violence were estimated at £412,150.[47]

A commission was established to investigate the disturbances. The report from the Wooding Commission, headed by Hugh Wooding, chief justice of Trinidad and Tobago, informed the subsequent Race Relations Act, which was based on Britain's 1965 and 1968 Race Relations Acts. But Bermuda's act was less interested in improving race relations and more in limiting black-led radical activism.

After the disturbances, Pauulu Kamarakafego (formerly Roosevelt Brown) contributed to growing Black Power on the island. Born in Bermuda in 1932, Kamarakafego studied at New York University, earned a PhD from California Tech-Pasadena, and taught in Tanzania, Kenya, and Uganda.[48] Alongside other PLP members, Kamarakafego attended Black Power conferences in New Jersey in 1967 and Philadelphia in 1968. He argued that the next Black Power conference should occur outside the US, specifically in Bermuda. The thought of Bermuda hosting a Black Power conference made the island's white elite uneasy—they argued it would damage the tourist industry. The US and Canada also loudly objected to the potential conference, citing security concerns. During the Cold War, the US and Canada wanted to ensure that any radical movements did not thrive so close to their respective borders. But the British government warned against Bermudians banning the conference, arguing that it would only inflame the situation and perhaps force Black Power to go underground, making it harder for them to maintain security on the island.[49]

Although it was agreed that the conference could take place in Bermuda in 1969, white elites took few chances. Immigration rules were tightened to prevent radical US or other Caribbean Black Power activists from attending the conference. Security was ramped up too. Canada moved two warships to Bermuda's waters, and once again British troops were sent to the island.[50] Despite the many restrictions, the conference went ahead relatively peacefully. It welcomed an array of activists and would come to impact the creation of the Black Beret Cadre (BBC) in Bermuda.

Formed by youths, some of whom were affiliated with the PLP to advance Black Power, the BBC became a highly influential group.[51] BBC members ranged in age between eighteen and thirty, and had around fifty members and one thousand associates.[52] The cadre's chief of staff, John Hilton Bassett Jr., had studied in the US and developed a close friendship with Fred Hampton and other US Black Panther Party members.[53] Other Black Beret leaders included Ben Aaharon, who alongside members challenged current inequalities in Bermuda, especially in the wake of the cost of living increasing sharply in the 1970s, rent hikes, and an overall land shortage. The BBC saw the necessity of armed struggle to wrench Bermuda from the United Bermuda Party and Britain and to engineer Bermudian independence. The group engaged in urban guerrilla warfare with security forces and spread their message through "liberation schools" and the newspaper *Black Beret*. They promoted an alcohol- and drug-free lifestyle and were heavily influenced by (and taught) works by Martinican activist Frantz Fanon as well as Che Guevara and Castro.[54]

British officials were deeply concerned about the BBC and other Black Power radical groups. A glimpse at their worries appears in an April 1970 report that argued "its racist bias is sinister and in its more extreme manifestations its aims are inimical to our interests ... it could prove disastrous to the interests of the region itself, where the increasingly tourist-based development of the economies of the islands could be badly set back by a loss of outside confidence."[55]

To undermine the BBC, the UBP worked alongside the Foreign and Commonwealth Office's Information and Research Department, developing propaganda to attack them.[56] Despite this collaboration, at times the FCO recognized the legitimacy of many BBC claims about the reality of racism under the UBP.[57] Richard Posnett, head of the FCO's West Indian Department, observed that the unequal constituency boundaries on the island favored white elite areas.[58] FCO officials also remarked on white Bermudians' "extreme racist attitudes" and commented that the "life styles of the more affluent whites [are] reminiscent of the worst aspects of the colonial era."[59]

Throughout 1970, the BBC increased their activism. As the months passed, the conflict between the state and the BBC grew more confrontational. In August, at a rally outside City Hall in the capital, BBC members burned the British flag in protest of the British decision to sell arms to South Africa and in commemoration of the 1960 Sharpeville massacre (when police officers fired at a peaceful group of demonstrators protesting against oppressive laws that forced black South Africans to carry documentation permitting their presence in certain areas, killing sixty-nine).[60] Although he did not burn the flag, Bassett was arrested under the Offensive Behaviour Act and received a six-month prison sentence.[61] The BBC was not alone in condemning Britain's relationship with South Africa. The Progressive Labour Party (PLP) echoed the BBC and protested against Britain's sale of arms to

South Africa. At this time, Prince Charles was due to visit the island, and the PLP boycotted events he attended, calling him "the supreme embodiment of British Colonialism and Imperialism."[62] In July 1971, Bassett was released from prison following his appeal for having "seditious literature."[63] Around this time BBC activity had decreased somewhat, but the group was also supposedly forging ties with criminal figures.[64]

Events turned deadly the next year. In September 1972, George Duckett, the police commissioner, was killed. Bassett fled the island, fearing that he would be falsely charged with murder.[65] (He never returned and died in the US in 1995.) Then in March 1973, Governor Sir Richard Sharples and his aide-de-camp were shot and killed.[66] These incidents alarmed Britain, the US, and Canada. The US FBI, the Royal Canadian Mounted Police, and Scotland Yard worked jointly to help find the suspects.[67] Suspicion for the killings fell on the BBC. Members were detained during the subsequent state of emergency. BBC associate "Buck" Burrows was linked to the murders, while another man, Larry Tacklyn, was accused of the subsequent murders of two shopkeepers.[68] Regardless of local and global protests, Burrows and Tacklyn were tried and hanged on December 2, 1977.[69]

In Bermuda, opinion on the hangings divided along racial lines, and uprisings spread throughout the island. The governor introduced a state of emergency, and 250 members of the Royal Regiment of Fusiliers arrived from Britain, joining another contingent from the British garrison on British Honduras.[70] Events on the island reverberated in Britain. In London, the Caribbean People's Solidarity Campaign criticized the hangings, describing them as "a continuing part of the suppression of the Black majority by the handful of English whites with the support of the Queen, and the British Labour Party in government."[71] A royal commission, established to investigate the island's problems, concluded by arguing that independence could help forge a better sense of national unity in Bermuda and proposed an independence conference.[72] But the UBP still feared that independence would undermine their grip on power, a stance they maintained into the 1980s and '90s. Black Power activism in Bermuda had a profound impact on the island's status, forcing the issue of independence much more vigorously. While it did not break the UBP's dominance, it did set in motion a tide of racial consciousness on the island.

Overall, Black Power activity in the Caribbean revealed the limits of constitutional decolonization, which in sovereign states left economic and racial inequality untouched. It also influenced non-sovereign parts of the Caribbean and the struggles there to end the racial-caste hierarchy. With Black Power, the masses took up the cause of secondary decolonization, and in response colonial and independent leaders again turned to violence to suppress these stirrings. Even so, Black Power left an enduring legacy across the Caribbean. In Jamaica, it would come to shape the rise of socialism and in Grenada it would lead to revolution.

MANLEY AND SEAGA'S JAMAICA

In Jamaica, the Black Power movement had a transformational impact on the leadership of the island's third post-independence prime minister, Michael Manley. Like his father, he spent time in Britain. During his time in 1940s London Manley served as a pilot officer with the Royal Canadian Air Force (1943–45), attended the London School of Economics and Political Science, worked at the BBC, and, on his return home, carved out a career in journalism and became involved in the trade union movement. In 1962 Manley accepted a senate position in the Jamaican parliament and five years later entered the house of representatives as MP for the Central Kingston constituency. He became leader of the People's National Party in 1969, following his father's retirement, and that, in turn, made him the leader of the opposition.

Although born into extreme privilege, with his light skin color, class, and father's surname securing his place in the upper echelons of the racial-caste hierarchy, Manley wrestled with his identity. According to his fourth wife, Beverley Manley (née Anderson), a dark-skinned woman from a working-class family, Michael Manley "wanted to be a black man more than anything else in the world."[73] Despite his mixed ancestry, many considered Manley a black leader because he embraced black working-class Jamaicans. Charismatic and populist, Manley carved out a distinctly unique political identity that quickly attracted many to the PNP's fold. Unlike his predecessors, Manley dispensed with European business-suit attire reminiscent of the colonial era, preferring a more informal and weather-appropriate Kariba suit. Manley pledged to bring meaningful change to the "sufferers," those at the bottom of Jamaican society struggling at a time when the unemployment rate was 24 percent, double that of a decade prior.[74]

During the 1972 election, Manley promised to make independence a reality. He sought to distribute wealth equally, expand public education, and enact land reform, drawing a vast following, with supporters comparing him to the biblical figure Joshua. The PNP won 56 percent of the votes and thirty-seven seats, in contrast to the JLP's 43 percent and sixteen seats.[75]

Once in office, Manley set about transforming Jamaican society and upending the racial-caste hierarchy. He developed new housing projects, improved literacy rates on the island, introduced new labor laws that increased incomes, and implemented a national minimum wage that led to a slight decrease in the unemployment rate. Manley also specifically addressed gender inequalities, introducing maternity leave legislation and passing the Status of Children Act, which ended legal distinctions between legitimate and illegitimate children. Feminists and the wider women's movement on the island and within the party played key roles in shaping these laws too. To promote African aspects of Jamaican culture, as many Black Power activists demanded, Manley recruited Jamaican scholar and choreographer Rex Nettleford as his cultural adviser. The PNP also restored social liberties suspended under the JLP, including ending bans on left-wing publications.

Michael Manley and Fidel Castro, Montego Bay, September 17, 1977.

In foreign policy, Manley was committed to the Non-Aligned Movement—a group of developing countries that chose not to align with a specific power bloc in the Cold War. Manley allied with the "Third World," reaching out to various countries in Africa, as well as Mexico and Venezuela, and strongly supported the New International Economic Order (NIEO), a set of initiatives by developing countries to end colonial economic dependency. Within the Caribbean, Manley supported projects designed to foster Caribbean unity, such as the Caribbean Community (CARICOM) founded in 1973, which promoted economic cooperation and integration among English-speaking Caribbean territories. He also developed a close bond with Fidel Castro. Crucially, Manley lent support to Cuba's decision to send troops to Angola in 1975, which irked the US. The decision came after the South African Defence Force invaded Angola during the Angolan Civil War (1975–91), with tacit support from the US, hoping to install an anti-communist client government that would preserve the cordon sanitaire between "Black Africa" and the apartheid regime. US secretary of state Henry Kissinger called on Manley to denounce Cuba's role in Angola, a request Manley refused. "We have that friendship with Cuba as part of a world alliance of Third World nations that are fighting for justice for poor people in the world," Manley reasoned in one speech. "As long as this party is in power we intend to walk through the world on our feet and not on our knees."[76] Manley often confronted the US, especially after 1974 when he announced that the PNP and, by extension, Jamaica, had adopted the policy of democratic socialism that focused on the "principles of social ownership over the means of production and societal equality of opportunity."[77]

Manley certainly brought about change in Jamaica but most of his lofty plans were forestalled by the global economic crisis of 1973. Global oil prices rose sharply due to the oil embargo imposed by the Arab Organization of the Petroleum Exporting Countries (OPEC) against parts of the Western world. In 1974 the island's oil bill amounted to $178 million, close to triple what it had been the previous year.[78] This led to increases in the price of goods and decreases in foreign exchange and the government's revenues, and a debt crisis. With the limits of the island's economic model exposed, Manley's government introduced a new levy on the production of bauxite that increased revenues to $170 million in 1974.[79] This was a boon for the government, but many bauxite companies and the US government opposed the levy. The US responded by limiting loans to the country. In 1975

Manley visited Cuba and agreed to joint development programs with the Cuban government. Cuban personnel came to Jamaica to assist in education, construction, healthcare, and housing. Yet by 1976, the economy was close to collapse.

Trucks loaded with police and soldiers rumble through the streets of Kingston, Jamaica, December 1976, as authorities tighten security during the general election. Jamaican voters were electing a new parliament after the most violent political campaigning in the island's history.

Jamaica's move toward democratic socialism contributed to economic problems too. Although it was more akin to the left-of-center position of Britain's Labour Party, many entrepreneurs and professionals, fearing the PNP would target their wealth, migrated abroad, especially to the US. According to scholar Brian Meeks, in 1976 the flight of capital by several means from Jamaica was estimated at $300 million.[80] Migration did have some positive benefit for those who stayed: some in the black middle class were able to move from jobs in the public sector into private sector managerial work. But those at the bottom socially and economically relied increasingly on the booming yet dangerous illegal drug trade (more on this later).

Foreign policy and the economy were major issues during the 1976 election. Voters had to choose between the socialist-orientated PNP, with support from Cuba; or the JLP, which would pursue a closer relationship with the US. When the JLP accused the PNP of financial mismanagement, the PNP responded that the economic problems stemmed from the 1960s and the legacies of colonialism. The PNP also blamed the unemployment rate on JLP propaganda that was undermining the economy and fueling destabilizing violence and argued that outside influence was impacting the economy—alleging that the CIA was involved in attempts to destabilize the island. On this point, there was evidence that the CIA and conservative forces on the island were undermining Manley's government and, coupled with US political pressure, played a destabilizing role by discouraging tourists and limiting aid and financial assistance.[81] Nonetheless, the PNP won the election, with 56.8 percent of the votes and forty-seven out of sixty seats, securing Manley another term in office.[82]

During Manley's second term, the economy continued to worsen because of the balance-of-payments crisis, leading Manley to turn to the International Monetary Fund (IMF), headquartered in Washington, DC.[83]

The IMF, as well as the World Bank and World Trade Organization, originated with a 1944 meeting at Bretton Woods in New Hampshire. It represented a new manifestation of Western and especially US-led imperialism in the guise of global finance that limited the ability of recently independent states to have a say in how they ran their own countries. The IMF placed more restrictions on loans to these countries than it did on European countries. Blaming non-Western nations for their economic problems without considering how colonialism and neocolonialism played important roles in causing underdevelopment, the IMF put stringent conditions on loans. The IMF's structural adjustment programs asked countries to introduce a raft of neoliberal economic measures, such as increasing foreign investment, introducing austerity measures, and devaluing local currencies.[84]

The IMF not only wielded economic control but also encroached on the political arena. During the Cold War, US influence in the IMF meant that it played a role in trying to stop the spread of global communism, oftentimes imposing fewer conditions on countries close to the communist bloc, especially in Asia and Africa.[85] Through controlling the economies of economically struggling countries, the IMF influenced their political agenda to ensure that they remained pro-West. The IMF had similarities with the World Bank, a development agency established to support underdeveloped countries and sway them away from the Soviet Union. The World Bank, also headquartered in Washington, DC, and financed by Western countries, especially the US, placed similar conditions on its loans.

Manley considered the conditions under which the IMF offered loans an affront to Jamaica's sovereignty. In a defiant speech in January 1977 he argued:

> the International Monetary Fund, which is the central lending agency for the international capitalist system, has a history of laying down conditions for countries seeking loans . . . This government, on behalf of our people, will not accept anybody anywhere in the world telling us what to do in our country. We are the masters in our house and in our house there shall be no other master but ourselves. Above all, we are not for sale.[86]

But by April, Manley realized he had few options, and negotiations with the IMF resumed. The IMF's structural adjustment policies forced Jamaica to reduce wages. After the government devalued the Jamaican dollar, the cost of imported goods rose.

But the economy still faltered, and the island failed a performance test in December. The cost of living rose between 1974 and 1980 by a staggering 320 percent, accompanied by increases in unemployment and a shortage of goods.[87] In these years, Jamaica's gross domestic product decreased by 16 percent.[88] The IMF's free-market economic policies did not improve the Jamaican economy, and businesses were still reluctant to invest in what they perceived to be an unstable country. In December 1979, the economy failed another performance test, and Manley's government severed its ties to the IMF to devise an alternative development path.[89]

With the economy in free fall, violence increased in advance of the October 1980 general election, with 750 people killed.[90] Given the economic and social chaos, the defeat of Manley's PNP was no surprise. When the JLP leader Edward Seaga came to office, he quickly turned attention to repairing the economy and pursued neoliberal economic policies. By April 1981, his government had agreed to a $698 million IMF loan for three years. The IMF treated Seaga much more favorably than they had Manley and imposed fewer restrictions—they did not stipulate the devaluation of the Jamaican currency, or price or wage controls.[91] By rebuilding links with the IMF, Jamaica under Seaga also received additional loans from the World Bank.

After he entered the White House in January 1981, Republican president Ronald Reagan recognized the importance of fostering friendly relations with Seaga as part of his agenda to contain Cuba and the alleged spread of communism in the Caribbean and encourage US investment on the island. Seaga was the first foreign leader Reagan invited to the White House, and he became known as "America's man in the Caribbean."[92]

Yet even with IMF and World Bank loans and support from the Reagan administration, the Jamaican economy struggled in the 1980s. The bauxite industry declined, and US investors remained wary of Jamaica due to its reputation as a place of violence and political instability and the balance-of-payments crisis. Seaga's economic policies increased poverty, migration, and violence.

The spiraling economic crisis worsened when, in June 1985, the island witnessed the first general strike since independence. Seaga turned again to the IMF, which provided another loan, this time $120 million from August 1985 to March 1987. Overall, Seaga's neoliberal strategy did not fully revive the Jamaican economy due to the limits of the island's capitalist class and institutions. In the February 1989 elections, the PNP and Manley were returned to power, but Manley was a changed man. Due to the economic context of the 1980s, the "new Manley" no longer preached democratic socialism but rather embraced a pro-US agenda that promoted deregulation and market liberalization. Dogged by ill-health during his third term, he resigned from office in 1992 and died five years later after suffering from prostate cancer.

Due to the pressures and strains of neoliberalism in 1980s Jamaica and the decline of export agriculture, the "informal economy" grew exponentially. Individuals and groups traded in foreign-made goods and pursued illegal activities such as drug trafficking, fraud, and smuggling. By 2001, the informal economy in Jamaica accounted for 43 percent of the GDP.[93] Cocaine trafficking, especially, increased wealth for organized criminals, and the security of the island was rocked as more citizens became addicted—some twenty-two thousand by the end of the 1980s.[94] Furthermore, drug use and trafficking exacerbated violent crime on the island. By 2005, Jamaica's murder rate was 58 per 100,000, making it the "most homicidal nation in the world."[95] The garrison-like politics stoked violence that was characteristic of urban gangs, but the island's economic stagnation caused violence related to the growth of urbanization, slums, youth poverty, and limited education.

The security of the island had been undermined as well by the power and control that drug gangs and influential "dons" (criminal non-state actors) began to amass, along with their powerful firearms, which were also trafficked into the country. Drug gangs have their origins in political gangs. There was a shift from politicians being the patrons, enacting clientelist practices through neighborhood dons, to drug dons being the ones with more resources. Enriched with drug money, gang leaders took control of politicians, who became clients of these drug dons since they needed their support during elections. In the 1980s, political gangs in Jamaica became involved in international drug cartels, and many migrated to the US and spearheaded the transnational drug community between the US (in places like Miami and New York) and Jamaica.[96] The dons spent their money in the garrisons and in many cases provided residents with improved facilities that the state could not.[97]

One of the most famous dons who threatened twenty-first-century state security was Christopher "Dudus" Coke, head of the "Shower Posse" gang, which was involved in shipping cocaine and marijuana to the US. In 2010 the US government sought to extradite him, and this created a crisis for the ruling JLP because Coke was based in Tivoli Gardens, an important center of Prime Minister Bruce Golding's constituency. After the Obama administration applied pressure, the JLP-led government used the military to try to find Coke, and conflict erupted between security forces and Coke's supporters in West Kingston. During the battle, over seventy-five civilians died, while those in the community place the number closer to two hundred.[98] Coke was later sentenced to twenty-three years in a US prison. In December 2017 Jamaica's prime minister, Andrew Holness, apologized to the individuals and families affected.[99]

The economic and political crises that plagued Manley and Seaga earlier arose less because of their differing ideologies and more because of overriding constraints caused by the island's entrapment in both neocolonialism and neoliberalism, as epitomized by the US, the IMF, and the World Bank. Ultimately, the dominance of these forces undermined Jamaica's sovereignty, making independence a mere myth, entrenching the island in Western powers, and propelling it further down the road of underdevelopment.

REVOLUTION AND INVASION

Meanwhile, in late 1970s Grenada, left-wing political activists were planning a revolution. With a population of under one hundred thousand, Grenada was heavily dependent on the export of nutmeg, cocoa, and bananas and, along with the rest of the Caribbean, was struggling economically. After independence, Grenada received a grant worth £2.5 million from Britain, but by 1978 that money was running out.[100] Furthermore, Prime Minister Gairy's behavior and public statements were becoming more erratic and bizarre. In one speech, he argued, "He who opposes me opposes God."[101] In other remarks, Gairy, a fervent believer in UFOs, urged the UN to designate 1978 as the "Year of the UFO."[102] By 1976, Maurice Bishop, head of the New Jewel Movement (NJM) that supported Black Power, won a seat in parliament. It was clear that fraud had contributed to Gairy's electoral victory that year. Realizing the difficulty of toppling Gairy constitutionally in an election, the NJM began to consider other options.

On March 10, 1979, rumors spread that Gairy planned to attack and arrest NJM leaders. Two days later Gairy left for New York to hold talks with UN secretary-general Austrian Kurt Waldheim. The NJM took advantage of Gairy's absence and on March 13, around fifty NJM members staged a coup, attacking the defense force barracks and taking control of the radio station in an encounter that killed three people. With pro-Gairy forces subdued, Bishop took to the radio to deliver his now famous "Bright New Dawn" speech, in which he informed the Grenadian people

"FLAG INDEPENDENCE"

of the revolution.[103] Bishop promised Grenadians: "this revolution is for work, for food, for decent housing and health services, and for a bright future for our children and great grandchildren. The benefits of the revolution will be given to everyone regardless of political opinion or which political party they support."[104] He vowed that "all democratic freedoms, including freedom of elections, religious and political opinion, will be fully restored to the people."[105] With these words, the People's Revolutionary Government (PRG) was installed, with Bishop serving as head and prime minister, while Bernard Coard (back home after his time spent in Britain) became deputy prime minister, his portfolio focusing on the economy.

Prime Minister of Grenada Maurice Bishop, 1983.

The Grenadian revolution was the first victorious armed revolutionary struggle in the independent Anglophone Caribbean. Britain tepidly accepted the revolution and recognized the PRG. In this instance, Britain put aside its fears about the NJM, given its deeper concerns about Gairy's authoritarian and violent rule.

But the revolution would cause more conflict not with its former colonial overlord but with its neighbor, the US. The revolution was one of three that year. In January 1979, the Iranian revolution led to the overthrow of the Pahlavi dynasty, which was replaced with the Islamic Republic ruled by Grand Ayatollah Ruhollah Khomeini, and in July, the Nicaraguan revolution saw the pro-US Somoza regime replaced by the Sandinista National Liberation Front. Socialist leaders came to power with the Grenadian and Nicaraguan revolutions, which the US deemed a threat to their political and economic interests.

Like Britain, the US under President Jimmy Carter recognized the PRG, believing that its promise to hold elections would restore democracy on Grenada. So too did neighboring Caribbean states. In the early days of the "Revo," as supporters affectionately called it, the PRG was widely popular. They challenged the Westminster model of politics by suspending the constitution of 1974 and replacing parliamentary democracy with participatory democracy, in the form of parish or workplace assemblies that enabled ordinary people to participate.[106] They created militias that prepared young people to defend the island; established women, youth, and farmers' groups; organized a mass literacy drive; improved adult education; and built new secondary schools. Yet although the PRG suspended the constitution, it kept Sir Paul Scoon as governor general, who acted as the Queen's representative as the ceremonial head of state. The PRG hoped that keeping the governor general, at least in the short term, would give the new government more international legitimacy and improve relations with the Commonwealth and Britain.

"FLAG INDEPENDENCE"

The PRG sought to develop a mixed economy with elements of local and foreign capital and tried to enlarge the tourist industry. The island's economy was aided by support from Venezuela, France, Canada, the Soviet Union, Syria, Libya, and Cuba.[107] Thousands of Cuban medical workers, teachers, and engineers moved to Grenada to assist in the development of the island and construct an international airport. And Castro and Bishop formed a close relationship, with the former regarding the latter like a son. Like Manley, Bishop and the PRG were part of the Non-Aligned Movement and supported Caribbean regional integration, evident in the support he gave to the formation in 1981 of the Organisation of Eastern Caribbean States (OECS). Founded to support economic integration and collective security, the OECS included Grenada, Dominica, Antigua and Barbuda, St. Vincent and the Grenadines, St. Lucia, St. Kitts and Nevis, and Montserrat.

But by 1981, the popularity of the Revo, and the PRG, was beginning to dwindle. Although Bishop's charisma and personality meant that he was still popular among Grenadians, no elections were held. The PRG also arrested its opponents. In addition, the NJM became more secretive as a group of leaders began to hold exclusive meetings to steer the revolution towards a more Marxist-Leninist platform.[108]

The problems facing the PRG were not only internal but also ideological. The US played a role, much as it did in Jamaica, in destabilizing Grenada. Wary of the close bond between Bishop and Castro, the Carter administration approved covert tactics in Grenada to undermine the PRG.[109] When Reagan took office, he refused to accept the legitimacy of the revolution and called on Bishop to break ties with Cuba and the Soviet Union. Reagan saw Grenada and Cuban relations as an affront to US hegemony, quipping: "It isn't nutmeg that's at stake in the Caribbean and Central America; it is the United States' national security."[110]

Like Manley, Bishop railed against the US, defiantly stating in a radio address that "No country has the right to tell us what to do or how to run our country or who to be friendly with . . . We are not in anybody's backyard, and we are definitely not for sale."[111] When Grenada did not demonstrate a more explicit commitment to non-alignment, the US isolated it financially.

Ultimately, however, divisions within the PRG from 1982 onward put an end to the revolution. In 1983, NJM members voted to elevate Bernard Coard, proposing that he and Bishop share power. Initially, Bishop accepted this but later reneged. In September, a rumor began spreading that Coard wanted to kill Bishop. It later became known that Bishop started the rumor, although he denied doing so. Believing that Bishop was trying to undermine the revolution, NJM leaders placed him under house arrest. Soon protests erupted that called on Bishop to be reinstated as prime minister. Bishop's supporters helped get him released from his residence, and the crowd proceeded to retake the military headquarters at Fort Rupert (renamed in honor of Bishop's father). But troops from another base arrived as part of an opposing NJM faction, and Bishop was murdered, along with other NJM allies. The military then imposed a curfew.

The violence in Grenada increased long-standing fears of regional insecurity that influenced the decision by the OECS, Barbados, and Jamaica to invite the US to help. Calls for US intervention were led by Caribbean leaders who sought a closer relationship with the superpower, including Dominican prime minister Eugenia Charles, then head of the OECS; Barbadian prime minister Tom Adams; and Seaga. Before approaching the US for military assistance, the OECS contacted British prime minister Margaret Thatcher, who argued that military intervention was not needed. But Secretary of State George Shultz supported US involvement because "the Caribbean is in our neighborhood."[112] Britain's attitude reflected a significant shift in Caribbean relations. In the words of Tom Adams: "In hemispheric terms, 1983 is bound to be seen as the watershed year in which the influence of the United States, willy-nilly, came observably to replace that of Great Britain in the old British colonies."[113]

Adopting Article 8 of the OECS treaty—concerned with responsibility for member states' collective defense—and with a letter seeking assistance from Grenada's governor general Scoon that was signed and backdated by him to October 24, Eugenia Charles and her allies in the Caribbean used it as legitimation for US intervention.[114] US troops alongside a small number of Caribbean soldiers participated in the invasion of Grenada known as "Operation Urgent Fury." Reagan justified the action in order to rescue 1,100 US citizens on the island and limit the rise of communism, as he labeled the island a "Soviet-Cuban colony being readied as a major military bastion to export terror and undermine democracy."[115]

US Marines guard a captured member of the People's Revolutionary Army during the invasion of Grenada, code-named Operation Urgent Fury, October 25, 1983, in St. Georges, Grenada.

Ultimately, the US invasion of Grenada presaged the island's entry into the US's orbit. Seeking to install a pro-US Grenadian government, the US supported Herbert Blaize, a barrister from Grenada's sister island of Carriacou, who established the New National Party (NNP), to prevent Gairy from returning to power from exile. In 1984, Blaize's NNP was elected, and his government developed a warm rapport with Reagan, even going so far as to hail him as a "national hero" of Grenada.[116]

After the invasion, US aid flowed into the island—$18.5 million in 1983 and the following year $57 million.[117] US favoritism toward Grenada undermined Caribbean unity, with Seaga arguing: "There is no way these investments can be put into Grenada and not into the rest of the OECS ... otherwise, all the islands will look to having a revolution and being rescued."[118] But by the late 1980s, international politics were drifting away from the Cold War and toward conflict in the Gulf, and the US no longer saw the Caribbean as a region central to their global power. Aid decreased to Grenada and islands in the Eastern Caribbean that supported the US invasion.

The events of 1979–83 in Grenada reveal once again the limits of constitutional decolonization. The short but seminal PRG tried to develop a model of governance that challenged US hegemony in the region, one of the legacies of British colonialism. However, this ultimately led to its undoing, with the invasion as the most explicit act of US imperialism. That Britain did not intervene reflects on the one hand its military insignificance in the Caribbean, perhaps as a result of the legacies of events such as those that occurred in Anguilla, but also the fear that if it did intervene, it would lead to blatant accusations of neocolonial imposition.

OFFSHORE PARADISE

While Jamaica and Grenada both struggled in the stranglehold of neocolonialism, neoliberalism, and US imperialism, other areas in the Caribbean—especially those that did not opt for constitutional decolonization—sought to benefit from the global changing tides. And this was no more true than in the Cayman Islands, which in the last four decades of the twentieth century transformed itself, as scholars Tony Freyer and Andrew P. Morriss have written, "from being one of the least developed, both legally and economically, jurisdictions in a poorly developed region to surpassing its former colonial power in GDP per capita terms, and developing a sophisticated body of financial law."[119]

The rise of offshore finance in the non-sovereign Caribbean reflected both the continuance of the British Empire and the perpetuation of increasing economic inequality and the racial-caste hierarchy within a neoliberal economic framework.

The growing wealth in the Cayman Islands (consisting of the islands Grand Cayman, Little Cayman, and Cayman Brac) had its roots in advancements in long-distance communication and airline travel that made it easier to do business globally. It was also linked to constitutional decolonization that saw the circulation of wealth from newly independent states to territories that still had ties to the British Empire, all of which aided its rise as an offshore financial center (OFC). OFCs are jurisdictions where most of the financial services are enacted by non-residents and where most of the financial institutions are owned by non-residents. Due to laws introduced in the Cayman Islands in the 1950s and '60s, it quickly became a tax-haven paradise. Offshore businesses, banks, and insurance companies in the Cayman Islands paid no taxes on income, capital gains, property, or inheritance.

The rise of the Cayman Islands as an OFC followed the Bahamas, which became an OFC in 1936.[120] The Bahamas served as a lucrative destination for British and Canadian financial institutions to protect their wealthy clients' investments. After the Second World War, as decolonization loomed, the Bahamas became an attractive tax haven for white settlers seeking to take their cash out of Southern Rhodesia and Kenya, fearful that black-African-led majority governments would seize their assets.[121] The transfer of these assets is a reminder, as historian Vanessa Ogle argues, that constitutional decolonization was not just a political event but also an economic one.[122] But when the Bahamas itself turned toward independence, wealthy individuals likewise feared that black majority rule there would lead to attacks on white-held wealth and property and began removing assets from the island.

Many turned to nearby islands that were still controlled by Britain, and in particular, the Cayman Islands, the British Virgin Islands, and Bermuda. As non-sovereign states, they received support financially from Britain through investment and aid, and they had preferential access to metropolitan markets and international free-trade zones. The Cayman Islands quickly surpassed other non-sovereign territories due to its combination of a relatively small population—around 10,500 in the 1970s—and its mixed-race composition.[123] This seemingly indicated political stability but overlooked the reality of the white merchant elites' maintenance of power at the expense, especially, of black and other working-class Caymanians.

The growth of the Cayman Islands' offshore financial activity was shaped by the deregulation of finance influenced by the rise of Euromarkets, a type of offshore market that developed as Britain chose not to impose regulations on the trading of foreign currencies in London banks. In the postwar era, British and Canadian lawyers helped write the Cayman Islands' tax codes and laws that would benefit its offshore financial activities. The first bank on the island, Barclays, opened in 1953, followed by the Royal Bank of Canada and the Canadian Imperial Bank of Commerce a decade later. After Bahamian independence in 1973, banks previously based there moved to the Cayman Islands, which quickly increased the number of banking institutions. In

1975 there were 194, by 1980 there were 324, and by 1991 there were 544.[124] The Cayman Islands also became a critical space for the offshore insurance industry and mutual and hedge funds.[125] By 2021, the Cayman Islands were one of the largest offshore centers in the world.

While OFC economic development saw a growth in jobs in the finance industry, the wealth hoarded by companies in the Cayman Islands did not improve the lives of average Caymanians. Indeed, although the local government benefits through income from incorporation fees and stamp duties, the cost of living and the dependency on imports have fed the growing resentment that Caymanians feel toward immigrant communities from different parts of the Caribbean, Britain, and the US who have moved to the area looking to benefit from the booming economy.

The success of the Cayman Islands and other British Overseas Territories that are tax havens have inspired independent territories to follow suit. Dominica, Barbados, and Antigua and Barbuda, among others, have looked to create their own tax havens, free-trade zones, low- or no-tax schemes, flags of convenience, shell banks, internet businesses, as well as promoting economic citizenship to generate much needed revenue.[126]

Nevertheless, OFCs and especially tax havens have a direct impact on global wealth inequality. Research shows that individual and corporate tax avoidance by moving money to areas with low- or no-tax jurisdictions impacts lower income countries in developing economies more than higher-income countries.[127] Furthermore, according to the Tax Justice Network, the Cayman Islands in 2020 were the "world's greater [sic] enabler of private tax evasion, alone causing a tax revenue loss of $47.6 billion globally."[128] In 2022, the British Virgin Islands topped the list as the world's leading tax haven. It was described as the "greatest enabler of corporate tax abuse," with the Cayman Islands coming in second and Bermuda third.[129]

Additionally, while tax havens offered a wealth of opportunities for legitimate businesses, they also provided avenues for money laundering linked to organized crime and drug trafficking, as the Caribbean region is both a consumer market for drugs as well as an important transit point for Central and South American producers and North American and European consumers. The contemporary illegal drugs market in the Caribbean creates an estimated income of $3.3 billion.[130] OFCs in the Caribbean show how legacies of British colonialism and economic policies continue to operate to provide the elite with opportunities to hide and hoard their wealth, while failing to improve the everyday lives of working-class communities in these territories.

The growth of OFCs occurred amid a rise in tourism in the Caribbean, which became another venue for the spread of neocolonialism. The rise of the Caribbean as a mass tourist destination took off from the 1950s onward, although its roots extend back to the late nineteenth and early twentieth centuries. In the mid-twentieth century, as passenger air travel increased, various islands invested in public sanitation programs that made the Caribbean a healthier destination for tourists.

In the Bahamas, for instance, US economic elites drove the surge by buying property and land and developing resorts. In the 1960s, US financier Laurance Rockefeller opened Rock-Resort in Virgin Gorda in the British Virgin Islands. Other wealthy investors purchased individual islands that would welcome members of Britain's royal family and rich politicians. In 1958, socialite Colin Tennant purchased the private island of Mustique in the Grenadines for £45,000. In the 1970s British billionaire Richard Branson, owner of the Virgin Group, purchased Necker Island in the BVI. As more wealthy investors began to pour into the region, creating hotels, restaurants, and resorts, they certainly provided employment opportunities: by the 1980s the tourist industry employed nearly half the Bahamian workforce.[131] The tourism boom proved lucrative for struggling economies and became a significant revenue source. By 2004, for instance, nearly half the BVI's GDP of $879 million derived from tourist returns.[132]

Although critical to Caribbean economies, tourism has also deepened economic and racial inequality. It has led the Caribbean to be dependent on Western money and visitors. Also, its heavy reliance on tourism means that the Caribbean suffers significantly from global recessions, pandemics, and environmental disasters. On this last issue, environmental disasters like hurricanes often deter tourists, and while the region's current experience of a water crisis with demand outpacing supply is impacted by various factors, tourism is a major contributor as it increases water consumption. When some parts of the region implement water rationing, water is often distributed first to tourist areas and hotels before it reaches locals.[133]

And accusations of anti-black racism have been a mainstay of the tourist industry. Some hotels and resorts have tended to only employ light-skinned people to cater to predominantly white vacationers. This has led Caribbean writers, especially Naipaul, to scathingly decry the effects of tourism in the contemporary Caribbean. In the 1960s he lamented:

> Every poor country accepts tourism as an unavoidable degradation. None has gone as far as some of these West Indian islands, which, in the name of tourism, are selling themselves into a new slavery. The élite of the islands, whose pleasures, revealingly, are tourist's pleasures, ask no more than to be permitted to mix with the white tourists, and the governments make feeble stipulations about the colour bar.[134]

Many tourists of different racial backgrounds bought into the stereotypical notions of the Caribbean, often conveyed in marketing campaigns of dark-skinned Caribbean people as exoticized, docile, and happy to serve wealthy elites.

In all, the final decades of the twentieth century and the early twenty-first revealed that the Caribbean's sovereignty was ultimately restricted and limited by the onslaught of neocolonialism, US imperialism, and neoliberalism, further entrapping the region under the control of external forces and powers and leaving unchecked, despite Black Power movements, the racial-caste hierarchy. Amidst the increased globalization of capital, older structures continued to shape the "new" global economy. Meanwhile, in Britain, the racial-caste hierarchy was deepening further, linked to the rise of post-colonial melancholia.

10

"Menace to society"
(Post)-Colonial Melancholia

David Oluwale was last seen running away from two police officers in Leeds on April 18, 1969. Just over two weeks later, on May 4, his body was found floating in the River Aire. Initially, the thirty-eight-year-old's death was not considered suspicious. But in 1970 a whistleblower within Leeds City Police claimed that Oluwale had been regularly physically and verbally abused by two senior police officers at Millgarth Police Station, who were seen with him on the last day he was sighted in public. Soon thereafter, Scotland Yard investigated his death and found substantial evidence that former inspector Geoffrey Ellerker and Sergeant Kenneth Kitching had on different occasions physically attacked and racially abused Oluwale.

In November 1971 Ellerker and Kitching went on trial for grievous bodily harm, perjury, assault, and manslaughter. During the trial, the judge showed as much contempt for Oluwale as the defendants, calling him a "menace to society."[1] Due to the actions of the judge and a lack of evidence, manslaughter charges were dropped. When the jury returned their verdicts, both officers were found not guilty of GBH. But Ellerker was found guilty of three assaults on Oluwale and Kitching of two. Ellerker was sentenced to three years in prison and Kitching twenty-seven months. The verdicts were the first prosecutions of British police officers in the death of a black person in Britain. But no one was convicted specifically of Oluwale's death.

Oluwale was born in Lagos, Nigeria, in 1930. In August 1949 he traveled to Britain as a stowaway on board the SS *Temple Bar*, a cargo ship heading to Hull. Under the 1948 British Nationality Act, he had the right to live and work in Britain, but when he arrived, he was charged as a stowaway under the Merchant Shipping Act and sentenced to twenty-eight days in prison. In October 1949 he tried to find work in the textile industry. In 1953 he had another run-in with the police when he was charged with disorderly conduct and assault, following a police raid on a nightclub, and served time in prison, during which he suffered hallucinations, perhaps because of the injuries he sustained in the raid. He was later transferred to a psychiatric hospital on the outskirts of Leeds, where he was detained for eight years and treated with numerous drugs and therapies, including electro-convulsive therapy. Upon his release, he struggled to keep a job and became homeless, often moving between Sheffield, London, and Leeds. In this last city, Oluwale frequently contended with police surveillance and harassment. In 1965 he was sent back to the hospital (the infamous High Royds, formerly Menston Asylum) and sectioned for a second time.[2] He stayed there for two years and after his release returned to sleeping on the city's streets until his untimely death.

Oluwale's life and death were marked by a combination of anti-black racism, police brutality, housing and employment precarity, as well as mental health challenges. While these issues were specific to Oluwale, they were also more broadly indicative of the experiences of black Britons (including those of African-Caribbean as well as African backgrounds), especially within working-class communities, and evidence of the intensification of state-led anti-black racism that infiltrated policies and practices around policing, immigration, housing, education, welfare, and health that characterized the last five decades.

After years of campaigning for recognition of the significance of what Oluwale endured, in 2022 a blue plaque commemorating him was placed by the Leeds Civic Trust on Leeds Bridge, where he was last seen alive. Within hours, however, the plaque was stolen, and detectives launched a hate-crime investigation. Racist graffiti was also found on the office buildings of the Leeds Civic Trust. In the intervening time, before the plaque was replaced, images of the blue plaque were displayed throughout the city on large digital screens. The theft of the plaque and racist graffiti reflected the ongoing debates over how to remember racist British histories that are intricately connected to the British Empire and whose legacies linger long into the present.[3]

What appears as central to the persistence of the racial-caste hierarchy in late twentieth and early twenty-first-century Britain is what scholar Paul Gilroy has termed "postimperial melancholia"—the inability to move on from the myth of imperial greatness that spawns a narrow and racially exclusive form of nationalism, based on a deliberate forgetting of both the historic and ongoing racism that has its roots in the British Empire.[4] In this era, it has shaped a narrative of black Britons as outsiders with an inherently criminal culture that threatens law and order. This supposed foreign black presence and culture inspired Margaret Thatcher's infamous 1978 remark (a year before she was elected prime minister) that she sympathized with voters who felt "rather afraid that this country might be rather swamped by people with a different culture."[5] Thatcher's words and subsequent policies drew on Powellite fears of Britain as a nation under threat from black and Asian Britons, who would, regardless of their nationality, always remain "immigrant" outsiders. This erasure—or particular form of "othering," where people of color are estranged from Britain, as if they have not been part of the British colonial culture for centuries—is not new but has taken on different forms over the last decades.

Furthermore, post-colonial melancholia has also taken the form of projecting racialized class and nationalist politics, which continues to pit black British communities against their white working-class counterparts. Over the last two decades especially, white working-class communities have been considered a disenfranchised indigenous group, "left behind" by a liberal multiculturalism that has been said to benefit undeserving minoritized outsider communities at their expense (an argument that also harkens back to Powellite ideas that racial groups were constantly in competition with one another for a limited set of rights and resources).[6] This is part of a deliberate attempt to foster, at a time of increased austerity, a zero-sum politics in which one community's illegitimate supposed gains lead directly to the loss of another group's legitimate rights.[7] A key tactic since the 1960s, it has been used especially since 2010 by right-wing Conservative governments who simultaneously deny that anti-black structural racism exists. Yet as scholar Robbie Shilliam has argued: "'white working class' is neither an indigenous constituency, nor its own progenitor, but a constituency produced and reproduced through struggles to consolidate and defend British imperial order, struggles that have subsequently shaped the contours of Britain's postcolonial society."[8] In other words, when politicians invoke the language of "white working class" they mobilize a type of reactionary politics that renders some Britons as legitimate and integral to the nation (yet often staying quiet about their economic subordination) and renders others, mostly people of color in Britain or those with migrant backgrounds, illegitimate interlopers.

These features of post-colonial melancholia did not happen in a silo. Rather, they were connected to the rise of neoliberalism that saw the introduction of market forces in welfare provision, cuts to public spending, rising austerity measures, neocolonialism, and white nationalism. And at the center of post-colonial melancholia, contestations over how to remember the history of the British Empire have become vital. In attempts to project a simplistic triumphalist narrative of British nationalism, the complexities and violence of the British Empire have been overlooked and replaced with a toxic brand of imperial nostalgia that has been used as a weapon, again and again, to denounce the persistence of systemic and subtle forms of anti-black racism.

Yet in the ongoing struggle between those who wanted to maintain the racial-caste hierarchy and those who aspired to demolish it, black youths in this era turned toward more demonstrations to protest their frustrations, especially against police injustice. While many labeled these activities violent riots, they were part of the longer trajectory of political protests against racist discrimination. Educational activism was another form of resistance. So too were the actions of aggrieved and bereaved parents who would lead judicial challenges for institutional change. Furthermore, in the late 2010s investigative journalists and Caribbean politicians would also expose the inherent anti-black racism at the heart of immigration policies that targeted Caribbean-born British residents. These actions culminated in 2020 when the largest anti-racist demonstrations in British history occurred, forcing historical and contemporary anti-black racism to the forefront of British society.

PROTESTING THATCHER'S BRITAIN

In the 1970s and '80s, working-class African-Caribbean men, in particular, continued to be labeled as dangerous and deviant. The media and the state whipped the public into a frenzy over high rates of crime in urban areas, increasingly comprising black communities. African-Caribbean culture and its links to crime had much to do with the rise of Rastafarian culture in Britain and the Caribbean, especially Jamaica, more broadly evidenced through the popularity of reggae bands and the Jamaican "rude boy" style that grew after the release of the Jamaican film The *Harder They Come* in 1972. Rastafarianism in Britain and the popularity of reggae music were construed as indications of widespread criminality rather than as critiques of inequality that they were long a part of. For those involved, the "rude boy" style and Rastafarianism were a cultural expression that can be seen as a form of resistance to anti-black racism. And in some cases, these cultural expressions would be adopted within white counterculture as well as black culture through the rise, for instance, of ska revival bands, such as the popular interracial two-tone band the Specials.

The supposed deviance and foreignness of African-Caribbean cultural practices as viewed by the state were also evident through family structures. Statistical and anecdotal evidence of black Caribbean family formations in Britain tended to reveal the dominance of female-headed households and absent fathers. With two-parent households and prescribed, patriarchal gender roles considered essential to social stability, it was argued that Caribbean family structures, deemed pathological, produced youths (especially males) who led undisciplined lives, making them more likely to drift into crime. Borrowing from tropes widely used in the postwar US, it was the "pathological" black family—rather than a deliberately exclusionary educational system or the color bar—that persisted, despite legislation to outlaw discrimination, that led young black male youths to commit crimes.[9] Factors like unemployment were also downplayed although they played a pivotal role.

Unemployment increased sharply in the 1970s. Figures show that unemployment stood at 628,000 in January 1974 and by January 1976 had risen to 1.4 million.[10] For black working-class communities, unemployment exacerbated poverty, and some turned to crime. A "moral panic"—defined as "excessive waves of fear and apprehension among sections of the public about a perceived threat to society itself and, in reaction, the recruitment of the agencies of social control and wider political structures to deal with it"—grew in relation to mugging, which, along with robberies, quickly became racialized: these were crimes supposedly committed especially by black youths and men in inner cities.[11] However, there is little statistical evidence that muggings increased dramatically in the early 1970s.[12]

In response to the perceived increase in mugging and the need to preserve law and order—fast becoming a Conservative Party trope—the police increased their surveillance and harassment of black communities. A large and disproportionate number of black youths were stopped and searched by the police in the 1960s and '70s under "sus" laws—shorthand for "suspicious behaviour." Sus laws dated from Section 4 of the Vagrancy Act of 1824 and gave the police the power to stop and search individuals suspected of intent to commit an offense. But to them, the people most likely to seem suspicious tended to be black youths—another example of how police discretion turns ostensibly race-neutral laws into tools of racist discrimination. Three-quarters of those arrested under "sus" between 1977 and 1979 were black.[13] Yet the police knew both the ineffectiveness of "sus" (and, later, stop and search) and the relatively low rates of crime among Caribbean communities. In the 1971–72 *Report on Police/Immigrant Relations*, the Select Committee on Race Relations and Immigration noted that the "West Indian crime rate is much the same as that of the indigenous population."[14] Nonetheless, the police continued to overpolice "high crime areas," which tended to overlap with black communities. These practices also linked with the fact that in the 1970s and '80s, moves were made in the judiciary toward a less reformist criminal justice system in England, with more punitive measures that captured black Britons in cycles of incarceration.

Caribbean communities made a concerted effort to challenge police practices. Black parents tried to challenge sus laws with the Black Parents Movement, from 1975 designing a "Scrap Sus" campaign against police harassment. But when black British men and women tried to confront police authorities to complain about their treatment, they encountered inadequate police complaints procedures.

While the police were concerned with disciplining black youth, this era also saw an increase in racist violence. In Britain, between 1976 and 1981, thirty-one black people lost their lives to attacks by racists.[15] Racist killings partly emerged out of the growth of right-wing and white nationalist organizations like the National Front (NF). Formed in February 1967 from the League of Empire Loyalists, the British National Party, and the Racial Preservation Society, the NF supported Enoch Powell's call for the repatriation of black and Asian people in Britain. They made inroads in local council elections in the 1970s, although they never won a seat in Parliament. In response, anti-racist, left-wing, and anti-fascist groups formed organizations too, from the musicians' campaign Rock Against Racism to the Anti-Nazi League, created in 1977.

Politicians, especially Margaret Thatcher in her remarks quoted earlier, rhetorically echoed the racist views of white nationalist groups. Thatcher made her sentiments known not only through words but also, and notably, in her immigration policies. Once she became prime minister in 1979, changes to immigration legislation were high on Thatcher's agenda, and she was committed to making it more difficult for people from former British colonies to reside and work in Britain. This stance was central to the 1981 British Nationality Act. The act repealed parts of the 1948 act, abolishing the status of "Citizen of the United

Kingdom and Colonies," and stipulated that a person born in Britain is a British citizen if at the time of birth their mother or father is a British citizen or settled in Britain. It perpetuated aspects of the 1971 Immigration Act that stated that only patrials—those born in Britain or with a parent born in Britain—had the right to reside in the country and excluded the concept of a larger political community based on the British Empire and Commonwealth.[16] In effect, the 1981 British Nationality Act reinforced the equation of Britishness with whiteness by redrawing the boundaries of Britain and distinguishing it from the colonies, strengthening further the rhetoric of CUKCs as immigrant outsiders. For those in Britain's territories that remained as colonies, the act created the new category of "British Dependent Territories."

Along with limiting immigration, Thatcher's policies exacerbated inequality in Britain. A firm believer that inequality was a natural part of modern society, Thatcher had little interest in addressing growing racial, religious, gender, or class discrepancies. In office, her attention focused on dismantling the welfare state, spreading a neoliberal economic agenda that increased privatization, cutting public expenditure (but increasing it relative to law and order and defense), and attacking trade unions, which she viewed as a threat to economic stability.

Thatcher's focus on law and order was attuned to an increase in crime. Recorded offenses increased from around 2.5 million to 4.5 million between 1979 and 1990.[17] Youth unemployment and desires for consumer goods were some of the factors contributing to this increase. Furthermore, the decline in Britain's manufacturing industries and the concomitant rise of the service industry particularly worsened unemployment in African-Caribbean communities. A 1984 study showed that the male Caribbean unemployment rate was 28.5 percent compared to 11 percent for white men, and 16.6 percent for Caribbean women compared to 10.1 percent for white women.[18] Black Britons also experienced housing inequality, exacerbated by the 1980 Housing Act, which gave council tenants who had been in their property for three years the right to buy the freehold of their house or the lease of a flat at a discounted price. By around 1995, 1.7 million tenants had purchased a quarter of the 1980 housing stock.[19] With many black Britons unable to afford to buy their own home, due to a lack of funds and difficulties in securing a mortgage, many were dependent on council housing. But as the stock of council property decreased, not enough new houses were built to replace them. Limited housing stock would be a major factor in the growing housing crisis. Racist discrimination also continued in employment, with more and more black and Asian workers who did find jobs working for low pay and in poor conditions as part of Britain's emerging outsourcing regime that was a critical part of neoliberal capitalism. For many of these workers, especially women, in catering and cleaning jobs, the racialized and gendered pay gap they faced and the precarity of their employment were indicative of racial capitalism.[20]

Unemployment, poverty, and anti-black racism were all factors that defined the disturbances that rocked major English cities in 1980 and 1981. The first disturbance took place in April 1980 in St. Pauls, a hub of Bristol's Caribbean community since the 1950s. It occurred after a police raid on the Black and White Cafe, a popular meeting place for locals. However, the police suspected the cafe was also a space for drug consumption and distribution and frequently raided it. On the afternoon of April 2, police officers entered the cafe. Some of the officers wore plain clothes while other reserve officers were nearby with dogs. At some point, a crowd began to gather outside the cafe and confronted the police with stones. As police reinforcements were sent in, they too were targeted, and one police car was set on fire. By around 6:30 p.m., the police attempted to remove the burned car and restore order, but they came under further attack and decided to withdraw from the area an hour later. Looting and arson soon followed and also involved white locals. The police returned around 11 p.m., and most of the disturbance was over by midnight.[21]

Events in Bristol shocked politicians and the public. The media quickly labeled the disturbance a "black riot," and most newspapers failed to see underlying anti-black racism or police injustice as causes.[22] The *Daily Telegraph* characteristically blamed the disturbance on "race-relations witch-finders and left-wing teachers and social workers."[23] The police's temporary withdrawal garnered criticism, with many arguing that they should have acted more decisively. Between April and November, more than 130 people were arrested and ninety faced charges in court, mostly for minor offenses.[24] Later a trial ended when five defendants were acquitted, and the jury remained deadlocked on the other counts.[25] There was no government public inquiry into the events in Bristol. Moreover, there was no substantial attempt to glean its underlying causes, which would later influence disturbances in other parts of the country.

On the morning of January 18, 1981, thirteen African-Caribbean youths between the ages of fifteen and twenty died and twenty-seven people were injured in a house fire in New Cross, southeast London, where a birthday party had taken place. In 1983, one of the survivors, who had been experiencing mental health difficulties, fell from a balcony in a possible suicide. The fire was said to have been a racially motivated firebomb attack by right-wing groups, but the police argued that it was started by a disgruntled black youth. Disappointed but not surprised by the police response, locals took matters into their own hands. On March 2, 1981, twenty thousand people were involved in the Black People's Day of Action, marching from the scene of the fire to the Houses of Parliament and calling for a full investigation. The police's response to the fire contributed to the worsening relations between black communities and the police and would go on to shape more protests in South London.

In the early 1980s, Brixton was associated with urban decay and increasing crime. Police statistics showed that violent theft and robberies had grown 138 percent in Brixton between 1976 and 1980 and that black people were "disproportionately involved."[26] In April 1981, plainclothes police in Brixton started "Operation Swamp 81," a term that shared connotations with Thatcher's earlier comments of the British public feeling swamped by those of a different culture. It consisted of ten days during which plainclothes police in Brixton made over a thousand stops and 150 arrests against violent street crime and used sus laws on anyone who they suspected was planning to commit a crime. This served only to increase tensions in a community already wary of police overreach.

The Brixton disturbances started around 6 p.m. on April 10, when a police officer stopped black youth Michael Bailey because of his supposed suspicious behavior. After a struggle between the two, the officer realized that Bailey had been stabbed. A crowd soon began to gather, believing officers were trying to arrest Bailey, and became hostile. Bailey then fled to a local house and asked for help. The family in the house tried to help Bailey and called a minicab to take him to the hospital. But the taxi was stopped by the police, who examined Bailey's wound and called an ambulance. Next, black youths began to gather at the scene and, thinking that the police were attacking Bailey or not offering to help him, seized him and took him to the hospital. Following this, black youths as well as more police gathered. An arrest was made for threatening behavior, and youths started throwing stones at the police. By April 11, the police had resumed Operation Swamp 81, and with their increased presence the situation spiraled. Growing tensions and another incident involving officers searching a minicab for drugs led to larger disorder of looting and burning that night and the next day. Eighty-two arrests were made on what was dubbed "Bloody Saturday," and 279 officers and forty-five members of the public were injured.[27]

Brixton disturbances, April 1981.

Afterward, police and mainstream media labeled the Brixton events senseless violence. Some politicians saw it as an indictment of immigration. A group of Conservative MPs in the "Monday Club" banded together and, like Powell, called for a voluntary repatriation scheme, whereby fifty thousand immigrants a year would be repatriated having been offered £5,000 as an incentive.[28] Although not taken up as official policy by political parties, calls for repatriation would influence the state's increasing power to deport putatively undesirable migrants and long-standing residents from Britain. However, given previous events in Bristol, the government established an inquiry, led by barrister and judge Leslie Scarman, to make some attempt to get a deeper understanding of the factors involved.

While Scarman was conducting his investigations, further disturbances occurred in the capital and beyond. At the beginning of July 1981, local Asian youth clashed with groups of white youths and skinheads "wearing National Front gear" in Southall, West London.[29] This area had previously seen racial incidents, including the 1976 murder of Sikh teenager Gurdip Singh Chaggar and New Zealander Blair Peach's death in 1979 during an anti–National Front march. Furthermore, that month disturbances broke out in Toxteth, Liverpool, that left 468 officers injured and five hundred people arrested. Moss Side in Manchester also experienced unrest, as did Blackburn, Birmingham, Derby, Leeds, Halifax, Nottingham, Reading, Portsmouth, Sheffield, Southampton, and Wolverhampton, among others. Disturbances also broke out once more in Brixton on July 15 following a police raid. Again, the media portrayed these events as an assault on Britain's peace and tranquility. The *Financial Times* described the nationwide unrest as being "Like an epidemic of some alien disease, to which the body politic has no immunity, street riots have erupted in different parts of England during the past ten days."[30]

When Lord Scarman's report was published in November 1981, he refrained from directly criticizing the police, despite widespread news of police abuse. His report argued that events in Brixton were an angry outburst by black youths against the police and that the disorders came from a mix of political, social, and economic disadvantage and racist discrimination, and drew heavily on the narrative of family dysfunction that linked culture to violence. Again, Scarman blamed racism on the supposed dysfunction of its victims, in a way that individualizes an affliction that is essentially systemic. Most of Scarman's suggested reforms related to further police training and the recruitment of black police officers but did not address the larger structural issues. In fact, although sus laws were scrapped after the disturbances, police gained new powers to stop and search following the Police and Criminal Evidence Act of 1984.

A year later, and unsurprisingly given new police powers, more disturbances occurred. In the autumn of 1985, disturbances took place in Handsworth, Brixton, Toxteth, and Tottenham. In Handsworth, an area in Birmingham made up predominantly of black and Asian communities, two days of disturbances occurred after the arrest of a black man following a police stop and search and a police raid nearby. Hundreds were involved, throwing firebombs and attacking property and police. Disturbances in London broke out after protests against police brutality. In Brixton, clashes erupted in response to a police search for a suspected firearm belonging to the son of Dorothy "Cherry" Groce, whom they shot, leaving her paralyzed from the waist down.[31] The following week, disturbances erupted on the Broadwater Farm housing estate in Tottenham, in north London. On October 5, police questioned twenty-four-year-old Floyd Jarrett. Later that day they raided and searched his home. During this search Floyd's mother, Cynthia Jarrett, who had a history of heart problems, collapsed and died. Jarrett's death came within a week of Groce's injuries and catalyzed more clashes between black youth and police.

Taken together, these disturbances showed the role that the police played in perpetuating the racial-caste hierarchy. The proposed solutions to the disturbances, such as employing more black police officers or state resources directed to black community activism, reveal too that this top-down imposed version of liberal anti-racism was more concerned with issues of inclusion and diversity that did little to radically destroy racist policies or structures but merely paid lip service to these issues. In addition, although in the aftermath of the disturbances, councils like the Greater London Council (GLC)—the largest council in Britain, led from 1981 to 1986 by Ken Livingstone, a member of the Labour Party—established municipal anti-racist programs, critics lamented that the groups were often fractured based on debates about class and political blackness and that, overall, the GLC had limited resources to fight for racial equality. A growing discourse about multiculturalism informed this version of moderate anti-racism and allowed the state to talk about racism while not actually addressing it—by instead focusing on diversity, culture, and identity. State-led, or what writers and activists Azfar Shafi and Ilyas Nagdee call "Antiracism from Above," was a process in which "radical antiracism was contained and incorporated into the mold of formal British politics, where gradualism and moderation prevailed, and where individual career trajectories substituted for social progress writ large."[32] Prime Minister Thatcher was no supporter of the GLC. She opposed Livingstone's financial spending and his attempt to use the council to support radical, feminist, and black organizations, and in 1986 she played a role in closing the GLC, along with seven other Labour-controlled metropolitan councils.[33]

While liberal anti-racist activism was developing locally, academic scholarship that centered on exposing the structural dimensions of anti-black racism in Britain flourished. The 1970s and '80s saw important developments in black British studies, driven especially by scholars at the Centre for Contemporary Cultural Studies, established at the University of Birmingham in 1964. During this time, those attached to the centre, including Stuart Hall, Paul Gilroy, and Hazel V. Carby, among others, published landmark texts about race, racism, the state, policing, feminism, gender, and decolonization. These included *Policing the Crisis: Mugging, the State, and Law and Order* (in 1978) and *The Empire Strikes Back: Race and Racism in 70s Britain* (in 1982).[34] These scholars' activism, publications, and public-facing work brought much-needed attention to the centrality of state-led racism in Britain. They were part of burgeoning intellectual studies that challenged the dominance of whiteness in academic fields like sociology and history, drew on global African diasporic perspectives, and expanded the field of post-colonial studies. While academic scholarship that tried to both expose and undermine post-colonial melancholia was appearing, within schools a sanitized view of colonialism was relayed to students that did not address the racism at the heart of the British Empire and instead focused on glorifying imperialism. This damaging rhetoric was exacerbated by the larger imperial nostalgia surrounding the Falklands War.

In 1982, the Falklands Islands in the South Atlantic archipelago, a self-governing British territory, was invaded by right-wing Argentinian dictator General Leopoldo Galtieri, and the Royal Navy was sent to defend the territory. After two months the Argentinians surrendered. The victory saw Thatcher ride a wave of imperial nostalgia, invoking the belief in white English national superiority. In this version of triumphalist imperialism, an overwhelming sense of pride in the British Empire tried to drown out notions of colonial loss or shame.

Meanwhile, progressive educators called for a more serious approach to teaching British colonialism, which grappled with the realities of white supremacy and which would perhaps help subvert the racist ideology that was having an impact on the everyday lives of Britain's Asian and black communities. In 1985 a report led by Michael (Lord) Swann, then chancellor of the University of York, titled *Education for All* was seen as "the boldest, most comprehensive statement on the subject of multicultural education so far produced in Britain."[35] The report discussed the need for culturally specific teaching that would include children from Asia, Europe, the Caribbean, and Africa, as well as Britain, and stressed the importance of educating young people and teachers for life in a multicultural society. But Lord Swann's calls provoked a backlash from the right. Debates especially about the teaching of imperial history in the national curriculum became entangled with British nationalism. Rather than associating the British Empire with the racial-caste hierarchy, a simplistic narrative that glorified the British past, designed to instill nationalistic pride, was promoted throughout the 1990s, 2000s, and arguably still today.

POLICE INJUSTICE AND ZERO-SUM POLITICS

In the 1990s, black communities' experiences of police injustice brought anti-black racism into the national spotlight, again exposing the state's violent role in enforcing the racial-caste hierarchy. On April 22, 1993 Stephen Lawrence, a young British student whose parents had moved from Jamaica to Britain in the 1960s, was stabbed to death in Eltham, in southeast London. Lawrence and his friend Duwayne Brooks had been visiting a relative and were waiting for a bus home when they were targeted by a group of white youths. Lawrence died from his injuries, while Brooks managed to escape. Hours after Lawrence's death, the police received the names of the suspects who were part of a local racist gang, but they failed to follow up on evidence from witnesses. Weeks later the police arrested the suspects, but enough time had lapsed that vital evidence was lost. A case against two suspects in July 1993 was dropped due to insufficient evidence.

Lawrence's murder was the third in two years to have been motivated by anti-black racism in southeast London.[36] This further frustrated black people in the local community, indicating a serious pattern of behavior whereby the police failed to properly investigate racially motivated murders. There were additional grievances against the police, including that when police officers first arrived at the scene, they did not give first aid to Lawrence while he lay dying.[37] They had also failed initially to recognize his death as racially motivated and treated Lawrence's family and Brooks insensitively. Stephen Lawrence's parents, Doreen and Neville, spearheaded a campaign for justice for their son. In 1994 they started a private prosecution against three of the suspects, but this civil case also collapsed in 1996. When an inquest into Stephen's death occurred in 1997, the suspects refused to answer questions. Following the election of a Labour government that year, Home Secretary Jack Straw called for a new public inquiry into the police's investigation, to be headed by Sir William Macpherson, a former High Court judge.

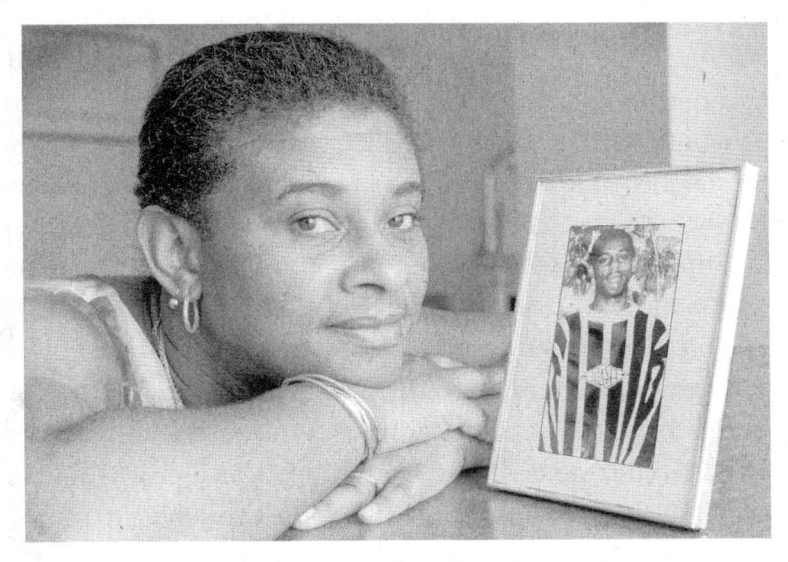

Doreen Lawrence with a photograph of her murdered son, Stephen, July 1999.

The 1999 Macpherson Report heavily criticized the Metropolitan Police's investigation and found Lawrence's murder "simply and solely and unequivocally motivated by racism."[38] It concluded that the investigation "was marred by a combination of professional incompetence, institutional racism and a failure of leadership by senior officers."[39] The report gained prominence because it pinpointed institutionalized racism, defining it as "the collective failure of an organisation to provide an appropriate and professional service to people because of their colour, culture or ethnic origin. It can be seen or detected in processes, attitudes and behaviour which amount to discrimination through unwitting prejudice, ignorance, thoughtlessness and racist stereotyping which disadvantage minority ethnic people."[40] Yet the report stopped short of linking institutional racism within the police force—which black communities had been arguing was the case since the 1950s—with wider structural racism within British society. Instead, the report focused on liberal multicultural policies—such as improving the recruitment of black as well as Asian police officers—rather than changing how the police responded to racist attacks. Diversifying the police force and improving police training, however, would do little to challenge the racial-caste hierarchy. And identifying institutionalized racism only in the police force minimized its widespread visibility within the state. It would take until 2012, after a cold-case review and new forensic evidence, for two men to be found guilty of Stephen Lawrence's murder.

Four months after Lawrence's murder in 1993, another case of police brutality made headlines. On July 28, at 7:40 a.m., forty-year-old Jamaican-born student Joy Gardner was sleeping next to her five-year-old son Graeme in Crouch End, in north London, when she was woken by five police and immigration officers. They were under orders to detain and deport Gardner back to Jamaica. Grabbing her, they forced her to the ground face down, tied her hands to her side with a leather belt and manacles, tied her legs together, and used surgical tape around her head.[41] Within minutes of being tied up, officers could not find Gardner's pulse. By 8:04 a.m. police officers called an ambulance and informed paramedics that she had collapsed and stopped breathing. At 8:15 a.m., a paramedic found Gardner without a heartbeat. They managed to revive her and took her to the local hospital, where she was placed on a life support machine. She was later taken to another hospital, where she stayed for four days. On August 1, Joy Gardner was pronounced dead. The autopsy reports showed that her death was linked to the mouth gag, oxygen starvation, and brain damage caused by asphyxiation.[42] In 1995 three police officers from the Aliens Deportation Group, a specialist unit within the Metropolitan Police, were tried on manslaughter charges. They argued that Gardner was a violent woman and their treatment of her was standard practice.[43] They were later acquitted.

Joy Gardner, 1984.

Like the Lawrences, Gardner's mother, Myrna Simpson, demanded justice for her child. Simpson had come to Britain in 1961 and left Joy with her grandmother in Jamaica. In 1987, Joy Gardner came to England on a six-month visit, during which she reunited with her mother, half brother, uncles, and aunts. She tried to stay longer on compassionate grounds, stressing the links she had to Britain and the fact that her son had been born here, but the Home Office rejected her application. After her daughter's death, Simpson wanted a public hearing and voiced the views of many black Britons when she said: "I didn't need the Lawrence inquiry to tell me the police were racist. But if the government is serious about change after Lawrence, then they will have to look at these cases. People are still dying. How many more Joy Gardners will there be?"[44] There was no public inquiry or inquest into Gardner's death.

The deaths of Lawrence and Gardner, to name just two, reminded Britons of the deadly extent of state anti-black racism and unease over the country's changing racial demographics. A year after the Macpherson Report, another report, *The Future of Multi-Ethnic Britain*, chaired by political theorist Lord Bhikhu Parekh and commissioned by Home Secretary Jack Straw, was released to much controversy. Parekh served on the Commission on the Future of Multi-Ethnic Britain, established in 1998 by the Runnymede Trust, an independent group created in 1968 to promote racial equality. The commission took stock of Britain at the millennium and identified the prevalence of post-colonial melancholia as a central aspect of contemporary British racism. According to their report, "expunging the traces of an imperial mentality from the national culture, particularly those that involved seeing the white British as a superior race, [remains] a much more difficult task. This mentality [had] penetrated everyday life, popular culture and consciousness."[45] One section of the report also noted:

The unstated assumption remains that Britishness and whiteness go together, like roast beef and Yorkshire pudding. There has been no collective working through of this imperial experience. The absence from the national curriculum of a rewritten history of Britain as an imperial force, involving dominance in Ireland as well as in Africa, the Caribbean, and Asia is proving from this perspective to be an unmitigated disaster.[46]

"Britain continues," the report lamented, "to be disfigured by racism; by phobias about cultural difference; by sustained social, economic, educational and cultural disadvantage; by institutional discrimination; and by a systematic failure of social justice or respect for difference."[47]

The commission's observation that Britain had not confronted its colonial past, and that Britishness remained equated with whiteness in an exclusionary way, provoked fierce backlash. Those on the right, selectively quoting from the report and taking points out of context, criticized the report for suggesting that "'British' is a racist word."[48] Indeed, politicians from across the spectrum criticized the report, and Straw distanced himself from arguments that racism was still a dominating force in Britain. The response to the report illustrated two competing visions of Britain: on the one hand, an insular island unaffected by empire, race, and racism; and on the other a long-globalized country connected through empire with various peoples, languages, and religions. The former served as a reflection of the attempt to erase the experience of empire entirely—a kind of self-exculpatory amnesia—rivaled by a highly distortive nostalgia that, likewise, erased the realities of empire. And over the coming decades, it would only grow louder, especially among ruling governments.

Anti-black racism would coexist, from the 2000s, with a larger wave of xenophobia that targeted migrants from the EU, whose numbers were on the rise. Some parts of the media stirred up xenophobia, claiming that the majority were coming simply to claim benefits, steal jobs and school places, and fill up NHS waiting lists that would undermine "deserving" (read "white") Britons.[49]

This anti-immigration narrative was akin to an anti-EU movement shaped by a combination of white nationalists and far-right politicians and crystallized in the United Kingdom Independence Party (UKIP) that campaigned for Britain to exit the EU and among Euroskeptics in the Conservative Party. European immigration numbers rose around the same time as refugees from war-torn areas sought asylum after 1999, especially from Kosovo, Sierra Leone, and, later, Sri Lanka and Iraq. These refugees were also frequently scapegoated as undeserving and unwanted. Anti-immigrant and anti-refugee narratives drew on long-standing xenophobic and racist sentiments long attached to black and Asian communities, as well as Islamophobia. They were also fueled by the rise of zero-sum politics, which fed into the narrative that white Britons, especially, were being disadvantaged. In reality, migrants were (and tend nearly always to be) much needed in Britain, boosting the economy and often working in precarious, low-paying, but essential jobs in hospitality, health, construction, social care, and agriculture. In fact, regardless of economic arguments or balance sheets, immigrants to Britain (historically and in the late twentieth century specifically) played a central role in developing and changing British society.

Nonetheless, hostility toward immigrants and refugees increased in the era of austerity. Austerity policies introduced by the Conservative-led coalition government after 2010 worsened the situation for immigrants, refugees, and working- and middle-class communities living in Britain. Austerity measures saw the loss of access to public services, a decrease in welfare payments, and limited pay raises for those in public sector jobs that, in combination with the rising cost of living, exacerbated poverty.

Service sector jobs were unregulated and became increasingly precarious and low-paid, with many working "zero-hours contracts" in the "gig economy." By 2009, a year after the economic recession, unemployment in Britain stood at above 2 million.[50] Crime also increased, and again black culture would be blamed.

Another moral panic arose, this time about gangs and knife crime and linked to aspects of black youth culture, such as garage, grime, and drill music, among inner-city youths. The "New Labour" government—seeking to be just as tough on law and order as the Conservative Party, which they believed was crucial to attracting the middle-class electoral base they sought—introduced new laws such as the 1998 Crime and Disorder Act, which created Youth Offending Teams to help young people avoid crime. Police and courts also received new powers, including issuing Antisocial Behaviour Orders (ASBOs) that banned individuals from areas where they had committed crimes, among other things. Police acquired increased powers to stop and search, although overwhelming evidence still suggests that this measure is largely ineffective in reducing crime.[51] As in the 1970s, politicians continued to make claims about the link between black culture and crime and to disregard the ways in which anti-black racism and class inequality—at the crux of the racial-caste hierarchy—impacted the families from which young offenders came and the broader social context that shaped their choices. In April 2007, speaking on the growth of knife crime in the capital, Prime Minister Tony Blair bluntly argued: "the spate of knife and gun murders in London was not being caused by poverty, but [by] a distinctive black culture."[52]

"Black culture" was again blamed for the disturbances that rocked Britain during the summer of 2011. And this came to impact the African-Caribbean as well as Britain's growing African population. (Since the start of the twenty-first century, Britain's black population has been linked more to Africa than the

Caribbean—the 2011 census showed that more black British people opt to classify themselves as black African.[53])

On August 4, 2011, a police officer shot dead twenty-nine-year-old Mark Duggan in Tottenham. Duggan had been followed by members of Operation Trident, a unit dealing with gun crime in Caribbean and African communities. It was reported that Duggan had fired at the police before he was shot, but this turned out to be false.[54] On Saturday, August 6, groups within the community assembled outside the Tottenham police station. Protests began peacefully but later turned violent, and two patrol cars were set on fire. Violence continued the following day, and unrest spread throughout the capital and farther afield to Liverpool, Birmingham, Nottingham, Bristol, and elsewhere. In response, police forces adopted military-style policing practices to quell the disturbances. Thousands were arrested, and in total five people died and sixteen were injured.[55] Most of those involved in the disturbances were handed heavy fines or draconian sentences, which accompanied rising rates of incarceration for young black, Asian, and mixed-race Britons. In 2019 more than a quarter of Britain's prison population were people of color, including 13 percent black, 8 percent Asian, and 7 percent of other racial groups.[56] Meanwhile, estimates for the larger population of England and Wales from the 2021 census show people of Asian ethnicity making up 9.3 percent of the population, those of black heritage 4.0 percent, those of mixed backgrounds 2.9 percent, and those listed as belonging to other ethnic groups 2.1 percent.[57]

Again, anti-black racism, police harassment, and social and economic factors were downplayed as pundits and politicians across the spectrum and media argued that the disturbances were just criminally motivated riots. Former prime minister Tony Blair claimed that pathological family structures were chiefly to blame; that those involved were people "from families that are profoundly dysfunctional, operating on completely different terms from the rest of society ... most of them are shaping up that way by the time they are in primary school or even in nursery."[58] The prime minister, David Cameron, also disregarded social context and echoed Blair in blaming "children without fathers" for the disturbances.[59] He called for increased police powers to address gang culture, a decision that only strengthened the link between blackness and criminality and furthered state-led anti-black racism that would continue to make headlines.[60] Yet in a powerful interview, veteran activist and former black British Panther Darcus Howe, who had been part of the Mangrove Nine in the 1970s, referenced the long history of anti-black racism that shaped the events, saying the police "had been stopping and searching young blacks for no reason" before the events of the summer of 2011.[61] In July 2017, for instance, police brutality was considered responsible for the controversial death of twenty-year-old Rashan Charles, who died following restraint by Metropolitan Police officers in Dalston, London.

HOSTILE ENVIRONMENTS

Anti-black racism, xenophobia, nativism, and anti-immigrant sentiment coalesced during the 2016 referendum over Britain's membership in the European Union. The "Vote Leave" campaign effectively stoked fears that Britain's continued membership would lead to more immigration and exacerbate (the politically created and maintained) competition in housing, health, and education. However, British exit—"Brexit"—was not just about present immigration issues but also about Britain's relationship to immigration historically; in other words, the British Empire loomed large throughout. Colonial metaphors were all the rage among Vote Leave campaigners. They argued that Britain's continued membership was limiting Britain's sovereignty—a far-fetched but easily digestible falsity. They invoked the idea that the people of Britain were under the colonial yoke of the EU's rule. Much of their anti-immigrant sentiment was related not just to Europeans but more broadly to descendants of migrants and people of color in Britain because of the deep equation of whiteness with Britishness.

Those who supported Leave drew heavily on a skewed interpretation of the history of the British Empire. Trying their best to leave aside the empire's tangible links to white supremacist violence and the racial-caste hierarchy, they leaned rhetorically on free trade. Leaving the EU, they argued, would allow Britain to forge more competitive and lucrative trade links with Commonwealth countries such as Australia, New Zealand, and Canada—with some using the acronym CANZUK to denote a new economic Anglosphere. In their vision, Brexit would herald the rise of "Global Britain."

Global Britain was shaped by historical amnesia. It reinforced colonial-era hierarchies that privileged former old Dominions over other Commonwealth countries in Africa, Asia, and the Caribbean. But just as much as historical amnesia and the racial-caste hierarchy shaped those Leave supporters, it also impacted "Remainers," albeit in a different way. Remain supporters invoked empire in their support of Britain taking a greater lead in Europe, as Britain had done when it led a vast colonial empire.[62] Others invoked the inclusivity of the Commonwealth and the potential for deepening ties with African, Asian, and Caribbean member countries.

When the votes were counted, it became clear that age, racial identity, class, geography, and education played a major role in the final decision. More affluent areas rather than deprived ones most heavily voted Leave, especially in the south of England with its large population of older voters, whose turnout tends to be high.[63] Younger voters and university graduates tended to opt for Remain. Places with high migrant populations, like major cities, were more inclined to vote Remain. It was clear that although the 51.89 percent of those who voted to leave the EU had various reasons for their votes, racism played a central role as well. In the immediate aftermath of Brexit, there were increased racist and xenophobic attacks, with the police recording a 57 percent increase in reported race crimes after the vote.[64]

Brexit and its colonial undertones would come to impact debates about racism and immigration beyond 2016, fueled especially by populist right-wing figures and political leaders who exacerbated the growing exclusionary nature of British nationalism. They would also contribute to the larger debates about the legacies of colonialism in Britain and the teaching of colonial history that captured headlines from 2014 due to student activist campaigns at universities across the country that grappled with the ongoing presence of colonial iconography—like the "Rhodes Must Fall" campaign at the University of Oxford, inspired by activism taking place in South Africa, and other campaigns such as "Why Is My Curriculum so White." These student-led protests showed the increasing desire among students especially to force academic places of learning to take seriously the institutional legacies of the racial-caste hierarchy and how Britain remembers its colonial past. They would be met, unsurprisingly, with loud dismissals that overlooked the long contestations over the legitimacy of a violent empire and doubled down further on a mythical and nostalgic history of the British Empire.

Before and amid the referendum campaign and "imperial history wars," the Windrush scandal, evidence once again of state-led anti-black racism, was unfolding. The scandal had its roots in the hostile environment legislation announced in 2012 and introduced in the Immigration Acts of 2014 and 2016 and earlier legal changes, designed to prevent undocumented migrants from accessing public services such as healthcare, employment, welfare aid, and housing.[65] This policy extended to Caribbean people who had been living in Britain for decades but who had no proof of their residency. Through the investigative journalism of the *Guardian*'s Amelia Gentleman and others, the activism of African-Caribbean Britons and their families, as well as Caribbean diplomats and politicians, it became known that from 2002 to June 2018 thousands of Caribbean nationals had been banned or deported from Britain. Others had been denied access to healthcare, housing, and employment. Some of those wrongly deported had died.[66] There were also cases of other Caribbean nationals being targeted before 2002. Most of the individuals impacted were middle-aged or elderly Caribbean men and women who had arrived in Britain before 1973. Many had joined relatives as children and did not have documentary evidence such as passports. Documentation that the Home Office should have held was also missing. The term "Windrush," referring to Caribbean men, women, and children who arrived in Britain in the postwar period, became a label to describe this group. However, it is slightly misleading since those most impacted by the scandal had arrived as part of a later wave of migration in the 1950s and '60s, and before the 1971 Immigration Act came into effect on January 1, 1973, and not all came from the Caribbean. Those who had entered Britain before 1973 should have had the right of abode but instead were treated as "illegal immigrants."

The scandal made headlines during a biennial Heads of Commonwealth meeting in London in April 2018. A formal request had been made by some Caribbean nations to meet with British prime minister Theresa May to discuss their concerns about Caribbean people and their disputes with the Home Office. However, their request was refused. The "diplomatic snub went on the *Guardian*'s front page, and the political response was instant," wrote Gentleman.[67] As more information became known, the scandal led to a government apology, the resignation of Home

Secretary Amber Rudd, and the creation of a task force and compensation scheme. According to Rudd's replacement, Sajid Javid, 164 people had been incorrectly detained for removal and eighty-three were wrongly deported.[68] An emergency hardship fund was established after the scandal came to light.

Jamaican grandmother Eulalee, who was detained in Yarl's Wood, at the front of the march from Downing Street on June 22, 2019, as seven UK cities take part in the National Windrush Day of Action, calling for justice and full compensation for victims of the Windrush scandal, their multigenerational families and other communities targeted, under the hostile environment policy, for detention and deportation.

However, as Gentleman admits, "we still don't know the true scale of what happened and we may never find out."[69] The Windrush compensation scheme remains woefully lacking in implementation. In 2020, nine people died before receiving payment.[70] Although the Home Office pledged to transform its culture, little change has occurred. In March 2022, following an independent inquiry into the scandal, a "lack of tangible progress or drive to achieve cultural changes required" was identified.[71] At the time of writing, many of those affected have still not received compensation, and problems continue to unfold.

Indeed, in late May 2022, the *Guardian* reported on a leaked government report that concluded that the origins of the Windrush scandal stemmed from thirty years of racist immigration legislation created to limit the population of people of color in Britain.[72] Yet within the media and among politicians, the Windrush scandal was presented as a mistake: the Conservative Party's hostile environment policies, it was suggested, were never designed to impact elderly, usually upstanding members of society—those deemed "good migrants." In this way, the scandal was seen as an administrative aberration. It was not. Rather it was a part of the state's long-standing promotion of anti-black racism and a direct consequence of the racial-caste hierarchy.

Furthermore, the Windrush scandal is part of a longer history of immigration control and exclusion that has seen increased rates of deportation. From the 1980s, the Home Office started to use minor violations of residency rules as justification for deportation.[73] Once considered exceptional, deportations now occur much more regularly and are a crucial part of the "hostile environment."[74] While sympathy was extended to victims of the Windrush scandal, it was not extended to vulnerable black youths, many of whom were born in the Caribbean but moved to Britain as children, who were (and are) especially targeted for automatic deportation after a criminal conviction of more than twelve months, despite appeals made to the Home Office following changes to immigration law in 2007.[75]

In the later twentieth century, "deportation" became a term often used interchangeably with "removal" and has become more widely used to limit migration. In the 1990s the number deported annually was around seven thousand; in 2004 there were 21,425 forced removals.[76] Regular news reports of activists trying to stop airplanes filled with men and women heading to Jamaica,

Ghana, or Nigeria have highlighted the British state's increased use of deportation, especially for those of Caribbean or African birth.[77] Many of those deported to the Caribbean are presented as dangerous foreign criminals, but not all are. Some have lived longer in Britain than anywhere else and consider themselves to be British. There is evidence that some have committed minor criminal offenses.[78] Some have also been deliberately harassed and followed by police officers who are well aware of their precarious migrant status.

Caribbean countries are implicated in the growing culture of deportation as well. In Jamaica, for instance, the National Organization of Deported Migrants, funded by the British government, helps deported individuals settle into new lives in Jamacia.[79] The island is also home to the Open Arms Drop-in Centre, a homeless shelter funded by the British government that houses black Britons and Jamaicans who are deported to the country. These organizations play an important role in helping deportees adjust to life in Jamaica, but they cannot always protect them from the violence many deportees face from members of the community and the police. Indeed, police violence in Jamaica is on the rise. Between 2000 and 2016, Amnesty International reported that around three thousand people were killed by law enforcement officials in Jamaica.[80]

Jamaica's involvement in Britain's deportation culture was evident during a state visit in 2015, when Prime Minister David Cameron sought to expand Britain's incarceration policies by offering to give the Jamaican government £25 million to create a new Jamaican prison, to which Britain could deport the six hundred Jamaican national prisoners being held in British prisons.[81] However, Jamaica would not be an equal partner with Britain in this venture. The offer was rejected by the Jamaican prime minister, Andrew Holness, once it was clear that his government would have to pay 60 percent of the costs of construction and management.[82]

The increasing use of deportation is evidence once again of how black men and women, some of whom might not have been born in Britain but certainly, because of long residence there, consider themselves to be black Britons, are deemed outsiders once they commit a crime, however minor, with no right to reside or belong here—an example of the devastation caused to individuals, families, and communities by anti-black racism.

By 2020, the onset of the Covid-19 pandemic exposed starkly the (literally) deadly nature of anti-black racism due to health disparities. In England, mortality figures among Asian and black groups were around 2.5 and 4.3 times higher than for white communities.[83] The higher rates of infection among Bangladeshi, Pakistani, and black Britons had little to do with biology and more to do with how their social, political, and economic conditions created health inequality. Since many black people in Britain live in overcrowded housing and have higher rates of poverty, lower incomes, and higher unemployment than white people, many had to go to work and interact with the public amid the pandemic, were exposed more frequently to the virus, and were less able to self-isolate. As the legacies of the pandemic continue to unfold, research still indicates that it has affected black and Asian communities the most.[84]

Racial disparities and protest against injustice came to a peak amid global Black Lives Matter (BLM) marches that occurred throughout the world from Britain to Brazil, the US, Australia, Liberia, and across Europe. Following the police murder of Black American George Floyd in May 2020 and of Breonna Taylor in Kentucky in March that year, and countless other black men and women and the racialized effects of the pandemic, thousands of protesters across Britain took to the streets against the growing anti-black racism that ruled the country. The largest demonstration occurred in June in London, attended by over thirty thousand people. BLM protests also railed against racist policing in Britain, with activists making demands to abolish the police and establish more community-driven policing practices in black communities.[85] Protests were not just about the present but also about the legacies of the colonial past. Later that month, hundreds of protesters assembled around the statue of Edward Colston, former director of the Royal African Company. They toppled it and threw it into Bristol Harbour. With this act they wanted to rid the city, once the center of Britain's involvement in the transatlantic slave trade, of visual reminders of racial slavery that are linked to today's struggles for racial justice.

The protests, along with blatant racial discrepancies made visible by the pandemic, forced the Conservative government under Boris Johnson to establish a commission to investigate racial and ethnic disparities, which was headed by Tony Sewell, an educational consultant whose parents were born in Jamaica. The result was a much-criticized report that the commissioners alleged had been edited by Downing Street to distort their findings and to repeat the fallacy that institutionalized racism did not exist in Britain.[86] The report deliberately misrepresented the overwhelming evidence of institutionalized racism and was afflicted with historical amnesia and inaccuracy. But it came as little surprise to many, following the long denials of state-led anti-black racism that helps maintain Britain's racial-caste hierarchy.

The previous Conservative government-driven politics of division, euphemistically called "culture wars," were predicated on zero-sum politics and blatantly reinforced the racial-caste hierarchy. In this context, political attacks rose on anti-racist activists, as well as on radical and progressive scholars, by those on the right who seemed to be obsessed with sovereignty, borders, the purity of the nation-state, the defense of the nuclear family, patriarchal masculinity, and with promoting an exceptionalism about an imagined past that relies heavily on colonial-derived hierarchies that in effect replicate the racial-caste order.[87] As historian Peter

Mitchell has so aptly said: "The imperial nostalgia of the Conservative Party itself, and of the class which dominates it, is more straightforwardly literal: the empire is something their ancestors built and governed, a fact in which it is possible to feel a personal and communal pride, and a model of a world arranged more or less as it should be."[88] And this nostalgia is not just perpetuated by white politicians and elites but increasingly by some members of the black and Asian middle class and elites, who draw on the rules of racial hierarchy to allow them access to spaces of power and control. Following the summer 2024 election, it remains to be seen whether the opposition Conservative Party will abandon or further the "culture wars" and what the response will be from the Labour government.

Overall, the final decades of the twentieth century and early twenty-first century in Britain have been marked by the dominance of post-colonial melancholia, which has simultaneously tried to overlook the persistence of anti-black racism that has its roots in the history of empire and that also fostered a politics of division, enhanced by zero-sum thinking that saw white and black Britons in competition. All of which is overwhelming evidence of the enduring presence of the racial-caste order.

Yet the growth of global movements for reparations and for radical anti-racism has the powerful potential to address the legacies of the British Empire and unravel the racial-caste hierarchy.

REPAIR AND RENEWAL

Calls for reparations for racial slavery and colonialism are not new. Enslaved Africans employed a variety of terms—such as "redress," "repayment," and "compensation"—to seek justice for the dehumanization they experienced.[89] In the 1950s and '60s, during constitutional decolonization and concurrent social movements, calls for reparations became increasingly popular, not just in the Caribbean but also internationally, which spurred an equally global resistance. In recent years, especially amid global black protest movements and the persistent poverty facing the Caribbean, those calls have grown louder from the public as well as political leaders.[90]

British political leaders have had to tread a very thin legal line so as not to admit responsibility for past deeds that might validate calls for financial compensation. Thus far they have only repeated statements of regret. In recent years, members of the British monarchy have joined politicians in these statements expressing "profound sorrow."[91] Other politicians have tried to avoid the issue altogether. During a state visit to Jamaica in September 2015, Prime Minister Cameron argued that Britain and Jamaica should "move on from this painful legacy."[92] Cameron's calls to overlook the past made headlines given his own family's involvement in racial slavery: after the passage of the Abolition of Slavery Act in 1833, his ancestor Sir James Duff received compensation for the 202 enslaved Africans he owned in Jamaica.[93]

While regret, sorrow, and calls to move on from a painful past abound in Britain, Caribbean leaders have been at the forefront of demanding not just an official apology but also wide-ranging reparations. In March 2007 the prime minister of Barbados, Owen Arthur, argued that reparations were an issue "not of retribution, but of morality," and called for the "need to bring equity to the emancipation process, and closure to the criminal activity that was racial chattel slavery."[94]

In 2014, the CARICOM (Caribbean Community) Reparations Commission (CRC) had equity and morality at its heart. With the involvement of and building on the pioneering scholarship of Caribbean historians like Hilary Beckles and Verene Shepherd, the CRC published a program targeting European countries, including Britain, France, Denmark, Portugal, the Netherlands, and Sweden.[95] The ten-point plan called for financial and symbolic reparations; a full and formal apology; repatriation for those who want to resettle in Africa; development programs for indigenous peoples; investment in cultural institutions; alleviation and support in dealing with public health crises; a program to eradicate illiteracy; an African knowledge program; psychological rehabilitation; technology transfer programs; and debt cancellations. These demands would take the form of "government-to-government legal process" and later be extended to include "those participating financial and social institutions that exist today as privileged beneficiaries."[96] For Beckles, "the objective of reparations is not to punish or penalize the offender, but to establish conditions for a just, reconciled future. Reparation is not an action of confrontation, but a search for unity, that is, the aim is repairing a damaged relationship."[97]

The CARICOM ten-point plan represents one version of reparations and is not one that is free from criticism, given how it currently overlooks the gendered dimensions of enslavement and colonialism. Indeed, there are many different visions of reparations. After protests for racial justice in 2020, for instance, the prime minister of Antigua and Barbuda, Gaston Browne, called for reparations from All Souls College at the University of Oxford. Browne argued that a bequest to the college in 1710 from slave owner Christopher Codrington that stocked and built the college's prestigious library was generated from the labor of enslaved Africans in Antigua and a lease he had acquired in Barbuda.[98] Browne called on All Souls to use reparations to fund scholarships and develop academic institutions in the Caribbean. His call underlines the indelible links between British academic institutions and racial slavery and colonialism that are being researched in increasing depth throughout the country. Banks, insurance companies, and religious institutions across Britain are also evaluating their involvement in racial slavery, with some taking steps to redress this. So too are city bodies. In March 2022, authorities in Glasgow apologized for the city's role in the transatlantic slave trade.[99]

As calls for reparations grow louder among a wider variety of voices, including descendants of slave owners, the British state's response of offering statements of regret will sound increasingly hollow, meaningless, and highly offensive.[100] While debates remain about the practicalities of reparations, it is undeniable that they are necessary, for they represent a meaningful step toward justice. Indeed, a recent report by the economic consultants group Brattle calculated that Britain owes £18.6 trillion—around eight times the country's annual GDP—for their involvement.[101] Yet reparations are just the beginning steps toward reconciliation, the first stage in the unfinished process of emancipation and decolonization, not the end.

In addition to reparations, other moves to address the lingering presence of colonialism in independent states are informing the current momentum toward republicanism, with more countries following the path of Dominica, Guyana, Trinidad and Tobago, and Barbados in removing the British monarch as the ceremonial head of state.[102] It remains to be seen whether this momentum will change or be accelerated; and to what extent it will be shaped by emerging research that shows in more detail the close links the British monarchy has to hereditary racial slavery.[103] However, while sovereign states in the region are trying to disentangle themselves from Britain, overseas territories continue to shy away from independence. While many bristle when Britain exercises its financial control over them, many wish to retain the colonial link.

Yet for reparations to be truly transformative, they need to deal not only with the past and present, but also with the future. And in considering the future, reparations must be linked to broader strategies to wrestle the Caribbean from the stranglehold of other powers that seek—similar to British colonialism and neocolonialism and US imperialism—to exploit the Caribbean. Over the last fifteen years, the Chinese government and businesses have been investing significantly throughout the Caribbean, building roads, tourist facilities, harbors, and ports and creating new markets for Chinese goods. China's encroachments into the Caribbean are on the one hand an attempt to gain economic entry into the region and on the other hand a way to undermine Taiwan's allies, especially in the Eastern Caribbean.[104] Chinese investment in the Caribbean, however, often leads to increasing debt for Caribbean states and further limits their autonomy. Reparations must help ensure that the Caribbean need not rely too heavily on external powers and grapple with the region's persistent economic dependency on the rest of the world, seen especially through the dominance of the tourist industry, which was seriously impacted during the Covid-19 pandemic.[105]

Reparations must look for ways also to redress the ecological damage wrought by the past that poses, amid the rapid climate crisis, an existential threat to the Caribbean.[106] The Caribbean is particularly vulnerable to continuing rising sea levels and changes in rain and temperature patterns that worsen the growing intensity of natural disasters. Any reparations arrangement must address the reality of the unequal consequences of climate crisis in the Caribbean, exacerbated by centuries of environmental destruction shaped by colonialism and contemporary "disaster capitalism"—defined by author and activist Naomi Klein as "orchestrated raids on the public sphere in the wake of catastrophic events, combined with the treatment of disasters as exciting market opportunities."[107]

While the reparations movement can address the continuance of colonialism in the independent Caribbean, radical anti-racism has the potential to undermine the racial-caste hierarchy. For meaningful change to occur, there needs to be a move away from liberal forms of anti-racism that focus on representation, diversity, and inclusion.[108] While there is some worthiness in considering these issues, they are ultimately limited because they are not predicated on the eradication of linked racist and class oppression. Rather, there needs to be a turn to a more radical form of anti-racism that seeks to upend racist exploitation that has been shaped by capitalism not just in Britain and the Caribbean but throughout the world.

Radical anti-racism is centered on confronting racist and class exploitation together and challenges the continuing reliance on the fictional concept of race. It seeks to move beyond racialized ways of thinking and fixed categories created by colonizers, which continue to divide rather than unite individuals and communities. And it is committed to challenging racial capitalism. Coupled with nonracial humanism—which seeks to move beyond a focus on race and skin color to consider the broader ties between individuals and communities—it can help, perhaps, erode racial hierarchies.[109] This move toward a nonracial humanism and radical anti-racism might not take place in this generation and would require nothing short of complete global transformation. However, it is possible—and necessary—to envisage a future where racial divisions and capitalist inequalities are not the defining features of our global social order.

The arguments and evidence recounted here, and histories of the British Empire more broadly, evoke powerful emotions. While feelings of shame, guilt, regret, horror, and anger dominate this history, these emotions should fuel rather than stifle attempts to grapple with its devastating consequences. For this is a history that is by no means over, and a history that is by no means limited to the protagonists and their descendants. This is a history hidden in plain sight, and it is one that haunts us all. Colonialism, capitalism, the legacies of enslavement, and linked racial, class, and gendered divisions are visible in nearly every facet of society in culture, politics, and the economy, not just in Britain and the Caribbean but across the world. Indeed, it is impossible to fully comprehend the world without reckoning with how it is still entangled with colonialism and the various permutations of the racial-caste hierarchy that have created a type of *living* history.

In these turbulent times of surging white supremacy, evidenced most explicitly in the August 2024 far-right violent riots that gripped major cities and towns in Britain, unraveling this living history comes with consequences, especially for historians. Detractors will, of course, deny these arguments; belittle, relegate, or misrepresent this history. This is not new. What is new is the increasing use of verbal and physical violence that those who write, study, and teach this history now face with more frequency. This abuse is indicative of just how critically necessary uncovering and telling this history is and, moreover, illustrative of the overarching political weight this history has for our times. From governments dictating that this history be taught in a skewed way, if taught at all, to book bans and author harassment, it mirrors the wider rise of authoritarianism that seeks not just to silence this history but to eradicate it. There is nothing to indicate that these attempts will soon stop. However, historical sources, some in their fragments, others in their abundance, data, statistics, oral testimony, personal and collective memory, and the everyday experiences of millions, attest to the realities of the pernicious, persistent presence of the British Empire and the racial-caste hierarchy. And in so doing force us—all of us—to reckon with the roles and responsibilities we have in *repairing* the present, for we cannot change the past.[110] This repair—a central part of reparatory history—is key to challenging not just colonialism and hierarchy but our present-day descent into despotism.

A global white supremacist system designed to divide and wage physical and psychological terror on the masses yesterday and today need not be a part of the future. Neither the British Empire nor the racial-caste system will persist forever. The struggle to end both endures.

Acknowledgments

Writing this book has proved a collective effort, and there are many people who deserve thanks for their help and advice. I would like to thank the many archivists and librarians at the Bermuda National Archives, the National Archives in Kew, Bishopsgate Institute, Mass Observation Archive, the Black Cultural Archives, and the LSE Library. At the Eccles Centre at the British Library, many thanks go to Polly Russell, Philip Abraham, Cara Rodway, and Jean Petrovic. For excellent research assistance, I am indebted to James Francis. For help with bringing the narrative together in a coherent way, I am grateful to Pamela Haag. For feedback on various drafts of the manuscript, I thank Oscar Webber, Grace Carrington, Jose Maria Hernandez Alvarez, Justine McConnell, Kate Quinn, Padraic Scanlan, Pat Thane, George Lawson, Bill Schwarz, Elizabeth Prochaska, Stephen Tuck, and Taylor Sherman. I am thankful, too, for the Department of International History at the London School of Economics who supported this research. For her wonderful help with sourcing the images in the book, I am indebted to Joanna Evans. For permission to use her stunning image on the front cover, I am grateful to Lubaina Himid and to creative director Suzanne Dean for designing a beautiful cover. For all their help, feedback, and advice, I am grateful to my editors, Michal Shavit and Kathryn Belden, as well as Seán Hayes; my agent, Chris Wellbelove; and copy editor, Kate Johnson. Most thanks go to my friends and family, who have provided enduring encouragement and support.

Illustration Credits

vii Library of Congress, Geography and Map Division, Washington, DC/licensed under CC0.
xiii Courtesy of the author.
3 Rijksmuseum, Amsterdam/licensed under CC0.
9 Album/Alamy.
26 NYPL/Schomburg Center for Research in Black Culture, Manuscripts, Archives and Rare Books Division/licensed under CC0.
34 Yale Center for British Art, Paul Mellon Collection/licensed under CC0.
45 Boston Public Library/licensed under CC0.
51 © The Trustees of the British Museum.
61 NYPL/Schomburg Center for Research in Black Culture, Photographs and Prints Division/licensed under CC0.
64 NYPL/Schomburg Center for Research in Black Culture, Photographs and Prints Division/licensed under CC0.
84 The Met/Harris Brisbane Dick Fund, 1932/licensed under CC0.
91 University of California Libraries/licensed under CC0.
94 © The Syndicate/Alamy.
107 Library of Congress Rare Book and Special Collections Division Washington/licensed under CC0.
107 Wikimedia Commons/licensed under CC0.
143 Janusz Pieńkowski/Alamy.
144 Wikimedia Commons/licensed under CC0.
153 Wikimedia Commons/licensed under CC0.
158 DeGolyer Library, Southern Methodist University/licensed under CC0.
170 Library of Congress Prints and Photographs Division Washington, DC/licensed under CC0.
173 Wikimedia Commons/licensed under CC0.
189 Hulton Archive/Getty Images.
197 Licensed under CC0.
213 Taylor/Imperial War Museums via Getty Images.
215 Imperial War Museums via Getty Images.
223 Daily Herald Archive/SSPL/Getty Images.

ILLUSTRATION CREDITS

238 Bettmann/Getty Images.
248 John Franks/Keystone/Getty Images.
252 Harry Benson/Express/Getty Images.
265 Associated Press via Alamy.
271 *Trinity Mirror*/Mirrorpix/Alamy.
284 Associated Press via Alamy.
286 Knoote/*Daily Express*/Hulton Archive/Getty Images.
288 Anthony Camerano/AP via Alamy.
289 *Trinity Mirror*/Mirrorpix/Alamy.
302 *Evening Standard*/Hulton Archive/Getty Images.
334 Associated Press via Alamy.
336 Associated Press via Alamy.
343 Keystone Press/Alamy.
347 DOD Photo/Alamy.
367 PA Images/Alamy.
373 *Trinity Mirror*/Mirrorpix/Alamy.
375 PA Images/Alamy.
385 Peter Marshall/Alamy Live News.

Notes

INTRODUCTION

1. Debate remains about the accuracy of Bassett's first name. In some records she is listed as Sarah or Sary, in others Sally. I use Sally as this is the name by which she is most commonly referred.
2. Bassett's trial is recorded in the Courts of Assizes minutes in: Court of Assize—AZ/102/6, Court Proceedings—Sally Bassett Case—1730, 221, Bermuda National Archives.
3. Quito Swan, "Smoldering Memories and Burning Questions: The Politics of Remembering Sally Bassett and Slavery in Bermuda," in Ana Lucia Araujo (ed.), *Politics of Memory: Making Slavery Visible in the Public Space* (New York, 2016), p. 73; Clarence V. H. Maxwell, "'The horrid villainy': Sarah Bassett and the poisoning conspiracies in Bermuda, 1727–30," *Slavery and Abolition* 21 no. 3 (2000): pp. 68–69.
4. James C. Scott, *Weapons of the Weak: Everyday Forms of Peasant Resistance* (New Haven, 1985), p. 29.
5. For a detailed account of the statue controversy see: Swan, "Smoldering Memories," pp. 71–91.
6. Swan, "Smoldering Memories," p. 84.
7. Tim Hall, "Race Row Swirls Around Statue: Why Did City Hall Turn Down Sally Bassett?" *Bermuda Sun*, November 14, 2008, p. 8.
8. Swan, "Smoldering Memories," pp. 86–87.
9. Tom Vesey, "A magnificent statue, in just the right place," *Bermuda Sun*, November 21, 2008, p. 9.
10. Tauria Raynor, "What Governor Said,", *Royal Gazette*, February 11, 2009, p. 6.
11. Tauria Raynor, "Governor's remarks were 'insensitive'—Commissiong," *Royal Gazette*, February 11, 2009, p. 1; Tom Vesey, "Governor, please explain what you meant about those statues," *Bermuda Sun*, February 13, 2009, p. 7.
12. Stuart Hall with Bill Schwarz, *Familiar Stranger: A Life Between Two Islands* (London, 2018), p. 97.

13 Gordon K. Lewis, *Main Currents in Caribbean Thought: The Historical Evolution of Caribbean Society in its Ideological Aspects, 1492–1900* (first published 1983; London, 2004), p. 9; Gordon K. Lewis, *Grenada: The Jewel Despoiled* (Baltimore, 1987), p. 7; Charles W. Mills, The Racial Contract (first published 1997; London, 2022), p. xxxii.

14 The construction of race in the context of the Caribbean built on earlier forms of human hierarchies that shaped medieval Europe and European contact with the Islamic world, see: Cedric J. Robinson, *Black Marxism: The Making of the Black Radical Tradition* (London, 1983), p. 2.

15 Frances L. Ansley, "Stirring the ashes: race, class and the future of civil rights scholarship," *Cornell Law Review* 74, no. 6 (1988–89), fn129, p. 1024.

16 For a fascinating contemporary take on some of these issues, see: Akala, *Natives: Race and Class in the Ruins of Empire* (London, 2019).

17 For more on the subtle forms of racism, see: Nicola Rollock, *The Racial Code: Tales of Resistance and Survival* (London, 2022).

18 Jane Burbank and Frederick Cooper, *Empires in World History: Power and the Politics of Difference* (Princeton, 2010), p. 11.

19 For an insightful discussion of caste similarities and differences in Germany, India, and the United States, see: Isabel Wilkerson, *Caste: The Lies that Divide Us* (London, 2020).

20 For a detailed study of the violence of British colonialism, see: Caroline Elkins, *Legacy of Violence: A History of the British Empire* (London, 2022).

21 For a fuller account of anti-colonial resistance, see: Priyamvada Gopal, *Insurgent Empire: Anticolonial Resistance and British Dissent* (London, 2019).

22 On the colonial mind, see: Robert Gildea, *Empires of the Mind: The Colonial Past and the Politics of the Present* (Cambridge, 2019).

23 As of August 2024, these currently include Antigua and Barbuda, the Bahamas, Belize, Grenada, Jamaica, St. Lucia, St. Kitts and Nevis, and St. Vincent and the Grenadines.

24 This figure is taken from https://worldpopulationreview.com/continents/caribbean-population (accessed 5/6/2024).

25 David Scott, "Modernity that predated the modern: Sidney Mintz's Caribbean," *History Workshop Journal*, Issue 58 (2004): pp. 191–210.

26 For a broad overview of the various empires operating in the Caribbean, see: Carrie Gibson, *Empire's Crossroads: A History of the Caribbean from Columbus to the Present Day* (London, 2015).

27 Oftentimes the region is divided into the Greater and Lesser Antilles. The Greater Antilles in the north include the Cayman Islands, Cuba, Haiti, the Dominican Republic, Puerto Rico, Jamaica, and the Lesser

Antilles in the south and east that include Antigua and Barbuda, Barbados, Dominica, Grenada, St. Kitts and Nevis, St. Lucia, St. Vincent, and the Grenadines, Trinidad and Tobago, Martinique, Guadeloupe, the US Virgin Islands, and Aruba, among others.

28 Richard Price, "Créolisation, Creolization, and Créolité," *Small Axe* 21, no. 1 (March 2017): p. 214. Edouard Glissant, "Creolisation and the Americas," *Caribbean Quarterly* 57, no. 1, (March 2011): pp. 11–20; Edward Kamau Brathwaite, *The Development of Creole Society in Jamaica, 1770–1820* (Oxford, 1971).

29 Marc T. Greene, "Slums of the Empire," Spectator, August 15, 1947, p. 7, http://archive.spectator.co.uk/article/15th-august-1947/7/-slums-of-the-empire (accessed 18/1/2024).

30 For more on the significance of the *longue durée* approach, see: Jo Guldi and David Armitage, *The History Manifesto* (Cambridge, 2014), pp. 14–37.

31 By focusing on Britain and the Caribbean, I wish to spotlight the centrality of both areas to the changing nature of racism while recognizing that they do not fully encapsulate everything there is to say on this issue.

32 Robert Booth, "UK More Nostalgic for Empire than Other Ex-Colonial Powers," *Guardian*, March 11, 2020, https://www.theguardian.com/world/2020/mar/11/uk-more-nostalgic-for-empire-than-other-ex-colonial-powers (accessed 28/4/2022).

33 Paul Gilroy, *After Empire: Melancholia or Convivial Culture?* (Oxford, 2004), pp. 102–3. It is also part of the "imperial history wars"; see: Dane Kennedy, *The Imperial History Wars: Debating the British Empire* (London, 2018).

34 Richard Drayton, "Where Does the World Historian Write From? Objectivity, Moral Conscience and the Past and Present of Imperialism," *Journal of Contemporary History* 46, no. 3 (2011): p. 685. For more on the ways in which the historical discipline has shaped the British Empire, see: Priya Satia, *Time's Monster: History, Conscience and Britain's Empire* (London, 2020).

35 Niall Ferguson, *Empire: How Britain Made the Modern World* (London, 2003); Nigel Biggar, *Colonialism: A Moral Reckoning* (London, 2023). There are recently published works that counter the narratives of Ferguson and Biggar; see: Gopal, *Insurgent Empire*; Sathnam Sanghera, *Empireland: How Imperialism Has Shaped Modern Britain* (London, 2021); Kehinde Andrews, *The New Age of Empire: How Racism and Colonialism Still Rule the World* (London, 2021); Kojo Koram, *Uncommon Wealth: Britain and the Aftermath of Empire* (London, 2022); Charlotte Lydia Riley, Imperial Island: *A History of Empire in Modern Britain* (London, 2023); Sathnam Sanghera, *Empireworld: How British Imperialism Has*

NOTES

Shaped the Globe (London, 2024); Alan Lester (ed.), *The Truth about Empire: Real Histories of British Colonialism* (London, 2024); Corinne Fowler, *Our Island Stories: Country Walks through Colonial Britain* (London, 2024).

36 Paul Gilroy, *The Black Atlantic: Modernity and Double Consciousness* (London, 1993).

37 Catherine Hall, "Doing reparatory history: bringing 'race' and slavery home," *Race & Class* 60, no. 1 (2018): p. 12.

CHAPTER 1

1 Bartolomé de Las Casas, *A Short Account of the Destruction of the Indies* (1552), edited and translated by Nigel Griffin (London, 1992), pp. 10, 9, 10.
2 Las Casas, *A Short Account*, pp. 11, 12.
3 Las Casas, *A Short Account*, p. 13.
4 Lawrence Clayton, "Bartolomé de las Casas and the African Slave Trade," *History Compass* 7/6 (2009): pp,1524–41.
5 Historia de las Indias, *Obras completas Bartolomé de las Casas*, 15 vols. (Madrid, 1988–98), V, 2324, translated by Parish and Sullivan, 203, as quoted in Clayton, "Bartolomé de las Casas," 1532.
6 Gad Heuman, *The Caribbean: A Brief History* (3rd edition; London, 2019), pp. 1–4; B. W. Higman, *A Concise History of the Caribbean* (2nd. edition; Cambridge, 2021), pp. 25–26.
7 I use the term "Taíno" while also recognizing its limitations and inaccuracies in failing to account for the diversity within indigenous people's societies. Recent archaeological research opts not to use the term "Taíno" as it imposes a uniformity that did not exist, as indigenous societies were highly diverse. But the term remains widely used. For more on the debate, see: William F. Keegan and Corinne L. Hofman, *The Caribbean Before Columbus* (Oxford, 2017), p. 115.
8 Heuman, *The Caribbean*, p. 4.
9 Higman, *A Concise History*, pp. 41–42.
10 Heuman, *The Caribbean*, p. 5.
11 Heuman, *The Caribbean*, p. 6.
12 Throughout this text, I will refer to them as Kalinagos.
13 *The Memoirs of Père Labat, 1693–1705*, translated and abridged by John Eaden (London, 1931), pp. 73, 79.
14 Heuman, *The Caribbean*, p. 2.
15 Higman, *A Concise History*, p. 61. However, the total population of the Caribbean when European encounter began remains a subject of debate.

NOTES

16 Higman, *A Concise History*, p. 68.
17 Luis Vidart, "Colón y Bobadilla: conferencia" (Madrid, 1892); Virginia Martín Jiménez, "El primer asentamiento castellano en América: el fuerte de Navidad," in *Estudios sobre América, siglos XVI–XX: Actas del Congreso Internacional de Historia de América*, 2005, pp. 463–82. I thank Jose Maria Alverez Hernandez for this reference and information.
18 *The Four Voyages of Christopher Columbus*, edited and translated by J. M. Cohen (London, 1969), p. 55.
19 *Four Voyages*, p. 56.
20 Heuman, *The Caribbean*, p. 8.
21 Higman, *A Concise History*, p. 75.
22 Vidart, "Colón y Bobadilla"; Jiménez, "El primer asentamiento castellano en América."
23 Heuman, *The Caribbean*, p. 8.
24 Heuman, *The Caribbean*, p. 8
25 Higman, *A Concise History*, p. 87.
26 Higman, *A Concise History*, p. 78.
27 Heuman, *The Caribbean*, p. 8
28 Heuman, *The Caribbean*, p. 9.
29 Heuman, *The Caribbean*, p. 8.
30 Higman, *A Concise History*, p. 90.
31 Higman, *A Concise History*, p. 90.
32 Higman, *A Concise History*, p. 94.
33 David Barker, "Geographies of Opportunity, Geographies of Constraint," in Stephan Palmié and Francisco A. Scarno (eds.), *The Caribbean: A History of the Region and Its Peoples* (Chicago, 2011), p. 34.
34 Heuman, *The Caribbean*, p. 20.
35 Heuman, *The Caribbean*, p. 20.
36 Matthew Restall, *Seven Myths of the Spanish Conquest* (New York, 2003), p. 54.
37 For more, see: Marcus Rediker, *Villains of All Nations: Atlantic Pirates in the Golden Age* (Boston, 2004).
38 James I, King of England, *A Counterblaste to Tobacco* (London, 1604), n.p.
39 Richard Ligon, *True and Exact History of the Island of Barbados—a Survey of the Natural, Social, and Economic Phenomena* (first published London, 1657, 2nd edition; London, 1673), pp. 43–44.
40 Ligon, *True and Exact History*, p. 43.
41 Howard A. Fergus, *Montserrat: Emerald Isle of the Caribbean* (London, 1983), pp. 6, 16.
42 Jenny Shaw, *Everyday Life in the Early English Caribbean: Irish, Africans, and the Construction of Difference* (Athens, GA, 2013), p. 63.

43 Heuman, *The Caribbean*, p. 19.
44 Hilary McD. Beckles, *White Servitude and Black Slavery in Barbados, 1627–1715* (Knoxville, 1989), p. 10.
45 Eric Williams, *Capitalism and Slavery* (first published 1944; third edition, Chapel Hill, 2021), p. 4.
46 Heuman, *The Caribbean*, p. 21.
47 Heuman, *The Caribbean*, p. 21.
48 Heuman, *The Caribbean*, p. 21.
49 For a moving personal account of Atlantic slavery more broadly, see: Saidiya V. Hartman, *Lose Your Mother: A Journey Along the Atlantic Slave Route* (London, 2006).
50 Olaudah Equiano, *The Interesting Narrative of the Life of Olaudah Equiano, or Gustavus Vassa, the African, Written By Himself* (first published 1789; seventh edition, London, 1793), p. 32. Debate remains about Equiano's origins. According to Vincent Carretta, Equiano's baptism certificate notes that he was born in South Carolina, see: Vincent Carretta, *Equiano, the African: Biography of a Self-Made Man* (Athens, GA, 2005), p. xi. Equiano's narrative might have been shaped by stories passed down to him, but it is still useful despite ongoing debates about his place of birth.
51 Equiano, *Interesting Narrative*, p. 33.
52 Colin A. Palmer, "The Slave Trade, African Slavers, and the Demography of the Caribbean to 1750," in Franklin W. Knight (ed.), *General History of the Caribbean*, Vol. III, *The Slave Societies of the Caribbean* (London, 1997), p. 23.
53 Robinson, *Black Marxism*, pp. 9–68.
54 Dalby Thomas, "May it please the Royal African Company," November 26, 1709, pp. 202–3, T 70/175, National Archives, Kew, United Kingdom (hereafter TNA).
55 Thomas, "May it please the Royal African Company," TNA.
56 James Houston, *Some New and Accurate Observations, Geographical, Natural and Historical ... Of the Situation, Product and Natural History of the Coast of Guinea* (London, 1725), pp. 33–34.
57 Alexander Falconbridge, *An Account of the Slave Trade on the Coast of Africa* (second edition; London, 1788), p. 23.
58 Equiano, *Interesting Narrative*, p. 46.
59 Quobna Ottobah Cugoano, *Thoughts and Sentiments on the Evil of Slavery, and Other Writings* (London, 1787), p. 15.
60 Ligon, *A True and Exact History*, p. 46.
61 On the figure, see: https://www.rmg.co.uk/stories/topics/history-transatlantic-slave-trade (accessed 02/09/2024). Yet it is difficult to know exactly the gendered dimensions of these figures. For a deep analysis of the challenges that remain in numbering enslaved black women, see:

NOTES

Jennifer L. Morgan, *Reckoning with Slavery: Gender, Kinship, and Capitalism in the Early Black Atlantic* (Durham, 2021), pp. 29–54.

62 For more on these figures, see: https://www.gilderlehrman.org/history-resources/teacher-resources/historical-context-facts-about-slave-trade-and-slavery (accessed 2/9/2024) and Transatlantic Slave Trade Database project https://www.slavevoyages.org/.

63 Heuman, *The Caribbean*, p. 25.

64 Heuman, *The Caribbean*, p. 26.

65 Palmer, "The Slave Trade, African Slavers, and the Demography of the Caribbean to 1750," p. 40.

66 Hilary McD. Beckles, *The First Black Slave Society: Britain's "Barbarity Time" in Barbados, 1636–1876* (Kingston, 2016), p. 16.

67 For more on the lives of Modyford and other white planters, see: Matthew Parker, *The Sugar Barons: Family, Corruption, Empire and War* (London, 2012).

68 Holly Brewer, "Not 'Beyond the Line': Reconsidering Law and Power and the Origins of Slavery in England's Empire in the Americas," *Early American Studies: An Interdisciplinary Journal* 20, no. 4, (Fall 2022): p. 630. Holly Brewer, "Slavery, Sovereignty, and 'Inheritable Blood': Reconsidering John Locke and the Origins of American Slavery," *American Historical Review* 122, no. 4 (October 2017): pp. 1038–78.

69 "Extracts from Henry Whistler's Journal of the West India Expedition," in C. H. Firth (ed.), *The Narrative of General Venables, with an Appendix of Papers Relating to the Expedition to the West Indies and the Conquest of Jamaica, 1654–1655* (London, 1900), pp. 145–47, as quoted in Richard S. Dunn, *Sugar and Slaves: The Rise of the Planter Class in the English West Indies, 1624–1713* (London, 1973), p. 77.

70 James A. Rawley with Stephen D. Behrendt, *The Transatlantic Slave Trade: A History* (revised edition; London, 2005), p. 6.

71 For more on the diverse lives of black people in the Tudor period, see: Imtiaz Habib, *Black Lives in the English Archives, 1500–1677: Imprints of the Invisible* (Burlington, VT, 2008); Onyeka, *Blackamoores: Africans in Tudor England, Their Presence, Status and Origins* (London, 2013) and Miranda Kaufmann, *Black Tudors: The Untold Story* (London, 2017).

72 *London Gazette*, No. 2270 (August 18–22, 1687), p. 4, as quoted in Peter Fryer, *Staying Power: The History of Black People in Britain* (London, 1984), p. 22.

73 *London Gazette*, No. 2605 (October 27–30, 1690), p. 2, as quoted in Fryer, *Staying Power*, p. 22.

74 Middlesex Sessions, Book 472, February 1690, 41, as summarized in W. J. Hardy, *Middlesex County Records: Calendar of the Sessions Books 1689 to 1709* (London, 1905), p. 6; and Fryer, *Staying Power*, pp. 23–24.

75 Fryer, *Staying Power*, p. 73; W. M. Thackeray, *The Four Georges* (London, 1856), p. 52.
76 Catherine Molineux, *Faces of Perfect Ebony: Encountering Atlantic Slavery in Imperial Britain* (Cambridge, MA, 2012), p. 31.
77 For more, see: Kim F. Hall, *Things of Darkness: Economies of Race and Gender in Early Modern England* (Ithaca, 1996).
78 Noémie Ndiaye, *Scripts of Blackness: Early Modern Performance Culture and the Making of Race* (Philadelphia, 2022), pp. 3, 10.
79 Molineux, *Faces of Perfect Ebony*, p. 11.
80 Molineux, *Faces of Perfect Ebony*, p. 24.
81 Molineux, *Faces of Perfect Ebony*, p. 24.
82 Molineux, *Faces of Perfect Ebony*, p. 5.
83 William Stapleton to Lords of Trade and Plantations, August 16, 1681, *Calendar of State Papers, Colonial, America and West Indies Volume 11 Series (CSPC)*, https://www.british-history.ac.uk/cal-state-papers/colonial/america-west-indies/vol11/pp98-105 (accessed June 15, 2022), and as quoted in Hilary McD. Beckles, *Britain's Black Debt: Reparations for Caribbean Slavery and Native Genocide* (Kingston, 2013), p. 25.
84 "Petition of Several Merchants of London on Adventures to the Caribbean islands to the Lords of Trade and Plantations," January 10, 1676, CSPC, https://www.british-history.ac.uk/cal-state-papers/colonial/america-west-indies/vol9/pp330-345 (accessed 15/6/2022) and as quoted in Beckles, *Britain's Black Debt*, p. 33.

CHAPTER 2

1 Beckles, First Black Slave Society, p. 47; Hilary Beckles, *Black Rebellion in Barbados: The Struggle Against Slavery 1627–1838* (Bridgetown, 1987), p. 34.
2 "An Act for the good governing of Servants, and ordaining the Rights between Masters and Servants," Barbados, September 27, 1661, pp. 35–42, CO 30/1, TNA.
3 "An Act for the good governing of Servants . . . ," TNA. Edward B. Rugemer, "The Development of Mastery and Race in the Comprehensive Slave Codes of the Greater Caribbean during the Seventeenth Century," *William and Mary Quarterly* 70, no. 3 (July 2013): p. 439. The Irish were not enslaved in the Caribbean; see: Jerome Handler and Matthew Reilly, "Contesting 'White Slavery' in the Caribbean: Enslaved Africans and European Indentured Servants in Seventeenth-Century Barbados," *Nieuwe West—Indische Gids/ New West India Guide* 91, no. 1/2 (2017): pp. 30–55.
4 Rugemer, "The Development of Mastery," p. 441.

NOTES

5 "An Act for the better ordering and governing of Negroes," Barbados, 1661, CO 30/2, pp. 16–26, TNA. Extracts of the act can also be found in Stanley L. Engerman, Seymour Drescher, and Robert L Pacquette (eds.), *Slavery* (New York, 2001), pp. 105–13.
6 Rugemer, "The Development of Mastery," p. 450.
7 Rugemer, "The Development of Mastery," p. 447.
8 "An Act for the better ordering and governing of Negroes," Clauses 1 and 20, TNA.
9 Michael Craton, *Testing the Chains: Resistance to Slavery in the British West Indies* (first published 1982, Ithaca, 2009), p. 296.
10 "An Act for the better ordering and governing of Negroes," TNA.
11 Susan Dwyer Amussen, *Caribbean Exchanges: Slavery and the Transformation of English Society, 1640–1700* (Chapel Hill, 2007), p. 135.
12 Bradley J. Nicholson, "Legal Borrowing and the Origins of Slave Law in the British Colonies," *American Journal of Legal History* 38, no. 1 (January 1994): pp. 39–41.
13 For more on the connections between these acts, see: Rugemer, "The Development of Mastery," pp. 429–58. Other colonial powers created their own versions of slave codes, such as the French *Code Noir* and the Spanish *Siete Partidas*. The Dutch also had similar laws. For more on slave laws, see: Elsa Goveia, *The West Indian Slave Laws of the 18th Century* (Kingston, 1970).
14 Manumission could occur for a variety of reasons: for instance, if a slave owner decided to reward an enslaved person for their loyalty. Manumission, however, did not always provide formerly enslaved people with unrestricted freedom as legal limitations were placed on free people of color and free blacks in part to ensure their inferior position to white elites.
15 Marisa J. Fuentes, *Dispossessed Lives: Enslaved Women, Violence, and the Archive* (Philadelphia, 2016), p. 2.
16 For more on the complexities of the Irish experience in the seventeenth century, see: Shaw, *Everyday Life in the Early English Caribbean*.
17 For more on female slave owners, see: Christine Walker, *Jamaica Ladies: Female Slaveholders and the Creation of Britain's Atlantic Empire* (Chapel Hill, 2020).
18 As listed in Table 6.4 in Kathleen Mary Butler, *The Economics of Emancipation: Jamaica and Barbados 1823–1843* (Chapel Hill, 1995), p. 102. For more on Dehany, see: https://www.ucl.ac.uk/lbs/person/view/2146632271 (accessed 7/8/2024).
19 Bryan Edwards, *The History, Civil and Commercial, of the British Colonies in the West Indies* (London, 1798), p. 137.
20 For more on Long's life and writings, see: Catherine Hall, *Lucky Valley: Edward Long and the History of Racial Capitalism* (Cambridge, 2024).

NOTES

21 Hannah Young, "Forgotten Women: Anna Eliza Elletson and Absentee Slave Ownership," in Kate Donington, Ryan Hanley, and Jessica Moody (eds.), *Britain's History and Memory of Transatlantic Slavery: Local Nuances of a "National Sin"* (Liverpool, 2016), pp. 83–101.
22 Beckles, *Britain's Black Debt*, pp. 82–108.
23 See especially: Padraic X. Scanlan, *Slave Empire: How Slavery Built Modern Britain* (London, 2020). For a recent book that grapples with Williams's arguments and also makes the case for the significance of slavery to the British industrial revolution, see: Maxine Berg and Pat Hudson, *Slavery, Capitalism and the Industrial Revolution* (Cambridge, 2023).
24 Scanlan, *Slave Empire*, p. 25.
25 Adam Smith, *An Inquiry into the Nature and Causes of the Wealth of Nations*, with an introduction and notes by Jonathan B Wight (Hampshire, 2007), p. 252.
26 Beckles, *Britain's Black Debt*, p. 91. The 2024 figures are based on real cost comparison using GDP deflation, estimated from https://www.measuringworth.com/ (accessed February 17, 2024).
27 Fryer, *Staying Power*, p. 34.
28 Rawley with Behrendt, *The Transatlantic Slave Trade*, p. 212.
29 Fryer, *Staying Power*, p. 36; Herbert S. Klein, "The English Slave Trade to Jamaica, 1782–1808," *Economic History Review* 31, no. 1 (February 1978): pp. 42–43.
30 Fowler, *Our Island Stories*, p. xi.
31 Beckles, *Britain's Black Debt*, pp. 110–11; Nicholas Draper, *The Price of Emancipation: Slave-Ownership, Compensation and British Society at the End of Slavery* (Cambridge, 2010), pp. 303–7.
32 Fryer, Staying Power, p. 70.
33 Edward Long, *The History of Jamaica, or General Survey of the Ancient and Modern State of that Island: with Reflections on its Situation, Settlements, Inhabitants, Climate, Products, Commerce, Laws, and Government*, Volume II (London, 1774), pp. 352–53.
34 Long, *The History of Jamaica*, Volume II, pp. 356, 370.
35 William Beckford, *Remarks upon the Situation of Negroes in Jamaica* (London, 1788), p. 38.
36 Beckford, *Remarks*, p. 60.
37 Beckford, *Remarks*, p. 98.
38 Ligon, *A True and Exact History*, p. 51.
39 For more on Sloane and his ties to the Caribbean, see: James Delbourgo, *Collecting the World: Hans Sloane and the Origins of the British Museum* (Cambridge, MA, 2019).
40 Hans Sloane, *A Voyage to the Islands Madera, Barbados, Nieves, S Christophers and Jamaica*, Vol 1 (London, 1707), p. lvii.

NOTES

41 Charles Leslie, *A New History of Jamaica, from the Earliest Accounts to the Taking of Porto Bello by Vice-Admiral Vernon in Thirteen Letters from a Gentleman to His Friend* (second edition; London, 1740), p. 305.

42 Prince made history when she became the first black woman to write and publish her autobiography in Britain in 1831. *The History of Mary Prince* was edited by white abolitionists who presented her as the perfect victim—a modest, married Christian woman. Although Prince and other enslaved people's narratives like Equiano's were heavily edited, that does not mean these sources should be dismissed. Nicole N. Aljoe argues that they could still create a "coherent, self-evident, self-conscious, commanding" voice; see: Nicole N. Aljoe, *Creole Testimonies: Slave Narratives from the British West Indies 1709–1838* (New York, 2012), p. 15.

43 *The History of Mary Prince: A West Indian Slave: Related by Herself*, first published London, 1831 (Chapel Hill, 2017), pp. 12, 19.

44 *The History of Mary Prince*, pp. 19–20.

45 Recent studies documenting the role of reproduction during slavery and abolition include Sasha Turner, *Contested Bodies: Pregnancy, Childrearing and Slavery in Jamaica* (Philadelphia, 2017) and Katherine Paugh, *The Politics of Reproduction: Race, Medicine and Fertility in the Age of Abolition* (Oxford, 2017).

46 For more on the experience and significance of enslaved women, see: Barbara Bush, *Slave Women in Caribbean Society, 1650–1838* (Kingston, 1990); Jennifer L. Morgan, *Laboring Women: Reproduction and Gender in New World Slavery* (Philadelphia, 2004); Fuentes, *Dispossessed Lives*; and Turner, *Contested Bodies*.

47 Morgan, *Laboring Women*, pp. 12–49.

48 Richard Hakluyt, *The Principal Navigations, Voyages, Traffiques and Discoveries of the English Nation*, Vol. XI, Africa, edited by Edmund Goldsmid (Edinburgh, 1889), p. 108.

49 Matthew Gregory Lewis, *Journal of a West India Proprietor 1815–1817*, edited and with an introduction by Mona Wilson (London, 1929), p. 76.

50 For more on Thistlewood, see: Heather V. Vermeulen, "Thomas Thistlewood's Libidinal Linnean Project: Slavery, Ecology and Knowledge Production," *Small Axe*, 55 (March 2018): pp. 18–38.

51 Tom Zoellener, Island on Fire: The Revolt That Ended Slavery in the British Empire (Cambridge, MA, 2020), p. 21.

52 Trevor Burnard, Mastery, *Tyranny, and Desire: Thomas Thistlewood and His Slaves in the Anglo-Jamaican World* (Chapel Hill, 2004), p. 176.

53 Burnard, *Mastery, Tyranny, and Desire*, p. 176.

54 Burnard, *Mastery, Tyranny, and Desire*, p. 173.

55 Zoellener, *Island on Fire*, pp. 20–21.

56 John Augustine Waller, *A Voyage in the West Indies: containing various observations made during a residence in Barbadoes, and several of the Leeward Islands; with some notices and illustrations relative to the city of Paramarabo, in Surinam* (London, 1820), p. 20.
57 Waller, *A Voyage in the West Indies*, p. 20.
58 *Lady Nugent's Journal of Her Residence in Jamaica from 1801 to 1805*, a new and revised edition by Philip Wright (Kingston, 1966), p. 98.
59 James Ramsay, *An Essay on the Treatment and Conversion of African Slaves in the British Slave Colonies* (first published London, 1784; Cambridge, 2013), pp. 243–45.
60 David R. Roediger, *The Wages of Whiteness: Race and the Making of the American Working Class* (first published 1991; London, 2007); W. E. B. Du Bois, *Black Reconstruction in America; An Essay Toward A History of the Part Which Black Folk Played in the Attempt to Reconstruct Democracy in America 1860–1880* (first published 1935; Oxford, 2007).
61 Statistics come from David W. Cohen and Jack P. Greene (eds.), *Neither Slave nor Free: The Freedmen of African Descent in the Slave Societies of the New World* (Baltimore, 1972), Appendix: Population Tables, p. 338.
62 Kay Dian Kriz, *Slavery, Sugar, and the Culture of Refinement: Picturing the British West Indies, 1700–1840* (New Haven, 2008), pp. 37–38.
63 Heuman, *The Caribbean*, p. 51.
64 Jerome S. Handler, "Joseph Rachell and Rachael Pringle-Polgreen: Petty Entrepreneurs," in David G. Sweet and Gary B. Nash (eds.), *Struggle and Survival in Colonial America* (Berkeley, 1981), p. 387.
65 For more on this point, see: Marisa J. Fuentes, "Power and Historical Figuring: Rachael Pringle-Polgreen's Troubled Archive," *Gender & History* 22, no. 3 (November 2010): pp. 564–84.
66 Heuman, *The Caribbean*, p. 50.
67 Heuman, *The Caribbean*, p. 50.
68 Heuman, *The Caribbean*, p. 50.
69 Heuman, *The Caribbean*, p. 50.
70 Heuman, *The Caribbean*, p. 54.
71 Heuman, *The Caribbean*, p. 47. For more on legal and racial distinctions and hereditary status among mixed-race people in Jamaica, see: Brooke N. Newman, *A Dark Inheritance: Blood, Race, and Sex in Colonial Jamaica* (New Haven, 2018), pp. 67–107.
72 Paul Lovejoy, "The Volume of the Atlantic Slave Trade: A Synthesis," *Journal of African History* 23, no. 4 (1982): p. 483.
73 *Negro Slavery Described by a Negro: Being the Narrative of Ashton Warner, A Native of St Vincents by S. Strickland* (London, 1831), p. 32.
74 Heuman, *The Caribbean*, pp. 37–38.
75 Beckles, *Britain's Black Debt*, p. 79.

NOTES

76 Heuman, *The Caribbean*, pp. 38–39.
77 *The History of Mary Prince*, p. 23.
78 Heuman, *The Caribbean*, p. 36.
79 On the nature of "elite" among the enslaved, see: Justin Roberts, "The 'Better Sort' and the 'Poorer Sort': Wealth Inequalities, Family Formation and the Economy of Energy on British Caribbean Sugar Plantations, 1750-1800," *Slavery and Abolition* 35, no. 3 (2014): pp. 458–473.
80 *The History of Mary Prince*, pp. 1–2.
81 Craton, *Testing the Chains*, p. 45.
82 See: Turner, *Contested Bodies*.
83 Vincent Brown, *The Reaper's Garden: Death and Power in the World of Atlantic Slavery* (Cambridge, MA, 2008), p. 13.
84 Heuman, *The Caribbean*, pp. 40–41.
85 *The Two Charters of the Society for Advancing the Christian Faith in the British West Indies . . . And in Mauritius . . .* (London, 1836), pp. 13–14.
86 Randy M. Browne, *Surviving Slavery in the British Caribbean* (Philadelphia, 2017), p. 3.
87 Heuman, *The Caribbean*, pp. 70–71.
88 Alison Carmichael, *Domestic Manners and Social Condition of the White, Coloured, and Negro Populations of the West Indies. By Mrs Carmichael, Five years a resident in St Vincent and Trinidad* Vol II (London, 1833), pp. 10–11.
89 For more on enslaved women's resistance, see: Stella Dadzie, *A Kick in the Belly: Women, Slavery and Resistance* (London, 2020); Bush, *Slave Women*; Hilary McD. Beckles, *Natural Rebels: A Social History of Enslaved Black Women in Barbados* (London, 1989).
90 For more on this, see: Diana Paton, *The Cultural Politics of Obeah: Religion, Colonialism, and Modernity in the Caribbean World* (New York, 2015).
91 Vincent Brown, *Tacky's Revolt: The Story of an Atlantic Slave War* (Cambridge, MA, 2020), p. 4.
92 Brown, *Tacky's Revolt*, pp. 89–90.
93 Brown, *Tacky's Revolt*, pp. 129–30.
94 Brown, *Tacky's Revolt*, pp. 4, 151.
95 Brown, *Tacky's Revolt*, p. 211.
96 Brown, *Tacky's Revolt*, p. 211.
97 Brown, *Tacky's Revolt*, p. 11.
98 Brown, *Tacky's Revolt*, pp. 207–36.
99 Heuman, *The Caribbean*, p. 72.
100 Alvin O. Thompson, "Gender and *Marronage* in the Caribbean," *Journal of Caribbean History* 39, no. 2 (2005): pp. 262–89.
101 Craton, *Testing the Chains*, p. 87.

102 Heuman, *The Caribbean*, p. 75.
103 Heuman, *The Caribbean*, pp. 71–75.
104 Thompson, "Gender and *Marronage* in the Caribbean," p. 274.

CHAPTER 3

1 James Walvin, *The Zong: A Massacre, the Law and the End of Slavery* (London, 2011), pp. 70–72.
2 Walter Johnson, "On Agency," *Journal of Social History* 37, no. 1 (2003): p. 116.
3 Letter in *The Morning Chronicle and London Advertiser*, March 18, 1783, reprinted in F. O. Shyllon, *Black Slaves in Britain* (London, 1974), p. 188.
4 Cugoano, *Thoughts and Sentiments*, p. 85.
5 For a wider examination on the role of liberalism in the anti-slavery movement, see: Scanlan, *Slave Empire*.
6 Thomas Holt, *The Problem of Freedom: Race, Labor, and Politics in Jamaica and Britain, 1832–1938* (Baltimore, 1992), p. xx.
7 For a detailed account of the West India Interest, see: Michael Taylor, *The Interest: How the British Establishment Resisted the Abolition of Slavery* (London, 2020).
8 Roxann Wheeler, *The Complexion of Race: Categories of Difference in Eighteenth-Century British Culture* (Philadelphia, 2000), pp. 288–302.
9 Norma Myers, *Reconstructing the Black Past: Blacks in Britain, 1780–1830* (London, 1996), p. 35.
10 Kathleen Chater, *Untold Histories: Black People in England and Wales during the Period of the British Slave Trade, c. 1660–1807* (Manchester, 2009), p. 238.
11 David Olusoga, *Black and British: A Forgotten History* (revised and updated, London, 2021), pp. 92–93.
12 For more on Lascars and the long Asian presence in Britain, see: Rozina Visram, *Ayahs, Lascars and Princes: Indians in Britain 1700–1947* (London, 1986).
13 As quoted in Fryer, *Staying Power*, p. 228.
14 Sadiah Qureshi, "Displaying Sara Baartman, the 'Hottentot Venus,'" *History of Science*, 42, no. 2 (2004): pp. 233–57.
15 Chater, *Untold Histories*, p. 95. The University of Glasgow has a database, "Runaway Slaves in Britain: Bondage, Freedom and Race in the Eighteenth Century"; see: https://www.runaways.gla.ac.uk (accessed February 5, 2024).
16 Fryer, *Staying Power*, p. 76; Charles Ryskamp and Frederick A. Pottle (eds.), *Boswell: The Ominous Years 1774–1776* (London, 1963), p. 118.

NOTES

17 See: David Dabydeen, *Hogarth's Blacks: Images of Blacks in Eighteenth Century English Art* (Surrey, 1985).
18 Lady Mary Coke, *Letters and Journals*, 1, pp. 194–95, as quoted in Vincent Carretta, "Julius Soubise (c. 1754–1798)," *Oxford Dictionary of National Biography*, https://www.oxforddnb.com/view/10.1093/ref:odnb/9780198614128.001.0001/odnb-9780198614128-e-60841 (accessed June 22, 2022).
19 Olusoga, *Black and British*, p. 109.
20 *A narrative of the most remarkable particulars in the life of James Albert Ukawsaw Gronniosaw, an African Prince, with a preface by W. Shirley* (Dublin, 1790), pp. 29–30.
21 *A narrative of the most remarkable particulars*, p. 30.
22 Equiano, *Interesting Narrative of the Life of Olaudah Equiano, or Gustavus Vassa, the African: written by himself* (first published 1789; Los Angeles, 2017), p. 7.
23 Ryan Hanley, *Beyond Slavery and Abolition Black British Writing, c. 1770–1830* (Cambridge, 2019), pp. 52–53.
24 Gretchen Gerzina, *Black England: Life Before Emancipation* (London, 1999), p. 33.
25 John Latimer, *The Annals of Bristol in the Eighteenth Century* (1893), p. 492.
26 Edward Long, *Candid reflections upon the judgement lately awarded by the Court of the King's Bench . . . on what is commonly called the Negroe-cause, by a planter* (London, 1772), pp. 48–49.
27 Philip Thicknesse, *A Year's Journey through France and Part of Spain*, Vol. II (London, 1789), p. 110.
28 Fryer, *Staying Power*, p. 74.
29 "Fielding's Penal Laws of London," in *The Retrospective Review*, Vol. XII, Part II (London, 1825), p. 221. London School of Economics and Political Science, Archive AP4.
30 *London Chronicle*, XVI/1214 (September 29–October 2, 1764), p. 317.
31 As quoted in Fryer, *Staying Power*, p. 152; David Hume, *Essays: Moral, Political, and Literary*, edited by Eugene F. Miller, Thomas Hill Green, and Thomas Hodge Grose (Indianapolis, 1987), p. 208.
32 Immanuel Kant, *Observations on the Feeling of the Beautiful and Sublime*, 1764, translated by John T. Goldthwait (Berkeley, 1991), p. 110.
33 Kant, *Observations*, p. 111.
34 As quoted in George M. Frederickson, *Racism: A Short History* (Princeton, 2002), p. 34.
35 As quoted in Granville Sharp, *The Just Limitation of Slavery in the Laws of God, compared with the unbounded Claims of the African traders and British*

American Slaveholders (London, 1776), Appendix 8, pp. 67–69 and as requoted in Fryer, *Staying Power*, p. 125.

36 Christopher Leslie Brown, *Moral Capital: Foundations of British Abolitionism* (Chapel Hill, 2006), p. 97.

37 Cugoano, *Thoughts and Sentiments*, p. 106.

38 Fryer, Staying Power, p. 201. These experiences of black Loyalists would later shape the development of Sierra Leone as a colony. For more, see: Padraic X. Scanlan, *Freedom's Debtors: British Antislavery in Sierra Leone in the Age of Abolition* (Yale, 2017).

39 Thomas Clarkson, *The History of the Rise, Progress, and Accomplishment of the Abolition of the Slave-Trade by the British Parliament* Vol I (new edition; London, 1808), p. 210.

40 Clarkson, *History*, p. 225.

41 For a more detailed study of the Haitian revolution, see: Laurent Dubois, *Avengers of the New World: The Story of the Haitian Revolution* (Cambridge, MA, 2005).

42 Heuman, *The Caribbean*, p. 77.

43 Heuman, *The Caribbean*, p. 81.

44 Heuman, *The Caribbean*, pp. 85–87.

45 Heuman, *The Caribbean*, pp. 86–87.

46 "Né dans l'esclavage, mais ayant reçu de la nature l'âme d'un homme libre," Toussaint report to Directory, 18 Fructidor an V (September 4, 1797), Archives Nationales, Paris AFIII 210, as quoted in Sudhir Hazareesingh, Black Spartacus: *The Epic Life of Toussaint Louverture* (London, 2021), p. 19.

47 Heuman, *The Caribbean*, pp. 82–83.

48 "*Constitution républicaine des colonies française* [sic] *de Saint-Domingue en soixante-dix-sept articles, concernant la liberté des nègres, des gens de couleurs et des blancs*, Port-Républicain," 19 Floréal an IX (May 9, 1801), Bibliothèque Nationale de France LK12–554, as quoted in Hazareesingh, *Black Spartacus*, p. 239.

49 Hazareesingh, *Black Spartacus*, p. 329.

50 "The Haitian Declaration of Independence, 1804, proclaimed by Jean Jacques-Dessalines, first read out by his secretary Louis Boisrond-Tonnerre," https://today.duke.edu/showcase/haitideclaration/declarations text.html (accessed June 22, 2022). The original is located in TNA: CO 137/111/1.

51 Seeking to place Haiti and events in the Caribbean at the center of analysis in the revolutionary period, Trinidadian writer and activist C. L. R. James's *The Black Jacobins* (London, 1938) was a significant piece of revisionist history that fervently argued for the importance of Haiti in the development of the modern world.

NOTES

52 Hazareesingh, *Black Spartacus*, p. 2.
53 Michel-Rolph Trouillot, *Silencing the Past: Power and the Production of History* (first published 1995; Boston, 2015), pp. 70–107.
54 David Geggus, "The Haitian Revolution," in K. O. Laurence (ed.), *General History of the Caribbean*, Volume IV: *The Long Nineteenth Century: Nineteenth Century Transformations* (London, 2011), pp. 31–32.
55 Lazaro Gamio, Constant Méheut, Catherine Porter, Selam Gebrekidan, Allison McCann, and Matt Apuzzo, "The Ransom: Haiti's Lost Billions," *New York Times*, May 20, 2022, https://www.nytimes.com/interactive/2022/05/20/world/americas/enslaved-haiti-debt-timeline (accessed October 9, 2023).
56 Kris Manjapra, *Black Ghost of Empire: The Long Death of Slavery and the Failure of Emancipation* (London, 2022), p. 45.
57 John Wesley, *Thoughts Upon Slavery*, 2nd. edition (London, 1774), p. 27.
58 Brown, *Moral Capital*, p. 335.
59 Brown, *Moral Capital*, p. 387.
60 Smith, *An Inquiry into the Nature and Causes of the Wealth of Nations*, p. 252.
61 Franklin W. Knight, "The Disintegration of the Caribbean Slave Systems 1772–1886," in F. W. Knight (ed.), *General History of the Caribbean*, Volume III: *The Slave Societies of the Caribbean* (London, 1997), p. 332.
62 Brown, *Moral Capital*, p. 110.
63 Brown, *Moral Capital*, p. 26.
64 Brown, *Moral Capital*, p. 27.
65 Emília Viotti da Costa, *Crowns of Glory, Tears of Blood: The Demerara Slave Rebellion of 1823* (Oxford, 1994), p. 5.
66 See: Clare Midgley, *Women Against Slavery: The British Campaigns 1780–1870* (London, 1992).
67 Olusoga, *Black and British*, p. 212. Hakim Adi, *African and Caribbean People in Britain: A History* (London, 2022), p. 79.
68 Robert Wedderburn, *The Axe Laid to the Root, or A Fatal Blow to Oppressors, Being an Address to The Planters and Negroes of the Island of Jamaica*, No. 1 (1817), in Iain McCalman (ed.), *The Horrors of Slavery and Other Writings by Robert Wedderburn* (Edinburgh, 1991), p. 82. He also published, in 1824, *The Horrors of Slavery*. But by 1831 Wedderburn's opinions on abolition had changed. In an 1831 pamphlet, *Address to Lord Brougham*, he argued for compensation for the slaveholders and gradual emancipation. Slavery was, in his mind, now a more preferable option to wage labor. Wedderburn argued that emancipation would leave the enslaved poor and powerless, and he preferred gradual emancipation with land rather than landless freedom. For more on Wedderburn's changing opinion on slavery and abolition, see: Ryan Hanley, "A Radical Change of Heart: Robert Wedderburn's Last Word on Slavery," *Slavery & Abolition* 37, no. 2 (2016): pp. 423–45.

69 Ryan Hanley, "'There to sing the song of Moses': John Jea's Methodism and Working-Class Attitudes to Slavery in Liverpool and Portsmouth, 1801–1817," in Donington, Hanley, and Moody (eds.), *Britain's History and Memory of Transatlantic Slavery*, pp. 39–59.

70 Ryan Hanley, "Slavery and the Birth of Working-Class Racism in England, 1814–1833," *Transactions of the Royal Historical Society* 26 (2016): p. 104.

71 Catherine Hall, *White, Male and Middle Class: Explorations in Feminism and History* (first published 1992; Cambridge, 2007), p. 208.

72 Morgan, *Reckoning with Slavery*, p. 153.

73 See: Turner, *Contested Bodies*.

74 Robert Isaac Wilberforce and Samuel Wilberforce, *The Life of William Wilberforce, with Extracts from His Diary, Journal, and Correspondence* (new edition, abridged; London, 1843), p. 501.

75 Padraic X. Scanlan, "Slaves and Peasants in the Era of Emancipation," Journal of British Studies 59, no. 3 (July 2020): p. 498.

76 Seymour Drescher's figures quoted in Kenneth Morgan, *Slavery and the British Empire: from Africa to America* (Oxford, 2007), p. 168.

77 Beckles, *Britain's Black Debt*, p. 94.

78 For more on this, see: Padraic X. Scanlan, "The Rewards of their Exertions: Prize Money and British Abolitionism in Sierra Leone, 1808–1823", *Past & Present* 225, no. 1 (November 1, 2014): pp. 113–42. Bronwen Everill, *Not Made by Slaves: Ethical Capitalism in the Age of Abolition* (Cambridge, MA, 2020).

79 For more, see: the British Library Partnership Agents of Enslavement, with the Barbados Department of Archives and Endangered Archives Programme, http://eap.bl.uk/ and use of fugitive ads, https://www.theguardian.com/world/2021/jul/18/secrets-of-rebel-slaves-in-barbados-will-finally-be-revealed and https://blogs.bl.uk/endangeredarchives/2021/07/help-trace-the-stories-of-enslaved-people-in-the-caribbean-using-colonial-newspapers.html (accessed April 5, 2022).

80 *The Report from a Select Committee of the House of Assembly, Appointed to Inquire into the Origin, Causes, and Progress, of the Late Insurrection* (London, 1818), p. 29.

81 Craton, *Testing the Chains*, pp. 264–65.

82 Sir James Leith, Governor of Barbados, to Earl Bathurst, September 21, 1816, CO 28/85, TNA.

83 Beckles, *First Black Slave Society*, 163; and *Remarks on the Insurrection in Barbados, and the Bill for the Registration of Slaves* (London, 1816), p. 8; *Report from a Select Committee . . . Progress, of the Late Insurrection*, (London, 1818), p. 14.

84 *Report from a Select Committee . . . Progress, of the Late Insurrection* (London, 1818), p. 15.

NOTES

85 Costa, *Crowns of Glory*, p. 177.
86 Heuman, *The Caribbean*, p. 92.
87 Costa, *Crowns of Glory*, p. 12.
88 Thomas Cooper, *Facts Illustrative of the Condition of the Negro Slaves in Jamaica with Notes, and an Appendix* (London, 1824), p. 20.
89 Costa, *Crowns of Glory*, p. 146.
90 John Smith, *Journal*, March 21, 1819, as quoted in Costa, *Crowns of Glory*, p. 153.
91 For more on the rebellion, see: Thomas Harding, *White Debt: The Demerara Uprising and Britain's Legacy of Slavery* (London, 2022).
92 Browne, *Surviving Slavery*, p. 37.
93 Costa, *Crowns of Glory*, pp. xvii–xviii.
94 Costa, *Crowns of Glory*, pp. 243–44.
95 Costa, *Crowns of Glory*, p. 244.
96 Costa, *Crowns of Glory*, p. 253.
97 Scanlan, *Slave Empire*, p. 240.
98 Elizabeth Heyrick, *Immediate, not Gradual Emancipation, or, An inquiry into the shortest, safest, and most effectual means of getting rid of West Indian Slavery* (London, 1824), pp. 27–28.
99 Heyrick, *Immediate, not Gradual Emancipation*, p. 24.
100 Scanlan, *Slave Empire*, p. 255.
101 Craton, *Testing the Chains*, p. 294.
102 Craton, *Testing the Chains*, p. 296.
103 For a full detailed account of the 1831 rebellion, see: Zoellener, *Island on Fire*. On the wider role of Caribbean revolts and how it shaped abolitionism in Britain, see: Gelien Matthews, *Caribbean Slave Revolts and the British Abolitionist Movement* (Baton Rouge, LA, 2006).
104 Gad Heuman, *The Killing Time: The Morant Bay Rebellion in Jamaica* (Knoxville, 1994), p. 131.
105 Craton, *Testing the Chains*, p. 313.
106 Craton, *Testing the Chains*, p. 314.
107 Craton, *Testing the Chains*, p. 312.
108 Craton, *Testing the Chains*, p. 323.
109 Craton, *Testing the Chains*, p. 297.
110 Holt, *The Problem of Freedom*, p. 40.
111 Holt, *The Problem of Freedom*, p. 21.
112 Holt, *The Problem of Freedom*, p. 28.
113 The 2024 figures are based on real cost comparison using GDP deflation, estimated from https://www.measuringworth.com (accessed February 17, 2024). For the legacies of British slave ownership that show where this money went, see: https://www.ucl.ac.uk/lbs/ and Catherine Hall, Nicholas Draper, Keith McClelland, Katie Donnington, and Rachel Lang,

Legacies of British Slave-Ownership: Colonial Slavery and the Formation of Victorian Britain (Cambridge, 2014). For more on slave ownership, see: Draper, *The Price of Emancipation*.
114 David Olusoga, "The Treasury's tweet shows slavery is still misunderstood," *The Guardian*, February 12, 2018, https://www.theguardian.com/commentisfree/2018/feb/12/treasury-tweet-slavery-compensate-slave-owners (accessed July 29, 2024).
115 Manjapra, *Black Ghost of Empire*, pp. 106–7.
116 Heuman, *The Caribbean*, p. 95.
117 Heuman, *The Caribbean*, p. 95.
118 Heuman, *The Caribbean*, p. 108.
119 *A Narrative of the Events since the First of August, 1834, by James Williams, an Apprenticed Labourer in Jamaica* (London, 1837), p. 1.
120 Joseph Sturge and Thomas Harvey, *The West Indies in 1837: being the journal of a visit to Antigua, Montserrat, Dominica, St Lucia, Barbados and Jamaica; undertaken for the purpose of ascertaining the actual condition of the Negro population of those islands* (London, 1838), p. 378.
121 *Negro Apprenticeship in the British Colonies*, published at the office of the Anti-Slavery Society (London, 1838).
122 *Negro Apprenticeship*, p. 27.
123 *Negro Apprenticeship*, pp. 30–31.
124 *Negro Apprenticeship*, p. 32.
125 Scanlan identifies an early use of the term "white supremacy" in anti-slavery writing; see: *Slave Empire*, p. 279.
126 As quoted in J. R. Oldfield, *Chords of Freedom: Commemoration, Ritual and British Transatlantic Slavery* (Manchester, 2007), p. 89.
127 Eric Williams, *British Historians and the West Indies* (Port-of-Spain, 1964), p. 182.
128 For more, see: Scanlan, *Slave Empire*.
129 For more on how anti-slavery sentiment shaped Victorian Britain, see: Richard Huzzey, *Freedom Burning: Anti-Slavery and Empire in Victorian Britain* (Ithaca, 2012).

CHAPTER 4

1 Thomas Carlyle, "Occasional Discourse on the Negro Question," *Fraser's Magazine* (December 1849), pp. 670, 671, 673.
2 Carlyle, "Occasional Discourse on the Negro Question," pp.675–76.
3 Thomas Carlyle, "Occasional Discourse on the Nigger Question" (London, 1853).
4 Expertus, "Negroes and the Slave Trade," *The Times*, November 21, 1857.
5 Expertus, "Negroes and the Slave Trade."

NOTES

6 Anthony Trollope, *The West Indies and the Spanish Main* (London, 1859), p. 92.
7 Catherine Hall, *Civilising Subjects: Metropole and Colony in the English Imagination, 1830–1867* (Cambridge, 2002), p. 440.
8 Woodville K. Marshall, "'We be wise to many more tings': Blacks' Hopes and Expectations of Emancipation," in Hilary Beckles and Verene Shepherd (eds.), *Caribbean Freedom: Economy and Society from Emancipation to the Present* (Kingston, 1993), pp. 12–20.
9 Holt, *The Problem of Freedom*, p. 117.
10 Douglas Hall, "A Population of Free Persons," in Laurence (ed.), *General History of the Caribbean*, Vol. IV, p. 54.
11 Higman, *A Concise History*, p. 204.
12 Higman, *A Concise History*, p. 205.
13 Beckles, *The First Black*, p. 224.
14 For more on banking and US imperialism in the Caribbean, see: Peter James Hudson, *Bankers and Empire: How Wall Street Colonized the Caribbean* (Chicago, 2017).
15 Pedro L. San Miguel, "Economic Activities other than sugar," in Laurence (ed.), *General History of the Caribbean*, Vol. IV, p. 122.
16 Holt, *The Problem of Freedom*, p. 348.
17 Holt, *The Problem of Freedom*, p. 348.
18 Holt, *The Problem of Freedom*, p. 350.
19 For more on Impey, see: Caroline Bressey, *Empire, Race and the Politics of Anti-Caste* (London, 2013).
20 Mary Seacole, *The Wonderful Adventures of Mrs Seacole in Many Lands* (London, 1857).
21 Fryer, *Staying Power*, p. 179.
22 Douglas A. Lorimer, *Science, Race Relations and Resistance in Britain 1870–1914* (Manchester, 2013), pp. 19–20.
23 Lorimer, *Science*, p. 50.
24 Lorimer, *Science*, p. 65.
25 Lorimer, *Science*, pp. 113–14.
26 For more on this, see: Angela Saini, *Superior: The Return of Race Science* (London, 2019).
27 W. E. B. Du Bois, *The Souls of Black Folk*, edited and with an introduction and notes by Brent Hayes Edwards (first published 1903; New York, 2008), p. 15.
28 Heuman, *The Caribbean*, p. 118.
29 Hall, "A Population of Free Persons," p. 48.
30 Bridget Brereton, "Social Organization and Class, Racial and National Conflicts," in Laurence (ed.), *General History of the Caribbean*, Vol. IV, p. 342.
31 Brereton, "Social Organization," p. 339.

32 Brereton, "Social Organization," p. 355.
33 Testimony of Saint Louis, n.d., Parliamentary Papers 1845, v 31 (146), p. 10, as quoted in Russell E. Chace Jr, "Protest in Post-Emancipation I: The 'Guerre Negre' of 1844," *Journal of Caribbean History* 23, no. 2 (1989): p. 130.
34 Quotes from Thomas Harvey and William Brewin, *Jamaica in 1866: a Narrative of a Tour through the Island: with Remarks on its Social, Educational and Industrial Condition* (London, 1867), p. 102.
35 JRC, Evidence of Cecilia Gordon, p. 180, as quoted in Heuman, *The Killing Time*, p. 8.
36 Heuman, The Killing Time, p. 137.
37 Parliamentary Papers: Report of the Jamaica Royal Commission, Part I 1866, p. 41, Bernie Grant Archive (Ref BG/ARM/16/2/17), Bishopsgate Library, London.
38 *The Times*, November 18, 1865.
39 *The Times*, November 18, 1865.
40 Bernard Semmel, *The Governor Eyre Controversy* (London, 1962), pp. 68–69.
41 James Anthony Froude, *The English in the West Indies, or The Bow of Ulysses* (London, 1888), pp. 50–51.
42 Froude, *The English in the West Indies*, p. 10.
43 *Jamaica's Jubilee: or, what we are and what we hope to be by Five of Themselves* (London, 1888), p. 83.
44 *Jamaica's Jubilee*, p. 12.
45 *Jamaica's Jubilee*, p. 21.
46 *Jamaica's Jubilee*, p. 111; Deborah A. Thomas, *Modern Blackness: Nationalism, Globalization and the Politics of Culture in Jamaica* (Durham, 2004), p. 36.
47 J. J. Thomas, *Froudacity: West Indian Fables by James Anthony Froude* (first published 1889; London, 1969), p. 55.
48 Brinsley Samaroo, "The Immigrant Communities," in Laurence (ed.), *General History of the Caribbean*, Vol. IV, p. 236.
49 Samaroo, "The Immigrant Communities," p. 237.
50 Samaroo, "The Immigrant Communities," p. 238.
51 Samaroo, "The Immigrant Communities," p. 242. Natasha Lightfoot, *Troubling Freedom: Antigua and the Aftermath of British Emancipation* (Durham, 2015), p. 171.
52 Samaroo, "The Immigrant Communities," pp. 247–48.
53 Walton Look Lai, *Indentured Labor, Caribbean Sugar: Chinese and Indian Migrants to the British West Indies 1838–1918* (Baltimore, 1993), p. 15. For more on the complex lives and legal status of "liberated Africans" across the Atlantic, see: Jake Christopher Richards, "Anti-Slave-Trade Law, 'Liberated Africans' and the State in the South Atlantic World c.1839–1852," Past and Present, no. 241 (November 2018): pp. 179–219.

54 Walton Look Lai, *The Chinese in the West Indies 1806–1995: A Documentary History* (Kingston, 1998), p. 9.
55 K. O. Laurence, "The Importation of Labour and the Contract Systems," in Laurence (ed.), *General History of the Caribbean*, Vol. IV, p. 199.
56 Laurence, "The Importation of Labour," p. 202.
57 Rhoda Reddock, "Indian Women and Indentureship in Trinidad and Tobago 1845–1917: Freedom Denied," *Caribbean Quarterly* 54, no. 4 (2008): p. 44.
58 Reddock, "Indian Women and Indentureship," p. 43.
59 Laurence, "The Importation of Labour," p. 203.
60 Ashutosh Kumar, *Coolies of the Empire: Indentured Indians in the Sugar Colonies, 1830–1920* (Cambridge, 2017), p. 80.
61 Verene A. Shepherd, *Maharani's Misery: Narratives of a Passage from India to the Caribbean* (Kingston, 2002), p. xxii.
62 Shepherd, *Maharani's Misery*, p. xxii.
63 As quoted in Shepherd, *Maharani's Misery*, p. 84.
64 As quoted in Shepherd, *Maharani's Misery*, p. 85.
65 Shepherd, *Maharani's Misery*, p. 72.
66 Shepherd, *Maharani's Misery*, p. 74.
67 Shepherd, *Maharani's Misery*, p. 32.
68 Look Lai, Indentured Labor, p. 52.
69 Laurence, "The Importation of Labour," p. 199.
70 Quoted in Parliamentary Papers, 1898, L (C.8657), "Report of the Royal Commission on the West India Sugar Industry," app. C, Pt 4 (Trinidad), sec. 295, as quoted in Look Lai, *Indentured Labor*, pp. 169–70.
71 Samaroo, "The Immigrant Communities," p. 250.
72 Prabhu P. Mohapatra, "'Restoring the Family': Wife Murders and the Making of the Sexual Contract for Indian Immigrant Labour in the British Caribbean Colonies, 1860–1920," *Studies in History* 11, no. 2 (1995): pp. 227–60.
73 Joseph Beaumont, *The New Slavery: an Account of the Indian and Chinese Immigrants in British Guiana* (London, 1871).
74 Beaumont, *The New Slavery*, p. 11.
75 Beaumont, *The New Slavery*, p. 14.
76 Beaumont, *The New Slavery*, p. 74.
77 Kumar, *Coolies of the Empire*, p. 4.
78 Heuman, *The Caribbean*, p. 119.
79 Samaroo, "The Immigrant Communities," p. 252.
80 Look Lai, *Indentured Labor*, p. 126.
81 Chinese indentured laborers also went to Cuba and the French Caribbean. For more on this, see: Christopher Bischof, "Chinese Labourers, Free Blacks, and Social Engineering in the Post-Emancipation British West Indies," *Past and Present*, no. 231 (May 2016): pp. 129–68.
82 Look Lai, *Indentured Labor*, p. 18.

83 Bischof, "Chinese Labourers," pp. 130–31, 137.
84 Laurence, "The Importation of Labour," p. 216.
85 Gaiutra Bahadur, *Coolie Woman: The Odyssey of Indenture* (London, 2016), p. 160.
86 Maria Del Pilar Kaladeen and David Dabydeen, Introduction: "My Father's Journey Made Me Who I Am," in Maria Del Pilar Kaladeen and David Dabydeen (eds.), *The Other Windrush: Legacies of Indenture in Britain's Caribbean Empire* (London, 2021), p. 2.
87 Samaroo, "The Immigrant Communities," p. 254.

CHAPTER 5

1 *The Federalist and Grenada People*, October 27, 1915, p. 2, as quoted in Glenford Howe, *Race, War and Nationalism: A Social History of West Indians in the First World War* (Kingston, 2002), p. 17.
2 Anne Spry Rush, *Bonds of Empire: West Indians and Britishness from Victoria to Decolonization* (Oxford, 2011), pp. 9, 1–15.
3 Richard Smith, "British West Indian Memories of World War One: From Militarized Citizenship to Conscientious Objection," in Shalini Puri and Lara Putnam (eds.), *Caribbean Military Encounters* (New York, 2017), pp. 39–47.
4 Howe, *Race, War and Nationalism*, p. 4. Full details of the Caribbean war effort may be found in: Sir Charles Lucas (ed.), *The Empire at War*, Vol. II (London, 1923), pp. 325–453.
5 Tyler Stovall, *White Freedom: The Racial History of an Idea* (Princeton, 2021), p. 138.
6 *Federalist and Grenada People*, June 19, 1915, p. 2, as quoted in Howe, *Race, War and Nationalism*, p. 34.
7 *The Boro of West Ham, East Ham and Stratford Express*, May 29, 1915, p. 2.
8 For more, see: David Killingray, "All the King's Men? Blacks in the British Army in the First World War, 1914–1918," in Rainer Lotz and Ian Pegg (eds.), *Under the Imperial Carpet: Essays in Black British History 1780–1950* (Crawley, 1986), pp. 164–81.
9 Dundonald to Lewis Vernon Harcourt, Secretary of State for the Colonies, November 23, 1914, CO 318/333, TNA.
10 Howe, *Race*, pp. 31–32. Dundonald to Harcourt, TNA.
11 Dundonald to Harcourt, TNA.
12 Lord Stamfordham (on behalf of George V) to Lewis Harcourt, April 17, 1915, CO 318/333, TNA.
13 Howe, Race, pp. 54–58.
14 Reena N. Goldthree, "'A Greater Enterprise than the Panama Canal': Migrant Labor and Military Recruitment in the World War I Era

Circum-Caribbean," *Labour: Studies in Working-Class History of the Americas* 13, nos. 3–4 (2016): pp. 57–82.
15 "West Indians and the War," *Panama Morning Journal*, May 18, 1917.
16 Goldthree, "A Greater," p. 67.
17 Goldthree, "A Greater," p. 59.
18 Howe, *Race*, p. 51.
19 C. L. R. James, *Beyond a Boundary* (first published 1963; London, 1966), p. 40.
20 For more on Jamaican volunteers in the war, see: Richard Smith, *Jamaican Volunteers in the First World War: Race, Masculinity and the Development of National Consciousness* (Manchester, 2004).
21 Dalea Bean, *Jamaican Women and the World Wars: On the Front Lines of Change* (Basingstoke, 2018), pp. 76, 33.
22 Bean, *Jamaican Women and the World Wars*, p. 79.
23 Howe, *Race*, p. 80.
24 Howe, *Race*, p. 80.
25 "Britain's Myriad Voices Call," *The West Indian* (Grenada), July 24, 1915, p. 4.
26 Harry M. Brown to Algernon Aspinall, December 5, 1917, underlined in original, CO 318/345, TNA.
27 Ernest Price to Jamaican governor, n.d., CO 137/725, TNA.
28 Howe, *Race*, pp. 106–7.
29 Howe, *Race*, p. 99.
30 "The Autobiography of Norman Washington Manley," *Jamaica Journal* 7, nos. 1–2 (March–June 1973): p. 7.
31 Sir Etienne Dupoch, *A Salute to Friend and Foe: My Battles, Sieges and Fortunes* (Nassau, 1982), p. 54.
32 "West Indian Jealousies," *Barbados Globe*, April 23, 1917, p. 3.
33 Gordon K. Lewis, *The Growth of the Modern West Indies* (first published 1968; Kingston, 2004), p. 5.
34 The British Honduras *Clarion*, March 9, 1916, p. 260.
35 "Autobiography of Norman Washington Manley," p. 6.
36 "English fond of the Dark Chaps," *Jamaica Times*, January 8, 1916, p. 6.
37 "Letter from Private G. J. Dadd," *Jamaica Times*, January 1, 1916, p. 17.
38 Governor Haddon-Smith to Viscount Milner, February 16, 1920, CO 318/353, TNA.
39 *Federalist and Grenada People*, May 25, 1918, p. 2, as quoted in Howe p. 172.
40 Howe, *Race*, p. 177.
41 Howe, *Race*, p. 161.
42 Enclosure in dispatch No. 27 of February 13, 1919, Re: Increase of Pay, CO 318/348, TNA.

NOTES

43 A. A. Cipriani, *Twenty-Five Years After: The British West Indies Regiment in the Great War 1914–1918* (reprint; London, 1993), p. 62, as quoted in Howe, *Race*, p. 166.
44 Cipriani, *Twenty-Five Years After*, p. 65, as mentioned in Howe, *Race*, p. 165.
45 Howe, *Race*, p. 165.
46 Howe, *Race*, p. 165. Base Commandant, Taranto to War Office, December 9, 1918, CO 318/347 TNA.
47 Howe, Race, p. 165. See: W. F. Elkins, "A Source of Black Nationalism in the Caribbean: The Revolt of the British West Indies Regiment at Taranto, Italy," *Science and Society* 34, no. 1 (Spring 1970): p. 102.
48 "Notes of meeting held at Cimino Camp Taranto Italy," December 17, 1918, CO 318/350, TNA.
49 Maj. Maxwell Smith to Maj. Gen. Thullier, Taranto, December 27, 1918, CO 318/350, TNA.
50 Letter from Sir Leslie Probyn to Downing Street, January 24, 1919, CO 318/350, TNA.
51 On the revolt, see: Howe, *Race*, pp. 155–71.
52 Reena N. Goldthree, "Writing War and Empire: Poetry, Patriotism, and Public Claims-Making in the British Caribbean," in Shalini Puri and Lara Putnam (eds.), *Caribbean Military Encounters* (New York, 2017), p. 57.
53 For a list of Caribbean soldiers who died in other regiments beyond the BWIR, see: Frank Cundall, *Jamaica's Part in the Great War, 1914-1918* (London, 1925), pp. 105–21, 144–45; "The West India Regiment WW1 Losses," Caribbean Roll of Honour, http://caribbeanrollofhonour-ww1-ww2.yolasite.com/west-india-regiment.php and "Caribbean WW1; "Casualties while serving with Regular Army Units," Caribbean Roll of Honour, http://caribbeanrollofhonour-ww1-ww2.yolasite.com/army-ww1.php (accessed June 6, 2022).
54 For more on the disturbances in British Honduras, see: reports re: "Riot at Belize," CO 123/296, TNA.
55 *Daily Record and Mail* (Glasgow), June 25, 1919, p. 2.
56 *Evening Times* (Glasgow), June 21, 1919, p. 2.
57 *South Wales Echo*, June 14, 1919, p. 1.
58 Lord Milner, "Memorandum on the Repatriation of Coloured Men," June 23, 1919, pp. 282–83, CO 323/814, TNA.
59 Jacqueline Jenkinson, Black 1919: *Riots, Racism and Resistance in Imperial Britain* (first published 2009; Liverpool, 2019), p. 167.
60 "Report of the Conference on the Repatriation of British Coloured Seamen," November 7, 1919, 2 CO 323/817, TNA.
61 Jenkinson, *Black 1919*, p. 157.

62 Laura Tabili, "The Construction of Racial Difference in Twentieth-Century Britain: The Special Restriction (Coloured Alien Seamen) Order, 1925," *Journal of British Studies* 33, no. 1 (1994): p. 56.
63 Tabili, "The Construction of Racial Difference," p. 88.
64 Tabili, "The Construction of Racial Difference," p. 91.
65 For more on this, see: Marc Matera, *Black London: the Imperial Metropolis and Decolonisation in the Twentieth Century* (Oakland, 2015).
66 Moody papers, "The story of my life," ms., dd early 1940s, as quoted in David Killingray, "To Do Something for the Race: Harold Moody and the League of Coloured Peoples," in Bill Schwarz (ed.), West Indian Intellectuals in Britain (Manchester, 2003), p. 54.
67 Moody papers, "The story of my life," in Killingray, "To Do Something for the Race," p. 54.
68 David A. Vaughan, *Negro Victory: The Life Story of Dr Harold Moody* (London, 1950), p. 33.
69 Moody, talk to the Baptist Union, Glasgow, May 1933; *Bulletin*, May 5, 1933, as quoted in Killingray, "To Do Something for the Race," p. 63.
70 *The Keys* 1, no. 1 (July 1933), front cover.
71 Amy Jacques Garvey, *Garvey and Garveyism*, introduction by John Henrik Clarke (London, 1970), p. 11.
72 Claude McKay, *Songs of Jamaica* (first published 1912; London, 2021), pp. 58–59.
73 Claude McKay, *A Long Way from Home* (first published 1937; New York, 1969), p. 76.
74 McKay, *Long Way*, p. 68.
75 McKay, *Long Way*, p. 70.
76 McKay to Marcus Garvey, December 17, 1919, copy in Hubert Harrison papers, as quoted in Winston James, "A race outcast from an outcast class: Claude McKay's experience and analysis of Britain," in Schwarz (ed.), *West Indian Intellectuals*, p. 85.
77 Una Marson, "Problems of coloured people in Britain," n.d., Una Marson papers box, 1944c, 1 National Library of Jamaica, as quoted in Alison Donnell, "Una Marson: feminism, anti-colonialism and a forgotten fight for freedom," in Schwarz (ed.), West Indian Intellectuals, pp. 120–21.
78 *The Keys* 1, no. 3 (January 1934): p. 50.
79 Delia Jarrett-Macauley, *The Life of Una Marson, 1905–1965* (Manchester, 1998), p. 48.
80 J. M. Kenyatta, "Hands Off Abyssinia!" *Labour Monthly: A Magazine of International Labour* 17, no. 9 (September 1935): p. 532.
81 Minkah Makalani, *In the Cause of Freedom: Radical Black Internationalism from Harlem to London 1917–1939* (Chapel Hill, 2011), p. 206; Matera, *Black London*, p. 110.

NOTES

82 George Padmore (ed.), *Colonial and . . . Coloured Unity, A Programme of Action: History of the Pan-African Congress* (London, 1947), p. 52.
83 For more on Padmore, see: Leslie James, *George Padmore and Decolonization from Below: Pan-Africanism, the Cold War, and the End of Empire* (Basingstoke, 2015).
84 George Padmore, *How Britain Rules Africa* (London, 1936), p. 4.
85 George Padmore, "The British Empire Is the Worst Racket Yet Invented by Man," *New Leader*, December 15, 1939.
86 As quoted in Makalani, *In the Cause of Freedom*, p. 213.
87 C. L. R. James, *Letters from London* (first published 1932; Oxford, 2003), p. 83.
88 St. Lucian economist Arthur Lewis authored an important pamphlet about the conditions facing workers in the Caribbean, in W. Arthur Lewis, *Labour in the West Indies: The Birth of a Worker's Movement* (London, 1938). The riots and disturbances in the 1930s also occurred in Cuba, Puerto Rico, and Guadeloupe.
89 W. M. Macmillan, *Warning from the West Indies: A Tract for Africa and Empire* (London, 1936), p. 13.
90 *Plain Talk*, January 18, 1936, p. 10, as cited in Ken Post, *Arise Ye Starvelings: The Jamaican Labour Rebellion of 1938 and its Aftermath* (London, 1978), pp. 209–10.
91 "4 Dead! 9 in Hospital!! 89 in Jail!!!" *Daily Gleaner*, May 3, 1938, p. 1.
92 "Report re: strike at Frome and shooting of Labourers, to Inspector General from Inspector O'Donoghue, officer in charge," Westmoreland, n.d., CO 137/826/9, TNA.
93 Colin A. Palmer, *Freedom's Children: The 1938 Labor Rebellion and the Birth of Modern Jamaica* (Chapel Hill, 2014), p. 52.
94 Palmer, *Freedom's Children*, p. 50.
95 "The West Indian Royal Commission," *International African Opinion* 1, no. 2 (August 1938): p. 1.
96 "The West Indian Royal Commission," p. 2.
97 "The West Indian Royal Commission," p. 2.
98 "Conclusions of a meeting of the War Cabinet held at 10 Downing Street, SW1, Tuesday, January 30, 1940, 11.30 a.m.," CAB 65/5/27, TNA.
99 "Conclusions of a meeting of the War Cabinet," TNA.

CHAPTER 6

1 Marika Sherwood, *Many Struggles: West Indian Workers and Service Personnel in Britain 1939–45* (London, 1985), p. 1; Adi, *African and Caribbean People in Britain*, p. 331.
2 Stephen Bourne, *Under Fire: Black Britain in Wartime 1939–45* (Cheltenham, 2020), p. 49.

NOTES

3 David Killingray, "Race and rank in the British army in the twentieth century," *Ethnic and Racial Studies* 10, no. 3 (1987): pp. 280–81.
4 Dr. Harold Moody to Malcolm MacDonald, December 7, 1939, CO 323/1692/4, TNA.
5 Annette Palmer, "Black American soldiers in Trinidad, 1942–44: wartime politics in a colonial society," *Journal of Imperial and Commonwealth History* 14, no. 3 (1986): p. 214.
6 This figure accounts for monetary gifts that the secretary of state was notified of and comes from Humphrey Metzgen and John Graham, *Caribbean Wars Untold: A Salute to the British West Indies* (Kingston, 2007), pp. 115–16.
7 Dudley J. Thompson with Margaret Cezair Thompson, *From Kingston to Kenya: The Making of a Pan-Africanist Lawyer* (Massachusetts, 1993), p. 22.
8 Thompson, *From Kingston to Kenya*, p. 23.
9 Thompson, *From Kingston to Kenya*, p. 21.
10 Gavin Schaffer, "Fighting Racism: Black Soldiers and Workers in Britain during the Second World War," *Immigrants & Minorities* 28, nos. 2–3 (2010): p. 248.
11 Figures from Rush, *Bonds*, pp. 129–30. Additional figures come from "West Indians Serving with the Forces in the United Kingdom," CO 968/74/14, TNA.
12 As quoted in Robert N. Murray, *Lest We Forget: The Experiences of World War II West Indian Ex-Service Personnel*, edited by Patrick L. Hylton (Nottingham, 1996), p. 97.
13 "Cy Grant," in Jim Pines (ed.), *Black and White in Colour: Black People in British Television Since 1936* (London, 1992), p. 44.
14 Cy Grant, *A Member of the RAF of Indeterminate Race: World War Two Experiences of a West Indian Officer in the RAF* (West Sussex, 2012), p. 28.
15 Grant, *A Member of the RAF*, p. 11.
16 *Manchester Guardian*, September 14, 1943, p. 4.
17 Michael S. Healy, "Colour, Climate and Combat: The Caribbean Regiment in the Second World War," *International History Review* 22, no. 1 (March 2000): p. 80.
18 "To: All ranks, 1st Bn Carib Regt; From: Officer Commanding 1st Bn Carib Regt," May 6, 1944, WO 176/41, TNA.
19 Healy, "Colour, Climate and Combat," p. 82.
20 Figures from Rush, *Bonds*, pp. 129–30.
21 "Grant" in Pines (ed.), *Black and White in Colour*, p. 44.
22 Thompson, *From Kingston to Kenya*, p. 31.
23 Bean, *Jamaican Women and the World Wars*, p.154.
24 Ben Bousquet and Colin Douglas, *West Indian Women at War: British Racism in World War II* (London, 1991), p. 2.

25 For more on Curtis and other Bermudians involved in the Second World War, see: http://www.bermuda-online.org/warveterans.htm (accessed June 24, 2022).
26 Bousquet and Douglas, *West Indian Women*, p. 107.
27 Bousquet and Douglas, *West Indian Women*, p. 109.
28 See: for instance, Letter from A. Pigott (War Office) to Norman Mayle (Colonial Office), February 17, 1943, CO 968/81/4, TNA.
29 Quoted in Amos A. Ford, *Telling the Truth: The Life and Times of the British Honduran Forestry Unit in Scotland 1941–44* (London, 1985), p. 58.
30 Letter from Harold Macmillan to Buccleuch, October 2, 1942, CO 876/41, TNA.
31 Wendy Webster, "'Fit to Fight, Fit to Mix': Sexual Patriotism in Second World Britain," *Women's History Review* 22, no. 4 (2013): p. 615.
32 Appendix A, "United States Negro Troops In The United Kingdom," 2, October 17, 1942, CAB 66/30 TNA and as quoted in Christopher Thorne, "Britain and the black GIs: racial issues and Anglo-American relations in 1942," *Journal of Ethnic and Migration Studies* 3, no. 3 (1974): p. 267.
33 Appendix A, "United States Negro Troops In The United Kingdom," 3, October 17, 1942, CAB 66/30 TNA and as quoted in Thorne, "Britain and the black GIs," 267.
34 George Orwell, "As I Please," *Tribune*, May 26, 1944, p. 12.
35 Schaffer, "Fighting Racism," p. 252.
36 Mass Observation Archive (hereafter MOA), "Race Directive 1939," D1346. Reproduced with permission of Curtis Brown Ltd, London on behalf of the Trustees of the Mass Observation Archive © The Trustees of the Mass Observation Archive.
37 MOA, "Race Directive," 1939, D1403.
38 MOA Observer No. 3484, Directive Replies, June 1943.
39 *Huddersfield Daily Examiner*, October 2, 1943, p. 2.
40 Webster, "Fit to Fight, Fit to Mix," p. 609.
41 "Attitudes to Coloured Races," File Report 1885, August 1943, MOA, as quoted in Webster, "Fit to Fight, Fit to Mix," p. 616.
42 Mary Louise Roberts, "The Leroy Henry Case: Sexual Violence and Allied Relations in Great Britain, 1944," *Journal of the History of Sexuality* 26, no. 3 (September 2017): p. 402.
43 Roberts, "The Leroy Henry Case," p. 408.
44 Roberts, "The Leroy Henry Case," p. 408.
45 Roberts, "The Leroy Henry Case," pp. 402–3.
46 Olusoga, *Black and British*, p. 484.
47 For more on the experiences of mixed-race children, see: Lucy Bland, *Britain's "Brown Babies": The Stories of Children Born to Black GIs and White Women in the Second World War* (Manchester, 2020).
48 Palmer, "Black American soldiers in Trinidad," p. 203.

NOTES

49 Palmer, "Black American soldiers in Trinidad," p. 203. For more on the US presence in Trinidad, see: Harvey R. Neptune, *Caliban and the Yankees: Trinidad and the United States Occupation* (Chapel Hill, 2007).

50 Major General Strong ACS G-2, for Chief of Staff, June 3, 1942, OPD 291.21, RG 165, National Archives, Washington, DC, as quoted in Graham Smith, *When Jim Crow Met John Bull: Black American Soldiers in World War II Britain* (London, 1987), p. 29.

51 "War Cabinet: Reports for the Month of December 1941 for the Dominions, India, Burma and the Colonies and Mandated Territories," January 24, 1942, 15, CO 968/1/2, TNA.

52 "Unemployment in the West Indies, Memorandum by the Colonial Office," 4, September 8, 1948, CO 1006/2, TNA.

53 A list of the HMT *Empire Windrush* passengers can be found at: https://www.gold.ac.uk/windrush/passenger-list/ (accessed 18/6/2022); https://www.rmg.co.uk/stories/windrush-histories/story-of-windrush-ship#:~: (accessed June 18, 2022).

54 Provision of hotel accommodation for Jamaican workers arriving in this country, letter from Listowel to Ness Edwards MP, June 5, 1948, LAB 26/218, TNA.

55 House of Commons Debate on the Commonwealth Immigration Bill, February 27, 1968, Vol. 759, Hansard, https://hansard.parliament.uk/Commons/1968-02-27/debates/357f59e5-0cfa-4b26-8d66-24d179630fac/CommonwealthImmigrantsBill (accessed 15/07/2022).

56 J. D. Murray, C. F. Grey, James Harrison, Frank McLeavy, R. W. G. Mackay, T. Reid, Louis Tolley, T. J. Brooks, J. R. Leslie, Percy Holman, Meredith F. Titterington to Prime Minister Clement Atlee, June 22, 1948, HO 213/244, TNA.

CHAPTER 7

1 As quoted in Cheddi Jagan, *The West on Trial: My Fight for Guyana's Freedom* (first published 1966; London, 2016), p. 125.

2 For more on this issue, see, Adom Getachew, *Worldmaking after Empire: the Rise and Fall of Self-Determination* (Princeton, 2019).

3 Spencer Mawby, *Ordering Independence: The End of Empire in the Anglophone Caribbean 1947–1969* (Basingstoke, 2012), pp. 233–53.

4 Katrin Norris, *Jamaica: The Search for an Identity* (London, 1962), p. 71.

5 Jagan, *The West on Trial*, p. 55. For more on Janet Jagan, see: Patricia Mohammed, *Janet Jagan: Freedom Fighter of Guyana* (Kingston, 2024).

6 Stephen G. Rabe, *US Intervention in British Guiana: A Cold War Story* (Chapel Hill, 2005), p. 21.

7 Rabe, *US Intervention in British Guiana*, p. 28.

NOTES

8 For a recent biography of Burnham, see: Linden F. Lewis, *Forbes Burnham: The Life and Times of the Comrade Leader* (New Brunswick, 2024).
9 PPP manifesto copies, which were forwarded to the US Department of State by William P. Maddox—Maddox was the American consul general in British Guiana—as quoted in: Colin A. Palmer, *Cheddi Jagan and the Politics of Power: British Guiana's Struggle for Independence* (Chapel Hill, 2010), p. 16.
10 Palmer, *Cheddi Jagan*, p. 15.
11 Oliver Lyttelton to Prime Minister, May 5, 1953, CO 1031/946, TNA.
12 Palmer, *Cheddi Jagan*, p. 25.
13 Secretary of State for the Colonies, Memorandum sent for the Prime Minister, September 27, 1953, PREM 11/827, TNA.
14 Memorandum to the Prime Minister from Secretary of State for the Colonies, London, October 2, 1953, PREM 11/827, TNA.
15 Jai Narine Singh, *Guyana Democracy Betrayed: A Political History 1948–1993* (Kingston 1996), p. 62.
16 "British Guiana: Statement by Her Majesty's Government," October 9, 1953, FO 371/103119, TNA.
17 Rabe, *US Intervention in British Guiana*, p. 51.
18 Palmer, *Cheddi Jagan*, pp. 58–59.
19 Palmer, *Cheddi Jagan*, p. 199.
20 Rabe, *US Intervention in British Guiana*, p. 61.
21 Rabe, *US Intervention in British Guiana*, p. 83.
22 Rabe, *US Intervention in British Guiana*, p. 80.
23 Rabe, *US Intervention in British Guiana*, pp. 91, 96.
24 Commonwealth Secretary Duncan Sandys to Prime Minister Harold Macmillan, January 11, 1962, PREM 11/3666, TNA.
25 Figures taken from Palmer, *Cheddi Jagan*, p. 232.
26 Bryan, Trinidad Legislative Council Deb, May 13, 1949, 936, as quoted in Jesse Harris Proctor, "Britain's Pro-Federation Policy in the Caribbean: An Inquiry into Motivation," *Canadian Journal of Economics and Political Science/Revue Canadienne d'Economique et de Science politique* 22, no. 3 (August 1956): p. 322; and Lewis, *Growth of the Modern West Indies*, p. 366.
27 Michele A. Johnson, "The Beginning and the End: The Montego Bay Conference and the Jamaican Referendum on West Indian Federation," *Social and Economic Studies* 48, no. 4 (1999): pp. 117–49.
28 Eric D. Duke, *Building a Nation: Caribbean Federation in the Black Diaspora* (Gainesville, 2016), p. 179.
29 Cheddi Jagan, *The Caribbean Revolution* (Prague, 1979), p. 35.
30 Grace Carrington, "Non-Sovereign States in the Era of Decolonisation: Politics, Nationalism and Assimilation in French and Caribbean Territories, 1945–1980," PhD Thesis, London School of Economics and Political Science (2019), p. 71.

NOTES

31 Elisabeth Wallace, *The British Caribbean: From the Decline of Colonialism to the End of Federation* (Toronto, 1977), p. 113.
32 Hilary McD. Beckles, *How Britain Underdeveloped the Caribbean: A Reparation Response to Europe's Legacy of Plunder and Power* (Kingston, 2021), p. 166.
33 For more on this point, see: Getachew, *Worldmaking after Empire*, pp. 107–41.
34 "West Indies Federate for Nationhood," *New York Amsterdam News*, September 27, 1947, p. 11, as quoted in Duke, *Building a Nation*, p. 171.
35 Alan Lennon-Boyd, "The West Indies," November 5, 1958, CO 1031/2311, TNA.
36 "Jamaican secession from the West Indies Federation," draft, n.d., CO 1031/4274, TNA.
37 Iain Macleod to Harold Macmillan, "The West Indies," September 22, 1961, CO 1031/3278, TNA.
38 For more on the role of ideology shaping Caribbean nationalists, see: Percy C. Hintzen, "Afro-Creole Nationalism as Elite Domination: The English-Speaking West Indies," in Percy C. Hintzen with Charisse Burden-Stelly and Aaron Kamugisha (eds.), *Reproducing Domination: On the Caribbean Postcolonial State* (Jackson, 2022), pp. 43–71.
39 Jamaica, Hansard 1962, 719, and 751, as quoted in Derek O'Brien, "The Post-Colonial Constitutional Order of the Commonwealth Caribbean: The Endurance of the Crown and the Judicial Committee of the Privy Council," *Journal of Imperial and Commonwealth History* 46, no. 5 (2018): p. 967.
40 For more on this point, see: Lewis, *Growth of the Modern West Indies*, pp. 169–444.
41 For more on republican transition in Britain's former African colonies, see: Philip Murphy, "The African Queen?: Republicanism and Defensive Decolonization in British Tropical Africa, 1958–1964," *Twentieth Century British History* 14, no. 3 (2003): pp. 243–63.
42 Norris, *Jamaica*, p. 71.
43 Norris, *Jamaica*, p. 72.
44 Kenneth Blackburne, *Lasting Legacy: A Story of British Colonialism* (London, 1976), p. 195.
45 "London Talks with Jamaica Delegation Concluded," July 7, 1962, CO 1031/3489.
46 Colin A. Palmer, *Eric Williams and the Making of the Modern Caribbean* (Chapel Hill, 2006), p. 149.
47 Sir Ellis Clarke, quoted in Barbados, *The Federal Negotiations 1962–1965 and Constitutional Proposals for Barbados*, para. 26, as quoted in Lewis, *Growth of the Modern West Indies*, p. 410. Clarke was the representative

NOTES

from Trinidad and Tobago on a subcommittee to the UN Committee on Colonialism.

48 For more on this process, see: Rafael Cox Alomar, *Revisiting the Transatlantic Triangle: The Constitutional Decolonisation of the Eastern Caribbean* (Kingston, 2009).

49 Spencer Mawby, "Overwhelmed in a very small place: the Wilson Government and the crisis over Anguilla," *Twentieth Century British History* 23, no. 2 (2012): p. 256.

50 Postscript, re: Anguilla, February 5, 1967, FCO 43/78, TNA.

51 Mawby, "Overwhelmed in a very small place," p. 262.

52 Mawby, "Overwhelmed in a very small place," p. 265.

53 NJM manifesto can be found online at: https://www.thegrenadarevolutiononline.com/73independence.html (accessed May 13, 2021).

54 https://www.thegrenadarevolutiononline.com/73independence.html (accessed May 13, 2021).

55 Grenada House of Commons Debates, December 11, 1973: https://hansard.parliament.uk/Commons/1973-12-11/debates/89f57852-c418-463f-aa40-97a5a60c52fe/Grenada?highlight=bernard%20braine#contribution-8a2884f2-f6b6-4043-921c-7338596d1d7e (accessed June 25, 2022).

56 For more on this, see: Phil Miller, "The Secret Story of Grenada's Independence," *Race & Class* 57, no. 2, (2015): pp. 101–8.

57 Miller, "The Secret Story of Grenada's Independence," p. 103.

58 Miller, "The Secret Story of Grenada's Independence," pp. 101–8.

59 Carrington, "Non-Sovereign States," p. 161. "Near-white" is a term often used in the Caribbean context to describe someone whose racial identity is closely aligned to whiteness although they might have mixed-race heritage.

60 Figures from: https://www.worldometers.info/world-population/turks-and-caicos-islands-population/ (accessed April 23, 2021).

61 Carrington, "Non-Sovereign States," pp. 124–25.

62 Carrington, "Non-Sovereign States," 124; see: "Policy in Commonwealth Caribbean," March 15, 1971, FCO 44/472, TNA.

63 Carrington, "Non-Sovereign States," p. 124.

64 Carrington, "Non-Sovereign States," p. 135; Martin Staveley in letter to Commonwealth Office, April 27, 1967, FCO 44/104, 1–2, TNA.

65 Benedict John-Paul William Greening, "'This Island's Mine': Anglo-Bermudian power-sharing and the politics of oligarchy, race and violence during late British decolonisation, 1963–1977," PhD Thesis, London School of Economics and Political Science (2014), p. 97.

66 Michael Craton and Gail Saunders, *Islanders in the Stream: A History of the Bahamian People*, Volume Two: *From the Ending of Slavery to the Twenty-First Century* (Athens, GA, 2000), pp. 337–41.

67 Craton and Saunders, *Islanders in the Stream*, p. 340.

68 Craton and Saunders, *Islanders in the Stream*, p. 358.
69 Craton and Saunders, *Islanders in the Stream*, p. 360.
70 Craton and Saunders, *Islanders in the Stream*, p. 360.
71 Craton and Saunders, *Islanders in the Stream*, p. 360.
72 Craton and Saunders, *Islanders in the Stream*, p. 360, quoted by Leonard Thompson to Steve Dodge in private interview, cited in Steve Dodge, "Independence and Separatism," in Dean W. Collinwood and Steve Dodge (eds.), *Modern Bahamian Society* (Parkersburg, 1989), p. 50, n23.
73 Richard Drayton, "Secondary Decolonization: The Black Power Moment in Barbados c.1970," in Kate Quinn (ed.), *Black Power in the Caribbean* (Gainesville, 2014), p. 117.

CHAPTER 8

1 Louise Bennett, *Selected Poems*, edited, with an introduction, notes, and teaching questions by Mervyn Morris (Kingston, 1983), pp. 106–07.
2 For more on the personal consequences of colonialism and decolonization, see: Jordanna Bailkin, *The Afterlife of Empire* (Berkeley, 2012) and Hazel V. Carby, *Imperial Intimacies: A Tale of Two Islands* (London, 2019).
3 On the global dimensions of Black Power, see: Nico Slate (ed.), *Black Power Beyond Borders: The Global Dimensions of the Black Power Movement* (New York, 2012).
4 Clair Wills, *Lovers and Strangers: An Immigrant History of Post-War Britain* (London, 2018), p. xii.
5 Kathleen Paul, *Whitewashing Britain: Race and Citizenship in the Postwar Era* (Ithaca, 1997), p. 119. For more on the impact of Caribbean migration on debates about race, see: Paul B. Rich, *Race and Empire in British Politics* (second edition; Cambridge, 1990).
6 Adi, *African and Caribbean People in Britain*, p. 403; A. Chater, *Race Relations in Britain* (London, 1966), pp. 33–35; *Forty Winters On: Memories of Britain's post war Caribbean Immigrants*, booklet written and produced by Lambeth Services, *The Voice* newspaper, and South London Press (1988 or 1989), p. 13.
7 Mary Chamberlain, "Introduction" in Mary Chamberlain (ed.), *Caribbean Migration: Globalised Identities* (London, 1998), p. 6.
8 Paul, Whitewashing Britain, p. 148.
9 W. David McIntyre, *The Commonwealth of Nations: Origins and Impact 1869–1971* (Minneapolis, 1977), p. 40.
10 Paul, *Whitewashing Britain*, p. 25.
11 *The Times*, February 17, 1943.
12 Louise London and Nira Yuval-Davis, "Women as National Reproducers: The Nationality Act (1981)," in *Formations of Nation and People* (London, 1984), pp. 216–17.

13 Richard Drayton and Andaiye (eds.), *Conversations: George Lamming: Essays, Addresses and Interviews 1953–1990* (London, 1992), p. 49.
14 Winston James, "Black Experience in Twentieth Century Britain," in Philip D. Morgan and Sean Hawkins (eds.), *Black Experience and the Empire* (Oxford, 2004), p. 349.
15 Wendy Webster, *Imagining Home: Gender, Race and National Identity 1945–1964* (London, 1998), pp. 123–27; Hazel V. Carby, "White Woman Listen! Black feminism and the boundaries of sisterhood," in Centre for Contemporary Cultural Studies, *The Empire Strikes Back: Race and Racism in 70s Britain* (London, 1982), pp. 212–35.
16 Z. Nia Reynolds, *When I Came to England: An Oral History of Life in 1950s and 1960s Britain* (London 2001), p. 16.
17 Donald Hinds, *Journey to an Illusion: The West Indian in Britain* (London, 1966), p. 35.
18 "Five Hundred Pairs of Willing Hands," *Daily Worker*, June 23, 1948, p. 3.
19 Paul, *Whitewashing Britain*, p. 148.
20 As quoted in Edward Pilkington, *Beyond the Mother Country: West Indians and the Notting Hill White Riots* (first published 1988; London, 2021), p. 24.
21 Pilkington, *Beyond the Mother Country*, p. 31.
22 Ruth Glass and Harold Pollins, *The Newcomers: The West Indians in London* (London, 1960), p. 31.
23 Learie Constantine, *Colour Bar* (Essex, 1954), p. 67.
24 Pilkington, *Beyond the Mother Country*, p. 28.
25 Brie's account is taken from Linda McDowell, *Migrant Women's Voices: Talking about Life and Work in the UK Since 1945* (London, 2016), p. 116.
26 As quoted in Joyce Egginton, *They Seek a Living* (London 1957), p. 101.
27 Pilkington, *Beyond the Mother Country*, p. 41.
28 Comments cited in Pilkington, *Beyond the Mother Country*, p. 42.
29 A. T. Carey, *Colonial Students—A Study of the Social Adaptation of Colonial Students in London* (London 1956), p. 62.
30 Michael Abdul Malik, *From Michael de Freitas to Michael X* (London, 1968), p. 93.
31 Pilkington, *Beyond the Mother Country*, pp. 53–54.
32 Paul, *Whitewashing Britain*, p. 157.
33 *Combat*, no. 2, January–March 1959, as quoted in Glass and Pollins, *Newcomers*, p. 177.
34 Ian Sanjay Patel, *We're Here Because You Were There: Immigration and the End of Empire* (London, 2021), 67. Ian R. G. Spencer, *British Immigration Policy Since 1939: The Making of Multi-Racial Britain* (first published 1997; London, 2010), p. 176 fn. 60, PREM 11/824, TNA.

35 "Immigration of British Subjects into the United Kingdom: Note by the Home Secretary," February 12, 1951, CAB 129/44/51, TNA.
36 Paul, *Whitewashing Britain*, p. 152.
37 Rita Sinclair interview quote from "Great Expectations," ORAL/2, Black Cultural Archives.
38 Pilkington, *Beyond the Mother Country*, p. 107.
39 Ron Ramdin, *The Making of the Black Working Class in Britain* (first published 1987; London, 2017), p. 205.
40 *The Times*, September 1, 1958.
41 Pilkington, *Beyond the Mother Country*, p. 113.
42 Pilkington, *Beyond the Mother Country*, pp. 117–18.
43 "White Mischief," *Spectator*, September 5, 1958.
44 *The Times*, August 28, 1958, p. 4.
45 *Daily Mail*, February 7, 1961, as quoted in Paul Foot, *Immigration and Race in British Politics* (Harmondsworth, 1965), p. 129.
46 George Lamming, *The Pleasures of Exile* (first published 1960; London, 2005), pp. 80–81.
47 "Note of a meeting held in the Home Secretary's Room on Monday 8 September 1958," CO 1032/196, TNA.
48 Norman Manley, "A challenge to Britain," *New Statesman*, September 13, 1958.
49 Pilkington, *Beyond the Mother Country*, p. 135.
50 Paul, *Whitewashing Britain*, p. 158.
51 For more on Jones, see: Carole Boyce Davies, *Left of Karl Marx: The Political life of Black Communist Claudia Jones* (Durham, 2007).
52 Kennetta Hammond Perry, *London Is the Place for Me: Black Britons, Citizenship and the Politics of Race* (New York, 2015), p. 130.
53 Perry, *London Is the Place for Me*, p. 133.
54 "Race tension increased by murder: Police say robbery was a likely motive," *The Times*, May 19, 1959.
55 Sanchia Berg, "Police knew murder suspect intended to kill a black man," BBC News, July 13, 2024, https://www.bbc.co.uk/news/articles/c2qox76e4ppo (accessed August 11, 2024).
56 Perry, *London Is the Place for Me*, pp. 126–52.
57 Letter from Alao Aka Bashorun to Harold Macmillan, May 18, 1959, CO 1028/50, TNA.
58 Pilkington, *Beyond the Mother Country*, p. 151.
59 Perry, *London Is the Place for Me*, pp. 150–52.
60 Paul, *Whitewashing Britain*, p. 164.
61 Paul, *Whitewashing Britain*, p. 164.
62 Paul, *Whitewashing Britain*, pp. 166–67.
63 Paul, *Whitewashing Britain*, p. 167.
64 Paul, *Whitewashing Britain*, p. 167.

65 "Commonwealth Migrants: Memorandum by the Secretary of State for the Home Department," October 6, 1961, CAB 129/107/3, TNA.
66 Paul, *Whitewashing Britain*, p. 169.
67 Paul, *Whitewashing Britain*, p. 176.
68 "What is the Afro Asian-Caribbean Conference," 6, *West Indian Gazette*, February 1962.
69 Perry, *London Is the Place for Me*, p. 178.
70 "Anti-Colour-Bill-Lobby—Feb 13," *West Indian Gazette*, February 1962.
71 https://hansard.parliament.uk/Commons/1961-11-16/debates/be2be54a-6786-4426-86df-72a6f183a482/ (accessed June 27, 2022).
72 https://hansard.parliament.uk/Commons/1961-11-16/debates/be2be54a-6786-4426-86df-72a6f183a482/CommonwealthImmigrantsBill?highlight=words%20africa%20inconsistent%20with%20action#contribution-8cd8fe84-01e8-4716-84d5-c024535951c9 (accessed June 27, 2022).
73 "West Indies Governments Oppose Colour-Bar Bill," 2, *West Indian Gazette*, December 1961.
74 "W. Indies protest to Macmillan," *The Times*, November 18, 1961.
75 Paul, *Whitewashing Britain*, p. 161. CAB 129/103/15, November 15, 1960, TNA. CAB 128/34/59 November 1960 TNA.
76 Figures taken from Paul, *Whitewashing Britain*, p. 172.
77 Paul, Whitewashing Britain, p. 168; Anthony M. Messina, *Race and Party Competition in Britain* (Oxford, 1989), p. 28.
78 Ramdin, *The Making of the Black Working Class*, p. 438.
79 Perry, *London Is the Place for Me*, pp. 191, 211.
80 "Race: The Unmentionable Issue," *Peace News*, September 25, 1964, p. 1.
81 *Birmingham Post*, February 13, 1965, p. 1. For more, see: Joe Street, "Malcolm X, Smethwick, and the Influence of the African American Freedom Struggle on British Race Relations in the 1960s," *Journal of Black Studies* 38, no. 6 (July 2008): p. 939; and "Britain's Most Racist Election: The Story of Smethwick 50 Years On," *Guardian*, October 15, 2014: https://www.theguardian.com/world/2014/oct/15/britains-most-racist-election-smethwick-50-years-on (accessed 27/6/2022).
82 "White Paper Gives Fuel to the Militants," Observer, August 8, 1965; "The Choice for Immigrants," *Guardian*, July 20, 1965; "Hit White Man Back, Says New Militant Group," *Observer*, July 4, 1965. For more on Michael X, see: Malik, *From Michael de Freitas to Michael X*; John L Williams, *Michael X: A Life in Black and White* (London, 2008).
83 Pilkington, *Beyond the Mother Country*, pp. 137–38.
84 "Tighter race laws for Britain," *The Times*, July 26, 1967.
85 For more on the rebellions that took place in the US in the 1960s and '70s and their impact on policing, see: Elizabeth Hinton, *America on*

NOTES

Fire: The Untold History of Police Violence and Black Rebellion Since the 1960s (London, 2021).

86 Pilkington, *Beyond the Mother Country*, p. 138.
87 *Black Power in Britain: A Special Statement by Universal Coloured People's Association* (London, 1967). A copy can be found in the British Library, London.
88 Rosalind Eleanor Wild, "Black was the colour of our fight: Black Power in Britain, 1955–1976," PhD Thesis, University of Sheffield (2008), p. 83. For more on Black Power in Britain, see: Rob Waters, *Thinking Black: Britain, 1964–1985* (Oakland, 2019).
89 R. E. R. Bunce and Paul Field, "Obi B Egbuna, C. L. R. James and the Birth of Black Power in Britain: Black Radicalism in Britain, 1967–1972," *Twentieth Century British History* 22, no. 3 (2011): p. 405.
90 Obi Egbuna, *Destroy This Temple: The Voice of Black Power in Britain* (London, 1971), p. 155.
91 A copy of this pamphlet can be found in CRIM 1/4962 TNA.
92 Waters, *Thinking Black*, pp. 40–41.
93 Bunce and Field, "Obi B Egbuna," p. 408.
94 Bunce and Field, "Obi B Egbuna," p. 408.
95 Bunce and Field, "Obi B Egbuna," pp. 408–9.
96 Louis Chase, "What Justice for the Mangrove Nine?" *Race Today*, February 1972, pp. 38–39.
97 A. Sivanandan, "The Heart Is Where the Battle Is: An Interview with the Author," in A. Sivanandan, *Communities of Resistance: Writings on Black Struggles for Socialism* (London, 1990), p. 10.
98 Interview: "Trinidad Implants in you this Wonderful Sense of Carnival," Bob Ramdhanie and Maria del Pilar Kaladeen in Kaladeen and Dabydeen (eds.), *The Other Windrush: Legacies of Indenture in Britain's Caribbean Empire* (London, 2021), p. 63.
99 For a recent work uncovering the work of Gerlin Bean, see: A. S. Francis, *Gerlin Bean: Mother of the Movement* (London, 2023).
100 Francis, *Gerlin Bean*, p. 62
101 For more, see: Kieran Connell, *Black Handsworth: Race in 1980s Britain* (Oakland, 2019) and Elizabeth Williams, *The Politics of Race in Britain and South Africa: Black British Solidarity and the Anti-Apartheid Struggle* (London, 2014).
102 As cited in Julia McNeal, "Education," in Simon Abbott (ed.), *The Prevention of Racial Discrimination in Britain* (Oxford, 1971), p. 123.
103 Sally Tomlinson, "West Indian Children and ESN Schooling," *Journal of Ethnic and Migration Studies* 6, no. 3 (1978): p. 238.
104 Bernard Coard, *How the West Indian Child is Made Educationally Sub-Normal in the British School System* (fifth edition, London 2021), pp. 3–4.

105 Coard, *How the West Indian Child*, p. 4.
106 Coard, *How the West Indian Child*, p. 10.
107 Coard, *How the West Indian Child*, p. 62.
108 Patel, *We're Here Because You Were There*, p. 84.
109 Mike Bower, "Do we risk discrimination against whites?" *Express and Star*, April 12, 1968, p. 6.
110 Enoch Powell, "To the annual general meeting of the West Midlands Area Conservative Political Centre, Birmingham 20 April 1968," in *Reflections of a Statesman: the Writings and Speeches of Enoch Powell, Selected by Rex Collings* (London, 1991), p. 376.
111 Shirin Hirsch, *In the Shadow of Enoch Powell: Race, Locality and Resistance* (Manchester, 2018), p. 14.
112 Enoch Powell, "To the Annual General Meeting of the West Midlands Area Conservative Political Centre, Birmingham 20 April 1968," in *Reflections of a Statesman*, p. 374.
113 Enoch Powell, "To the Annual General Meeting of the West Midlands Area Conservative Political Centre, Birmingham 20 April 1968," in *Reflections of a Statesman*, p. 377.
114 Enoch Powell, "To the Annual General Meeting of the West Midlands Area Conservative Political Centre, Birmingham 20 April 1968," in *Reflections of a Statesman*, p. 377.
115 Enoch Powell, "To the Annual General Meeting of the West Midlands Area Conservative Political Centre, Birmingham 20 April 1968," in *Reflections of a Statesman*, p. 379.
116 Enoch Powell, "To the Annual General Meeting of the West Midlands Area Conservative Political Centre, Birmingham 20 April 1968," in *Reflections of a Statesman*, p. 378.
117 Enoch Powell, "To the Annual General Meeting of the West Midlands Area Conservative Political Centre, Birmingham 20 April 1968," in *Reflections of a Statesman*, p. 379.
118 "Powell out of Shadow Cabinet," *The Times*, April 22, 1968.
119 "Unions, MPs and dockers line up," *Guardian*, April 27, 1968.
120 "An Evil Speech," April 22, 1968, *The Times*, p. 11.
121 Stuart Hall, "A torpedo aimed at the boiler-room of consensus," *New Statesman*, April 17, 1998.
122 Dilip Hiro, "The young are ready to hit back," *Observer*, July 14, 1968.
123 Camilla Schofield, *Enoch Powell and the Making of Postcolonial Britain* (Cambridge, 2013), p. 249.
124 Nadine El-Enany, *(B)ordering Britain: Law, Race and Empire* (Manchester, 2000), p. 120.

NOTES

CHAPTER 9

1 George Beckford, "The Pot Boils Again," *Abeng* 1, no. 3, 15 (February 1969).
2 William R. Lux, "Black Power in the Caribbean," *Journal of Black Studies* 3, no. 2 (1972): p. 215.
3 "Intelligence Memorandum, 'Black Radicalism in the Caribbean,'" Directorate of Intelligence, CIA Washington, DC, 1970, as quoted in Anthony Bogues, "The *Abeng* Newspaper and the Radical Politics of Postcolonial Blackness," in Kate Quinn (ed.), *Black Power in the Caribbean* (Gainesville, 2014), p. 79.
4 Walter Rodney, *The Groundings with My Brothers* (first published 1969; London, 2019), p. 24.
5 Kate Quinn, "Black Power in Caribbean Context" in Kate Quinn (ed.), *Black Power in the Caribbean* (Gainesville, 2014), p. 26.
6 Victoria Pasley, "'The Black Power Movement in Trinidad': an Exploration of Gender and Cultural Changes and the Development of a Feminist Consciousness," *Journal of International Women's Studies* 3, no. 1 (November 2001): pp. 24–40.
7 Drayton, "Secondary Decolonization," pp. 117–35.
8 Alan A. Block and Patricia Klausner, "Masters of Paradise Island: Organized Crime, Neo-Colonialism, and the Bahamas," *Dialectical Anthropology* 12, no. 1 (1987): p. 86; Richard Peet, *Unholy Trinity: The IMF, World Bank and WTO* (2nd edition, London, 2009), p. 9.
9 For more on neoliberalism's complexity, see: Daniel Rodgers, "The Uses and Abuses of 'Neoliberalism,'" 2018, https://www.dissentmagazine.org/article/uses-and-abuses-neoliberalism-debate (accessed June 11, 2022).
10 Rodgers, "Uses and Abuses of 'Neoliberalism.'"
11 David Harvey, *A Brief History of Neoliberalism* (New York, 2005), p. 119.
12 Norris, *Jamaica*, pp. 75–76.
13 "The Caribbean: Tourism is Whorism," *Time*, August 3, 1970, http://content.time.com/time/subscriber/printout/0,8816,876687,00.html (accessed April 5, 2022).
14 Quito Swan, *Black Power in Bermuda: The Struggle for Decolonization* (New York, 2009), p. 56.
15 Swan, *Black Power in Bermuda*, p. 56.
16 Stanley Reid, "An Introductory Approach to the Concentration of Power in the Jamaican Corporate Economy and Notes on its Origin," in Carl Stone and Aggrey Brown (eds.), *Essays on Power and Change in Jamaica* (Kingston, 1977), pp. 15, 15–44; Anthony J. Payne, *Politics in Jamaica* (revised edition; New York, 1994), p. 18.
17 Payne, *Politics in Jamaica*, p. 18.
18 Orlando Patterson, *The Confounding Island: Jamaica and the Postcolonial Predicament* (Cambridge, MA, 2019), p. 133.

19 Deborah A. Thomas, *Exceptional Violence: Embodied Citizenship in Transnational Jamaica* (Durham, 2011), p. 174.
20 Rodney, *Groundings*, p. 5.
21 Payne, *Politics in Jamaica*, p. 20.
22 Payne, *Politics in Jamaica*, p. 18.
23 Norris, Jamaica, p. 93.
24 Rodney, *Groundings*, p. 63.
25 Rodney, *Groundings*, p. 26.
26 Rodney, *Groundings*, p. 26.
27 "Shearer Tells house of Guyanese's Castro Plot," *Daily Gleaner*, October 18, 1968, p. 1.
28 Rupert Lewis, "Jamaican Black Power in the 1960s," in Kate Quinn (ed.), *Black Power in the Caribbean* (Gainesville, 2014), p. 67.
29 Lewis, "Jamaican Black Power in the 1960s," p. 65.
30 Ralph Gonsalves, "The Rodney Affair and its aftermath," *Caribbean Quarterly* 25, no. 3 (1979): pp. 8–9.
31 Gonsalves, "The Rodney Affair and its aftermath," p. 9.
32 Swan, *Black Power in Bermuda*, p. 51.
33 Heuman, *The Caribbean*, p. 174.
34 Lewis, "Jamaican Black Power in the 1960s," p. 70.
35 Brinsley Samaroo, "The February Revolution (1970) as a Catalyst for Change in Trinidad and Tobago," in Kate Quinn (ed.), *Black Power in the Caribbean* (Gainesville, 2014), p. 100.
36 Samaroo, "The February Revolution (1970)," p. 100.
37 Samaroo, "The February Revolution (1970)," pp. 106–7.
38 Eric Williams, "*Nationwide Broadcast*, March 23, Port-of-Spain, Trinidad: Government Printery 1970, 4," as quoted in Samaroo, "The February Revolution (1970)," pp. 108–9.
39 Eric Williams, "*Nationwide Broadcast*," 6, quoted in Samaroo, "The February Revolution (1970)," p. 109.
40 Eric Williams, "*Nationwide Broadcast*," May 3, 1970, 3, quoted in Samaroo, "The February Revolution (1970), p. 109.
41 Samaroo, "The February Revolution (1970)," p. 110.
42 Samaroo, "The February Revolution (1970)," p. 110.
43 Eric Williams, "*Independence Day Message*, 31 August 1970," Eric Williams Collection, University of West Indies Library, St. Augustine File 1961, quoted in Samaroo, "The February Revolution (1970)," pp. 110–11.
44 Kate Quinn, "Conventional politics or revolution: Black Power and the radical challenge to the Westminster model in the Caribbean," *Commonwealth and Comparative Politics* 53, no. 1 (2015): pp. 86–87.

45 Swan, *Black Power in Bermuda*, pp. 16–17.
46 Swan, *Black Power in Bermuda*, p. 26; "British Troops Form A Reserve," 1, *Royal Gazette* (Bermuda), April 29, 1968.
47 Swan, *Black Power in Bermuda*, p. 26.
48 For more on Kamarakafego, see: Quito J. Swan, *Pauulu's Diaspora: Black Internationalism and Environmental Justice* (Gainesville, 2020).
49 Quito Swan, "I & I Shot the Sheriff: Black Power and Decolonization in Bermuda, 1968–1977," in Kate Quinn (ed.), *Black Power in the Caribbean* (Gainesville, 2014), pp. 201–2.
50 Swan, "I & I Shot the Sheriff," p. 202.
51 Swan, "I & I Shot the Sheriff," p. 206.
52 Swan, *Black Power in Bermuda*, p. 109.
53 Swan, "I & I Shot the Sheriff," p. 206.
54 Swan, "I & I Shot the Sheriff," p. 208.
55 *Black Power in the Caribbean*, April 1970, FCO 63/380, TNA.
56 Swan, *Black Power in Bermuda*, p. 124.
57 Swan, *Black Power in Bermuda*, p. 114.
58 Swan, *Black Power in Bermuda*, p. 94; R. N. Posnett, Head of West Indies Department, to D.A. Scott, April 20, 1971, FCO 44/546, TNA.
59 P. C. Duff letter on Bermuda to FCO, December 21, 1977, FCO 44/1465, TNA; Swan, *Black Power in Bermuda*, p. 180.
60 Swan, "I & I Shot the Sheriff," p. 212.
61 Swan, "I & I Shot the Sheriff," p. 212.
62 Swan, Black Power in Bermuda, p. 140; "PLP Members to Boycott Royal Visit Events," 1, *The Royal Gazette* (Bermuda), October 16, 1970.
63 Swan, *Black Power in Bermuda*, p. 159.
64 Swan, *Black Power in Bermuda*, pp. 160–61.
65 Swan, "I & I Shot the Sheriff," p. 213.
66 Swan, "I & I Shot the Sheriff," p. 213.
67 Swan, *Black Power in Bermuda*, p. 167.
68 Swan, "I & I Shot the Sheriff," pp. 213–14.
69 Swan, "I & I Shot the Sheriff," p. 214.
70 Swan, *Black Power in Bermuda*, p. 178.
71 Caribbean People's Solidarity Campaign Statement, FCO 44/1464, TNA; Swan, *Black Power in Bermuda*, p. 177.
72 Swan, *Black Power in Bermuda*, p. 181.
73 Beverley Manley, *The Manley Memoirs* (Kingston, 2008), p. 93.
74 Laurent Dubois and Richard Lee Turtis, *Freedom Roots: Histories from the Caribbean* (Chapel Hill, 2019), p. 284.
75 David Panton, *Jamaica's Michael Manley: The Great Transformation (1972–92)* (Kingston, 1993), p. 33.

NOTES

76 Michael Manley speeches shown in BBC Film documentary, *Blood and Fire*, presented by Robert Beckford, Channel 4, 2002, see: https://www.youtube.com/watch?v=-cdCCJtoAMQ (accessed June 29, 2022).
77 Panton, *Jamaica's Michael Manley*, p. 39.
78 Dubois and Turtis, *Freedom Roots*, p. 290.
79 Dubois and Turtis, *Freedom Roots*, p. 290.
80 Brian Meeks, *Narratives of Resistance: Jamaica, Trinidad, the Caribbean* (Kingston, 2000), p. 124.
81 Payne, *Politics in Jamaica*, pp. 56–57.
82 Carl Stone, "The 1976 Parliamentary Election in Jamaica," *Caribbean Studies* 19, nos. 1–2 (April–July 1979): p. 33.
83 Patterson, *The Confounding Island*, p. 17.
84 Payne, *Politics in Jamaica*, pp. 72–73.
85 On this argument, see: Ariel Akerman, João Paulo Pessoa and Leonardo Weller, "The West's Teeth: IMF conditionality during the Cold War," *The World Economy* 45 (2022): 2034–51.
86 Michael Manley, "Speech to the nation, 5 January 1977," mimeo (Kingston, 1977), as quoted in Payne, *Politics in Jamaica*, p. 70.
87 Payne, *Politics in Jamaica*, p. 75.
88 Payne, *Politics in Jamaica*, p. 75.
89 Payne, *Politics in Jamaica*, p. 74.
90 Payne, *Politics in Jamaica*, p. 2.
91 Payne, *Politics in Jamaica*, p. 82.
92 Anthony Payne, "Seaga's Jamaica after one year," *World Today* 37, no. 11 (November 1981): p. 437; Payne, *Politics in Jamaica*, p. 12.
93 Diana Paton and Matthew J. Smith, "Jamaica in the Age of Neoliberalism," in Diana Paton and Matthew J. Smith (eds.), *The Jamaica Reader: History, Culture, Politics* (Durham, 2021), p. 364; "The Informal Sector in Jamaica," Inter-American Developmental Bank, Region 3, *Economic and Sector Studies*, December 2006, p. 1.
94 Axel Klein, "The Search for a New Drug Policy Framework: From the Barbados Plan of Action to the Ganja Commission," in Axel Klein, Marcus Day, and Anthony Harriott (eds.), *Caribbean Drugs: From Criminalization to Harm Reduction* (London, 2004), p. 24; Carl Stone, "Extract and Summary of the National Survey on Use of Drugs in Jamaica (1990)," *The Jamaican Nurse*, 29, no. 1 (1991): p. 56.
95 Patterson, *The Confounding Island*, p. 120.
96 Thomas, *Exceptional Violence*, p. 3.
97 Thomas, *Exceptional Violence*, p. 6.
98 Deborah A. Thomas, *Political Life in the Wake of the Plantation: Sovereignty, Witnessing, Repair* (Durham, 2019), p. xi.

99 "Mixed Reactions from West Kingston's residents to PM's apology," Radio Jamaica News, December 7, 2017, https://radiojamaicanewsonline.com/local/mixed-reactions-from-west-kingston-residents-to-pms-apology (accessed July 31, 2024).
100 Hugh O'Shaughnessy, *Grenada: Revolution, Invasion and Aftermath* (London, 1984), p. 75.
101 As quoted in O'Shaughnessy, *Grenada*, p. 53.
102 O'Shaughnessy, *Grenada*, p. 75.
103 https://www.thegrenadarevolutiononline.com/bishspkbrghtdawn.html (accessed May 13, 2021).
104 https://www.thegrenadarevolutiononline.com/bishspkbrghtdawn.html.
105 https://www.thegrenadarevolutiononline.com/bishspkbrghtdawn.html.
106 Quinn, "Conventional politics or revolution," p. 72.
107 Steve Clark, "Grenada's workers' and farmers' government: Its achievement and its overthrow," in Bruce Marcus and Michael Taber (eds.), *Maurice Bishop Speaks: The Grenada Revolution and its Overthrow 1979–83* (first edition 1983; New York, 2020), p. 39.
108 Merle Collins, "What Happened? Grenada: A Retrospective Journey," in Patsy Lewis, Gary Williams, and Peter Clegg (eds.), *Grenada: Revolution and Invasion* (Kingston, 2015), p. 27.
109 Dubois and Turtis, *Freedom Roots*, p. 301.
110 Ronald Reagan, "Remarks on Central America and El Salvador at the Annual Meeting of the National Association of Manufacturers," March 10, 1983, Public Papers of the Presidents of the United States, American Presidency Project, https://www.presidency.ucsb.edu/documents/remarks-central-america-and-el-salvador-the-annual-meeting-the-national-association (accessed May 12, 2021).
111 Maurice Bishop, "In nobody's backyard," April 13, 1979, address broadcast on Radio Free Grenada, as quoted in Bruce Marcus and Michael Taber (eds.), *Maurice Bishop Speaks: The Grenada Revolution and its Overthrow, 1979–1983* (New York, 1983; 2020 edition), p. 123.
112 Patrick E. Tyler and David Hoffman, "US invades Grenada, Fights Cubans," *Washington Post*, October 26, 1983. For more on Charles's response, see Imaobong Umoren, "Eugenia Charles, the United States, and Military Intervention in Grenada," in Christopher McKnight Nichols and David Milne (eds.), *Ideology in US Foreign Relations: New Histories* (New York, 2022), pp. 231–45.
113 Edward Cody, "Caribbean Aid," *Washington Post*, December 17, 1983.
114 Gary Williams, "The Tail that Wagged the Dog: the Organisation of Eastern Caribbean States' Role in the 1983 Intervention in Grenada," *European Review of Latin American and Caribbean Studies/Revista Europea de Estudios Latinamericanos y del Caribe*, no. 61 (December 1996): pp. 95–115.

115 Transcript of address by President (Reagan) on Lebanon and Grenada, *New York Times*, October 28, 1983, https://www.nytimes.com/1983/10/28/us/transcript-of-address-by-president-on-lebanon-and-grenada.html (accessed June 29, 2022). Umoren, "Eugenia Charles, the United States, and Military Intervention in Grenada," p. 236.
116 James Ferguson, *Grenada: Revolution in Reverse* (London, 1990), p. x.
117 Williams, "The Tail that Wagged the Dog," p. 107; Ferguson, Grenada, p. 19.
118 Cody, "Caribbean Aid."
119 Tony Freyer and Andrew P. Morriss, "Creating Cayman as an Offshore Financial Center: Structure and Strategy since 1960," *Arizona State Law Journal*, 45 (2013): p. 1300.
120 Robert Goddard, "Tourism, Drugs, Offshore Finance, and the Perils of Neoliberal Development," in Stephan Palmié and Francisco A. Scarano (eds.), *The Caribbean: A History of the Region and its Peoples* (Chicago, 2011), p. 577.
121 For more on this, see: Vanessa Ogle, "Funk Money: The End of Empires, the Expansion of Tax Havens, and Decolonization as an Economic and Financial Event," *Past and Present*, no. 249 (November 2020): pp. 227–32.
122 Ogle, "Funk Money," pp. 213–49.
123 John Bradley, "Cayman Islands: Peaceful and Prosperous," *Financial Times*, September 17, 1971, p. 27.
124 John Connell, "The Cayman Islands: Economic Growth and Immigration in a British Colony," Caribbean Geography 5, no. 1 (1994): pp. 52–53.
125 Vanessa Ogle, "Archipelago Capitalism: Tax Havens, Offshore Money, and the State, 1950s–1970s," *American Historical Review* 122, no. 5 (December 2017): p. 1454. For other statistics, see: https://blogs.lse.ac.uk/latamcaribbean/2017/11/02/the-cayman-conundrum-why-is-one-tiny-archipelago-the-largest-financial-centre-in-latin-america-and-the-caribbean/ (accessed December 20, 2021).
126 Goddard, "Tourism, Drugs, Offshore Finance, and the Perils of Neoliberal Development," p. 577.
127 Vanessa Ogle, "The end of empire and the rise of tax havens," *New Statesman*, December 18, 2020, https://www.newstatesman.com/ideas/2020/12/end-empire-and-rise-tax-havens (accessed January, 2022).
128 *The State of Tax Justice 2020: Tax Justice in the time of COVID-19*, November 2020, p. 54, https://taxjustice.net/wp-content/uploads/2020/11/The_State_of_Tax_Justice_2020_ENGLISH.pdf (accessed July 30, 2024)
129 Phillip Inman, "UK overseas territories top list of world's leading Tax Havens," *Guardian*, March 9, 2021, https://www.theguardian.com/business/2021/mar/09/uk-overseas-territories-top-list-of-worlds-leading-tax-havens (accessed April 5, 2022).

130 Michael Platzer with Flavio Mirella and Carlos Resa Nestares, "Illicit Drug Markets in the Caribbean: Analysis of Information on Drug Flows Through the Region," in Klein, Day, and Harriott (eds.), *Caribbean Drugs*, p. 189.
131 Block and Klausner, "Masters of Paradise Island," p. 87.
132 Colleen Ballerino Cohen, *Take Me to My Paradise: Tourism and Nationalism in the British Virgin Islands* (New Brunswick, 2010), p. 3.
133 Farah Nibbs, "Thirsty in paradise: Water crises are a growing problem across the Caribbean Islands," *The Conversation*, May 13, 2024, https://theconversation.com/thirsty-in-paradise-water-crises-are-a-growing-problem-across-the-caribbean-islands-227345 (accessed September 3, 2024).
134 V. S. Naipaul, *The Middle Passage: Impressions of Five Colonial Societies* (first published 1962; London, 2011), p. 198.

CHAPTER 10

1 Kester Aspden, *The Hounding of David Oluwale* (London, 2008), p. 221.
2 Aspden, *Hounding of David Oluwale*, p. 53.
3 For more detailed information about Oluwale's life, and efforts to remember his legacy, see: https://rememberoluwale.org (accessed February 13, 2024). For a recent work uncovering more on Oluwale, see: Kennetta Hammond Perry, "The Sights and Sounds of State Violence: Encounters with the Archive of David Oluwale," *Twentieth Century History* 34, no. 3 (2023): pp. 467–90.
4 Gilroy, *After Empire*, pp. 107–16.
5 Granada Television, *World in Action*, January 30, 1978, as cited in Charles Husband and Jagdish M. Chouhan, "Local Radio in the Communication Environment of Ethnic Minorities in Britain," in Teun A. van Dijk (ed.), *Discourse and Communication: New Approaches to the Analysis of Mass Media* (Berlin, 1985), p. 276.
6 Robbie Shilliam, *Race and the Undeserving Poor: From Abolition to Brexit* (Newcastle, 2018), pp. 6–7.
7 Gargi Bhattacharyya, Adam Elliott-Cooper, Sita Balani, Kerem Nisancioglu, Kojo Koram, Dalia Gebrial, Nadine El-Enany, and Luke De Noronha, *Empire's Endgame: Racism and the British State* (London, 2021), pp. 163, 162–70.
8 Shilliam, *Race and the Undeserving Poor*, p. 6.
9 The controversial argument about Black American families and pathology was shaped by then assistant secretary of labor for policy, planning, and research Daniel Patrick Moynihan's 1965 report, "The Negro Family: The Case for National Action."

NOTES

10. Pat Thane, *Divided Kingdom: A History of Britain, 1900 to the Present* (Cambridge, 2018), p. 317.
11. Stuart Hall, Chas Critcher, Tony Jefferson, John Clarke, and Brian Roberts, *Policing the Crisis: Mugging, the State, and Law and Order* (first published 1978; 2nd edition, London, 2013), p. xii.
12. Hall et al., *Policing the Crisis*, p. 15.
13. Simon Peplow, *Race and Riots in Thatcher's Britain* (Manchester, 2019), p. 36.
14. Quoted in the Metropolitan Police memorandum of March 1976 to the Select Committee on Race Relations and Immigration, as cited in Cecil Gutzmore, "Capital, 'black youth,' and crime," *Race & Class* 25 no. 2 (1983): p. 20.
15. Fryer, *Staying Power*, p. 395.
16. Paul, *Whitewashing Britain*, p. 183.
17. Thane, *Divided Kingdom*, p. 387.
18. Statistics from Labour Force Survey, cited in Table 10.3 in Mark R. D. Johnson, "Ethnic Minorities and racism in welfare provision," in Peter Jackson (ed.), *Race and Racism: Essays in Social Geography* (London, 1987), p. 245.
19. Thane, *Divided Kingdom*, p. 353.
20. James Vernon, "Heathrow and the Making of Neoliberal Britain," *Past and Present*, no. 252 (August 2021): p. 233.
21. Peplow, *Race and Riots in Thatcher's Britain*, pp. 53–54.
22. *Daily Telegraph*, April 3, 1980.
23. *Daily Telegraph*, April 7, 1980, as cited in Michael Rowe, *The Racialisation of Disorder in Twentieth Century Britain* (Aldershot, 1998), pp. 7–8.
24. Peplow, *Race and Riots in Thatcher's Britain*, p. 86.
25. Peplow, *Race and Riots in Thatcher's Britain*, p. 89.
26. Lord Scarman, *The Scarman Report: The Brixton Disorders 10–12 April 1981* (London, 1981), pp. 83–84; Peplow, *Race and Riots in Thatcher's Britain*, p. 101.
27. Peplow, *Race and Riots in Thatcher's Britain*, p. 114; "Britain: Bloody Saturday," Time, April 20, 1981, https://content.time.com/time/subscriber/article/0,33009,952979-2,00.html (accessed 29/6/2022); *Scarman, Report*, p. 65.
28. Lee Lawrence, *The Louder I Will Sing: A Story of Racism, Riots and Redemption* (London, 2020), pp. 48–49.
29. R W Apple Jr, "Neo-Nazis Accused in London Riots," *New York Times*, July 5, 1981 https://www.nytimes.com/1981/07/05/world/neo-nazis-accused-in-london-riots.html (accessed July 30, 2024).
30. "Outbreak of an alien disease," *Financial Times*, July 11, 1981.
31. For more on Groce, see: the memoir of her son and carer, Lawrence, *The Louder I Will Sing*.

32 Azfar Shafi and Ilyas Nagdee, *Race to the Bottom: Reclaiming Antiracism* (London, 2022), p. 41.
33 Thane, *Divided Kingdom*, p. 365.
34 Hall et al., *Policing the Crisis*.
35 Shirley Williams, "Foreword" in Gajendra K. Verma (ed.), *Education for All: A Landmark in Pluralism* (London, 1989), p. vii.
36 "Stephen Lawrence," in David Dabydeen, John Gilmore and Cecily Jones (eds.), *The Oxford Companion to Black British History* (Oxford, 2007), p. 253.
37 "Lawrence" in Dabydeen, Gilmore and Jones (eds.), *Oxford Companion*, p. 253.
38 *The Stephen Lawrence Inquiry: Report of an Inquiry by Sir William MacPherson* Cm 4262–I (London, 1999), p. 19, https://assets.publishing.service.gov.uk/government/uploads/system/uploads/attachment_data/file/277111/4262.pdf (accessed June 29, 2022).
39 *Stephen Lawrence Inquiry*, p. 365.
40 *Stephen Lawrence Inquiry*, p. 369.
41 Heather Mills, "A life without Joy," *Guardian*, March 7, 1999, https://www.theguardian.com/celldeaths/article/0,2763,195387,00.html (accessed March 9, 2021).
42 "Death in Police Custody of Joy Gardner," *Amnesty International*, August 1995, 4–5, AI INDEX: EUR 45/05/95. This report can be found at: https://www.amnesty.org/en/documents/eur45/005/1995/en/ (accessed February 13, 2024).
43 Mills, "A life without Joy."
44 Mills, "A life without Joy."
45 *The Future of Multi-Ethnic Britain: Report of the Commission on the Future of Multi-Ethnic Britain* (London, 2000), p. 24.
46 *Future of Multi-Ethnic Britain*, p. 25.
47 *Future of Multi-Ethnic Britain*, p. 36.
48 Andrew Pilkington, *Racial Disadvantage and Ethnic Diversity in Britain* (Basingstoke 2003), p. 269.
49 Thane, *Divided Kingdom*, p. 440.
50 Thane, *Divided Kingdom*, p. 465.
51 Statistics from 2018 show that black people are 4.3 times more likely than white people to be stopped and searched by the police. "Met police 'disproportionately' use stop and search powers on black people," *Guardian*, January 26, 2019, https://www.theguardian.com/law/2019/jan/26/met-police-disproportionately-use-stop-and-search-powers-on-black-people (accessed February 17, 2022).
52 Patrick Wintour and Vikram Dodd, "Blair blames spate of murders on black culture," *Guardian*, April 12, 2007, see: www.theguardian.com/politics/2007/apr/12/ukcrime.race (accessed February 10, 2022).

53 Adi, *African and Caribbean People in Britain*, p. 489.
54 "Why so many find the Mark Duggan verdict hard to accept," *Guardian*, January 19, 2014, https://www.theguardian.com/commentisfree/2014/jan/19/mark-duggan-lawful-killing-inquest-verdict (accessed June 29, 2022).
55 James Trafford, *The Empire at Home: Internal Colonies and the End of Britain* (London, 2021), p. 71.
56 Prison Reform Trust, "Prison: the facts," Bromley Briefings, Summer 2019, p. 7. https://prisonreformtrust.org.uk/wp-content/uploads/old_files/Documents/.pdf (accessed July 30, 2024).
57 2021 statistics can be found here: https://www.ethnicity-facts-figures.service.gov.uk/uk-population-by-ethnicity/national-and-regional-populations/population-of-england-and-wales/latest/ (accessed September 3, 2024).
58 Tony Blair, "Blaming a moral decline for the riots makes good headlines but bad policy," *Observer*, August 21, 2011, https://www.theguardian.com/commentisfree/2011/aug/20/tony-blair-riots-crime-family (accessed April 4, 2022).
59 Janaki Mahadevan, "Riots blamed on absent fathers and poor school discipline," *Children and Young People Now*, August 15, 2011, https://www.cypnow.co.uk/news/article/riots-blamed-on-absent-fathers-and-poor-school-discipline (accessed June 8, 2022).
60 For more on policing, see: Adam Elliott-Cooper, *Black Resistance to British Policing* (Manchester, 2021).
61 Darcus Howe interview can be found at: www.youtube.com/watch?v=mzDQCT0AJcw (accessed January 10, 2024).
62 For more on this, see: Robert Saunders, "Brexit and Empire: 'Global Britain' and the Myth of Imperial Nostalgia," Journal of Imperial and Commonwealth History 48, no. 6 (2020): pp. 1140–74.
63 Danny Dorling and Sally Tomlinson, *Rule Britannia: Brexit and the End of Empire* (London, 2020), p. 348.
64 Sally Tomlinson, *Education and Race: From Empire to Brexit* (Bristol, 2019), p. 214.
65 For more, see: Maya Goodfellow, *Hostile Environment: How Immigrants Became Scapegoats* (London, 2020).
66 Kevin Rawlinson, "Windrush: 11 people wrongly deported from the UK have died—Javid," *Guardian*, November 12, 2018, https://www.theguardian.com/uk-news/2018/nov/12/windrush-11-people-wrongly-deported-from-uk-have-died (accessed June 29, 2022).
67 Amelia Gentleman, *The Windrush Betrayal: Exposing the Hostile Environment* (London, 2020), p. 198.
68 Gentleman, *Windrush Betrayal*, p. 249.
69 Gentleman, *Windrush Betrayal*, pp. 286–87.

70 Jack Fenwick, "Windrush: At least nine victims died before getting compensation," November 2, 2020, BBC News, https://www.bbc.co.uk/news/uk-politics-54748038 (accessed September 3, 2022).

71 Amelia Gentleman, "Windrush: Home Office has failed to transform its culture, report says," *Guardian*, March 31, 2022, https://www.theguardian.com/uk-news/2022/mar/31/windrush-home-office-has-failed-to-transform-its-culture-report-says (accessed April 4, 2022).

72 Amelia Gentleman, "Windrush scandal caused by '30 years of racist immigration laws'—report," Guardian, May 29, 2022, https://www.theguardian.com/uk-news/2022/may/29/windrush-scandal-caused-by-30-years-of-racist-immigration-laws-report (accessed June 8, 2022).

73 Bailkin, Afterlife of Empire, p. 234.

74 Luke de Noronha, *Deporting Black Britons: Portraits of Deportation to Jamaica* (Manchester, 2020), pp. 11–13.

75 https://www.ukmigrationlawyers.com/deportation-of-convicted-criminals.html (accessed June 30, 2022).

76 De Noronha, Deporting Black Britons, pp. 11–12.

77 Peter Walker, "Disproportionate 'targeting' of Jamaicans for deportation from UK, data suggests," Guardian, July 25, 2021, https://www.theguardian.com/uk-news/2021/jul/25/disproportionate-targeting-of-jamaicans-for-deportation-from-uk-data-suggests (accessed April 4, 2022).

78 For more on deportations, see: Noronha, *Deporting Black Britons*.

79 Noronha, *Deporting Black Britons*, p. 27.

80 Amnesty International, *Waiting in Vain: Jamaica: unlawful police killings and relatives' long struggle for justice* (2016), p. 11, https://www.amnesty.org/en/documents/amr38/5092/2016/en/ (accessed June 29, 2022).

81 Gentleman, *Windrush Betrayal*, p. 267.

82 Jovan Scott Lewis, *Scammer's Yard: The Crime of Black Repair in Jamaica* (London, 2020), p. 147.

83 Gary Younge, "What Covid taught us about racism—and what we need to do now," *Guardian*, December 16, 2021, https://www.theguardian.com/society/2021/dec/16/systemic-racism-covid-gary-younge (accessed April 5, 2022). For figures, see: Lucinda Platt and Ross Warwick, "Are some ethnic groups more vulnerable to Covid-19 than others?" Institute of Fiscal Studies, May 2020, https://ifs.org.uk/inequality/wp-content/uploads/2020/04/Are-some-ethnic-groups-more-vulnerable-to-COVID-19-than-others-V2-IFS-Briefing-Note.pdf (accessed April 5, 2022).

84 Nazia Parveen, "Covid job losses show structural racism of UK labour market, says TUC," *Guardian*, February 28, 2021, https://www.theguardian.com/society/2021/feb/27/covid-job-losses-show-structural-racism-uk-labour-market-tuc (accessed April 5, 2022).

85 The broader abolitionist movement seeking to end systemic violence and oppression has its roots in ongoing movements, often spearheaded by black feminist abolitionists; see: Angela Y. Davis, Gina Dent, Erica R. Meiners, and Beth E. Richie, *Abolition. Feminism. Now* (London, 2022).

86 "Downing Street suggests UK should be seen as a model of racial equality," *Guardian*, March 31, 2021, https://www.theguardian.com/world/2021/mar/31/uk-an-exemplar-of-racial-equality-no-10s-race-commission-concludes (accessed April 5, 2022).

87 Peter Mitchell, *Imperial Nostalgia: How the British Conquered Themselves* (Manchester, 2021), pp. 7–10.

88 Mitchell, *Imperial Nostalgia*, p. 66.

89 On the long and global history of reparations for transatlantic slavery, see: Ana Lucia Arajuo, *Reparations for Slavery and the Slave Trade: A Transnational and Comparative History* (London, 2017); Jacqueline Bhabha, Margareta Matache, and Caroline Elkins (eds.), *Time for Reparations: A Global Perspective* (Philadelphia, 2021); and Manjapra, *Black Ghost of Empire*.

90 For more on debates about reparations in the US, see: Randall Robinson, *The Debt: What America Owes to Blacks* (New York, 2001); and Ta-Nehisi Coates, "The Case for Reparations," *The Atlantic*, 2014, https://www.theatlantic.com/magazine/archive/2014/06/the-case-for-reparations/361631 (accessed February 25, 2022).

91 "Prince William expresses 'profound sorrow' over slavery in Jamaica speech," BBC News, March 24, 2022, https://www.bbc.co.uk/news/uk-60856763 (accessed April 19, 2022). During the 2022 royal tour, the Duke and Duchess of Cambridge were met with protesters calling for reparations; see: https://www.theguardian.com/uk-news/2022/mar/21/jamaican-campaigners-call-for-colonialism-apology-from-royal-family (accessed April 5, 2022).

92 "David Cameron rules out slavery reparations during Jamaica visit," BBC News, September 30, 2015, http://www.bbc.com/news/uk-34401412 (accessed February 11, 2022).

93 Caroline Davies, "How do we know David Cameron has slave owners in family background?", *Guardian*, September 29, 2015, https://www.theguardian.com/world/2015/sep/29/how-do-we-know-david-cameron-has-slave-owning-ancestor (accessed October 17, 2023).

94 Caribbean Community Secretariat, Government of Barbados, "Address by the Rt. Hon. Owen Arthur Prime Minister of Barbados in Commemoration of the 200th Anniversary of the Abolition of the Trans-Atlantic Slave Trade," Holy Trinity Church, Hull, England, March 25, 2007.

95 For CARICOM ten-point plan for reparatory justice, see: https://caricom.org/caricom-ten-point-plan-for-reparatory-justice/ (accessed June 29, 2022).

96 Beckles, *Britain's Black Debt*, p. 163.

97 Beckles, *Britain's Black Debt*, p. 17.
98 See: https://antiguanewsroom.com/antigua-and-barbuda-pm-seeks-reparation-from-all-souls-college/ (accessed April 5, 2022).
99 See: https://www.theguardian.com/uk-news/2022/apr/01/glasgow-apologises-for-role-in-slave-trade-saying-its-tentacles-are-in-every-corner-of-city (accessed April 6, 2022).
100 On calls made by descendants of slave owners for reparations, see: the group "Heirs of Slavery," https://www.heirsofslavery.org (accessed February 13, 2024).
101 Kenneth Mohammed, "Don't listen to the critics: reparations for slavery will right historical wrongs," *Guardian*, August 21, 2023, https://www.theguardian.com/global-development/2023/aug/21/dont-listen-to-the-critics-reparations-for-slavery-will-right-historical-wrongs (accessed October 17, 2023). For the report see https://www.voice-online.co.uk/wp-content/uploads/2023/07/The-Brattle-Report_compressed.pdf (accessed October 17, 2023).
102 Republicanism sits alongside other changes, like replacing the British High Court, known as the Judicial Committee of the Privy Council, as the final judicial authority for the island with the Caribbean Court of Appeal.
103 Brooke Newman, "The British monarchy's ties to slavery are writ large in the historical archives," *Guardian*, April 6, 2023, https://www.theguardian.com/commentisfree/2023/apr/06/british-monarchy-ties-slavery-historical-archives-slaves (accessed October 17, 2023).
104 For more on the role of China in the Caribbean, see: https://www.pri.org/stories/2011-04-22/why-china-spending-billions-caribbean and https://www.theguardian.com/world/2015/dec/24/beijing-highway-600m-road-just-the-start-of-chinas-investments-in-caribbean (accessed April 27, 2022).
105 Kenneth Mohammed, "Reparations to the Caribbean could break the cycle of corruption—and China's grip, *Guardian*, January 27, 2022, https://www.theguardian.com/global-development/2022/jan/25/reparations-caribbean-cycle-of-corruption-china (accessed April 5, 2022).
106 For more on the links between reparations and climate change, see: Olúfemi O Táíwò, *Reconsidering Reparations* (New York, 2022). Bernard Ferguson, "Climate change is destroying my country: the nations causing it must help," *New York Times*, June 23, 2021, https://www.nytimes.com/2021/06/23/magazine/climate-change-impact-bahamas.html (accessed April 7, 2022).
107 Naomi Klein, *The Shock Doctrine: The Rise of Disaster Capitalism* (London, 2008), p. 6.

108 For more on how elites have co-opted anti-racism and identity politics, see: Olúfémi O Táíwò, *Elite Capture: How the Powerful Took Over Identity Politics (And Everything Else)* (London, 2022).
109 Paul Gilroy, *Against Race: Imagining Political Culture Beyond the Color Line* (Cambridge, MA, 2001), pp. 11–53.
110 David Scott, "Preface: A Reparatory History of the Present," *Small Axe* 21, no. 1 (March 2017): pp. vii–x.

Index

Page numbers in *italics* indicate illustrations

Aaharon, Ben, 329
Abaco Islands, 263–64
Abbas, Zainab, 303
Abeng (newspaper), 315, 324
abolitionism, 58–59, 79–81, 96–97, 103–27
    Abolition of Slavery Act (1833), 121–23, 129, 391
    apprenticeship system, 122–24
    capitalism and, 104, 110
    Christianity and, 103–6, 109, 114–17, 120
    class and, 106
    gradualism, 110, 113, 118
    Orders-in-Council, 113, 117, 118
    racism and, 80–81, 96, 106, 122
    revolts and, 111–20
    Slave Registration Act (1819), 111–13
    Slave Trade Act (1807), 110
    white supremacy and, 80–81, 106, 108, 125–26
Abolition of Slavery Act (1833), 121–23, 129, 391
abortion, 70
absentee planters, 47–48, 81
Accra, Gold Coast, 77
Act for the Abolition of the Slave Trade (1807), 110
Act of Union (1707), 5

Adams, Grantley, 242, 294
Adams, Peter, 251
Adams, Tom, 346–47
Adi, Hakim, 105
African Association, 139
African Friends of Ethiopia (IAFE), 188
African Races Association of Glasgow (ARAG), 183
African Times and Orient Review, 139, 190
Afro-Asian-Caribbean Conference (AACC), 293
Air Jamaica, 324
Albury, Arnold, 263–64
Ali, Dusé Mohamed, 139, 190
Aliens Deportation Group, 375
Allanshaw (ship), 155–57
Allen, William, 109, 113
All Souls College, Oxford, 392
Almanzora, SS, 222–23
Almaze, Joseph, 105
American Civil War (1861–65), 134
American colonies (1606–1776), 18, 20, 23, 31, 37, 49, 86, 94–95
American Revolutionary War (1775–83), 94, 105
Ammere, Cojoh, 105
Anglicanism, 21, 68, 104
Anglo-American Commission, 221

455

INDEX

Anglo-Dutch Wars
  1652–54, 21
  1665–67, 21
Anglo-Spanish Wars
  1585–1604, 17, 18
  1654–1660, 21
  1796–1802, 99
  1804–1808, 99
Angola, 335
Anguilla, 250–53
Anomabo fort, Gold Coast, 29
Ansley, Frances Lee, xv
Anti-Caste (journal), 136
anti-fascism, 188, 195, 196
Antigua, 20, 29
  apprenticeship system and, 122
  Christianity in, 68
  Closer Association conference (1947), 242
  finance sector, 351
  free people in, 61
  free villages in, 140
  labor unrest (1935), 200
  Maroons in, 73
  Portuguese community, 152
  protests (1858), 142
  provisions, supply of, 65
  reparations movement in, 392
  Second World War (1939–45), 221
  Slave Code (1702), 43
  sugar crisis (c. 1838–70), 134
  sugar industry, 30
  West Indies Federation (1958–62), 244, 250
Anti-Nazi League, 362
Antiracism from Above, 370
anti-racist movements, xxiii, 167, 186–99, 295–308, 362, 369–70, 394–95
anti-Semitism, 260, 271, 277, 279
Anti-Slavery Society, 113, 120, 159

Antisocial Behaviour Orders (ASBOs), 379
apaan jhaat ("vote your own race"), 237
apartheid, 138, 269, 293
apprenticeship system, 122–24, 140
Arawakan, 6
Artisans' Union, 149
Aruba, 254
Ashwood, Amy, 190, 195–96, 289–90
Associated States, 250–56
Association for the Advancement of Coloured People (AACP), 289–90
Attlee, Clement, 311
Auker, Katherine, 33
Austen, Jane, 47
austerity, 358, 359, 378
Australia, 120, 125, 126, 137–38, 194, 247, 269, 272, 382
Auxiliary Territorial Service (ATS), 214–15, *215*

Baartman, Saartjie, 82
Babington, Thomas, 109
Back to Africa, 191
Bahadur, Gaiutra, 162
Bahamas, xx, 259
  Columbus's exploration (1492–93), 7, 8
  finance sector, 350
  independence (1973), 261–63
  Lucayans in, 14
  Maroons in, 73
  Second World War (1939–45), 221
  segregation in, 141
  shipwreck salvaging, 65, 141
  West Indies Federation and, 242, 243
Bailey, Michael, 366

456

INDEX

Bailey, W. F., 149
Baker, Baron, 275
Baker, Lorenzo, 136
bananas, 135, 200, 342
Bandung Conference (1955), 245
Bangladesh, 228
banking, 48, 349–52
Bank of England, 49
Bank of London and Montreal, 324
Baptiste, Mona, 223
Baptists, 68, 97, 103, 120, 132, 140, 144
Baptist War (1831), 118–20, 322
Barbados, xx, 14, 19–24, 29–31, 39, 40, 56, 86
   abolition in, 134
   Bussa's rebellion (1816), 111–12
   Closer Association conference (1947), 242
   crops, 63
   emigration from, 134
   finance sector, 351
   First World War (1914–18), 169, 171–72
   free blacks in, 60
   Grenada intervention (1983), 346
   independence (1966), 250
   labor unrest (1935), 200
   Maroons in, 73
   neocolonialism in, 316
   Quakers in, 68
   reparations movement in, 391
   Slave Code (1661), 40–43
   West Indies Federation (1958–62), 244, 250
Barber, Francis, 81–82
Barbuda, 65, 122, 250
Barclay, Alexander and David, 49
Barclays, 350
Barrow, Errol, 250
Barry, Wales, 182
Bassett, John Hilton, Jr., 329

Bassett, Sally, xi–xiv, *xiii*, xxiii, xxv, 70
Bathurst, Henry, 3rd Earl, 116, 118
Bathurst, Richard, 81–82
Battle of Blood River (1838), xiv
bauxite, 232, 241, 319, 335, 339
Bay Street Boys, 141
Bean, Gerlin, 303–4
Beaumont, Joseph, 159
Beckford, George, 315
Beckford, Richard, 82
Beckford, William, 52, 82
Beckles, Hilary, 391–92
Beese, Barbara, 301, *302*, 303
Beginner, Lord, 223
Behn, Aphra, 35
Belize, xx, 65, 264
Belize Town, British Honduras, 181
Belle, Dido Elizabeth, 92–93, *94*
Belle, Maria, 92
Belmore, 2nd Earl (Somerset Lowry-Corry), 119
Benezet, Anthony, 96
Bennett, Louise, 267
Berbice, 100
Berlin Conference (1884–85), 149
Bermuda, xi–xiv, xx, 18, 173, 259–61
   apprentice system and, 122
   Black Power movement in, 269, 317, 327–32
   finance sector, 350, 351
   Hotel Keepers' Protection Act (1930), 259–60
   Second World War (1939–45), 221
Bernard, Carey, 180
Biggar, Nigel, xxiii
Bird, V. C., 242
Birmingham, England, 105, 274, 368, 380
Bishop, Maurice, 254, 342–46, *343*
Black Beret Cadre (BBC), 329–31

457

INDEX

black Britons, xxi, 32–34, 167
   Georgian period (1714–1837), 33–34, 81–97
   Interwar period (1919–39), 182–99
   Modern period (1980–present), 362–90
   Postwar period (1945–79), 222–26, 267–313, 355–62
   Second World War (1939–45), 207–17
   Victorian period (1837–1901), 136–39
Blackburn, England, 368
Blackburne, Kenneth, 249
black internationalism, 188
Black Liberation Front, 303
Black Lives Matter, 359, 388–89
Black Man, The (magazine), 191
Black Panther Party, 269, 329
Black Parents Movement, 362
Black People's Alliance, 312
Black Power, 266, 268–69
   in Caribbean, 315–17, 319–25, 332, 333, 342
   in United Kingdom, 295–308
Black Star Line, 191
Black Unity and Freedom Party, 303
Black Writers Conference, 323
Blair, Tony, 379–81
Blaize, Herbert, 348
Bloomsbury Group, 192
Blyden, Edward Wilmot, 139
Bobadilla, Francisco de, 12
Bogle, Paul, *143*, 144, 145
Bogle-L'Ouverture, 304
Booker Brothers, McConnell & Co., 231–32
Boston Fruit, 136
bottles, 49
bounty hunters, 42
Boyce, Rupert Glasgow, 301, 302, *302*

Bradford, England, 274
Bradshaw, Robert, 251
Braine, Bernard, 255
Bramble, Austin, 257
Bramble, W. H., 257
branding, 41
Branson, Richard, 352
Brathwaite, Edward Kamau, xx, 304
Brattle, 393
Brazil, 13, 101, 125, 126, 134
Bretton Woods Agreement (1944), 337
Brexit, 381–83
Bridgetown, Barbados, 39, 112
Bristol, England, 24, 49–50, 87, 186, 274
   Bus Boycott (1963), 295
   Colston statue toppling (2020), 389
   national riots (2011), 380
   St. Pauls riot (1980), 364
Britain, *see* England; Great Britain; United Kingdom; unrest in Britain
British Black Panther Movement (BBPM), 300–301
British Broadcasting Corporation (BBC), 195, 268, 282, 298, 304
British Caribbean Welfare Service, 274
British Coloured Association, 295
British Empire, xvii–xix, xxi–xxiv, 5, 151, 166, 204, 395–96
   American colonies (1606–1776), 18, 20, 23, 31, 37, 49, 86, 94–95
   Antigua (1632–1981) (*see* Antigua)
   Australia (1788–1986), 120, 125, 126, 137–38, 194, 247, 269, 272
   Bahamas (1648–1973) (*see* Bahamas)

458

INDEX

Barbados (1625–1966) (*see* Barbados)
Bermuda (1609–present) (*see* Bermuda)
Brexit and, 381–83
Canada (1763–1982), 37, 94, 125, 172, 224, 247, 272
Cayman Islands (1670–present), 65, 122, 257–59, 318–19, 348–51
civilizing mission, xxii, 148
Dominica (1763–1978), 37, 43, 60, 73, 75, 141, 244, 250, 256
Gold Coast (1821–1957), 238–39, 247
Grenada (1763–1979) (*see* Grenada)
Guiana (1831–1966) (*see* British Guiana)
Honduras (1783–1981), 65, 161, 181, 200, 211, 216, 243, 264
Indian colonies (1612–1947), 85, 147, 154–63, 228
Jamaica (1655–1962) (*see* Jamaica)
Kenya (1895–1963), 228, 238, 247, 309, 350
Malaya (1826–1957), 153, 234, 238
Montserrat (1632–present), 20, 29, 30, 244, 250, 257
New Zealand (1840–1986), 125, 137–38, 247, 272
Nigeria (1861–1960), 238, 247
nostalgia for, 359, 371, 377, 381–83, 390
St. Kitts (1623–1983) (*see* St. Kitts)
St. Lucia (c. 1803–1979), 99, 117, 162, 200, 221, 244, 250
St. Vincent (1763–1979), 37, 43, 60, 75, 99, 142, 149, 200, 244, 250

Tobago (1762–81; 1814–1962), 37, 43, 60, 75, 149, 244, 248–49
Trinidad (1797–1962), 99, 109, 134, 154, 200, 244, 248–49
Turks and Caicos (1783–present), 65, 141, 257
Virgin Islands (1672–present), 62, 68, 243, 259, 350–53
British Guiana (1831–1966), 100, 109, 211–12, 226–42
  abolitionism in, 117
  Chinese community, 161, 232
  Closer Association conference (1947), 242, 243
  coup d'état (1953), 227–29, 233–37
  free villages, 140
  independence (1966), 241
  Indian community, 154, 155–58, 162, 232, 233, 237, 240
  labor unrest (1935), 200
  Portuguese community, 152–53, 232
  riots (1896; 1905), 149
  Second World War (1939–45), 211–12, 221
  sugar crisis (c. 1838–70), 134
British Guiana Labour Party (BGLP), 232–233
British Honduras (1783–1981), 65, 161, 181, 200, 211, 216, 243, 264
British Hotels and Restaurants Association, 276
British India (1612–1947), 85, 147, 154–63, 228
British Museum, London, 53
British Nationality Act (1948), 209, 224–25, 270, 273
British National Party (BNP), 285, 362
British Society for Coloured Welfare, 295

British South Asians, 272, 279, 303, 388
British Union of Fascists, 279
British Virgin Islands, 62, 68, 243, 259, 350–53
British West Indies Regiment (BWIR), 169–82, *173*
   Belize riots (1919), 181
   Taranto revolt (1918), 179–81
Brixton, London, 288, 366–69
Brixton Black Women's Group, 303–4
Brockway, Fenner, 287, 292
Brookes (ship), 108
Brooks, Duwayne, 372
Brougham, Henry, 109
Brown, Harry, 174
Brown, Prince, 296
Brown, Robert, 138
Browne, Gaston, 392
Bruce, Charles, 156
Bruce Golding, 341
Brunias, Agostino, 60, *61*
Bryan, Beverley, 303–4
bubonic plague, 12
Buccleuch, 8th Duke (Walter Scott), 216
Burma, 182, 223, 228
Burnham, Linden Forbes, 231–34, 237, *238*, 240–41
Burrows, Buck, 331
Bussa's rebellion (1816), 111–12
Bustamante, William Alexander, 201–2, 242, 246, *248*, 249, 323
Bustamante Industrial Trade Union (BITU), 201–2, 324
Butler, Milo, 262
Buxton, Charles, 147
Buxton, Thomas Fowell, 113
Byron, Vincent, 251

Calcutta, Bengal, 85, 153–55
callaloo, 135
calypso music, 223, 317
Camden Town, London, 282
Cameron, David, 381, 387, 391
Campaign Against Racial Discrimination (CARD), 296
Canada, 37, 94, 125, 172, 224, 247, 272, 319, 325, 345, 382
Canadian Imperial Bank of Commerce, 324, 350
Canadian Presbyterian Mission, 162
Canary Islands, 7–11, 13–14
Canning, George, 113
Caonabó, 11, 12
Cape Coast (sloop), 29
Cape Verde, 8
capitalism, xv, xvii, xix, xxi, 23, 27, 37, 48–50, 104, 110
   liberalism, 31, 80, 104, 110, 126, 131–32, 150, 166
   neoliberalism, xxi, 317–19, 337–40, 342, 348–54, 364
Carby, Hazel, 370
Cardiff, Wales, 178, 182, 184, 274
Carew, Jan, 295, 298
Caribbean Artists Movement, 304–5
Caribbean Carnival, 288
Caribbean Community (CARICOM), 334–35, 391–92
Caribbean identity, 176–77, 214
Caribbean Labour Congress (CLC), 242
Caribbean League, 180–81
Caribbean Regiment, 212–14
Caribbean Voices (radio program), 282, 304
Caribs, 6
Carlisle, 1st Earl (James Hay), 19
Carlyle, Thomas, 130, 131, 147, 148, 149, 281
Carmichael, Alison, 70
Carmichael, Stokely, 269, 299, 323

INDEX

Carriacou, 348
Cartagena, 16
Carter, Jimmy, 344, 345
Carter, Martin, 227, 233
cassava, 135
caste, xvii–xviii
castration, 41
Castro, Fidel, 239, 320, 323, 329, *334*, 345
Catholicism, 8, 19, 20, 27, 45, 57
Cayman Islands, 65, 122, 257–59, 318–19, 348–51
Central Intelligence Agency (CIA), 240, 316, 337
Centre for Contemporary Cultural Studies, 370
Ceylon, 228
Chaggar, Gurdip Singh, 368
Chamberlain, Neville, 203
Charles, Eugenia, 256, 346–47
Charles, Rashan, 381
Charles I, England, Scotland, and Ireland, 19, 21
Charles II, England, Scotland, and Ireland, 21
Charles III, King of the United Kingdom, *265*
Chase, Ashton, 232, 233, *238*
Chester, England, 50
Chicago, Illinois, 189, 230
China, 393–94
  Chinese people, xx, 132, 153–54, 161, 162, 176, 182, 232, 271
  in Jamaica, 161, 320, 321
chocolate, 49
cholera, 134, 142, 155
Christian Democratic Party (Cayman Islands), 258
Christianity, 4, 8, 11, 15
  abolitionism and, 103–6, 109, 114–17, 120
  Catholicism, 8, 19, 20, 27, 45, 57

  colonial identity and, 166
  indentured labor and, 162
  Protestantism, 17, 20, 21, 32, 57, 114
  slavery and, 4, 15, 40–41, 45, 50, 68
Churchill, Winston, 234, 280, 311
Church of England, 20, 68, 103
Citizens of the United Kingdom and Colonies, *see* CUKCs
civilization, xxii, 80, 131, 148
civil rights movement (1954–68), 269, 285, 296, 327–28
Clapham Sect, 109
Clarendon, Jamaica, 46
Clarkson, Thomas, 96–97, 113, 126
class, xv–xvii, 273
  abolitionism and, 106
  anti-racist movements and, 167–68, 187–88, 192, 200
  colonial identity and, 151, 166
  labor unrest and, 200
  nationalism and, 204, 226
  pan-Africanism, 150
  racial-caste hierarchy and, 150–51, 212
climate crisis, 394
Closer Association conference (1947), 242
Coard, Bernard, 307–8, 343, 346
cocaine, 340–41
Cochrane, Kelso Benjamin, 290
cocoa, 30, 63, 157, 342
Codrington, Christopher, 47, 392
coffee, 20, 35, 63
Coke, Christopher, 341
Coke, Mary, 84–85
Cold War (1947–91), 226, 266
  Bermuda and, 328–29
  British Guiana and, 226–42
  Grenada and, 256, 318, 332, 342–48

INDEX

Cold War (1947–91) (*cont.*)
   IMF and, 338
   Jamaica and, 339
   Non-Aligned Movement, 334, 345
   West Indies Federation and, 244, 253
Coleridge-Taylor, Samuel, 137
Collingwood, Luke, 78
colonial identity, 151, 166, 204
"Colonization in Reverse" (Bennett), 267
color bars, xvi, 88–89, 167–68, 186–87, 192, 198, 207, 268, 275–78, 360, 364
Colored Alien Seamen Order (1925), 185–86
Coloured People's Progressive Association, 290
Colston, Edward, 389
Columbus, Christopher, 7–12
Committee for the Black Poor, 95
Committee of African Organisations (CAO), 289–90, 293, 300
Committee of Gentlemen, 95
Commonwealth, 272, 382
Commonwealth Immigrants Act (1962), 291–95, 297
Commonwealth Immigrants Act (1968), 308, 312
Commonwealth Immigration Advisory Council, 306
communism, 196–97, 227–42, 287–88, 299, 324, 338, 339
Communist Party of Britain, 233
Communist Party of the Soviet Union, 197
Communist Party USA, 288
Connor, Pearl, 293
Conservative Party (UK)
   culture wars, 389–90

education policies, 280
Euroskepticism, 378
immigration legislation and, 291, 367
imperial nostalgia, 390
law and order, 284–85, 379
Windrush scandal (2018), 386
zero-sum politics, 358
Constantine, Learie, 276
contraception, 70, 304
"coolies," 157
Cooper, Anna Julia, 139
Cooper, Thomas, 114
copper, 49
Cornwall estate, Jamaica, 47
Coronmantees, 71
Cosmopolitan, The (journal), 194
Costa, Emília Viotti, 116
Costa Rica, 135
cotton, 20, 30, 32, 49, 63, 65, 126
Country Party (Jamaica), 140
Courteen, William, 19
Covid-19 pandemic (2019–23), 388, 394
creole society, xx, 14, 58, 62, 67, 69, 70, 152
Crichlow, Frank, 301, 302
crime, 357, 359–62, 363, 365–66, 379–81
Crime and Disorder Act (1998), 379
Crimean War (1853–56), 137
Cromwell, Oliver, xiv, 21
Cropper, John, 113
Cruelty of the Spaniards in Peru, The (D'Avenant), 35
Cuba
   Angolan Civil War (1975–91), 335
   Castro government (1959–2008), 239, 320, 323, 329, 335, 345
   Grenada, relations with, 345
   Guantánamo Bay, 221

INDEX

Jamaica, relations with, 320, 323, 329, 335–37
   Revolution (1952–59), 228, 269
   Spanish period (1511–1898), 4, 5, 7, 8, 11, 13, 37, 101, 126, 134
   US occupation (1898–1902), 134–35
Cudjoe, 73
Cugoano, Quobna Ottobah, 29, 79, 86–87, 96, 105
CUKCs (Citizens of the United Kingdom and Colonies), 225, 278–79, 292, 312, 363
culture wars, 389–90
Curtis, Lobelia, 214–15
cutlery, 49
Cuvier, Georges, 82
Cypriot people, 270, 279

Dadzie, Stella, 303–4
D'Aguiar, Peter, 239
Dahomey (c. 1600–1904), 137
Daily Argosy, 234
Dartmouth, England, 50
Darwin, Charles, 137
D'Avenant, William, 35
Davis, Angela, 299
decolonization, xviii–xix, 227–67, 317
   Bahamas, 261–63
   British Guiana, 227–42
   British Honduras, 264
   Dominica, 256
   Grenada, 254–56
   Jamaica, 246–49
   St. Kitts-Nevis-Anguilla, 250–53
   Trinidad and Tobago, 248–49
Dehany, Mary, 46
Delany, Martin Robison, 139
Demerara, 100, 115–17
Democratic Labour Party (Barbados), 250

Denham, Edward, 201
Denmark, xix, 124, 183, 209, 391
Depo-Provera, 304
deportations, 386–88
Derby, England, 368
Derby's dose, 56
Dessalines, Jean-Jacques, 101
destroyers for bases deal (1940), 221
Dickens, Charles, 147
Dingwall, R., 149
disaster capitalism, 394
diseases, 12, 25–26, 28, 67, 155, 157–58, 174
Dominica, xx
   abolition of slavery, 130
   Columbus' exploration (1493), 11
   finance sector, 351
   free people in, 60
   Grenada intervention (1983), 346
   Guerre Negre (1844), 141
   independence (1978), 256
   indigenous people, 19, 37
   Maroons, 73
   protests (1893), 149
   republicanism, 393
   slavery in, 43
   Treaty of Paris (1763), 75
   West Indies Federation (1958–62), 244, 250
Dominican Republic, 209
Dominica Passage, 11
Dominions, 168, 224–25, 247, 272, 280
Doran, James, 86
Douglass, Frederick, 136
Dowling, Carlos, xii
Drake, Francis, 17
Drax, James, 20–24, 30
Drayton, Richard, 266
drivers, 65
drug trade, 337, 340–41, 352

INDEX

Du Bois, W. E. B., 59, 139
Duckett, George, 331
Duff, James, 391
Duggan, Mark, 380
Dunmore, 4th Earl (John Murray), 94
Dupoch, Etienne, 176
Dutch Antilles, 221
Dutch Republic (1579–1795), 18, 21–22
Dutch Revolt (1566–1648), 17
Duvalier, François, 254
dysentery, 25, 28, 155

East India Company, 147
Eden, Anthony, 238, 311
education, xxi, 121, 141, 192, 357, 359
   colonial period, 47, 82, 83, 85, 150, 162, 186, 212
   post-colonial period, 305–8, 371, 383
Educationally Subnormal (ESN) schools, 307–8
Education for All (1985 report), 371
Edwards, Bryan, 46
Egbuna, Obi, 299
Egypt, 175, 179, 238
Eisenhower, Dwight, 285
Elephant and Castle, London, 283
Elizabeth I, Queen of England, 17
Elizabeth II, Queen of the United Kingdom, 247, 250, 259, 264, 327
Ellerker, Geoffrey, 355–56
Elletson, Anna Elizabeth, 47
Emigrants, The (Lamming), 282
Empire Day, 151, 166, 201
Empire Strikes Back, The (Centre for Contemporary Cultural Studies), 370
Empire Windrush (ship), 223, 223–24, 275

encomienda, 3, 13
England, Kingdom of (886–1707), xxi, 4, 17–22, 32–33
   Civil Wars (1642–51), 21, 22, 45
   Dutch War (1652–54), 21
   Dutch War (1665–67), 21
   Glorious Revolution (1688–89), 32
   racial-caste hierarchy in, 31
   Spanish War (1585–1604), 17, 18
   Spanish War (1654–60), 21
   Tudor period (1485–1603), 32
Enlightenment (c. 1637–1815), 90, 104
Enriquillo, 14
environmental destruction, 394
Equiano, Olaudah, 25, 26, 44, 86, 96, 105
Essequibo, 100
Ethiopia, 188, 195, 196, 200
eugenics, 138, 208
Euromarkets, 350
European Economic Community (EEC), 294, 313
European Union (EU), 378, 381–83
European Voluntary Workers, 270, 273
Evangelical Christianity, 103, 104, 109, 115
Evans, Audley, 296
evolution, 137
executions, 28, 35, 37, 41, 72, 112
Exeter, England, 50, 105
Expedition of Humphry Clinker, The (Smollett), 47
Eyre, Edward, 144, 145–48
Ezzrecco, Frances, 290

Fabian Society, 192
Falconbridge, Alexander, 28
Falklands War (1982), 371
family structures, 203, 360, 380–81

INDEX

Fanon, Frantz, 329
fascism, 188, 195, 196, 198, 279, 283, 285, 287, 396
Fascist Italy (1922–43), 188, 195, 196
Faubus, Orval, 285
Federal Bureau of Investigation (FBI), 331
Federalist (newspaper), 165, 169, 178–79
Fédon, Julien, 99
feminism, 192, 269, 303–4, 333, 370
Ferdinand II, King of Aragon, 3, 7, 10, 16
Ferguson, Niall, xxiii
Fielding, John, 89
First Africa Corps, 321
First World War (1914–18), 162, 163, 165–82, 204
Fisher, Nigel, 293–94
"flag independence," 315–16
Flamingo (newspaper), 295
Fletcher, John, 192
Florence Mills Social Parlour, London, 196
Florida, 16, 37, 48
Floyd, George, 388
Forbes Bonetta, Sarah, 137
Foster, Sarah and Thomas, xi
Fowler, Corinne, 50
France, xix, xxii, 17, 29, 36, 98–103
  abolition of slavery (1848), 125
  Grenada, relations with, 345
  Napoleonic Wars (1803–15), 121
  reparations movement and, 391
  Revolution (1789–99), 98, 109
  Saint-Domingue (1697–1804), 98–102
  Seven Years' War (1756–63), 37, 72, 75, 99
  Suez Crisis (1956–57), 238
Franklin, Benjamin, 83
Fraser, Hugh, *248*

free blacks, 43, 60–63, 124–25
free villages, 140
Freitas, Michael de, 278, 298, 299
Frome estate, Jamaica, 200–201
Froude, James Anthony, 147–50
"Future of Multi-Ethnic Britain, The" (Parekh), 376–77

Gainsborough, Thomas, 85
Gairy, Eric, 254–56, 342–44, 348
Galtieri, Leopoldo, 371
Gandhi, Mohandas, 161
Gardner, Joy, 374–76, *375*
Garvey, Amy Ashwood, 190, 195–96, 289–90
Garvey, Amy Jacques, 191
Garvey, Marcus, 190–92, 199–200, 297, 322
Gegansmel, Boughwa, 105
Gentleman, Amelia, 384–85
George I, King of Great Britain, 33
George IV, King of the United Kingdom, 117
George V, King of the United Kingdom, 169
Georgia Colony (1733–76), 37
Germany, xxii, 197, 208
Gerzina, Gretchen, 87
Ghana, 238, 247, 293, 387
gibbeting, 41
Gibraltar, 223
Gilroy, Paul, 357, 370
ginger, 30, 49, 63
Gittens, Odessa, 215
Gladstone, John, 116, 122
Glasgow, Scotland, 50, 182–84, 392
glass, 49
Glass, Ruth, 275
Glean, Marion, 296
Glissant, Martinican Édouard, xx
Global Britain, 382
globalization, xix

INDEX

Glorious Revolution (1688–89), 32
gold, 8, 10, 13, 16
Gold Coast, 26, 29, 77
Gomes, Albert, 242
Gonsalves, Ralph, 323–24
Gordan, Rhodan, 301, 302, *302*
Gordon, Garnet, 294
Gordon, George William, 141, 145–47
Gordon, R., 149
Goree, Jasper, 105
Gozney, Richard, xiv
Granada Emirate (1232–1492), 10
grand marronage, 73
Grant, Cy, 211–13, 275
Great Britain, Kingdom of (1707–1800), 32–38, 75–98
    anti-black racism in, 76, 80, 81
    black community, 33–34, 81–97
    racial-caste hierarchy in, 75–76
    Seven Years' War (1756–63), 37, 72, 75
    slavery, legality debate, 83, 90–93
    Zong trial (1783), 77–80, 96, 97
Great Depression (1929–39), 199
Greater Antilles, 62
Greater London Council (GLC), 369–70
Gregson, William, 77–79
Grenada, 37, 75, 99, 254, 342–48
    First World War (1914–18), 178–79
    independence (1974), 254–56
    Indian community, 162
    protests (1895), 149
    Revolution (1979), 256, 332, 342–46
    United Labour Party (GULP), 254
    US invasion (1983), 318, 347–48
    West Indies Federation (1958–62), 244, 250
Grenada National Party (GNP), 254

Grenadines, 352
Grenville, William, 1st Baron, 109
Grey, Charles, 120
Griffiths, Peter, 297
Grig, Nanny, 111
Groce, Dorothy, 369
Gronniosaw, James, 85
Guacanagarí, 7–8, 12
Guadeloupe, 11, 99
Guam, 134
Guanahaní, 7
Guanahatabeys, 7
Guanches, 13–14
Guantánamo Bay, Cuba, 221
Guatemala, 264
Guerre Negre (1944), 141
Guevara, Ernesto "Che," 323, 329
Guiana Industrial Workers' Union (GIWU), 235
Guiana Sugar Workers' Union (GSWU), 240
guns, 49
Guppy, Robert Lechmere, 157–58
Gutch, John, 227
Guyana, xx, 19, 241, 316, 393

Hackett, Roy, 296
Hailes, 1st Baron (Patrick Buchan-Hepburn), 245
Haiti, 7, 98, 100–103, 209, 254
Halifax, England, 368
Halifax, Nova Scotia, 172–73
Hall, Catherine, xxv
Hall, Chuck, 263–64
Hall, Stuart, ix, xv, 311, 370
Ham, 15
Hamilton, Bermuda, xi–xiv
Hampton, Fred, 329
Handsworth, West Midlands, 369
Harder They Come, The (film), 360
Hardwicke, Edward, 156
Harlem, New York, 190

INDEX

Harvey, Thomas, 124
Hassan, Leila, 303
Hawkins, John, 17
Hay, James, 1st Earl of Carlisle, 19
Hazareesingh, Sudhir, 101
Heart of the Race, The (Dadzie et al.), 304
Heath, Edward, 255
Henry, Claudius, 320–21
Henry, Leroy, 219–20
Henry, Owen, 296
hereditary racial slavery, xxii, xxiv, 5, 26–27, 37–38, 40, 110. *See also* slavery
    capitalism and, xv, 27, 37, 47–50, 104
    Christianity and, 50
    reproduction and, 26, 54–55, 66–67
    resistance to, 69–76
    skin color and, 40–41
    violence of (*see* violence)
    white supremacy and, 52, 80–81
Heyrick, Elizabeth, 117–18
Hibbert, George, 106
Hinds, Donald, 274
Hinduism, 154, 162
Hiro, Dilip, 312
Hirsch, Shirin, 309
Hispaniola
    Dominican Republic (1844–present), 209
    French Saint-Domingue (1697–1804), 98–102
    Haiti (1804–present), 7, 98, 100–103, 209, 254
    Spanish Santo Domingo (1492–1865), 3, 5–7, 11–17, 21, 100
Hitler, Adolf, 197, 210
Hogarth, William, 83
Hogg, Quintin, 225
Holness, Andrew, 341, 387

Holt, Thomas, 121
Home, Baron (Alexander Douglas-Home), 311
hookworm, 158
Hope Plantation, Jamaica, 47
Hordley estate, Jamaica, 47
Horton, James Africanus Beale, 139
Hotel Keepers' Protection Act (Bermuda, 1930), 259–60
housing, xxi, 277–79, 357, 364
Housing Act (1980), 364
Houston, James, 27–28
Howe, Darcus, 301–2, *302*, 381
Hubbard, J. M., 232
Hugues, Victor, 99
Hull, England, 182
Hume, David, 90
Huntley, Jessica and Eric, 304
hurricanes, 267, 353
Hutson, Eyre, 181
Huxley, Thomas, 147

Igbo people, 25
immigration, 222–26, 267–313, 357
    deportations, 386–88
    employment and, 274–77, 364
    fascism and, 279, 283, 285, 287
    housing and, xxi, 277–79
    interracial relationships, 273, 280
    legislation on, 209, 224–25, 270, 273, 291–95, 308, 383–84
    racist violence and (*see* racist violence)
    remittances, 281
    virginity tests, 304
    Windrush scandal (2018), 383–86
Immigration Act (1971), 312, 384
Immigration Act (2014), 383
Immigration Act (2016), 383
Immigration and Nationality Act (US, 1952), 270–71

467

imperial nostalgia, 359, 371, 377, 381–83, 390
Impey, Catherine, 136, 139
indentured labor, 19, 23, 40, 41, 45, 59, 122, 126, 152–63
India, 85, 147, 154–63, 228, 269, 271–72
Indian National Congress, 161, 230
Indian people, xx, 132, 154–63, 176
　Britain, 271–72, 279, 303, 388
　British Guiana, 154–58, 162, 231–33, 237, 240
Indian Workers' Association, 293
indigenous peoples, 1–15, 36–37
　diseases, susceptibility to, 12, 16
　encomienda, 3, 13
　intermarriage, 14
　resistance, 14, 19, 75, 99
　slavery and, 4, 13–14
indigo, 20, 42, 63
industrialization, 48
Industrial Workers of the World (IWW), 192
influenza, 12
Inkle and Yarico (opera), 35
Innis, Anthony Carlisle, 301, 302
Innocent Mistress, The (Pix), 35
Institute of Race Relations (IRR), 303
insurance, 48
International African Friends of Abyssinia (IAFA), 196, 198
International African Service Bureau (IASB), 188, 198, 202–3, 207
International Afro Restaurant, London, 195
International Club, 192
International Conference of Negro Workers, 197
International Monetary Fund (IMF), 337–40, 342
Interracial Friendship Coordinating Council (IRFCC), 291
interracial relationships
　First World War (1914–18), 178–79, 183
　Georgian period (1714–1837), 88
　indigenous peoples and, 14
　Postwar period (1945–79), 273, 280
　Second World War (1939–45), 208–9, 216–20
　slave trade and, 25, 56, 63, 81
Ipson, Robert, 156
Iran, 344
Iraq, 378
Irish people, 19, 20, 27, 45, 57, 270, 277, 279
Isaac Hobhouse and Company, 50
La Isabela, Hispaniola, 11, 12
Isabella I, Queen of Castile, 3, 7, 10
Islam, 8, 10, 154
Islamophobia, 378
islandism, 176–77
Israel, 238
Italian people, 270
Italy, 188, 195, 196

Jagan, Cheddi, 231–34, 237–41, *238*
Jagan, Janet, 231–33, *238*, 239, 241
Jamaica, xx, 52–55, 140–41
　Baptist War (1831), 118–20, 322
　Black Power movement in, 317, 319–25, 332, 333
　Chinese community, 161, 320, 321
　Closer Association conference (1947), 242–43
　Columbus's exploration (1494), 11
　crops, 30, 63–64, 135–36
　Cuba, relations with, 320, 323, 329, 335–37
　democratic socialism in, 335–39
　deportations and, 387

INDEX

drug trade, 337, 340–41
emigration, 223, 267–68, 281, 320, 336
free blacks in, 60, 62, 125
Grenada intervention (1983), 346
Hurricane Charlie (1951), 267
IMF in, 337–40, 342
independence (1962), 246–49, 258, 259
Indian community, 154, 157, 162
labor unrest (1935–38), 200–201
Maroons in, 72–75, 119, 145, 322, 324
Morant Bay Rebellion (1865), 142–49
neocolonialism in, 316, 319–25, 337–42
neoliberalism in, 339–42
non-alignment, 334
Obeah in, 70, 72, 73
Portuguese community, 152–53
protests (1848; 1860), 142
Quakers in, 68
Rastafarianism, 200, 317, 320–21, 324, 360
reggae music, 317, 320–21
reparations movement in, 391
riots (1902), 148
Rodney riots (1968), 315, 323–25
Second World War (1939–45), 221
Slave Acts (1664; 1684), 42
slavery in, 30, 42–43, 45, 46–47, 52–55, 71–73, 118–20
Spanish rule (1509–1655), 13, 14, 21
Tacky's Revolt (1760–61), 71–72
tourism, 319
US, relations with, 135–36, 142, 319, 339
voting rights in, 141
West Indies Federation (1958–62), 244, 246–49, 258

Jamaica Advocate (newspaper), 151
Jamaica Committee, 147
Jamaica Labour Party (JLP), 202, 246, 320, 321, 324, 334, 339
Jamaica's Jubilee (Gordon et al.), 149–50
James, C. L. R., 172, 196, 198, 299
James II, King of England, Scotland, and Ireland, 24, 32
James VI and I, King of Scotland, England, and Ireland, 18
James Rogers and Associates, 50
Japan, xxii
Jarrett, Cynthia, 369
Jarrett, Floyd, 369
jaundice, 25
Javid, Sajid, 385
Jenkins, Roy, 298
Jews, 27, 260, 271, 277, 279, 320
Jim Crow laws (1874–1965), 171, 190, 192, 212, 216, 221, 229
John, Patrick, 256
Johnson, Boris, 389
Johnson, James Weldon, 184
Johnson, Linton Kwesi, 301
Johnson, Samuel, 82, 85–86
Johnston, Louisa, *271*
Johnston, Violet, *271*
Joint Council, 192
Jones, Claudia, 288, *288*, 290, 293
Jones, Thomas, 105
Jones, Viola, 300
Jones, Whitfield, 274
Jones-Lecointe, Altheia, 300–303, *302*
Jordan, Edward, 141
Judicial Committee of the Privy Council (JCPC), 247

Kalinagos, 6–8, 11, 16, 18–19, 36–37, 73, 75, 99, 169
Kalipuna, 6

INDEX

Kamarakafego, Pauulu, 260, 328
Kant, Immanuel, 90
Karifuna, 37
Keane, Augustus, 138
"Keep Britain White" campaign, 279
Keith, Minor Cooper, 136
Kennedy, John Fitzgerald, 239
Kentish, Rothwell, 301, *302*
Kenya, 228, 238, 247, 309, 350
Kenyatta, Jomo, 196
Keys, The (Marson), 193–94
Khomeini, Ruhollah, 344
Kincaid, Jamaica, ix
King, Martin Luther, Jr., 296
King, Robert, 86
King, Sydney, 233, *238*
Kingsley, Charles, 147
Kinloch, Alice, 139
Kissinger, Henry, 335
Kitchener, Lord, 223
Kitching, Kenneth, 355–56
Klein, Naomi, 394
Knox, Robert, 137
Kosovo, 378
Ku Klux Klan, 191, 279
Kwayana, Eusi, 233

labor unrest, 142, 168, 199–204, 232, 235
Labour Party (Guiana), 232–33
Labour Party (Jamaica), 202, 246, 320, 321, 334, 339
Labour Party (Montserrat), 257
Labour Party (St. Kitts), 251
Labour Party (UK), 196, 222, 287, 290, 298, 324, 379
Lambey, Theo, 216
Lamming, George, 273, 282
Lancaster, England, 24, 50
La Rose, John, 304–5
Lascars, 82, 95
Las Casas, Bartolomé de, 1–6, 12, 15

Latchmansingh, J. P., *238*
Latvian people, 270
Lawrence, Doreen, *373*
Lawrence, Stephen, 372–74
League Against Imperialism (LAI), 196
League of Coloured Peoples (LCP), 188, 193–95, 207, 220
League of Empire Loyalists, 279, 362
Lebanese people, xx, 153, 320
Lee, Robert Edward, xiv
Leeds, England, 105, 274, 355–57, 368
Leeward Islands, 29, 36, 61
Leeward Islands People's Association, 295
Leeward Maroons, 73
left-wing politics, *see* socialism
Leicester, England, 274
Lennox-Boyd, Alan, 245
Leslie, Charles, 53
Lesser Antilles, 6, 11, 18–19
Lewis, Gail, 304
Lewis, Gordon, 177
Lewis, Matthew, 46–47, 55
Lewsam, Amelia, 82
liberalism
    post-colonial period, 269–70, 280, 287, 294, 303, 308, 311, 358, 369, 374, 394
    slave trade and, 31, 80, 104, 110, 126, 131–32, 134, 147, 150, 166
Liberia, 139
Libya, 345
Ligon, Richard, 19–20, 29
Lilley, Irene Maude, 219
Lindsay, John, 92
Linnaeus, Carl, 90
Listowel, 5th Earl (William Hare), 224
Lithuanian people, 270

470

INDEX

Little, Louise, 297
Little Rock crisis (1957), 285
Liverpool, England, 24, 49, 50, 81, 105, 178, 182, 189, 225, 274
    riots in, 368, 369, 380
Livingstone, Ken, 369
Lloyd George, David, xxi
London, England, 81, 86, 178, 188, 194–96, 198
    abolition movement in, 105
    color bars in, 88–89, 278
    Greater London Council (GLC), 369–70
    housing in, 278
    riots in, 182, 281, 286, 365–69, 379–81
    slave trade and, 24, 49
London Assurance, 49
London Missionary Society (LMS), 115–17
London Transport, 276
Lonely Londoners, The (Selvon), 282
Long, Edward, 46, 51, *51*, 74, 87–88, 311
Lorimer, Douglas, 138
Louisiana, 126
Louverture, Toussaint, 100–101
Love, Joseph Robert, 150–51, 190
Loyalist Claims Commission, 95
Lucayans, 7, 14
Lucky Valley, Jamaica, 46
Lyttelton, Oliver, 234, 235

Macau, 153–54
Macaulay, Zachary, 109, 113
MacDonald, Malcolm, 203
Macleod, Iain, 246
Macmillan, Harold, 216, 238, 278, 287, 290, 294, 311
Macmillan, William, 199
Macpherson, William, 373
Macpherson Report (1999), 373, 376

Madeira, 13–14
Madeiros, Sutherland, xiii
Madras, India, 155
Magnet (newspaper), 295
malaria, 12, 28, 157
Malaya, 153–54, 234, 238, 293
Maltese people, 270, 279
Manchester, England, 24, 105, 189, 274, 368
Mandeville, George Robert, 105
Mangrove Nine, 301–3, *302*
Manjapra, Kris, 103
Manley, Beverley, 333
Manley, Edna, 324
Manley, Michael, 324–25, 332–40, *334*
Manley, Norman, 175–77, 201–2, 242–43, 246–47, *248*, 286
Manley, Roy, 176
Manning, Sam, 196
Manpower Citizens' Association (MPCA), 234, 235, 239
Mansfield, 1st Earl (William Murray), 79, 92–93, 294
Mansfield Park (Austen), 47
manumission, 43, 60, 66, 111, 113–14
March for Dignity (1969), 312
Marley, Bob, 317, 320
Maroons, 14, 72–75, 119, 169, 322
marronage, 69, 72–73
Marryshow, Theophilus Albert, 196, 242
Marson, Una, 194–95, 268
Martinique, 99
Martonmere, 1st Baron (John Roland Robinson), 260
Marxism, 230, 232, 233, 299, 301, 345
Marxist International Congress, 299
Maryland Colony (1632–1776), 23, 31, 37
Massachusetts Colony (1629–1780), 49

INDEX

Mass Demonstration of Interracial Friendship, 287
Mass Observation, 217–19
Maudlin, Reginald, *248*
Mau Mau rebellion (1952–60), 228
Mauritius, 154
May, Theresa, 384
McCarthy, Joseph, 288
McKay, Claude, 132, 192–93
McNeil, Roy, 324
McTaggart, Roy, 258
measles, 12, 28, 155
Meeks, Brian, 336
mercantilism, 50
Merren, Ducan, 258
mestizo, 14
Methodism, 68, 97, 103, 115, 140
Metropolitan Police, 301, 373, 375
Mexico, 16, 48, 334
MI5, 256
middle class, 150–51, 166, 167, 187, 226
    nationalism and, 204, 226, 230, 316
    racial-caste hierarchy and, 150–51, 212
Migrant Services Division, 274
Military Service Act (1916), 169
militias, 42, 58
Mill, John Stuart, 147
Millet, Godfrey, 301, *302*
Milliard, Peter, 196
Mills, Florence, 196
Milner, Alfred, 1st Viscount, 184–85
Mimic Men, The (Naipaul), 282
missionaries, 114–17, 140, 162
Mitchell, Colin, 264
Mitchell, Peter, 390
mixed-race people, xi, xxiv, 14, 140–41, 145, 148, 150, 204
    in Britain, 87–88, 137, 178, 187, 208–9, 220, 273, 280

slave trade and, 25, 43, 56–57, 63–66, 81, 82, 87, 92–93
modernization, xxii
Modyford, Thomas, 20, 30
molasses, 30
Molineux, Catherine, 36
monarchy, 151, 247, 250, 264, 327, 391, 393
Monday Club, 367
Mongoose Gang, 254
Monk, The (Lewis), 46–47
monogenesis, 137
Montagu, Mary, Duchess of, 85
Montesinos, Antonio, 4
Montgomery Bus Boycott (1955), 296
Montreal, Quebec, 325
Montserrat, 20, 29, 30, 244, 250, 257
Montserrat Labour Party (MLP), 257
Moody, Charles Arundel "Joe," 207
Moody, Harold, 186–87, *189*, 193–94, 208, 211
Moore, Richard B., 245
Moore, W. A., 169
Morant Bay Rebellion (1865), 142–49
Moravians, 103
More, Hannah, 87
Morris, Olive, 303–4
Morrison, Majbritt, 283
Morrison, Raymond, 283
Mosley, Oswald, 279
Mosquito Coast, 86
Moss Side, Manchester, 368
Movement for Colonial Freedom (MCF), 287, 292–93
Moyne, 1st Baron (Walter Guinness), 202
mulatto, 63
Mulatto Kitty, 66
multiculturalism, 308, 358, 370, 374
Multiracial Britain, 296

INDEX

Murray, Elizabeth, 92–93, *94*
Murray, John, 116
muskets, 49
Mussolini, Benito, 188
mustee, 63
musteefino, 63
Mustique, 352
Myal, 70

Nagdee, Ilyas, 370
Naipaul, V. S., 282, 353
Nanny of the Maroons, 322
Napoleonic Wars (1803–15), 121
National Association for the Advancement of Colored People (NAACP), 220
National Democratic Party (Cayman Islands), 258
National Front (NF), 311, 362, 368
National Health Service (NHS), 276
National Joint Action Committee (NJAC), 325–27
National Labour Party (UK), 279, 285
National Organization of Deported Migrants, 387
La Navidad, Hispaniola, 11
Navigation Act (1651), 21–22
Nazi Germany (1933–45), 197, 208
Ndiaye, Noémie, 35
Necker Island, 352
Negro Bureau of the Red International, 197
Negro Welfare Association (NWA), 188
neocolonialism, xviii, 256, 267, 317–19, 322, 337–42, 354, 359
neoliberalism, xxi, 317–19, 337–42, 348–54, 364
Netherlands, xix, 17, 18, 21, 22, 100, 391
Nettleford, Rex, 334

Nevis, 20, 29, 30, 68, 252, 253, 345
New Beacon Books, 305, 307
New Calabar, 28
New Cross house fire (1981), 365
New International Economic Order (NIEO), 334
New Jewel Movement (NJM), 254–55, 342–48
New National Party (Grenada), 348
New Netherland (1614–67), 21–22
Newport, Wales, 182
New Providence, Bahamas, 73
New Slavery, The (Beaumont), 159
Newton, Huey, 269
New World Group, 325
New York City, 189, 190
New Zealand, 125, 137–38, 247, 272, 382
Nicaragua, 344
Nicholas V, Pope, 15
Nigeria, 25, 28, 85, 86, 238, 247, 293, 387
1917 Club, 192
Nollekens, Joseph, 86
Non-Aligned Movement, 334, 345
Nonconformists, 114, 147, 149
Norris, Katrin, 230, 322
Northbrook Estate, British Guiana, 140
North Carolina Colony (1712–76), 37
North London West Indian Association (NLWIA), 307
nostalgia, 359, 371, 377, 381–83, 390
Nottingham, England, 274, 282, 289, 368, 380
Notting Hill, London, 278, 279, 282–87, 289, *289*, 300
Notting Hill Carnival, *289*
Nova Scotia, 75, 95, 172–73
Nugent, George and Maria, 58
nutmeg, 99, 342, 345

473

INDEX

Obama, Barack, 341
Obeah, 70, 72, 73
Obi, Liz, 303
"Occasional Discourse" (Carlyle), 130, 131
offshore financial centers (OFCs), 349–52
Ogle, Vanessa, 350
oil crisis (1973), 335
Oliver, Michael, 264
Oluwale, David, 355–57
Open Arms Drop-in Centre, Kingston, 387
Operation Sheepskin (1969), 252
Operation Swamp (1981), 366
Operation Trident (2011), 380
Operation Urgent Fury (1983), 319, 347–48
Orders-in-Council, 113, 117, 118
Organisation of Eastern Caribbean States (OECS), 345, 346, 348
Organisation of Women of African and Asian Descent (OWAAD), 304
Organization of the Petroleum Exporting Countries (OPEC), 335
Ormonde, SS, 222–223
Oroonoko (Behn), 35
Orwell, George, 217
Osborn, Robert, 141
Osborne, Cyril, 284–85
Osborne, John, 257
"Our Countrymen in Chains" (Whittier), 107
"Out of Many, One People" motto, 322
Ovando, Nicolás de, 12–13, 16
Oxford, Thomas, 105

Pacific Islanders, 126
Padmore, George, 196–97
Pakistan, 228, 272
Pan-African Conference, 139, 196
pan-Africanism, 139, 150, 187, 190–92, 196, 199
Panama, 16, 171, 213
Panama Canal, 135, 171, 209
Pan-American Airlines, 324
Pankhurst, Sylvia, 192
Panton, Ormond, 258
Parekh, Bhikhu, 376
Paris, France, 189
Parks, Rosa, 296
Paul, Kathleen, 278
Peach, Blair, 368
Penang, Malaya, 153–54
Penn, William, 21
People's Action Movement (Anguilla), 251
People's Liberation Movement (Montserrat), 257
People's National Congress (Guiana), 237, 239, 241
People's National Movement (Trinidad and Tobago), 300, 327
People's National Party (Jamaica), 202, 320, 321, 324, 332–40
People's Solidarity Campaign, 331
Peru, 16
petit marronage, 69
Philip II, King of Spain, 1
Philippines, 134
Phillips, James, 107
Phoenix Foundation, 264
Piercefield House, Monmouthshire, 82
Pindling, Lynden, 261–63, *265*
Pitt, David, 290, 293
Pitt, William, 109
Pix, Mary, 35
plantains, 135
Platt Amendment (1901), 135

474

INDEX

Plymouth, England, 50, 81, 85, 105
poison, xii, 69–70
Poland, 183
Police and Criminal Evidence Act (1984), 369
policing, xxi, 356–57, 361–62, 366–76, 379–81, 389
Policing the Crisis (Hall), 370
Polish people, 270
Political Affairs Committee (Guiana), 232
politics of difference, xvii, 160, 176, 237, 240
Pollins, Harold, 275
polygenesis, 137
Poole, England, 50
Portsmouth, England, 368
Portugal, 13, 16, 17, 152, 232, 391
Posnett, Richard, 330
post-colonial melancholia, 357–59, 371, 390
post-colony states, 266
Powell, Enoch, 309–12, 358, 362, 367
Powell, John, 19
Preston, England, 50
Price, Ernest, 174
Price, Richard, xx
Prince, Mary, 44, 54, 65, 66, 68
Pringle-Polgreen, Rachael, 60
privateers, 17–18
Progressive Democratic Party (Montserrat), 257
Progressive Labour Party (Bermuda), xii–xiii, 260, 330–31
Progressive Liberal Party (Bahamas), 261–63
Progressive People's Party (Guiana), 227–28, 233–41
property rights, 31
prostitution, 56, 58, 60, 83

Protestantism, 17, 20, 32, 57, 114
pseudoscience, 90, 137–38, 150, 156, 208
Puerto Rico, 5, 6, 13, 37, 134, 209, 221
Puritanism, 21

quadroon, 63
Quaker, Leicester, 117–18
Quakers, 49, 68, 86, 96, 97, 104, 107, 124, 192
Queensberry, Duchess (Catherine Hyde), 84
Queensland, Australia, 126
Queen's Own Royal West Kent Regiment, 207
Quinn, Kate, 316
quinteron, 63
Quisqueya, 7

Race & Class (journal), 303
Race Relations Act (Bermuda, 1969), 328
Race Relations Act (UK, 1965), 298, 299, 309, 310
race riots, *see* unrest
Rachman, Peter, 278
Racial Adjustment Action Society (RAAS), 298–99
racial-caste hierarchy, xv–xxv, 30–31, 37–38, 40, 43–68, 75–76, 162, 261, 354, 396
  abolition and, 108, 125–26
  Black Power and, 303, 305, 308, 327, 332
  Brexit and, 382
  Cold War and, 229, 328
  crime and, 379
  culture wars and, 389–90
  decolonization and, 229–30
  education and, 308, 359, 383
  elite whites, 44–59
  enslaved people, 63–68

INDEX

racial-caste hierarchy (*cont.*)
  First World War and, 165, 167, 178, 204
  free blacks, 43, 60–63
  immigration and, 152, 287, 311
  independence and, 256
  interracial relationships and (*see* interracial relationships)
  middle class, 150–51, 212
  mobility within, 43–44, 141, 151
  neocolonialism and, 317
  Nonconformists and, 114
  policing and, 369, 372, 374
  poor whites, 59–60
  reparations and, 394–95
  Second World War and, 208, 210, 216, 219, 221
  Windrush scandal and, 386
Racial Preservation Society, 362
racism, xxi, xxiii, 23, 52, 75–76, 80–81, 129–33, 376–77
  abolitionism and, 80–81, 96, 106, 122
  anti-racist movements, xxiii, 167, 186–99, 295–308, 362, 369–70, 394–95
  Black Power and, 269, 295–308
  Brexit and, 381–83
  Covid-19 pandemic, 388
  education and, 305–8
  Enlightenment and, 90
  First World War and, 165–82
  immigration and, 268, 273–313, 362, 377–78
  inquiries into, 376–77, 389
  interracial relationships and (*see* interracial relationships)
  labor competition and, 88–90, 183, 268
  liberalism and, 129–33
  policing and, xxi, 356–57, 361–62, 366–76, 379–81, 389

  pseudoscientific, 90, 137–38, 150, 156, 208
  Second World War and, 207–9, 216–20
  structural, xvii, 204, 358, 370, 374, 389
  tourism and, 353–54
  zero-sum politics and, 358, 378
racist violence, 268–270, 282–291, 362
  Cochrane murder (1959), 290–91
  Gardner murder (1993), 374–76
  Lawrence murder (1993), 372–74
  nationwide riots (1919), 182–85
  nationwide riots (2024), 396
  Nottingham riots (1958), 282, 289
  Notting Hill riots (1958), 282–90
  "Rivers of Blood" speech (1968), 311
Ramdhanie, Bob, 303
Ramsay, James, 58–59, 97
rape, *see* sexual violence
Rastafarianism, 200, 317, 320–21, 324, 360
Reading, England, 368
Reagan, Ronald, 339, 345
Red Cross, 172
Red Scare (1947–57), 230–31
Reform Act (1832), 120–21
Reformation (1517–1648), 17
refugees, 378
reggae music, 317, 320–21, 360
Reid, J. H., 149
remittances, 281
Remond, Sarah Parker, 136
Renison, Patrick Muir, 237
reparations, xxiii, 87, 118, 150, 250, 255, 390–95
reparatory history, xxv
repartimiento, 11
reproduction, 26, 54–55, 66–67

INDEX

republicanism, 393
"Rhodes Must Fall" campaign (2015), 383
rice, 32, 42
Rich, Robert, 33
riots, *see* unrest
"Rivers of Blood" speech (Powell), 310–12
Roatán Island, 75
Robinson, John Roland, 260
Rock Against Racism, 362
Rockefeller, Laurance, 352
Rock-Resort, British Virgin Islands, 352
Rodgers, Daniel, 318
Rodney, Walter, 315, 316, 322–23
Roediger, David, 59
Roma, 27
Roman Britain (43 AD–c. 410), 32
Rose, Jack, 258
Rose Hall, Jamaica, 45, 45
Royal African Company, 24–25, 27, 35, 389
Royal Air Force (RAF), 172, 207, 210
Royal Bank of Canada, 350
Royal Canadian Mounted Police, 331
Royal Exchange Company, 49
Royal Naval Hotel, Bridgetown, 60
Royal Navy, 42, 110, 172, 207, 211
Rudd, Amber, 385
rum, 30, 35, 49, 105
Runnymede Trust, 376
Russian people, 183
Russian Revolution (1917), 192
Rustin, Bayard, 296

Saint-Domingue (1697–1804), 98–102
Salford, England, 182
Salkey, Andrew, 304–5
Samaroo, Brinsley, 152
sambo, 63

Sancho, Ignatius, 85
Sandinista National Liberation Front, 344
Sandys, Duncan, 240
San Fernando, Trinidad, 157
San Salvador, 7
Sansom, Philip, 97
Santa María (ship), 7, 11
Santo Domingo (1492–1865), 3, 5–7, 11–17, 100
São Tomé, 13
Savage, Alfred, 234, 237
Sawh, Roy, 298
Scafe, Susanne, 304
Scanlan, Padraic, 108
Scarman, Leslie, 367–68
scientific racism, 90, 137–38, 150, 156, 208
Scobie, Edward, 295
Scoon, Paul, 344, 347
Scotland, 5, 50, 182–84, 211, 216, 392
Scott, James, xii
Scramble for Africa (1885–1914), 110
Seacole, Mary, 136–37
Seaga, Edward, 339–41, 346, 348
Seale, Bobby, 269
Second World War (1939–45), 207–22
    interracial relationships and, 208–9, 216–20
Selassie, Haile, Emperor of Ethiopia, 195, 200
Selvon, Sam, 273, 282
Senegal, 37
servants, 33–35, 37, 39–41, 83, 88–90
Seven Years' War (1756–63), 37, 72, 75
Sewell, Tony, 389
sexual relations, *see* interracial relationships

477

sexual violence, xii, 29, 41, 42, 54–56, 63, 155–57
Shafi, Azfar, 370
Sharp, Granville, 79, *91*, 91–92, 95, 97
Sharpe, Sam, 119, 322
Sharpeville massacre (1960), 330
Sharples, Richard, 331
Shearer, Hugh, 323
Sheffield, England, 105, 368
Shepherd, Verene, 155, 391
Sherkerley Mountains, Antigua, 73
Shilliam, Robbie, 358
shipbuilding, 48, 50
shipwrecks, 65, 141
Shower Posse gang, 341
Shultz, George, 346
Sierra Leone, 17, 95–96, 175, 378
Simpson, Myrna, 376
Sinclair, Rita, 281
Singh, Jai Narine, 236, *238*
Sir George Williams University, 325
ska music, 360
skin color, 40–41, 62
Slave Registration Act (Barbados, 1817), 113
Slave Registration Act (UK, 1819), 111–13
slavery, xi–xv, xix, xxi–xxii, xxiv, 5, 22–38, 40
  abolitionism (*see* abolitionism)
  Africans, 4–5, 15–16, 22
  British Empire, 22–76, 103–27, 390–95
  capitalism and, xv, 27, 37, 48–50, 104
  chattel principle, 27, 40
  Christianity and, 4, 15, 40–41, 45, 50, 68
  flight from, 18, 33, 39, 69, 73, 74, 75
  indigenous peoples and, 4, 13–14

reparations, xxiii, 87, 118, 150, 250, 255, 390–95
  resistance to, 69–76
  skin color and, 40–41
  Spanish Empire, 4–5, 15–16, 48
  triangular trade, 49
  violence and (*see* violence)
  writing on, 46
Slave Trade Act (1807), 110
Slavs, 27
Sloane, Hans, 53
smallholders, 133, 135, 141
smallpox, 12, 28, 142
Smeathman, Henry, 95
Smethwick, England, 297–98
Smith, Adam, 49, 104
Smith, John, 115–17
Smollett, Tobias, 47
socialism, 188, 192, 196–97
  British Guiana, 227–42
  Grenada, 256, 332, 342–48
  Jamaica, 335–39
Society for Effecting the Abolition of the Slave Trade, 97, 108, 109
Society of West Indian Planters, 47
Somalia, 183
Somerset, James, 92–93
Somoza, Debayle Anastasio, 344
Sons of Africa, 105
Sonthonax, Léger-Félicité, 98–100
Soubise, Julius, 84–85
South Africa, 161, 269, 272, 293–94, 330, 335, 383
Southall Black Sisters (SBS), 304
Southampton, England, 50, 368
South Asians, *see* British South Asians
South Carolina Colony (1629–1776), 23, 32, 37, 42
Southerne, Thomas, 35
Southern Rhodesia (1923–65), 350

INDEX

South Sea Company, 48
South Shields, England, 182, 183
Soviet Union (1922–91), 197, 229, 239, 241, 338, 345
Spanish Empire, xx, 1–17, 36, 100
   abolition of slavery (1886), 125
   American War (1898), 134
   Anglo-Spanish War (1585–1604), 17, 18
   Anglo-Spanish War (1654–60), 21
   Columbus's voyages (1492–1504), 7–12
   Dutch Revolt (1566–1648), 17
   gold mining, 8, 10, 13, 16
   Santo Domingo (1492–1865), 3, 5–7, 11–17, 100
   Seven Years' War (1756–63), 37, 72, 75
   slavery, 4–5, 15–16, 48
   Treaty of Utrecht (1713), 48
Spanish Netherlands (1556–1714), 17
Special Restriction Order (1925), 185–86
Specials, The (band), 360
Spence, Thomas, 106
Spencer, Herbert, 137, 147
spices, 49
Spirit of Freedom (statue), xii–xiv, *xiii*
spirits, 49
Sri Lanka, 228, 378
St. Barthélemy, 124
St. Christopher, 18–19
St. Elizabeth, Jamaica, 55
St. Kitts, 18–20, 29, 30, 58, 73, 123, 134, 149, 200, 253, 345
St. Kitts-Nevis-Anguilla, 244, 250–53
St. Lucia, 43, 99, 117, 162, 200, 221, 244, 250
St. Thomas, 139

St. Vincent, xx, 178
   free people in, 60, 99
   indigenous people, 19
   labor unrest in, 142, 149, 200
   Portuguese community, 152
   slavery in, 43, 70
   Treaty of Paris (1763), 37, 75
   West Indies Federation (1958–62), 244, 250
Standing Closer Association Committee (SCAC), 243
Stanley Despatch (1945), 242
Stapleton, William, 36
Status of Children Act (Jamaica, 1976), 333
Staveley, Martin, 259
Stephen, James, 109
Stephenson, Paul, 295
Sterne, Laurence, 85–86
Stewart, Charles, 92
stop and search, 361, 369, 379, 381
Straw, Jack, 373, 376–77
Strong, Jonathan, 91
structural racism, xvii, 204, 358, 370, 374, 389
Student Nonviolent Coordinating Committee, 269
Sturge, Joseph, 124
Suez Crisis (1956–57), 238, 313
suffragettes, 192
sugar
   post-abolition period, 134–36, 141, 157, 232, 234, 235, 240
   slave trade period, 5, 8, 13–14, 20–24, 29–32, 35, 46–49, 63–64, 105, 115, 126
Sugar Duties Act (1846), 134
Sugar Equalization Act (1854), 134
Suriname, 22
sus laws, 361
Swann, Michael, 371
Sweden, xix, 124, 183, 391

sweet potatoes, 6, 135
Swing Riots (1830), 120
Syria, 345
Syrian people, xx, 153, 320

Tabili, Laura, 185
Tacklyn, Larry, 331
Tacky's Revolt (1760–61), 71–72
Taíno, 6–14, 16
Taiwan, 394
Taranto revolt (1918), 179–81
Tax Justice Network, 351
Taylor, Breonna, 388
Teachers against Racism, 308
Teddy boys, 281, 282
Temple Bar, SS, 356
tenancy-at-will system, 133
Tennant, Colin, 352
Tennyson, Alfred, 147
textiles, 49
Thatcher, Margaret, 346, 357, 362–63, 371
theater, 35
theft, 69
Thicknesse, Philip, 88
Thistlewood, Thomas, 55–56
Thomas, Dalby, 27
Thomas, John Jacob, 150
Thompson, Dudley, 210–11
Thompson, Leonard, 263
Thompson, Thomas John, 139
Thornton, Henry, 109
timber, 20, 65, 200, 211, 216
Tivoli Gardens, Kingston, 320, 341
tobacco, 18–20, 30, 32, 35
Tobago, 37, 43, 75, 149
Tottenham, London, 369, 380
tourism, 319, 353–54, 394
Towerson, William, 55
Town Party (Jamaica), 140
Toxteth riots (1981), 368, 369
Trade Union Congress (Guiana), 240

Tranter, Olive, 187
travel literature, 35
Treaty of Breda (1667), 22
Treaty of Paris (1763), 37, 75
Treaty of Paris (1898), 134
Treaty of Rome (1957), 294
Treaty of Utrecht (1713), 48
Trelawny War (1795–96), 74
Trench Town, Kingston, 320
triangular trade, 49
Trinidad, 5, 14, 19, 99, 109, 134
Trinidad and Tobago, 23
  Black Power revolution (1968–70), 317, 325–27
  calypso music, 223
  Chinese community, 161
  Closer Association conference (1947), 242
  First World War (1914–18), 169, 171–72
  independence (1962), 248–49
  Indian community, 153–54, 157–58
  labor unrest (1935), 200
  neocolonialism in, 316
  Portuguese community, 152
  Second World War (1939–45), 211, 221–22
  UK, migration to, 223
  West Indies Federation (1958–62), 244, 248–49
Trinidad Workingmen's Association, 149
Trollope, Anthony, 131
Trouillot, Michel-Rolph, ix, 102
Tucker, Henry, 260–261
Tudor period (1485–1603), 32
Ture, Kwame, 269
Turks and Caicos, 65, 141, 257
Turner, Sasha, 67
Tuskegee Institute, 192
two-tone music, 360

INDEX

Udah, David, 300
UFOs, 342
Ukrainian people, 270
unemployment
  Britain, 120, 277, 279, 360–61, 363, 378
  Caribbean, 120, 134, 161, 179, 214, 222, 232, 244, 267, 333, 337–39
Union Movement, 279
United Bahamian Party (UBP), 261–63
United Bermuda Party (UBP), xii, 260, 329, 332
United Force (Guiana), 239, 241
United Fruit Company, 136, 201
United Kingdom, xxi–xxiv
  Abolition of Slavery Act (1833), 121–23, 129, 391
  black community (*see* black Britons)
  Black Power movement in, 295–308
  Brexit (2016–20), 381–83
  British Nationality Act (1948), 209, 224–25, 270, 273
  British Nationality Act (1981), 363
  Commonwealth Immigrants Act (1962), 291–95, 297
  Commonwealth Immigrants Act (1968), 308, 312
  Crime and Disorder Act (1998), 379
  emigration, 271–273
  Falklands War (1982), 371
  Grenada crisis (1979–83), 344, 346, 348
  immigration to, 222–26, 267–313, 357
  policing in, 355–57, 361–62, 366–76, 379–81
  Race Relations Act (1965), 298, 299, 309, 310
  racial-caste hierarchy in, xvi–xviii, 167, 354, 357
  Reform Act (1832), 120–21
  reparations movement and, 390–95
  Second World War (1939–45), 207–22
  Slave Registration Act (1819), 111–13
  Slave Trade Act (1807), 110
  Suez Crisis (1956–57), 238, 313
  Swing Riots (1830), 120
  unrest in, 182–85, 192, 225–26, 282–83, 359, 364–70, 379
  welfare state, 274, 278, 357, 359
  white working class, xvi, 167, 182, 272–73, 281–83, 297, 311, 358, 378
  Windrush scandal (2018), 383–86
United Kingdom Independence Party (UKIP), 378
United Nations, 249, 260, 264
United States, xviii, 134–35, 209, 229
  Angolan Civil War (1975–91), 335
  Black Lives Matter movement (2013–present), 388
  Black Power movement (1966–80s), 269
  British Guiana, relations with, 239
  civil rights movement (1954–68), 269, 285, 296, 327–28
  Civil War (1861–65), 134
  Cold War (1947–91) (*see* Cold War)
  Grenada invasion (1983), 318, 347–48
  Immigration and Nationality Act (1952), 270–71
  Jamaica, relations with, 135–36

481

INDEX

United States (*cont.*)
    Jim Crow laws (c. 1874–1965), 171, 190, 192, 212, 216, 221, 229
    Little Rock crisis (1957), 285
    neocolonialism, 316, 318–20, 338, 342, 347–48, 354
    Panama Canal construction (1904–14), 171
    race riots (1919), 184
    Red Scare (1947–57), 230
    Revolutionary War (1775–83), 94, 105
    Second World War (1939–45), 216–22
    slavery in, 125, 126, 136
    Spanish War (1898), 134
    Universal Negro Improvement Association, 190–91
    War of 1812, 113
United States Virgin Islands, 209, 221, 259
Universal Coloured People's Association (UCPA), 299–300
Universal Negro Improvement Association (UNIA), 190–91
universities, 48
University of Birmingham, 370
University of Cambridge, 96–97, 188
University of Edinburgh, 188
University of Glasgow, 188
University of Oxford, 188, 383, 392
University of the West Indies (UWI), 322, 324
unrest in Britain
    1919 nationwide, 182–85, 192, 225
    1954 Camden, 281
    1958 Nottingham; Notting Hill, 282–90
    1980 St. Pauls riot, 364
    1981 nationwide, 365–68
    1985 nationwide, 369
    2011 nationwide, 380

2020 BLM protests, 359, 388–89, 392
2024 far-right violence, 396
urbanization, 199

Vagrancy Act (1824), 361
Venables, Robert, 21
Venezuela, 334, 345
Verdala, SS, 172–73
Victoria, Queen of the United Kingdom, 137, 142, 151
violence, slave trade, xii, 29, 35–36, 41–42, 52–56. *See also* racist violence
    executions, 28, 35, 37, 41, 72, 112
    sexual violence, xii, 29, 41, 42, 54–56, 63, 155–57
    whipping, 41, 54, 65, 114, 117, 123
    wife murders, 159
Virgin Gorda, British Virgin Islands, 352
Virgin Group, 352
Virginia Colony (1606–1776), 18, 20, 23, 31, 37, 86, 94
virginity tests, 304
voting rights, 141

Waddington, E. J., 233
Waldheim, Kurt, 342
Walker, Patrick Gordon, 297
Wallace, George, 105
Waller, John, 56
Walpole, Horace, 87
Walrond, Humphrey, 39, 45, 46, 52–53
Ward, Arnold, 188
Warner, Ashton, 63, 68
Warner, Philip, 37
Warner, Thomas, 19
War of 1812, 113
War of the Spanish Succession (1701–13), 48

INDEX

Washington, Booker T., 192
Washington, S. J., 149
water supplies, 353
Watkins, Errington, 263
Wealth of Nations, The (Smith), 49, 104
Webster, Ronald, 251–52
Webster, Wendy, 219
Wedderburn, Robert, 105–6
Wedgwood, Josiah, 97, 106–7
welfare, 274, 278, 357, 359
Wellington, 1st Duke (Arthur Wellesley), 120
Wells, Ida, 136
Wells, Nathaniel, 82
WerBell III, Mitchell, 264
Wesley, John, 103
Wesleyan Missionary Society, 115
West African Students' Union (WASU), 188, 207
West India Interest, 81
West Indian Development Council, 296
West Indian Gazette (newspaper), 298
West Indian National Association, 295
West Indian Standing Conference, 290
West Indian Students' Union, 289, 293, 299
West India Royal Commission (1938–45), 204
West Indies Act (1967), 253
West Indies Federation (1958–62), 244–49, 257–59, 294
West Midland Engineering Employers' Association, 309
Wheatley, Phillis, 83
whipping, 41, 54, 65, 114, 117, 123
Whistler, Henry, 31
White, Sarah, 305

White Defence League (WDL), 279, 285
white supremacy, xv–xvi, xxii–xxiii, 52, 68, 162, 376, 396
   abolition and, 80–81, 106, 108, 125–26, 132
   First World War and, 165, 175–76
   interracial relationships and (*see* interracial relationships)
   politics of difference and, xvii, 160, 176, 237, 240
   scientific racism, 90, 137–38
white working class, xvi, 167, 182, 272–73, 281–83, 297, 311, 358, 378
Whitlock, William, 252
Whittier, John Greenleaf, 107
"Why Is My Curriculum so White" campaign, 383
wife murders, 159
Wilberforce, William, 97–98, 108, 111, 113, 118, 126
William IV, King of the United Kingdom, 60
Williams, Eric, 23–24, 48, 126, 249, 326–27
Williams, Henry Sylvester, 139
Williams, James, 123
Willis, R. E., 180
Wilson, Harold, 253, 298, 311
"Wind of Change" speech (Macmillan), 238
Windrush scandal (2018), 383–86
Windward Islands, 154
Windward Maroons, 73
Wolmer's Free School, 186
Wolverhampton, England, 274, 276, 368
women, xi–xii, xvii, 42, 46, 54–55
   Black Power movement, 303, 317
   domestic servants, 66, 69–70
   feminism, 192, 269, 303–4, 333, 370

women (*cont.*)
  First World War (1914–18), 170, 172
  indentured laborers, 154–59
  interracial relationships and (*see* interracial relationships)
  Maroons, 73–74, 322
  planters, 46, 54, 56
  Second World War (1939–45), 214–15
  sexual violence against, xii, 29, 41, 42, 54–56, 63, 155–57
Women's Auxiliary Air Force (WAAF), 214
Wong, Clinton, 233
Woodbine, Lord, 223
Wooding, Hugh, 328
Workers' Dreadnought (newspaper), 192
Workers' Socialist Federation (WSF), 192
working class, 80, 179
  Bermuda, 259–60
  British, black, 151–52, 267, 358
  British, white, xvi, 167, 182, 272–73, 281–83, 297, 311, 358, 378
  British Virgin Islands, 259
  Cayman Islands, 350, 351
  Jamaica, 320, 333
  pan-African movement, 139
  Second World War, 166
  socialist movements, 192, 200
World Bank, 337, 338, 339
World Trade Organization, 337
World War I, *see* First World War (1914–18)
World War II, *see* Second World War (1939–45)
Worthy Park, Jamaica, 66

X, Malcolm, 297–98, 300, 323
X, Michael, 298–300
xenophobia, 377, 381, 383

yams, 6, 131, 135
yellow fever, 12
Yemen, 183
Young, William, 60
Youth Offending Teams, 379
Yucatan peninsula, 5

zero-sum politics, 358, 378, 390
Zong massacre (1781), 77–80, 96, 97
Zulu Kingdom (1816–97), xiv

About the Author

Imaobong Umoren is a historian of the Caribbean, Britain, and wider African diaspora. She is an associate professor at the London School of Economics and Political Science.